THE PSYCHOLOGY OF STRESS & NUTRITION

by

Sarah A. Culton, Ed.D.

NATIONAL BOOK COMPANY

PORTLAND, OREGON

Appendix reprinted by permission of
Cooperative Extension, WSU, Pullman, Washington

345000

0-89420-281-2

Library of Congress Catalog Card Number
91-62175

To Verlen, for Patience, Devotion, and Understanding

PROGRESS CAN ONLY BE MADE BY
IDEAS WHICH ARE
VERY DIFFERENT
FROM THOSE ACCEPTED
AT THE MOMENT

~

Hans Selye

CONTENTS

PREFACE

In 1990, even though we had an 80's "fitness boom" that seemed to be of unprecedented proportions, we ate 5 percent more than we did ten years ago; and we are rounder by an average of 6 pounds — in fact, one-third of us are overweight! Along with all of this, our stress levels are up, and our fitness levels are down — we live more with disease than with ease!

Man has the innate intelligence to live in the very best way possible, but he needs to better understand the relationship between stress and nutrition.

In the past, there has been a "hodge-podge" of seemingly contradictory "hoopla" — so much so, that many have given up! In this book, I have painstakenly attempted to single out and make clear what the problems are, why we have problems, and what to do about them — the stress-nutrition connection! We need more stress controlled life-styles that will give us more quality as well as quantity of life. I can point you in the right direction, and then with sufficient desire and motivation to change your own life style, you will be able to do it. I have confidence that if one can understand the "why," then one should be willing to accept the responsibility for any desired change.

This book is written in such a way that each chapter is a mini-book all of its own. If you wish, you can read any section you would like, first, and then the others in any order you might desire — the more you enjoy, the more you will profit!

One fascinating thing about any science is that we are sometimes confronted with surprises, data which don't fit earlier thinking or which may even appear to contradict what we think we already know. Sometimes, truth is stranger than fiction. Then we must decide whether to modify our old thinking or even to abandon it. That is what learning is all about — it always involves change.

Furthermore, many of the concerns that arise from a book like this can only be explained in terms of psychological, sociological, anthropological, biological, physiological, and chemical reactions that take place inside the human body. Many books have been written that do not make for pleasant recreational reading. They are no fun!

However, I shall try to give you an interesting, meaningful, and useful coverage of the stress reaction and how it relates to our struggle for well-being. This is something that has never been done in the way that I shall be doing it; and I feel that it is long overdue. Some may criticize me for oversimplification and/or misrepresentation; but we could criticize them for making this information so sticky and so "ivory tower" that it has not seeped through and been synthesized, so that it can be understood by the typical average American. I have every confidence that what I have to say will "open doors" for many people.

Even though I have endeavored to write this book in a comprehensive way, it has been difficult, if not impossible, at times, to translate the professional "jargon" into meaningful terms.

However, I did try. If I had to use professional terms, I tried to give a translation. If you do get "bogged down," I wouldn't blame you. Just move on to another section and come back later after your next good meal or exercise, when your brain cells are better nourished and oxygenated! Have confidence. We will get it together.

Many times, I have felt like the mother who said, "Before I was married, I had six theories about how to raise children. Now I have six children and no theories!" When I was in graduate school studying psychology, I learned many theories about adjustment and health, most of which had merit, but somehow did not seem to do the "trick" in actual practice. For instance, people have been known to have been in psycho-therapy for years and years with no apparent appreciable changes!

What I have learned in recent years has added a great deal to my background in orthodox psychology. Yes, I am an academic psychologist (with a doctoral degree) in the field, who looked over the fence and found that the "grass" was, indeed, "greener." I have also looked beyond the scope of academic nutrition and orthodox medicine in my quest for insights.

True, there is no theory that can be proven beyond a reasonable doubt, and the evidence for some is more skimpy than for others. However, all have their advocates, based on some degree of evidence. Some seem controversial, but I find a thread of commonality among them all — control your stress by eating right! We'll see why this is true as we travel along together through some of the seemingly "mishmash" of studies, opinions, and assumptions on the interplay of diet and well-being.

What complicates matters for the researchers is that they can't stick people in a study and give them what is a toxic level, nor can they deprive them of food. That's just bloody unethical. So, we wait for people to report adverse effects, and then sneak back into their history to see what they did.

Another complicating factor is that we are not necessarily what we think or eat. We are also the genes we inherited, and environment we live in, the pressures of life, and how happy we are.

The science of nutrition is only two hundred years old; the science of psychology is much younger than that. In fact, psychology noted its one-hundredth birthday in 1979. Both sciences are very complicated and very new; and combining the two has just now begun.

In my attempt to "leave no stone unturned," I should say that all of us know "invulnerables" who drink, chase the opposite sex, do all the so-called wrong things, and still live to be a 100! Some try to do all of society's "right" things, and drop dead at 30!

However, there are risk reductions for doing the right things, if we look at a very large group as a whole. No one can say that this or that will happen to anyone.

For example, I have two acquaintances whose nicknames attest to their "wayward" lifestyles — "Wish" and "Bum" — hardy souls they seem to be! Perhaps they have strong genetic endowments, lower stress levels, or maybe they don't care what people think. Maybe their reputations are their "claim to fame," or perhaps exercise is their "ace in the hole." Who knows? I do know that they dance like crazy! They must have something going for themselves.

We do have some seemingly invulnerable individuals. However, they are probably the ones who, if they choose to do so, could extend their life expectancies by 30 percent.

This book is written for informational and educational purposes. It is intended to be a self-help book in so far as it offers a better understanding of the complex mechanisms involved in maintaining better health — stress control through exercise, relaxation, and nutrition. It is not intended to be a total encyclopedia of knowledge in these areas, but a guide for inspiration and encouragement for all who seek to better their lives through stress control.

Welcome aboard!

Sarah A. Culton, Ed.D

1.

INTRODUCTION

As a psychologist and a professional educator, I am charting a new course. This task has never been accomplished in my field — merging the psychology of stress, the physiology of stress, and nutrition, our ultimate source of energy — in any comprehensive way.

As Dr. Diespecker, psychologist at the University of Wollongong, in Australia, says, there's an "interconnectedness between everything that exists — whether biological, psychological, or physical."[1] He explains that psychology has a lot of catching up to do, because of all the new scientific and technological changes. But so, too, do nutrition and stress. Psychology can only be powerful when it can promote healthful change. This is my concern with nutrition and psychology. If we understand stress and its effects on the body and the role that nutrition has to play in bringing about positive change, then great progress can and will be made.

By the same token, our prevailing poor nutrition is now detrimental and an added stress on already over-burdened individuals in our modern-day culture. Psychologists are only responsible when they support the bio-chemical model. Only when psychology attends to the other sciences, can it become capable of guiding healthful change.

According to Dr. Diespecker,

> The most important notions - still largely ignored in our science - are 1) the intrinsically dynamic nature of the universe of which we are parts; and 2) the interrelatedness, interconnections, and interdependence of everything."[2]

Psychology does have a new emerging field of health psychology. Now we specifically need nutritional psychology, to help us deal with stress and stress-related disorders. We must draw from the specialists all we can in order to describe, explain, predict, and offer ways of controlling human behavior — the four goals of psychology.

From Where We Have Come

A glimpse into "yesteryear" shows us that people have long been concerned about tension and the importance of relaxation. Selye gave us a definition of stress in 1956;[3] but earlier it was said that if one could sit back, right at the moment, shut one's eyes, and snooze in the midst of activity all around and then become aware, say in five minutes, one was an unusual person, indeed. If you could do this, you were considered to be one who knew the restorative effects of relaxation and were profiting from them. More than likely, even at that time, many people were "tensed-up" or under stress, even when they thought that they were sitting down to relax, "take five," "light up," and perhaps read something about relaxation. They worked hard and they played hard, never really taking time to relax or to unwind. There were some folks who could, but they seemed few and far between.

However, one famous and popular personality in our history was Teddy Roosevelt who had this exceptional gift. On his campaign tours, he could drop into a passenger seat in the railroad car, completely unaware of the commotion all around him. As the train would start slowing for a stop, he would start moving and rubbing his eyes. By the time the wheels of the train were grinding to a stop against the rails, he was in the aisle, making his way toward the rear platform. Still groggy, he would head through the doorway, then throw his head up high. He would hear the applause of the crowd and shout out "Bully!" He was then the dynamic Teddy that the voters loved. Instead of playing hard and then trying to work hard, which is a very poor combination, he was relaxing and then working with all his might.

Anyone can improve his/her ability to work hard by first learning how and when to relax. People like Roosevelt, who have done well in the past, have had a rhythmical beat to their activities. They would really "go for it," then retreat and relax. These fortunate people compared the benefits of their efforts against what it was costing them in terms of wear and tear. They had a precise understanding of values and could prioritize their responsibilities. They know when to work and when to rest! In other words, those individuals could relax the muscles of their bodies and get the necessary sleep or "snooze" whenever they felt the need. Other notables with this same ability were William Jennings Bryan, Thomas Edison, and Winston Churchill. In addition to their night's sleep, they also achieved getting restful breaks during the day.

Earlier in history yet, the Bible includes coverage concerning the term "worry" and says that it's a sin. From this standpoint, worry is a "diffused cloud" or generalized fear that we now call anxiety. It is seen as a sinful perversion of a good emotion — concern.

Concern turns into worry when it is directed toward the wrong day — tomorrow. In Matthew 6:34 Jesus said, "Therefore do not worry about tomorrow, for tomorrow will worry about itself. Each day has enough trouble of its own." The fact that tomorrow isn't here yet does not allow an opportunity for the energy and/or anxiety generated by the worry to find a release. There is no way to channel it productively. The result is what we now call *stress,* with its many negative consequences and/or grief.

Continuing in Matthew 6:37, Jesus said, "We could worry from now until the day we die about the length of our life, but we will nevertheless not add one hour to it." The Bible thus indicates that it is useless to worry. The results are fatigue and dissatisfaction that have led to the stress-related disorders that we know today.

However, worry can be overcome. We should, according to this view, focus our concern productively on the immediate tasks of the day. We should look ahead to tomorrow, but not worry about tomorrow! To eliminate worry, we should plan for tomorrow. We should attempt to do as we planned; but if obstacles intervene, not worry, and see what we can learn from such obstacles. If we can do this, we will feel tired, but satisfied, and be able to sleep well without worry keeping us awake all night.

In summary, mankind has always had a concern about stress. Today, children and adults alike are under a great deal of stress in our society; probably more than ever before. It seems there are more pressures as time goes on and more problems, as a result of these, to the extent that we must become concerned and make every effort to "stem the tide." There is a sense of urgency about the matter. We can hope that what is to follow will provide the understanding and the skills necessary for accomplishing this critical task.

Bumbling Matilda

Before the topic of nutrition can have any meaning or validity, it is necessary to describe and explain the stress response, in order to have a thorough and comprehensive understanding of stress and its psychological components. Then the role of nutrition can be clearly discernable.

First, let's take a look at an example of the outward manifestations of stress which are so common in our society.

There was a Dr. Matilda who at one time went "waltzing" along, but more recently that could not be said. One morning she had overslept, having spent much of the night worrying about the sabbatical leave decision that was to be announced soon by the college president. If anyone's application deserved to be accepted, she thought that hers did. After all, she had devoted 19 years of teaching and counseling above and beyond the call of duty, but one of the administrators might not see it that way! So Dr. Matilda "wolfed down" her coffee and toast, checked to see if her pantyhose had any runners or if her nose was shiny, grabbed her lecture notes, raced out the door, jumped into her 70's vintage car, and headed for school.

Her neck started cramping as she alternatively switched her view from left to right, right to left, and then to her speedometer, as she came through a 45-mile-an-hour zone in Airway Heights and startled a pedestrian. He yelled obscenities. She kept on going.

After miraculously reaching the college grounds, she found the upper parking lot full and had to run a considerable distance to get to her office. Eight minutes late in the door of her Introduction to Psychology class, she said to the students, "Don't run away, I am here." Some had already left.

The lecture went poorly. She could not concentrate or get herself calmed down. She felt guilty and told the remaining students, "Well, I'll do a better job tomorrow."

During her office hours, her son called, saying that he had been laid off from his construction job; and her daughter called from the South Pacific, asking for more money. About that time, a student came by to have a drop slip signed and another one to argue for another point on a test. She took some Tylenol for her headache, which got progressively worse as the day wore on.

After somehow finding her way home, she had an "overdraw" statement from her bank, with ten days to pay day! Must be the calculator wasn't working right when she balanced the account, she rationalized. Then she fantasized about how she might borrow or what antique she might sell. Then, off came a shoe which flew across the kitchen, hit the microwave, bounced off the cupboard door, and landed on the cat! He yowled and scrambled to safety under the coffee table.

She heaved a sigh of relief. Some of the anxiety had just been alleviated. "Bumbling" Matilda fell into a heap on the living room couch.

This modern-day college professor seems far removed from the ivory towers of yesteryear. She is suffering from the stresses of our modern times. It is safe to say that we probably have more stresses to deal with than ever before in history. Matilda showed the emotional responses of frustration, irritation, and anger; the behavioral changes of poor concentration, forgetting, and poor performance; the physiological changes of headache and neckache. She felt helpless. She was gaining weight!

Obviously, this individual was eating a poor diet, not getting proper rest and relaxation, working at a taxing job, commuting to work, and spending more than she earned.

These all had a variety of negative consequences which were debilitating and, over time, would prove even more so. What is important to understand is that all of us have a certain amount of stress and anxiety in our lives. It is part of the human condition. However, it is most certainly possible to make wiser choices than did Dr. Matilda. Through a better understanding of the dynamics of stress and nutrition, this can be done. Prevention is the key.

Prevention is not just a "buzz" word; it is a "shout" word that is echoing across the land. It can be a wonderful life with prevention. Most of us were born healthy, but most of us do stupid things, over the years, to jeopardize that good health. Technology and the medical profession cannot protect us from our blatant disregard for the laws of nature and basic health rules. Hopefully, some are starting to wake up, but the confusing array of technology and much self-serving information is complicating matters. It is difficult to maintain our own good health and add years to our lives; but it can be done. It is not easy, though, when we are faced with a multimillion-dollar ripoff, says Rosenfeld in his book, *Modern Prevention, The New Medicine.*[4]

Some of the greatest minds in advertising approach us breathlessly, but with bright eyes. In a free enterprise system, if there's a buck to be made, there will be a whole flock going after it. Millions of dollars are spent in convincing us that one product is better than another, and multi-millions are reaped. The public is vulnerable and naive. It is nearly impossible to sort the wheat from the chaff in the present state of affairs. It seems that for every grain of wheat, there is a ton of chaff!

Someone needs to take the responsibility for giving solid, practical information about *prevention*.

Because this hasn't been done, the public is looking for such information wherever it can — advertisements, magazines, and television. A profit-seeking publisher can put a book on the best-seller list, but this does not necessarily mean that the author is right! Some who are more nearly correct never get published. Sometimes the truth does not sell well.

Oftentimes, there is some legitimate information, but it is lumped together with countless pitches for health fads, diets, and life-extension plans. Some of these are worthless, and some are outright dangerous. This book is dedicated to solving the dilemma we face.

The cost of health care has skyrocketed in the last decade. Insurance companies were picking up the tab, as if everything were free. Medical procedures were ordered regardless of their cost. But this wasteful system is starting to collapse, as insurance companies are beginning to make cost and coverage changes.

Consider for a moment that one-tenth of the price of a new compact car goes for autoworkers' health programs, according to Califano, the former Secretary of Health, Education, and Welfare. He also noted that in 1984, the U.S. spent $1,580 per person on health care. Compare this with West Germany at $900, Japan at $500, and Great Britain at $400. The health care in these other countries is also sophisticated and modern, perhaps not as high as ours; but life expectancy is just as high and the infant mortality rates are lower.[5]

The medical training field is showing some long-awaited signs of change. The importance of listening to a patient without causing the patient to feel that he is "weird" or that it's "all in his head" is evident in a few places, such as Wellness Associations in Spokane, Washington, where the patient is allowed and encouraged to be a partner in his or her own health care.

It does no good, and many times much harm, to tell a patient certain things. Many sincere and trusting patients are being told, in so many words, that they are at fault for making themselves ill. Granted, there is definitely a psychosomatic component to illness, as well as wellness; but it is something that is not willfully chosen, for the most part. How much better it is to help patients understand something about how stress is inevitable, and how it affects their bodies and feelings.

Researchers have found that a humane and caring physician who listens to the patient and allows that patient to actively participate in his or her recovery, sees that patient get well faster. Patients' attitudes are much more positive; and they are more likely to comply with mutually arrived at instructions for changes in lifestyles that will be conducive to improved health.

Dr. Krupat says, "As a result of such efforts, young physicians may learn that it does not necessarily take any more time to deal with a patient as a whole person, and even when it does require additional time, it is a good investment in positive results such as patient compliance."[6] No longer is one compelled to stay with anyone, including the physician, who is not willing to listen and be a friend. Nor is that other person obligated to take any undue abuse. If a doctor does not seem to have time to listen to you, in respect to your dignity and peace of mind, as well as that of the physician, it makes sense to find another!

Please realize that the normal defenses of the body will take care of your health, if you learn to do the *right* things, not the *wrong* ones. Then outside help is less likely to be needed. Besides, there are self-diagnostic kits available to test for such things as blood sugar level and salt concentration, among others. What we really need to do is take more responsibility for ourselves.

As we shall see, we will want to learn to control our internal stress levels. This can be done through our own thought processes of thinking *well*, not *ill*, by not smoking, and by controlling our intake of salt, sugar, and fat of all kinds. Then add to this list proper rest, relaxation, and plenty of exercise — the kind that makes us "huff and puff" a bit. Given the motivation and the necessary information, this can all come to pass. We'll each be able to slow down the aging process and much personal suffering.

Reasons for Concern

People are suffering. They are physically and psychologically crippled. Too little is known about the etiological factors involved. According to an article in the Spokesman Review on January 6, 1986, heart disease was the leading cause of death in this country in 1984, being responsible for 37.6 percent of all deaths. Non-heart circulatory diseases accounted for 9.9 percent. Cancer was second, being responsible for 22.2 percent of deaths. Other causes of death were: diabetes, 1.3 percent; influenza and pneumonia, 2.9 percent; chronic liver disease and cirrhosis, 1.3 percent; other diseases, 17.3 percent.[7] There is impressive evidence, as we shall see, that all of these disease states are caused or aggravated by stress and/or poor nutrition.

According to a Department of Agriculture report in 1986, Americans may think that they are eating better; but they continue to consume large quantities of foods which are known to have harmful effects. In 1983, the average person drank 40 gallons of soft drinks — an increase of 13 gallons since 1973. The consumption of ice cream and red meat also rose in the ten-year period.[8]

However, there is some indication of a decline during the past three years, according to a study done at the University of California in 1986. It reports that Americans have reduced their intake of sugary foods by 29 percent, bacon by 21 percent, and eggs and beef by 16 percent.

Consumption of salty foods, butter, and other fats also went down. More fruits, vegetables, poultry, and fish were eaten during the same period. Although this is an encouraging sign, the average American diet in 1970 was 44 percent fat, when 23 to 40 percent or less is recommended, according to Bailey.[9] When one considers that even these decreases represent extremely high consumptions, it becomes clear that we haven't made much progress.

Even so, it is certainly a move in the right direction.

Despite concerns about nutrition, eating habits haven't changed significantly. Basically, what we see from surveys over the last few years is that Americans have cut down on one bad habit, but have increased another. Even though the consumption of coffee, eggs, and whole milk has decreased, Americans are still consuming higher amounts of soft drinks, sugar, and fats.

A recent Gallup Organization study, conducted in January of 1985, shows that despite the current attention given to the relationship between diet and health in the public media, the majority of people pay no attention. Lack of attention seems to be due to the confusion that exists.[10] Basically, people want to do what's right, but they must first know what it is that is in their best interest. Many of them have a greater motivation along these lines after they have "hurt" long enough or severely enough from not doing what's best!

To the behavioral psychologist, this phenomenon is known as aversive conditioning. Unfortunately, much damage may have already resulted, but fortunately, as Pelletier says, "If a pathological pattern can be detected early enough, it becomes possible to rectify the pattern and prevent the degenerative progress toward disease."[11] This is our hope — prevention — through education and understanding.

Another finding of the Gallup Organization was that "Given America's obsession with diet and fitness, it was surprising to discover that when Gallup asked 1,557 adults to choose their favorite method of preparation for veal, shrimp, and chicken, a great many people chose a fat-and-calorie-laden method."[12] These are the very same people who eat billions of double cheeseburgers, french fries, and milk shakes every year.

In the same study, it was found that 31 percent liked their chicken fried, 22 percent liked it cooked in the oven, and 18 percent liked it barbecued. For 40 percent of the people, frying is also the favorite cooking method for shrimp, whereas only 18 percent prefer it broiled. The preference for fried foods is particularly true in the South.

Furthermore, fewer people were interested in low-calorie and low-salt food than just three years ago. When asked what they would order when eating out, only 19 percent (compared with 38 percent of those 18 to 24 years of age, in 1983) were interested in low-calorie foods; and only 18 percent (as compared with 28 percent in 1983) were interested in low-salt foods.

This makes me think of a conversation I overheard in a local country restaurant, recently. A customer, apparently in the 18 to 24 age bracket, said, "I would like a piece of banana cream pie." Another piped up, "Don't you know that'll make you fat?", to which the first responded, "At my stage in life, I'm far past worrying about that!"

In addition, the study also found that interest in low-salt, low-calorie food had decreased for the 25 to 34 and 35 to 49 age groups. The only group to show greater interest were the people over 50 years of age. This is true because as they age people become more concerned about strokes, heart attacks, and cancer. What a shame that they wait until after the fact! These disease processes may have been going on for some 10, 20, 30, or 40 years!

Some interesting sex and race differences showed up in this same study. More women were concerned about diet, but part of this could be that women store more fat than men as part of their genetic programming for child bearing and preservation. More muscle mass in the male requires a greater supply of energy. It is a fact that, on the average, a man can eat almost half again as much as a woman.

Twice as many women as men choose a low-calorie meal. Less than 25 percent of the men said they would choose low-salt food, although they, as a rule, are more likely to have high blood pressure. This compares with a third of the women who would choose low-salt food.

Blacks are more likely than whites to have high blood pressure; and they, likewise, are more likely to choose high- salt entrees.

Another study was conducted for the National Association for the Specialty Food Trade. In the October 15, 1985 issue of their journal, called *Showcase,* findings were reported that nearly 85 percent of 2,600 adults who were surveyed engaged in some kind of physical fitness. However, only 17 percent said they avoided carryout foods, which contain high amounts of sodium, fat, and calories. Of this group, only 11.9 percent said they did not buy this type of food because of additives and artificial ingredients.[13]

However, the report showed that many people were concerned about alcohol. Now, whether this is the result of stricter drunken driving laws or health concerns may be debatable; but the result is the same. More are turning to alternatives for hard liquor, such as wine coolers which are a mixture of wine and fruit juices; wine spritzers, which consist of wine and club soda; and kir which is white wine mixed with sweet liqueur.

Even though the demand is growing for cocktails that contain no so-called hard liquor, one should realize that every glass of beer and every glass of wine contains the same amount of alcohol as a jigger of hard alcohol such as whiskey, rum, vodka, and gin. It does not appear that the switch would prove advantageous. At any rate, Americans do seem somewhat more concerned about the ill effects of alcohol than regular food on the table; but it doesn't appear that they are doing much about it. Again, this state of affairs exemplifies the need for more education.

It Looks Like Trouble

Problems are not only found in middle-aged and older people. Kuntzleman reported, in January of 1986, that our young people have been showing declining health since the 1960's. They are flabby and don't show proper cardiovascular tone. They can't run as long on a treadmill, because they are not physically fit. Blood pressure is now significantly higher among all boys and girls than it was in the 1960's. This is true for black and white, poor and wealthy young people alike. In fact, twice as many had high blood pressure as in the sixties.[14]

According to a study done in 1986, which included 360 children ranging in age from 7 to 12, risk factors for heart disease start early. Forty-two percent had high blood cholesterol levels; 31 percent had elevated triglycerides; and 15 percent of the subjects had at least one risk factor for heart disease. Over half of them had three or more risk factors. As grade levels went up, so did the risk factors. Too much fat had been consumed by 68 percent of the children.[15]

In addition to the high pressure to perform in our society are: 1) poor eating habits, 2) insufficient sleep, and 3) inadequate exercise. Even though a national study conducted by the Department of Agriculture's Food and Nutrition Service in April of 1983 concluded that students who do eat school lunches have significantly higher energy levels than those who don't, only 50 percent of high school students eat school lunches. The other 50 percent are suffering from nutritional deficiencies which can affect their academic performance. For example, lack of iron reduces attention and, subsequently, achievement.[16]

Some instruction is presently given in science and health classes on the ill effects of too much sodium and saturated fats and the benefits of more fiber, but somehow this knowledge doesn't seem to be transferring into real life. The kids go to the fast food chains (such as McDonald's or Wendy's) where they "pig-out" on fats, sugars, and salt that are major threats to their cardiovascular and glandular functioning, by putting stress on the body. Some fast-food outlets are now making available to the public the nutritional content of their foods, but I'm not sure how meaningful that information is to either kids or adults.

The hearty, well-balanced meal of yesteryear is now more of an exception than a rule. More and more families are not eating home-cooked meals together. As the children watch TV (on the average) about six hours per day, they are munching down commercially prepared snack-oriented foods. Most teenagers scramble out of bed just in time to catch a ride to school, thus skipping breakfast. This practice has been found to reduce the ability to solve problems, especially reflective and analytical abilities.

An increase in quality food intake is necessary during the growth spurt of adolescence, particularly for the hormone system. If nutritional needs are not met, sexual development may be arrested in both males and females; and later chronic diseases may develop. Therefore, it should be clear that poor diet is a reality for many of our young people and most certainly stresses their bodies.

Moreover, our young people generally are not getting enough sleep in order to restore their bodies from the stresses of life. For one thing, the high-decibel sounds that have invaded the bedroom are far from the lullabies of yesteryear. Parents may think their children are asleep, not realizing that the earphones may be camouflaging the truth — that the kids are listening to music and/or watching TV until maybe 2:00 a.m. Many times they fall asleep to find their ears still plugged when the alarm goes off in the morning. This happened to my own son, on many an occasion! This is appalling when one considers that the actual sleep needs of most teenagers is the same as when they were 12 years of age — approximately nine hours per night.

According to a study conducted by the Stanford University Sleep Center, young people who don't get this much sleep lack energy during the day. The conclusion of Dr. William Dement, Director of the Stanford Center is, "Both parents and adolescents, especially college-age adolescents, need to be educated as to the vital importance of getting enough sleep, and the consequences of improper sleep habits, which are typical of most teenagers today."[17]

Another consideration is that of physical exercise, which is very necessary for controlling the effects of stress on the body. The President's Council on Physical Education and Sports has recommended a minimum of 30 minutes of vigorous physical activity per day, for all students. However, what is happening, according to the council, is that 90 percent of the students are meeting the physical education requirements with two or three classes a week in a nonaerobic sport, instead of aerobics, such as gymnastics and calisthenics, which were once required. More and more schools are not requiring any physical education classes after the 10th grade.[18]

Lack of exercise does not occur only in the school setting. During the 60s, youngsters were spending more time in outdoor physical activities, such as walking or riding their bikes to and from school, and then playing outdoors. As mentioned earlier, the average adolescent today spends six hours a day in front of the TV at home or with peers.

In addition to all of the above, the emotional health of our young people is not up to par. Parents are spending less and less time with their children — no more than an average of 10 to 20 minutes per day! This short time usually takes the form of criticizing or giving orders, and the parents are not given them the emotional help and guidance that is needed. This, in turn, can lead to drug abuse.[19]

Mann reported in March of 1986 that "Prior to 1962, less than two percent of the entire U.S. population had any experience with an illegal drug. By 1985, 54 percent of high school seniors had smoked 'pot,' and 17.3 percent had used cocaine."[20]

According to Richard Jessor, Director of the Institute of Behavioral Science at the University of Colorado in Boulder, teenage drug users have increased sexual activity by almost 50 percent over the non-users. This trend is continuing, and sexually transmitted diseases have reached epidemic proportions for millions of adolescents.[21] When one thinks about the evidence that drugs impair the immune system, then the AIDS epidemic takes on additional significance!

In 1979, the death rate had gone down significantly since 1960, for all age groups *except* the 15-24 year olds, according to the U.S. Surgeon General. This report also indicated that 75 percent of our kids died as the result of traffic accidents which were primarily alcohol and/or drug related, other accidents, suicide (which has tripled since 1976), and homicide. This same report also concluded that the present lifestyles of the young could very well affect their susceptibility to disease in later life.[22]

As a teaching and counseling psychologist for many years, as well as a parent of two young adults, I am duly concerned about the health and productivity of our young people. It is at an extremely low ebb right now, at a time when never before in history has there been a greater need for energy and power for living. I have also observed that the emotional health of our young people is not what it should be. College kids are definitely not the same as they once were. Some observers say that it is difficult to even get a "good fight" out of them. The antipathy of the 60s was more like apathy in the 80s! Today, they seem more anxious, but "stressed-out" and lethargic.

We must do something to "stem the tide." An improvement in any one of the areas discussed — emotions, diet, exercise, and sleep — would increase the ability to function and to cope on the part of young people, the adults of tomorrow.

As Dr. Robert Dupont, an international expert on public health, has noted, "We must never forget that health practices acquired during adolescence persist throughout life."[23]

2.

UBIQUITOUS STRESS

Even though a varied and substantial amount has been written about stress, it still remains vague and not well understood. In order to begin the process of better understanding, it would be well to consider two truths. In the first place, stress is not always harmful. Our lives are full of it, and we cannot escape from it. Secondly, it is how we deal with it that counts. Poor reactions certainly are harmful and do bring on many disease states.

At this point in time, people have about 25 years to grow up and 40 years to do their "thing." Then we tend to slide along or go down hill until "check out time." Many of us are obsessed with earning the highest possible marks for our achievements within the unknown (but short time that we have); and we drive our hearts and minds at a killing pace. We can, indeed, do ourselves a favor at any stage in life, by not overworrying about ourselves and our troubled times, by not smoking, and by not over- or under-eating.

It is possible to extend our lives by 50 percent, according to Walford. "Age is a time of ripeness and wisdom,"[1] he says. Functionally, older people can be happy and productive as they engage in new social roles, pursue more leisure time, re-education, and multiple careers. We hope society will be ready for us, because here we come, ready or not!

Today, only 83 percent of the population live to be 60 years or older.[2] We can, indeed, have more quality (as well as quantity) time, with a better understanding of stress and its control.

Life is Stress

It's not just the major catastrophes like loss of a job, serious illness, divorce, or death that cause stress. The little stresses we cope with every day, like running out of time, dealing with distractions, and waiting our turn, add up to "killer" dimensions. On the average a person reacts to stress 125 and 150 times a day.

As we shall see, every time this happens a surge of catecholamines and steroids flood the bloodstream. If this build-up is not allowed to subside, it eventually "snow-balls." When we realize that this can be going on in the body 24 hours a day, 7 days a week, 52 weeks a year, it should become clear that stress is our biggest source of pain and an unseen killer.

The stress response in the body itself is natural, but the environments is abnormally high in stressors. Therefore, there is an incongruence, or imbalance, and the body is asked to deal with an insurmountable task — too much stress. It's the effect of stress on the *weakest* body links that first creates a problem. A genetic predisposition for cardiovascular problems, or gastrointestinal, or skeletal-muscular, or metabolic, or neurological, could provide a certain vulnerability to stress-related disease states. That's why stress seems to effect people in different ways, or why people respond to stress in various modes.

Some of us are "hot reactors." Probably one out of five healthy people approach every situation as if it were "mortal combat." This can happen 30 or 40 times a day. The autonomic nervous system seems to be "trigger happy." We are the ones who are more likely to need medications, counseling, relaxation, and diet therapy.

James E. Skinner, a neuroscientist at Baylor College of Medicine in Houston, is researching to find out if there's a neuropeptide or enzyme in the frontal lobe of the brain, responsible for determining when a fight-or-flight response is appropriate. Perhaps an over supply of this, if it exists, could lead to problems. Skinner believes that a breakthrough is close at hand.[3]

Meanwhile, from the research conducted at MIT by the Wurtman's, we know that the diet can regulate the production of serotonin in the brain, a very powerful neurotransmitter that prevents surges of the catecholamines and steroids that overwhelm the body when one is terrified or angry.[4] Research in this area is also being conducted at Harvard by a team of cardiologists, neurologists, and psychologists. This is our protection, then, in addition to our knowledge about cognitive therapy, relaxation, and proper exercise in controlling the adverse reactions to stress.

Definition

The concept of stress is a slippery one. It is many times thought of as the threats and challenges to which we are exposed. These can have positive effects by arousing and motivating us, or harmful effects, by lasting too long or being too severe. Usually, when we are pressured or in conflict, our bodies and minds experience stress. It can take the form of physical, cognitive, or social stress; but more often than not, it is a combination of all three or more.

If the stress is great enough to cause one to expend more energy, whether it be biological, mental, emotional, or behavioral, then one would, under normal circumstances, undoubtedly be experiencing stress, perhaps more appropriately called *strain*.

Any stimulus from the environment that causes physical or psychological activity is a stressor. These stressors do produce physiological arousal, tension, and sometimes anxiety. Not only do environmental stimuli cause arousal and sometimes failure to adapt, but there are also internal demands that sometimes can exceed the capacity of the organism to adapt.

Anything perceived as a catastrophe (either minor or major) in one's life can cause this kind of strain. Basically, stress can be viewed as any reaction or set of reactions to a real or perceived threat to one's safety.

However, it must be realized that we all should function at a positive state of motivation or arousal. This level is tolerable and non-pathological; but it can be changed to the opposite by incessant stressors, either psychological, physical, or environmental. These can cause a malfunction in the psychological and/or physiological system, usually thought of as hyper-activation; but it can also take the form of hypo-activation.

Disorders caused by stress usually occur after a fairly long time and, therefore, are believed to be developmental. Pelletier says, "If a pathological pattern can be detected early enough, it becomes possible to rectify the pattern and prevent the degenerative progress toward disease."[5]

Another position which has some merit is this: man is a combative animal and will undoubtedly always be one. This predisposition attracts him to all kinds of competition. Modern man's way of life affects him profoundly as he works all day and worries at night, when he should be sleeping. Jarvis says, "The way of living he has created will not wreck him, however, if he learns how to control the energy expending mechanisms of his body."[6]

We have as part of our innate or inherited biochemical programming, the predisposition to prepare to strike back or run away whenever we perceive a danger, a demand, or a problem — anything that threatens us! Our ancestors passed this down to us through natural selection, a process that gave us physical ability to deal with an environment that is often competitive and/or hostile. This is known as the "fight-or-flight" response, which activates that part of our autonomic nervous system known as the sympathetic division, designed to provide the necessary energy. The other part is called the parasympathetic, to give us calm, rest, and recuperation. The problems come when there is too much sympathetic activation and not enough parasympathetic function.

Some New Ideas

Modern man's mind creates stress in a rather phenomenal way, but we do not create stress intentionally. Today's man is very different from his caveman ancestors. In order to survive, humans have evolved from primitive beings who probably reacted more to direct and immediate physical dangers , then gradually, to more intelligent ones, hopefully, with the ability to foresee dangers. This should be in his best interest if the dangers become reality and he can expend the pent-up, generated energy in coping with them. But man has the ability to synthesize information from all of his senses and then react to the image or picture that he has created in his own mind; and if he does not find appropriate ways of reacting and a release for this stress, difficulties do occur.

The modern, sophisticated human can project his conscious awareness from today to tomorrow. All of this information is stored in the brain and becomes the memory. One is not usually "consciously" aware of this information unless some stimulus triggers or activates the recall. Even then, one probably is not aware of the influence that it's having on his/her thoughts and actions. Therefore, this part of man's functioning is usually referred to as the sub-conscious mind or the subliminal mind; but it is always there to influence an individual's future behavior — inwardly and outwardly. The stress is there, *somewhere!*

Unconscious motivation, then, is a very real thing. Many times, we do not know why we feel the way we do or act the way we do. The behaviors may take the form of *generalized* anxiety.

Moreover, today's human is also different from those of earlier times and from any other form of life — in another very distinct way. Our species has created a highly complex social structure — an environment of mental thoughts, ideas, and images. This condition expands, more and more, as time goes on; and we look at this decade of the 90s.

Constantly we are trying to cope with such social situations as making a living, getting along with people, and living by the rules. Those of us who believe that these things are important are said to have a social conscience. We are more likely to suffer from duress when we see others (or ourselves) not living up to the dictates of our moral beliefs. We are either fearful or angry about the whole state of affairs! Many times, out of moral restraints, we do nothing. We may have a fear of "rocking the boat." This can be interpreted by others as a "don't care" attitude, and situations can become worse instead of better. These are very different, indeed, from the more physical stressors of our ancestors. Albeit, they had theirs, too, but the times have changed.

Difficulties in dealing with the social environment occur primarily when we lack the information necessary for understanding. When this happens, we feel threatened! Our very survival and/or well-being is at stake, and we continue to live under duress. It seems absolutely incredible that man would produce such a "monster" of a social environment and not have the foresight to simultaneously achieve the where-with-all to cope with it! Quite obviously, as the result of this dilemma, man has more diseases than any other form of life and more hazards to deal with than ever before known in history. However, we do plan to survive.

Obviously the road to "stressland" is conceptual, but so is the road out! It behooves us to use our conceptualizing mentality. This means understanding and awareness of our society, our culture, our experiences, our conditioning (learning), and thinking. Our stresses are manufactured out of the raw material of life and existence. Since intelligence actually gets us in trouble — our intelligence can get us out! We have emotions (feelings), both positive and negative, because we are intelligent human beings. To be emotional is to be human. An emotion is the result of thinking, not a primitive reflex. This is the crux of the human stress response. We think ourselves into it — we must think ourselves out! To do this, it is mandatory that we explore our resources and alternatives, secure relevant information, and increase our awareness, so that we can cope. It is not simple, but it can be done! The human brain is a marvelous creation.

As we try to conceptualize stress, we find that is very difficult. It is a complex mixture of the mind, body, our inborn nature, and social conditions. Out of all of this comes pain and unhappiness; seeming, somehow, to pop up out of nowhere, and causing us to abuse the functioning of our minds and bodies.

The operations of the mind form such a tight circle of incessant rumination and morbid preoccupation that perceptions become distorted and unreal. The modus operandi of the mind is that it generates feelings that can really "rattle your cage." Rumination keeps *attention* on the problem, rather than solving it. The mind becomes so preoccupied with "gloom and doom" that things are no longer as they are, but as they seem to fit some disastrous outcome. We hear only what we want to hear and see only what we want to see. The signals (as to our internal state) become inhibited, and we cannot detect the tensions building up in our bodies.

The higher brain cannot do its job because blood is leaving the higher brain and going, instead, to the primitive or reflex brain. This is to prepare us for immediate "fight" or flight!" Muscles continue adapting to higher and higher levels of tension. Because the mind is ruminating on its difficulties, the muscles of the body stay tense and ready to take action. Over time, this whole process of dis-ease becomes disease. These threats to our personal well-being are not "out there," but "in here."

It has been said that stress is in the "eye of the beholder." In other words, it is our *perception* of the environment; that is, the meaning we attach to what we sense, whether we see it, hear it, and/or feel it. Our senses give us information about the world, but our brains perceive it. New information is always associated with that gained from previous experience and stored in the memory. This gives us a picture of what is going on "out there," but it may or may not be correct. Barbara A. Brown, in her book, *Between Health and Illness,* gives a convincing account of how stress is in the mind.[7]

Achiever's Disease

In the beginning, stress comes out of the hopes and dreams that we have been taught to have; but in their pursuit, life presents us with challenges. We join society in demanding more and better performances, successes, and achievements — and the demand never ends! We tend to feel that any failures must be weaknesses in ourselves. This has become known as "Achiever's Disease" and is common in people who are super-conscientious. Many are hard-driving professionals who have lost control of the stress in their lives, according to Susan Zarrow.[8]

Common complaints are headaches, insomnia, indigestion, low back pain, shoulder and neck pain, chest pain, and high blood pressure. These people feel discouraged, angry, rushed, distracted, and frustrated. They start forgetting things; and their thinking is scattered, with lack of focus. They seem almost totally overwhelmed, and many actually shed tears from the pressure and frustration.

There is one very good reason why those with Achiever's Disease have problems. They put too much pressure on themselves! They want to do a good job! They over schedule themselves at work and at home, never taking time to relax. They don't even know what the word means, let alone what's happening to their bodies! They are not mentally ill in the popular sense of the term, but their bodies start to fall apart. Perhaps this is partly because they do have active intellects. They are very bright, achieved good grades in college, and are successful. Their brains are super-strong, but the rest of the body starts to crumble.

Research has demonstrated that when people enter a stress-reduction program designed to help each one understand, individuals do get control again. The process involves learning to quantify their stress and become aware of situations which provoke the stress response. Then they can cognitively talk themselves out of a negative thought and replace it with a positive one. An example of this might be to say something like, "Oh, this is ridiculous to feel angry! It's only temporary," when faced with an anxiety-arousing situation.

Since all high achievers are *self-stimulators*, they should not consume massive amounts of coffee, "sweets," and cigarettes. This provides the perfect combination for anxiety.

The hypoglycemic diet is the diet of choice. It calls for protein in the morning, eating all three meals each day or dividing the food up into six small meals each day, and refraining from large amounts of simple sugar. This should be accompanied by some low-impact aerobic exercise that is enjoyable. People feel better, and the world looks better when they exercise!

Controlling the physiological response to stress through relaxation is also very effective. This slows down the thinking, the talking, the bodily processes, and improves performance.

Stress inoculation is possible, wherein one learns not to get excited. We can switch from a high-stress state to a low-stress one, that allows us to cope, feeling calm and thinking clearly. The tools are available for dealing with the world in a more calm, cool, and collected manner.

Self-Fulfilling Prophesies

It has been found that pessimists handle stress more poorly than do optimists. This has to do with the theory of self-fulfilling prophesies. Individuals tend to conform to others' expectations of them, which is known as the "Pygmalion effect." This is also true for the expectations that people have for their own lives, and it is transformed into visceral and emotional qualities.

People whose explanatory style is to blame themselves for their misfortunes are more susceptible to disease. The health of pessimists usually starts to decline quickly during middle-age. The attitude of "helplessness" is associated with weakening of the immune system, and pessimists have more tumors and infections. They also tend to neglect themselves more through poor nutrition, smoking and drinking more, and exercising less.

Optimists, on the other hand, have an explanatory style of seeing a failure as something that they can do something about or as something that they can change. Stress is not as devastating to them.

Martin Seligman, a psychologist at the University of Pennsylvania, says, "It is the combination of reasonable talent and the ability to keep going in the face of defeat that leads to success.... What you need to know about someone is whether they will keep going when things get frustrating."[9]

Pessimists make a mess of their lives. They talk gloom and doom, "turn off," and the self-fulfilling prophesy manifests itself. More bad things happen to them; like break-ups, family troubles, and failure in school and the work-place, leaving them estranged from people and lonely. They are less likely to "bounce back" from trouble than the optimists.

However, cognitive therapy that identifies and corrects false habits of thought has met with some successes. Some former pessimists have been found to still be optimists one year after therapy. The program requires that subjects monitor their automatic thoughts in reaction to things that bother them and then to replace them with ones that are more realistic. Hopelessness and helplessness can be replaced with hopefulness and helpfulness!

With a combination of wisdom and humor, Lawrence Galton sums it up well when he gives tips on effective handling of stress. These ideas originally came from Dr. Robert S. Elliot of the University of Nebraska Medical Center. They are as follows:

(1) The bottom line of stress is not to upset yourself.

(2) Develop a thick skin. Why hate when a little dislike will do...have anxiety when you can be nervous...have rage when anger will do the job...be depressed when you can be sad?

(3) Rule number one is: Don't sweat the small stuff.

(4) Rule number two is: It's all small stuff.

(5) If you can't fight and you can't flee, flow.[10]

There Is More To It Than That

Several medical doctors are now questioning that emphasis which has been placed only on emotional stressors. For instance, Dr. Charles T. McGee of Coeur d'Alene, Idaho says "If there ever was a time when humans were under stress it must have been in Europe during World War II. Cities were destroyed. People were bombed, displaced, shot, and starved. But death rates from diabetes and heart attacks fell in Europe during the war, instead of rising, as would be anticipated by following the stress theory: ... sugar became unavailable, and whole wheat bread replaced white bread so as to save energy. Nutritional quality was improved by the elimination of refined carbohydrates and a general reduction in caloric intake...if there is anything we have adapted to on this earth, it is stress ... emotional stress will not produce organic disease in a well-nourished individual."[11]

Dr. John A. McDougal, practicing in Kailua, Hawaii says, "When people are exposed to difficult or challenging situations that they cannot immediately resolve or escape from, they will often experience mental-emotional stress. The history of the human race is marked by stressful daily experiences forced upon us from so many sources that one must conclude that stress is a natural and expected condition we must learn to live with. Stress is functional and necessary in that it creates an environment that motivates us to get the job done and the situation resolved. When satisfactory progress is not being made in resolving the stress-producing situation, health problems may be the consequence. Unfortunately, stress has become the scapegoat for an infinite number of physical and mental health problems. The scientific evidence to support the theory of stress as the immediate cause of disease is insufficient in most cases. Although stress in itself is only a small factor in the processes that lead directly to disease, it can have significant indirect effects. Stress frequently brings on self-destructive behavior, that is characterized by the above, of food, tobacco, alcohol, and drugs. When people placed under stress abandon a health-supporting diet and lifestyle, they become physically ill. Stressful situations also can bring on an interesting form of behavior where one rewards or comforts one's self by indulging in harmful habits to compensate for all the suffering one is going through."[12]

Dr. Carl J. Reich, practicing in Calgary, Alberta, Canada says, "Diseases arising for reason of psychological or physical stresses do not occur because of the exhaustion of the endocrine adaptive response of the body. Instead, these disease states occur because, prior to the advent of this stress, the adaptive potential of the tissue which becomes diseased had already been rendered imperfect by chemical deficiencies and/or excesses usually inflicted by the diet. The disease therefore is not so much a 'stress adaptive disease' as it is 'deficiency-stress maladaptive disease'."[13]

Common Pitfalls

All drugs which are psychic energizers or "uppers" usually facilitate or increase nerve transmission in the autonomic nervous system. They make us more active, physically and mentally. As we know, this increases our breathing, heart rate, and so forth. Caffeine is probably the most commonly used stimulant drug in our society. Coffee, black tea, chocolate, and colas are all high in caffeine content. Caffeine chemically induces a "fight or flight" response by stimulating the adrenal glands the same way as an emotional response of fear or anger. If we are already trying to cope with stress, caffeine will make matters worse. It also depletes the body of the "B" vitamins.

A more dangerous class of drugs are called "pep pills" or diet pills, because they depress the appetite. Some trade names for these are Benzedrine, Dexadrine, and Methedrine. When used illicitly, they are referred to as "speed." Continued use of these amphetamines can cause a severe mental disorder called paranoid schizophrenia. Every cigarette, every "hit" from a "joint," and every "snort" of cocaine has the same stress on the nervous system, in varying degrees, of course.

Sugar should be used sparingly or avoided, because it is a highly refined simple carbohydrate, with no starch, fiber, vitamins, or minerals and provides nothing, nutritionally, except calories.

The average American consumes an average of 128 to 160 pounds of sugar a year. A twelve ounce can of Coca-Cola contains nine teaspoons of it. When under stress, the body may already have too much glucose. There is no wonder that the incidence of degenerative diseases is so high. The number of people who are pre-diabetic or pre-hypoglycemic is now believed to be three out of five — that's 60 percent. This may be due to the abuse of the pancreas, to say nothing about the cardiovascular system.

Many of us are very sensitive to changes in blood sugar level. When we eat foods which are high in refined sugar, our blood sugar level goes shooting up. This gives us a small burst of energy and a restless feeling. The pancreas has to secrete insulin, to counteract the sugar in the blood. With a great amount of sugar, the pancreas can over-react and produce too much insulin which will bring the blood sugar level too low. This condition is then known as hypoglycemia — resulting in dizziness, irritability, depression, tremor, nausea, or anxiety.

There are also hunger pangs to motivate us to have another sweet. We may experience a 20 minute high, but then a two hour crash! Over and over again! With the environmental or emotional stress which usually goes along with this, we are virtually on a stress "roller coaster." Sugar is the fuel that keeps it going, and we are taken for one wild ride!

Besides sugar, there are other refined foods or simple carbohydrates to avoid. Saliva in the mouth immediately turns these foods sweet. They are white flour, white rice, processed cereals, processed fruit products, and over-cooked vegetables. Milling, refining, processing, and cooking removes much of the fiber, vitamins, minerals, and starch. Some starch may be left, but also a lot of sugar.

Thus, refined carbohydrates are higher in calories and lower in nutrients than the whole foods from which they come. Enrichment does not put back all that was destroyed.

Alcohol leaches out necessary water soluble vitamins and minerals as it dehydrates the tissues. Even though alcohol is a central nervous system depressant, the pancreas and liver treat it just as they do sugar. Anytime alcohol is consumed with food, more glucose is changed into glycogen and stored in the fat cells.

Contrary to popular opinion, alcohol does not induce sleep. It interferes with sleep and dreaming, so necessary for a hold on sanity.

The human body needs no more than 250 milligrams to 5 grams of sodium per day. Yet children and adults consume up to 10 to 20 times that amount! The body already has an abundance of salt in a stress reaction, which leads to high blood pressure, as we know. Table salt contains 40 percent sodium. Almost all processed foods contain sodium, as does baking soda, baking powder, and many medications, such as antacids. It has been found that hypertensive patients consume much more sodium than those with normal blood pressure. So, this is another stressor to avoid.

In addition, aspirin has been linked to the malabsorption and depletion of vitamins and minerals. When we are under stress, we require more of all the vitamins and minerals. Especially important are the B vitamins. Also, deficiencies in vitamin C, calcium, and magnesium have been linked to insomnia, irritability, depression, and fatigue — all stress-related symptoms. The absorption of vitamin E is hampered by chlorinated water.

Fat is also a problem in stress-related disorders. In most cases, at least in the early progression of disease, the body stores too much fat, causing many problems, including those of a cardiovascular nature. A large body of research indicates that too much saturated fat in the diet is not healthy for the heart. There is new evidence indicating that unsaturated fats are deleterious to the immune system. Of course, the body needs essential fatty acids; but these can be obtained with as little as one teaspoon of fat intake per day!

Saturated and unsaturated fats do differ. However, they can both be very dangerous. Saturated fat is solid at room temperature. It contains all the hydrogen it can possibly hold. Polyunsaturated fats are liquid at room temperature. When these are substituted for the saturated fats, cholesterol levels may drop tremendously, decreasing the likelihood of a heart attack.

However, over-consumption of polyunsaturated fats can cause problems in other ways, such as conditions associated with a weak immune system — tumors, cancers, infectious diseases, and yes, AIDS. The wise thing to do is to avoid the saturated fats, including margarine and Crisco or Crisco-like products, but also to avoid the polyunsaturates!

Manufacturers turn liquid vegetable fat into a solid by adding hydrogen to the oil. This process changes the fatty acids by altering some of their components into unnatural forms. Abnormal fatty acids also tend to collect in the cardiovascular system, and polyunsaturated fats damage the immune system. It would be a far better choice to eat a small amount of butter, mixed with cold-pressed safflower or rape seed oil, which would be much more compatible with the human body — "better butter!"

The latest stressors that we have learned about are silver amalgams, or fillings in our teeth, with which we chew our food. In addition to the toxicity of the mercury attaching itself to the sites in the red blood cells which carry oxygen (not being compatible with protein and altering the immune system) it has a galvanic effect.

The environment in the mouth can be compared to a storage battery. Amalgams contain dissimilar metals that are contained in an acid solution provided by the saliva, which acts as the electrolyte; and together they generate an electrogalvanic current. These electrical impulses, which are measured in microamps, may affect the function of the brain.

Dr. Robert Stephan, of Spokane, Washington, explains that brain impulses are measured at about seven or eight microamps. Therefore, if a tooth can emit 40 to 50 microamps, "We are talking about a considerably larger amount of electricity that is actually carrying messages around in the brain. The neurological implications are, as far as I know, somewhat unknown."[14]

Dr. Stephan described patient improvements since he stopped using amalgams five years ago. "Some of the major symptoms which we have seen disappear instantly include headaches, muscular aches and pains, a feeling of overall lowered energy levels, and itching and skin rashes."[15]

Well, there is no doubt that stress is a major problem in our society. I would say that probably 75 percent or more of bodily disease is stress-related. This situation is undoubtedly costing us billions of dollars every year. It is difficult to put a dollar sign on the unhappiness, irritability, and dissatisfaction in our lives, but the price is there. How much better off we would all be if we could learn to control our stress level through relaxation and proper nutrition!

More Stress In The Name of Less

There are a number of ways in which some individuals try to eliminate or control stress and actually wind up creating more! For instance, the only way to dispose of fat is to burn it up through muscular activity; but if one exercises too much, too much glucose is used up and the brain suffers from too little sugar or hypoglycemia. One can get woozy, dizzy, have blurred vision, and maybe even faint from lack of brain food.

After all, the brain is a glucose "hog" — it needs 66 times as much glucose as one pound of muscle, even though it may weigh as little as one pound itself! While one is unconscious from "passing out," the liver converts protein to glucose — a very dangerous phenomenon. One loses muscle and, if the diet is low in carbohydrates and calories, one will lose muscle even faster.

The reason for this is that amino acids are also burned in muscles by the oxidative enzymes, if the body can't get enough energy from fats, or glucose from sufficient carbohydrates; and, therefore, valuable protein, which should be reserved for tissue repair, is burned. Therefore, inappropriate exercise can be very dangerous in terms of loss of muscle.

In all cases, those excercising should be sure their diet is balanced. They need to eat up to 60 grams of protein a day, which should be 8 to 12 percent of their calories, but if their carbohydrate intake is low, protein will be used for the making of glucose, instead of tissue repair. Three-fifths, or 60 percent, of one's total caloric intake should be from the complex carbohydrates found in whole grains, vegetables, pasta, etc. This leaves 30 percent of the calories from fat.

However, there are some recent findings that indicate that it would be far better to decrease the fat intake down to as low as 10 percent or less; and increase the complex carbohydrates. In view of recent findings, it would appear that all fats are very deleterious to the cardiovascular system, as well as to the immune system; I would therefore suggest keeping the fat intake as low as possible, until more definitive findings are in.

At the present time, the RDA (Recommended Daily Allowances) of the American Heart Association and the Academy of Science if for 30 percent fat; but I would predict that this will change in the future.

Exercise stimulates hunger in an overweight person as mostly glucose is burned, causing temporary low blood-sugar. Overweight people lack fat-burning enzymes. They have an insulin insensitivity, and their blood-sugar shoots up because the glucose has trouble entering the muscle and goes to the fat cells instead. Here, the sugar is converted into triglycerides.

So overweight people who exercise heavily can't burn the fat they are trying to shed. Again, stress causes trouble! What these people do is exercise mildly and eat complex carbohydrates that enter the blood stream slowly. Such food should be in small quantities and eaten six or more times a day.

As one gets fat, bodily changes cause one to get fatter. In fat people, both blood-sugar level and insulin are high. This causes the person's tissues to be insensitive to his or her own insulin. The muscles can't respond to insulin, and the glucose which is circulating in the bloodstream goes to the fat cells — they become a glucose "reservoir."

Inside the fat cells, this glucose is converted to glycerol, that attaches to three fat molecules, which equals glycerol plus three fatty acids. These are then known as triglycerides, which are the neutral, stable, and good kind of fat that the body needs. However, in excess they cause physical and emotional problems. No one wants to be fat! It is paradoxical, indeed, that the individual with the least need for the storage of energy stores it the fastest!

If one is physically ill or has an emotional problem coupled with a poor diet, exercise will do no good! It would only be another stressor and would cancel out any beneficial outcomes. Doing such a thing would be like "whipping a tired horse!" No one should allow himself or herself to be coerced into exercising when they are not able.

Furthermore, recent biochemical evidence indicates that exercising isolated muscles, as is done in weight lifting, actually stimulates intense glucose burning, but synthesizes fats in the muscles. Again, another kind of stress that causes the accumulation of fat, but one about which so few people are aware.

Competitive exercise causes maximum stress and is known as anaerobic stress. Here, blood flow to the digestive organs is restricted and digestion is impeded — a pure and direct physiological stress reaction! This accounts for the fact that if one exercises vigorously after eating, one gets sick! The muscles are more likely to cramp because of the radical change in blood flow, digestion, and adrenalin secretion.

Gentle exercise, known as aerobic, does not do this. Furthermore, aerobic exercise after a sensible meal can be beneficial, whereas anaerobic exercise shuts off all fat burning and causes the muscles to use glucose instead of fat. Therefore, weight is not lost!

Technically, this is what happens. If exercise causes the pulse rate to exceed 80 percent of maximum, which can be determined by taking the number 220 minus one's age, one is in trouble!

For instance, if a person is 40 years of age, then his or her maximum heart rate would be 180. This is the fastest that one's heart should beat. Never, but *never,* exercise at this rate! That would constitute an anaerobic exercise that would be very dangerous and certainly would not contribute to weight loss.

If the pulse rate exceeds 80 percent of maximum, the heart and lungs cannot keep up with the oxygen requirements of the muscles. Then the glucose is broken down to pyruvic acid, which cannot be burned; and it accumulates in the muscle where it is converted into lactic acid. This can be very painful. In smaller amounts, it makes us feel tired; but in excessive amounts, it causes pain, often very intense, and damage occurs. Only one-fifth of the acid can be converted back into pyruvic acid after the exercise, when oxygen again enters the muscles. The other four-fifths is converted into fatty acids or triglycerides.

Many "fitness freaks" over-stress themselves to their own detriment. Glucose burning in anaerobic exercise requires little oxygen, but the enzymes needed in aerobic exercise for fat breakdown need a great deal of oxygen. Enzymes break up the fatty acid to get energy out of it in an orderly sequence called a *chemical pathway* or *beta oxidation pathway*. In intense exercise beyond 80 percent of maximum heart rate, DNA (deoxyribonucleic acid) synthesis of enzymes is not possible. The enzymes cannot proliferate. One simply does not have the oxygen necessary to use fats.

Famine Adaptation

Another faulty but very common practice in weight control is that of eating fewer than 800 calories each day. Many diets propose creative ways to starve one's self. Some of these diets consist of no carbohydrates, or all grapefruit, or are limited to several kinds of fresh fruits, or even to all eggs! They are not successful in keeping the weight off, as many people have learned the hard way.

What many people do not know is that these starvation diets set off a reflex mechanism known as *famine adaptation*. When this occurs, the metabolic rate is lowered within 48 hours of beginning a low-calorie diet. The BMR (Basic Metabolic Rate) is decreased by 20 percent within two weeks and up to 30 percent as one continues to diet. People "starve" in Ethiopia, but we "diet" in America. The real fact is that the BMR can still be depressed as long as six months following cessation of the diet. However, with exercise, the BMR can be reversed or increased again by the end of one month, even while still on the diet. To be effective in raising the BMR, the exercise must be continuous for 30 minutes a day!

With a lowered metabolic rate, there is more efficient use of energy and a general feeling of tiredness. This all leads to decreased physical activity. The body is doing its job well! The ability to store food is a great advantage, like having money in the bank, because it increases our chances for survival — it's a safety mechanism.

In prehistoric times, man was forced to "live off his hump" like the camel. This was necessary in order to endure famines, which were usually short. Modern man, a highly evolutionary species, has evolved even better ways of doing it! He has many biochemical routes for the synthesis of fat and ways of saving it.

Our caveman ancestors often had to go days without eating. The ones who survived were probably the ones who adapted to the sparse supply of food. They did so by carrying a little extra fat to use in times of need. They were very active, so they didn't carry too much and get fat, but we have inherited that ability to store fat; and, in so doing, tuck away a few calories out of every meal.

Therefore, under the conditions of famine adaptation, we don't eat much, we don't lose much and, if we do, we easily gain it back! Here, then, is another example of what physiological stress does to the body. Stress of any kind or description is always countered with an increase in the deposition of fat and a decrease in the utilization of stored fat.

Fasting, in terms of greatly reduced caloric intake on a temporary basis, is another stress that makes one think that one is getting thinner, but in actuality, one is getting fatter, with all of its dangerous consequences. However, man also has a highly developed brain; he can and should understand and make wise choices.

Still another dietary calamity is the practice of skipping meals. Daily famines of 18 to 20 hours trigger the process of famine adaptation. If one skips breakfast, the very meal that is necessary to "break the fast," one can easily create the 18 to 20 hour daily famine. This practice is very common among women. They tend to think that they are too busy, that it stimulates their appetites, that they get upset stomachs, or that nothing sounds good. What many do not realize is that this practice of skipping breakfast actually brings on the famine adaptation process whereby the fat they wish so much to lose is actually stored!

Animal and human research alike provide evidence that eating more often is correlated with weight loss, not gain! Six small feedings of breakfast, snack, lunch, snack, dinner, and snack is now becoming the "name of the game." People who do this have more energy all day and do not store excess fat. Of course, staying within the RDA (Recommended Daily Allowances) and exercising intelligently are also very important.

Don't forget! Even temporary fasting is a stress. One meal per day is the same as a 23 hour fast, during which time a higher percentage of the food you eat is made into fat. When less food is available for energy and tissue repair, one is in trouble! However, another expensive mistake is often made by people who think that they are doing the "right" thing.

Another known fact is that all diets high in protein and low in carbohydrates are interpreted as emergency situations — the alarm reaction, "fight" or "flight" and there is an increase in the deposition of fat and other health problems. Covert Bailey, in his book, *Fit Or Fat,* does an outstanding job explaining these concerns and recommends that no more than 12 percent of our daily calories should come from protein.[16] Too many Americans are eating too much meat, and the excess amount of protein is being translated into stress by the body!

The River Of Drowning People

Imagine for a moment standing on the bank of a river. Many people are floating by waving their arms and screaming for help. They're drowning! Naturally, we dive in and try to pull them to shore. However, for every one we rescue, two more come drifting down, screaming for help. More good swimmers are recruited, and we resuscitate the unconscious. A lot of money is spent, as we try to help everyone. Power boats are needed in order to reach more people, and more hospitals are needed to treat them. Obviously, if these people had known how to stay out of the river in the first place or had known how to swim, none of this would have been necessary!

The state of health care in America seems analogous to the river of drowning people. This is also the thinking of Dr. David Sobel, an M.D. who is an authority on preventive medicine at Kaiser-Permanente Medical Center in San Jose, California. At a recent conference, he spoke on "The Healing Brain." He said causes that are "upstream" — such as lifestyle, behavior and environmental pollution — are leading to disease states. The medical system is overwhelmed, trying to treat all of these cases. The way we think and what we do also have profound effects on our health. Therefore, some upstream changes are necessary. Even with all the high technology of modern medicine, chronic degenerative diseases still run rampant. Many diseases, particularly heart disease and cancer, continue to plague Americans.[17]

In exploring some of the reasons for this, studies have shown that there is a link between lifestyle and health. Those individuals who eat at least three meals a day or six small ones, do eat breakfast, do get moderate exercise, do get adequate sleep, do not smoke, do control their weight, and drink little or no alcohol tend to be much healthier than the average. Life expectancy is greater by at least 10 years for those who have all seven of the good habits, as compared with those who only practice two or three of them. Those who practice good habits seem to be protected to a substantial degree.

Research also shows that emotional stress is a major factor in setting the stage for disease, but many people with many stressful life-events still stay healthy. Continuous minor hassles may be more detrimental than major events in breaking down health, and the number of hassles is almost endless! Some with the seemingly greatest amount and intensity of stress still stay healthy. What is more important to measure is what goes on in the brain — the perceptions and appraisals of stressful events in one's life. This is a crucial factor in determining the actual effects of stress. (See Figure A, "Emotions and Stress," Appendix, p. 188.)

Resistance resources help some to cope and lessen the adverse effects of stress. Social support and social ties are probably the most important. For instance, a study shows that the Japanese of San Francisco have five times the heart disease as do those in their own home country of Japan. Both San Francisco and Japan are highly urbanized. This fact rules out urbanization as a cause. Those fortunate ones in San Francisco who do not succumb to heart disease have extensive social networks with the Japanese community, as do those in Japan. These people, whether in our country or in their homeland were, in a sense, immune to developing heart disease. The social network factor was independent of other factors, such as smoking, cholesterol level, or lack of exercise. Other studies also support these findings. There is a high correlation between social ties and good health. In fact, the death rate is two and one-half times less!

Those with social support systems have someone they can count on for money or a place to stay in times of need. They are also respected in the sense that people ask them for their opinions or advice. However, the people with many social relationships can actually experience more stress, as they have more loved ones to lose, either through relocation or death. One can see that there must be something else "upstream." In spite of their additional losses, they stay healthy!

Another study demonstrated that executives who remain healthy under stress have "high hardiness." By this is meant that they have the CCC's of *commitment, control,* and *challenge.* They believe in the truth and importance of what they are doing and who they are. They are involved with their work, family, and community; and they have a sense of purpose. They also have confidence that their actions make a difference. They realize that they can't control everything, but that they can influence the course of events. They view their lives as processes of change, with opportunities for growth that include novelty and flexibility.

An Israeli researcher, Aaron Antonovsky, concluded that coherence, or a sense that one's life is characterized by comprehensibility, is a deterrent to damage by stress. The demands of life make sense for those with coherence, and they are orderly and predictable. If one has manageability, there are available resources for meeting the demands of life. These resources are believed to be available from someone who is benevolent — yourself, or your spouse, or your "significant other," or God! Finally, there is meaningfulness. Not only do things make sense, but one cares! People who do not have these characteristics tend to break down under the stresses of living.[18]

Summary

Stress is everywhere! It need not be devastating to our health and well-being. To live is to be stressed! We are programmed for "fight," "flight," or "flow," from the time we are conceived. We are intelligent human beings who can "come to grips" with the powerful forces within ourselves. This can be done through understanding the dynamic interactions of our existence here on this earth. Cognitive problem-solving is the foundation upon which we can build. Once we can describe and explain what is happening and see cause-and-effect relationships, then we are in a position to exert some control over our destiny. Yes, the tools are at our disposal. First, a change in beliefs may be necessary. Pessimists can become optimists, as they begin to feel better — a real reward so necessary for behavior modification to take place.

The effects of emotional stress are certainly magnified by our health habits — poor diet, lack of appropriate exercise, and lack of sufficient rest and relaxation. Our insistence on using social drugs has staggering consequences. The research on nutrition and stress emphatically shows that Americans consume too many refined foods, sugar, salt, fat (saturated and unsaturated), and protein! Some of these may come as a surprise, especially the protein. Degenerative diseases of many descriptions — which affect both mind and body — are the result. More complex carbohydrates (in place of the massive amounts of simple sugars, fats, and proteins that we consume) are in order.

Many mistakes are being made by well-meaning but misinformed individuals. There are beneficial ways to eat, exercise, and rest. We should be able to identify them and practice them. Last, but not least, social support systems are a necessity for good health. Every living human being should believe that someone cares! *I do believe and I do care!* If this is also true for you, please read on. It will be well worth your time.

3.

THE PHYSIOLOGY OF STRESS

Before we can understand and visualize the effect of stress on our bodies, good or bad, and the importance of nutrition, we need to understand a few things concerning the fields of anatomy and physiology.

The Autonomic Nervous System

The autonomic nervous system is not a nervous system set off by itself. The cerebral cortex, part of the central nervous system, has autonomic centers which are first connected to like centers in the hypothalamus. By way of explanation, the cerebral cortex gives us our conscious awareness of "calm" or "storm"; the thalamus is a switching station for the many nerve impulses; and the hypothalamus is the autonomic or automatic control center for bodily functions.

Perhaps, at this point in time, your "system" is beginning to feel a bit "nervous!" Well, let me attempt to make this section as meaningful as possible without sacrificing important information. If you do get "bogged down," as I mentioned earlier, just move on to another section and come back to this a bit later when you are more refreshed or relaxed.

To continue, the hypothalamus has two basic parts, one of which is the anterior and medial portion, which controls the parasympathetic division. If "all is well upstairs," that is, if our cognitive awareness senses no immediate danger, this area is in control, bringing about, among other measures, normal heart rate, blood pressure, eyesight, and digestion of food.

Contrary to much popular thinking, it is the parasympathetic division that should "reign supreme," that is, be in operation most of the time. It is the one that maintains an adequately functioning state and conserves body energy. Even though it is called a "rest-repose system," it is by no means inactive. It keeps us going quite happily and merrily along our way.

However, it is sometimes necessary that we become active, especially when confronted by stress. Here is where the sympathetic has a very important role to play. It is this division that has the job of preparing the body for "fight or flight." In other words, it comes up with energy in the right places, to get the job done. This is known as *reflex action,* which is necessary for our self-preservation. It is the sympathetic division, in contrast with the parasympathetic, that is involved with the expenditure of energy, not the conservation of it. The time involved should be only long enough to get the necessary bodily strength to take care of the threat, and then the parasympathetic should resume control.

Nonetheless, during extreme or prolonged stress, the sympathetic dominates, and the body's store of energy is quickly consumed. For a time, bodies become alert and possess unusual strength. Fear or anger usually triggers this response, and the posterior and lateral portions of the hypothalamus are stimulated, thereby increasing the visceral activities. Among other measures, there is an increase in heart rate, a rise in blood pressure, dilation of the pupils, and inhibition of the digestive tract. The first can lead to heart and circulatory malfunctions and vision irregularities. The last action can lead to gastro-intestinal problems during chronic stress.

Before moving on, it is well to realize that if the cortex perceives an extremely dangerous situation, it apparently overstimulates the sympathetic division (which is housed in the rear portion of the hypothalamus) and this electro-chemical surge then "spills over" to the parasympathetic, which is housed in the front of the hypothalamus. This can result in a profound reaction — vasodilation of blood vessels, a lowering of blood pressure, and possible fainting. This is the way stress can cause hypo-activation, mentioned earlier. It seems that nature is "pulling us down" to protect us. Primitive man would have been left for dead by the wild animals, and modern man is usually no longer assaulted by his attackers. This is known as shock reaction, and it can occur in varying degrees, from trembling to death itself. Death can occur as the result of a lack of oxygen to the brain and the stopping of the heart. There are some individuals who live under such conditions of constant fear that they are continually in a state of semi-shock, and the consequences are pathetic. They are always "shot down" and have a terrible time coping with the exigencies of life.

Just how the sympathetic nervous system brings about the bodily changes is the result of information coming from the hypothalamus to the adrenal glands, which mediate the stress response. Two electro-chemical reactions are set off.

First, and very quickly, the catecholamines (epinephrine and norepinephrine) are secreted by the adrenal glands to give instant energy, cause blood clotting, and increase pulse rate and blood pressure. This is brought about by direct nerve innervation. Over time, these actions can put a great burden on the cardiovascular system, but in the short run, they serve beneficial effects — more energy, protection from bleeding in case of a wound, and delivery of more oxygen and nutrients.

In contrast, the other way is more complex and takes longer. In this case, the cortex sends a message by way of the thalamus to the hypothalamus. Then, the hypothalamus releases a chemical messenger called CRF (corticotrophic hormone-releasing factor) which stimulates the pituitary gland, that is located just under the brain over the roof of the mouth. This pituitary gland discharges ACTH (adreno-corticotrophic hormones) into the blood stream which, in turn, stimulates the outer portion or cortex of the adrenal glands that are located on top of the kidneys. They then release corticoids such as cortisol and cortisone (steroids) into the blood stream.

These steroids give "get-up-and-go" and control inflammation, but over long-term and chronic stress, they hamper the functioning of the immune system and are implicated as causes for infectious and autoimmune diseases. They may also be responsible for leaching calcium out of the bones — osteoporosis - - as more is needed for increased nerve transmission. In fact, muscles can't relax properly with a calcium deficiency.

The Powerful Catecholamines

We now know that there are, indeed, two routes from the hypothalamus to the adrenal glands. In the first line of defense, the adrenal medulla or inner core of the adrenal glands is stimulated. This part then secretes the catecholamines, mainly epinephrine (adrenalin) and norepinephrine (nor-adrenalin). These "juices" help with the release of energy stores of sugar, cause blood coagulation to control bleeding in the case of injury, an increased pulse rate and blood pressure through vaso-constriction, to get more blood flow to the muscles for "fight" or "flight."

An extremely important phenomenon occurs here — one which is grossly misunderstood! Blood is diverted out of the higher cognitive centers of the brain and into the primitive "reptile" brain, which is the center of our reflexes. This makes it possible for us to use our muscles and act quickly (reflexively), without having to take the time to think (cognitively) — a cumbersome and time-consuming task when one's life is at stake. The reptilian brain serves one well if there is a masked gunman leaping from behind a car or building, but it doesn't work well when this mechanism is triggered while trying to solve a problem of any kind, whether it be as complex as giving a speech or as simple as trying to recall someone's name.

One's learning capacity is likewise crippled when the thinking brain is shut down by the non-thinking brain! Don't think for a moment that I don't know what can and does happen. After many years of being a student myself and then teaching others, I am convinced of this! Stress does not enhance our intellectual abilities. It does just the opposite! One does not have enough blood to the brain to know enough to come in out of the rain!

In our society, stress has become an addiction. It is imperative that we break that addiction before it breaks us! Nonetheless, there is a place for reflexive and quick action. Without it, we could not survive, but neither can we survive for long, if we allow it to totally consume and overwhelm us to the point where good judgment and wise decisions cannot be made.

The catecholamines are designed to stimulate the nervous system for quick action. Their route from the hypothalamus in the brain to the adrenal glands uses direct nerve innervation. This fact accounts for the speed with which the message can travel.

However, there is another interesting finding. C. Van Toller states that back in the 1950's, there was evidence which indicated that there is a differential response to fear versus anger. When we are angry, there is a noradrenalin or a mixture of an adrenalin/noradrenaline-like reaction; and when we are fearful, there is an adrenalin-like patterning. Therefore, stress that involves exhilarating or aggressive reactions (anger) is associated with increased levels of noradrenalin, and we are like lions and fight back. Stress that involves apprehension, pain, or general discomfort (fear) is associated with increased levels of adrenalin, and we are like rabbits and run away. The face may be "flushed" with anger and "pale" with fear.[1]

Both of the above reactions are necessary in our everyday encounters and our bodies usually vacillate back and forth, depending on the existing conditions and our perceptions of them. Sometimes, it is more intelligent to be fearful and not to "rush in where angels fear to tread!" Other times, we need to be more assertive (socially acceptable aggressiveness) to get the job done.

However, stress, when elicited by adverse influences or over-stimulation from pleasant circumstances, does, indeed, cause a massive release of epinephrine and norepinephrine in our bodies. As a result of this speeded-up metabolism of the "fight" or "flight" state, people can even become depleted of these adrenal gland "juices" and suffer a collapse — Selye's state of exhaustion. Some of the subsequent degenerative diseases are possibly schizophrenia, depression, infections, cancer, arthritis, and atherosclerosis. Immune system functioning is definitely impaired.

Whether we "run away" or "go for it," whichever the case may be, we have more energy for self-preservation. This is accomplished through changes in blood flow. The blood vessels on the skin and viscera constrict (vaso-constriction), and the rest of the blood vessels dilate (vaso-dilation). This reaction brings about a rise in blood pressure, as more blood is forced into the muscles, heart, lungs, and lower (reflex) brain.

All blood pressure medications are designed to counteract the effects of the catecholamines on the cardiovascular system. The causes of high blood pressure begin in the periphery of the body, as blood vessels constrict and force the blood back into the center of the body. The heart rate increases as the heart pumps faster to push the now increased volume of blood to the bodily organs that are used in running away or fighting back. The breathing rate increases to allow for more air to move in and out of the lungs.

More oxygen is needed in the decomposition reactions of catabolism, the counterpart of metabolism. More carbon dioxide is eliminated that has been produced as a sub-product of catabolism. Sweat glands are stimulated to increase perspiration and cool the body, which gets warmer as circulation increases. Profuse sweating also helps to eliminate waste products that accumulate as the result of increased metabolism and catabolism. The spleen discharges blood into general circulation. Red blood cells are increased in number, and the blood clots more easily, in order to combat bleeding. The blood actually becomes thicker and, over time, can lead to circulatory problems.

There is a limit to the length of time that the body can withstand this pressure! War has been declared! The defense plants are in operation, and survival is the "name of the game." Other processing plants not essential for combat are slowed down or shut down. This is particularly true for the gastro-intestinal tract. The salivary, gastric, and intestinal glands are constricted. The throat is dry. There is decreased motility in the stomach and intestines.

The common belief that ulcers are caused by too much hydrochloric acid seems repudiated by this explanation. More than likely, as some new research indicates, there is not enough bicarbonate of soda! Taking aspirin and drinking alcohol also causes ulcers! The pancreas inhibits the secretions of digestive enzymes. No wonder that highly stressed people have digestive problems! Some need temporary administration of digestive enzymes, hydrochloric acid, and bicarbonate of soda!

Other changes also occur. The blood vessels of the kidneys constrict, causing decreased urine volume. Over prolonged periods of time, toxins can build up in the blood stream. The muscular wall of the urinary bladder relaxes to accommodate more volume, while the sphincter muscle contracts to retain the contents — a reservoir during the ensuing drought. This causes great stress on the urinary tract; but we can't even cry about this whole state of affairs because the tear glands are constricted.

It is only after one relaxes a bit that crying takes place. Our hair literally "stands on end" as the hair follicles erect, and we produce "goose pimples" — a cooling effect. The blood vessels of the skin constrict and we feel cold and clammy.

Sexual functions are adversely affected. In the female, contraction of the uterus is inhibited if nonpregnant, but stimulated if pregnant. No time for that now, but if already pregnant, the load may be too heavy to carry, as one is faced with protecting the self. Undue stress during this time can lead to premature labor. In the male, erection of the penis may not be possible. At this juncture, perpetuation of the species is not the number-one concern. Self-preservation comes first. The male simply "can't get it up," or if he does, he has a difficult time maintaining it.

Sexual dysfunctions and many social problems may be the result of this disorder — marital discord, marital separation, divorce, and possibly sexual abuse. Some actual rapes, with the use of a "dildo," could occur. Mental aberrations, of course, are part of this alarming picture.

Fortunately, those with an adequately developed super-ego or conscience, who care about the welfare of others, would be far less likely to engage in any anti-social behavior. However, this deterrent to harm others would not negate the toll that this kind of stress could take on the self. Much of our concept of self is measured in terms of our sexuality.

The workings of the catecholamines are marvelous, indeed, and serve us well. However, proper use and abuse are two different things. We need to know how and why things go wrong, in order to exercise some prudent judgment concerning the care of our bodies and avoid unnecessary wear and tear. A proper balance between exercise and relaxation is important; but it is also through good nutrition (our source of energy) that our bodies can maintain themselves appropriately. Stress is a fact of life, but control of *it* is life!

The Steroids In Action

The steroids are the second line of defense. In addition to suppressing inflammation, they cause the release of stored energy necessary for adaptive reactions. This is accomplished by stimulating the liver to "kick out" glycogen (stored sugar) into the blood stream, so that there is fuel for "fight" or "flight." This glycogen has previously been stored by the action of insulin from the pancreas. The adrenal glands are responsible for converting the glycogen back into glucose (blood sugar), the fuel needed for nerve and muscle activity.

When blood sugar levels drop, certain cells are activated, and one feels hungry. As one eats and digests a meal, the sugar or glucose goes through the blood stream to the liver. Then, because the glucose level of the blood has increased, one is no longer hungry. One feels satiated. It is in the liver that glucose is converted into glycogen, which is *fat* soluble, not water soluble. This is how food is converted into reserve energy, and stored in the liver and muscles for future use.

Insulin helps us to utilize the fuel at the rate we need it, by turning it from glucose to glycogen. Glucose cannot be stored until it meets with insulin. Sugar in the blood (coming from the intestines) stimulates the pancreas to release insulin. This insulin goes to the liver and converts glucose coming from the digestive tract into the glycogen, for storage.

Not all is stored, however. The amount that the body needs is left in the blood. When an emergency arises, the adrenal hormones, which are epinephrine and norepinephrine, raise the blood sugar level by forcing glycogen (fat soluble) back into glucose (water soluble). When the blood sugar level is low, other cells of the pancreas are stimulated by the adrenals to secrete glucagon which speeds up the process of sending sugar (which has been stored in the liver) back into the bloodstream. This release of the adrenal hormones is responsible for the internal feelings of alarm or anxiety.

Over-stimulation of the pancreas as the result of this sympathetic nervous system activity, causes the pancreas to release an excessive amount of insulin; and this in turn causes the glucose level to plunge below the level at which the body can still function normally. This condition is known as hypoglycemia or low blood sugar. There is not enough fuel for the body to carry out its activities.

In the process, the adrenal glands are over-stimulated in an attempt to raise the blood sugar level. This overload can lead to adrenal exhaustion. The result is chronic fatigue, with its many allied disorders, some of which are shakiness, blurred vision, depression, and difficulty in breathing. Severe stress or an "anxiety attack" can trigger this awesome experience.

In addition, the over-stimulation of the pancreas, over time, may result in malfunction and eventual exhaustion. This, then, could lead to the inability to produce insulin to control the blood sugar level, and the result could be high blood sugar, called hyperglycemia or diabetes.

The elevated blood sugar goes into the kidneys and then into the urine. This is the reason for a urine test, in diagnosing diabetes. The concept was known even during the Middle Ages. Practitioners, back then, were known as "piss prophets," because they knew that sweet urine attracted ants and that spelled diabetes!

Even though physicians, researchers, and educators do not know the *cause* of diabetes, it could very well result from the stress response repeated time and again. The diet that is heavy in sugars and fats further complicates matters. Emotional stress can cause the deposition of fat, regardless of the amount of fat and sugar consumed. Current medical theory (Kilo) does state that an obese patient is insulin-resistant; that is, insulin intake at the receptor sites is impaired because of an imbalance in the release-receptor mechanism, brought on by expanded body mass. The pancreas can't produce enough insulin for the massive amount of tissue.[2]

However, of the ten million Americans who have diabetes, about one million are not fat! They are normal in weight or even lean, but they are, nonetheless, diabetic. What could possibly account for this discrepancy? We now know that stress produces endorphins, which stimulate the appetite and also cause a greater storage of fat for future use. But, we also know that norepinephrine can act as an appetite depressant in some people; so there would not be as much fuel to be stored. Could it not be that the lean diabetic might be one of these people? Obviously, his/her pancreas isn't functioning properly, but perhaps for a different reason.

It seems to me that injecting massive amounts of any stimulants — sugar, caffeine, nicotine, etc. — continuously would pose a hazard to the pancreas. The genetic factor helps to account for the fact that some do, and some do not, succumb to the disease. However, "since 1965, both the prevalence and the incidence of diabetes have increased by more than 50 percent," says Kilo.[3]

The "average per capita sweetener intake in 1975 was about 40 pounds per year. Now it's about 120 to 130 pounds per person per year," according to Prichard on January 20, 1987. At no time in history have Americans eaten more sweeteners than they do today, and at no time in history has there been a greater incidence of diabetes.[4]

The plight of the American Indian populations attests to the severity of the situation. At the beginning of the century, there was virtually no known diabetes among the nations' 266,760 Indians, according to Kronholm.[5] Even 30 to 40 years ago, it was still considered relatively rare. Today, however, more than half of all the Pimas in Arizona over the age of 35 have diabetes. This is the highest documented incidence in the world. It is an increase of 42 percent in the last 10 years. While the average white American has one chance in five of developing the disease, the American Indian has one chance in four!

The diets of today's Native Americans are extremely high in simple carbohydrates (sugars, including alcohol), and diabetes has become a major health concern. Since I have lived on the Spokane Indian Reservation for 12 years and the Colville Indian Reservation for one year, I can relate to their problems firsthand. Nutritionally, Native Americans have the worst profile of any minority group in the nation. The massive consumption of commercial, convenience, and "fast foods" is incredible.

For thousands of years, Native Americans lived off the land and adapted genetically to feast or famine. In times of real feast (summer months), their bodies stored energy for the forthcoming real famine (winter months). They still have that super-efficient storage system, along with the added stress of living in a "white man's world" and eating the "white man's diet." Their health is deteriorating rapidly. They are basically survivors, in a sense, or "easy keepers" who cannot tolerate too heavy a load to carry, which is much the same for any of us.

Overall, every American has one chance in five of developing diabetes. It is a blood vessel disease. Dr. Charles Kilo says, "We have photomicroscopic evidence of thickened muscle-capillary basement membranes in humans."[6] There is increased capillary permeability of the microcirculation, causing small blood vessel disease. The effects of glucotoxicity are also seen on red blood cell membranes and to hemoglobin, which prohibits the release of oxygen. Because they can't release oxygen, the red blood cells cannot change shape in order to pass through the narrow capillaries. Their flexibility that allows them to change from circular to oblong is lost when they are coated with glucose. The poor circulation (as the result of blood vessel disease) can lead to blindness, renal diseases, gangrene, glaucoma, heart attack, or stroke. Therefore, this marvelously designed part of the autonomic nervous system does wreak havoc when abused by stress, including that of an inappropriate diet.

One more thing (as was noted earlier), the sugar or glucose in excess of what the body can use is stored in the liver and muscles, as glycogen. However, there is a limit to how much can be stored there, and the excess is changed into fat and stored in the adipose tissue. This is how people get fat.

All overweight people have too much insulin, in a form of hyperinsulinism. The over-burdened fat cells are not responsive to insulin, as are normal-sized cells; meanwhile the pancreas produces more insulin. Thus, the fat get fatter.

The diet also determines the amount of insulin produced — either too much or too little. Insulin does deposit glycogen and fat. It's not that our emotions can cause the hypothalamus to get out of balance and stimulate an abnormal appetite, so that we eat more and more and get fat — the old view. Overeating is *not* the only cause for obesity. So is the internal physiological component to stress, a cause for fatness. When we combine overeating with the internal stress reaction of storage, we then are in "double trouble."

During stress, epinephrine mobilizes some glycogen and fat, but stress also causes the production of steroids, especially a well-known one, called cortisone. Its purpose is to fight inflammation, but it also fights insulin. This causes the pancreas to produce more insulin, which in turn causes an accumulation of fat. Those who have taken Prednisone (cortisone) for arthritis may have developed a "moonface," as extra fat was deposited under the skin.

So, too much cortisone, whether produced in the body as the result of stress or administered as medication does (or can) have deleterious side effects — in this case, an over-abundance of fat. Here is a very good reason for controlling our stress reactions, and also for the caution that some physicians now have about prescribing Prednisone. In short-term treatment, it may be the treatment of choice; but long-term use is quite another matter. It does bring the stress response, with its many dangers.

The question as to whether eating sugar can cause diabetes comes up many times. Don't be fooled by the claim that there is no evidence that sugar causes diabetes. This is more or less a "cop-out." Granted, there is no confirmed and conclusive evidence that there is a direct cause-and-effect relationship that is acceptable to the medical community. Nonetheless, an excess consumption of sugar, as well as other foods, particularly fat, and also protein, do lead to obesity. Obesity is a risk factor for developing diabetes. The condition of hyperinsulinism, where the pancreas is over-stimulated to produce too much insulin is comparable to the emotional stress response. In this case, the pancreas is also overstimulated to produce an excessive amount of insulin. In both cases, too much sugar in the bloodstream may be causing the pancreas to overwork, become ineffective, and finally reach a state of exhaustion. Then, it would not be able to produce insulin to control the blood sugar, and the blood sugar level would elevate — constituting hyperglycemia or diabetes.

Weight control is the best prevention against diabetes, and the treatment of choice for those with the disease. In addition, there's some very good news for diabetics. Research reported by the National Institute of Health, in December of 1986, indicates that for diabetics, up to five percent of the carbohydrate calories could come from table sugar![7] This would translate into nine grams a day, about two and one-third teaspoons! These figures are based on the assumption that carbohydrates provide 50 percent of one's calories. If carbohydrate consumption is raised to 65 percent or more, then proportionately more table sugar!

Keep in mind that total carbohydrates should supply 65 percent or more of the calories, fats should supply 23 percent or less, an protein should supply 12 percent or less (Bailey).[8] Please realize that the amount of sugar now allowed is a very small amount of the total carbohydrate category. Moderation is the key!

Another danger is that unused sugar raises the level of blood fats and cholesterol; and these accumulate in already diseased arteries and help to make plaque. This condition is known as atherosclerosis, or hardening of the arteries. Animal studies and a few studies with humans suggest that excess animal protein will also raise cholesterol levels. According to Prichard, "Animal studies have shown that doubling the protein intake with animal protein raises cholesterol, but soy protein does not have the same effect. In human diets, animal protein is always associated with fat intake."[9] Calcium and other minerals such as lead, mercury (which can come from silver-amalgam fillings in teeth), and copper attach to this fatty matrix. Other polluting chemicals from air, water, and food sources also attach. A heart attack can occur as the result of arterial plaquing when the coronary artery is blocked, so that proper blood flow does not reach the heart muscle. If this same plaquing occurs in the brain, reducing blood supply and oxygen, then a "stroke" may occur.

Steroids known as cortisol and cortisone are responsible for all of the above, and still more. The brain reacts to the steroids by producing endorphins, which are the body's natural opiates that give temporary relief from pain. In large amounts, the endorphins can bring about a trance or state of euphoria. The "runner's high" and "positive addiction" to exercise may be the result of this state. "Binge-eating" can do the same thing.

When we are stressed, endorphin production increases rapidly and prolifically to kill or dull any pain that might occur. Of course, this is good in moderation, as it helps us to get through a trying time and "to get on with it." However, we are also not aware of the discomfort and damage that stress is causing. A "silent killer" is on the loose!

Unexpressed anger can threaten one's self-control, and food can sooth the spirits until one is back in command. Some people find it very difficult to express anger directly, because of feelings of anxiety. They do not have the necessary skills for being assertive without seeming aggressive; or else they're in a situation where no matter how diplomatic, yet assertive, they are, their actions would be interpreted as aggressive by other persons. In this case, constructive physical activity is the best solution, until such time as other options can be explored. It is not desirable to add food when the body is already storing too much. Even though food, much like a mood-altering drug, can be a 'quick fix' when you're feeling blue, it isn't worth the price you must pay.

People who eat during stress are caught in a vicious cycle. Stress and stress-eating both lead to weight gain; the weight gain itself induces more stress; the stress stimulates more eating, to relieve the tension; and on and on! Nothing is gained but unwanted pounds and ensuing health problems. How much better it would be to get out from under some of the pressure, by eliminating that which is possible to eliminate or delegating some stressful responsibilities to others. We unconsciously try to gratify our own egos by being indispensable; in fact we are not indispensable! To try to be so is costly in terms of our well-being.

Indeed, the over-production of endorphins can have negative, as well as positive effects. To control the less than desirable consequences of the endorphins, non-eating activities are a wise choice. Some of these might be visiting with a good friend who will "lend an ear;" plan one small pleasurable activity each day; or do something that you've put off for a long time. Exercise of any kind, preferably the new, low-impact aerobics, which put less strain on the joints, is highly desirable. Walking three or four times a week will provide a sense of well-being, because of the moderate increase in endorphin levels in the blood. Depression, the "common cold" of the emotional disorders, can be controlled.

By way of explanation, endorphins raise the level of insulin in the blood, and we already know what that can do. However, the point is that when the insulin reduces the blood sugar level, we feel hungry. That triggers the psychological motivation to eat, so we eat — in response to stress — not because we really need any more food. We really have the "munchies." The food consumed causes the pancreas to produce even more insulin, which in turn lowers the blood sugar level.

Many people are caught in this stress-related cycle in which the act of eating causes them to eat more. McConnell says that people get overweight because their bodies produce too many endorphins.[10] However, this is not always the case. Norepinephrine, which is produced as the result of stress, can act as an appetite suppressant. This would more than likely be the result of shock that can occur in either the alarm or exhaustion phase. Amphetamines can do the same thing.

Many hyperkinetic children who take Ritalin, an amphetamine-like drug, do not get hungry. Phenylalanine, an amino acid found in about everything we eat, stimulates the production of norepinephrine. "Phenylalanine is chemically related to amphetamine and phenylethylanine, the mood-altering stimulant found in cocoa and chocolate," according to Haas.[11] Therefore, stress of various kinds can cause suppression of the appetite. Phenylalanine is one of the essential amino acids that we get from our food; but when consumed in excess, it can cause trouble.

There is another big price to be paid for the temporary relief of pain, brought about by the production of endorphins. These morphine-like substances block the activity of the natural killer cells, which are the lymph cells that recognize and destroy tumor cells. This is the body's immune system against infection and disease. These cells, which are called "T" cells, because they mature in the thymus gland, are acutely sensitive to the corticoids. Abnormally high levels will either damage or destroy these cells or induce their movement out of the thymus, causing it to shrink.

Lymphocytes or T cells respond best to antigens or invaders when the circulating corticoids are least in amount. Hall and Goldstein — Nicholas R. Hall and Allen L. Goldstein — explain that corticoids, in high concentrations, mute the immune response and, in small amounts, have been known to activate it. Acute stress can cause immunosuppression, whereas chronic stress sometimes enhances the immune response.[12]

Cancer is an example of a disease that is caused by *suppression* of the immune response; and any autoimmune disease, such as rheumatoid arthritis, serves as an example of an over-response of the immune system. The "silent killer" moves on!

The mineral, calcium, is necessary for nerve transmission involved in muscle contractions during the "fight" or "flight" response, including that of the heart. It can be used up rapidly. If there is a cellular deficiency of calcium, the steroids literally draw it out of the bones, where it is stored. Over-demineralization of the bones can lead to osteoporosis. The excess calcium which is not used by neural activity, deposits in *abnormal* locations, such as the joints, and causes arthritis. It settles in the plaque and contributes to arteriosclerosis. This was mentioned earlier in the discussion on unused fat. Many medical practioners are now "frowning" on the practice of administering cortisone or steroid injections, or giving medications such as Prednisone, by prescription, for this very reason. Cortisone does control inflammation, but the negative aspects, over long-term use, far outweigh the positive.

There is still another way that the immune system is weakened. Often overlooked in the consideration of stress is that the hypothalamus also responds to a stressor by stimulating the thyroid to secrete thyroxin, which is needed to catabolize carbohydrates. So vitally important for the production of glucose, the corticoids promote the formation of glucose or blood-sugar, the fuel needed for nerve and muscle activity. In so doing, some fats and proteins are also broken down or metabolized, to make more fuel available. This is adaptive in the short run, but the increased use of protein to make fuel may be maladaptive because proteins are needed in the manufacture of new cells.

Stress, whether physical and/or emotional, decreases recuperative powers. Protein is not utilized appropriately. There is, in fact, a distinct increase in protein waste in the urine of stressed subjects. Especially vulnerable are the white blood cells, which are essential for fighting infection. They have a short lifespan and must be continuously replaced. If the protein supply is deficient, then infectious diseases may be the result.

In summary, the steroids produced by the action of the sympathetic nervous systems are powerful, indeed. Nature intended for them to serve us well, and indeed they do. However, with continued abuse over time, their massive powers are destructive. By yielding to this powerful foe, many times out of ignorance, we slowly but surely do commit suicide! The "great reaper" continues to cut a wide swath. The body self-destructs, like an ill-guided missile.

GAS Spells Trouble

The many physical responses that the body makes to stressful situations follows an adaptive pattern called the General Adaptation Syndrome, first outlined more than 40 years ago by Canadian Scientist Hans Selye.[13] It has since then been updated, as science has given us more information.

Basically, the GAS has three stages or parts, which consist of the alarm, the resistance, and the exhaustion. They can be compared to what happens when one gets into very cold water. First, it seems unbearable, and one's impulse is to run. Then one becomes used to it and can even swim about. Finally, the ability to resist the effects of the numbing cold becomes exhausted and, hopefully, one hurries out! Moreover, the body is constantly bombarded in real life, again and again and again. Stress is not a one-time occurrence, and its effects are accumulative.

In the first stage, the responses are designed to counteract immediate danger by mobilizing the body's resources. This is accomplished through the massive amounts of glucose and oxygen which power the human machine. The responses are immediate and short-lived, being powered by the catecholamines. We can accomplish feats requiring great strength because of increased circulation and catabolism for energy production. However, if we suffer from severe stress or trauma, our bodies and minds can go into a state of shock. This is where the parasympathetic function (discussed earlier) takes over. Temperature and blood pressure drop, the tissues swell with fluid, and muscles lose tone. We can't think clearly and we lose the ability to store information into long-term memory. If the stress is great enough, we may faint. If the body mechanisms are not able to cope, we may even die right "off the bat."

During alarm or shock, kidney function is curtailed because there is less blood circulating to the kidneys. This decrease in urine production invokes the production of mineralcorticoids, which cause the sodium ions to be conserved by the body. This increase in sodium (salt) by the body, as well as the increase in toxins in the bloodstream, as the result of decreased kidney function, leads to water retention and swelling. Here is one reason why some individuals are "salt sensitive," particularly when they are under increased stress.

It is a known fact that salt intake can be detrimental while the body is responding to any stressful situation. High blood pressure is maintained as the heart tries to cope with the increased volume of blood. The positive aspect of this is that the body can make up for fluid, which may be lost through bleeding. However, if there is no bleeding, one can see what the consequences can be. Hydrogen ions also build up and make the blood more acidic, which changes the pH level. It is to be hoped that we survive the initial alarm.

The second phase (called the resistance stage) enables the body to continue fighting long after the initial "blow." It speeds up the life processes. Blood pressure remains abnormally high, because of the volume of blood. However, blood chemistry returns to almost normal, as the cells use glucose at the same rate it enters the bloodstream. Blood pH is brought back under control as the kidneys excrete more hydrogen ions.

By way of explanation, the normal pH level of the blood is 7.4, slightly alkaline, not an acid solution. Herman Aihara explains that this level of alkalinity needs to be kept almost constant, as minor fluctuations are dangerous. If the hydrogen ion concentration in the blood rises to pH 6.95 (barely over the line on the acid side), coma and death can occur. If the hydrogen ion concentration in the blood falls from pH 7.4 to pH 7.7, convulsions occur. Either the heart relaxes and ceases to beat (parasympathetic function) or it contracts and ceases to beat (sympathetic function).[14]

It is most fortunate that blood pH is kept under control. This is normally maintained by buffers, which are substances that combine with H+ ions when the hydrogen ion concentration decreases. Usually, the ingestion of acidic or alkaline foods would not affect the pH balance. However, it is now postulated that over-consumption of either acids or alkaloids can and does, indeed, upset this delicate balance. There are certain high-stress foods, just as there are high-stress emotions. Many foods are highly acid or alkaline forming, and it all goes into the bloodstream. Foods are carriers of these two forces, according to Aihara. Too much in one direction or the other can produce antagonistic reactions (stressful) in our cells, our nerves, our organs, and our very thoughts. Acid and alkaline are both very necessary, but it is also necessary that they be balanced for our well-being.[15]

Even though I do not have verification for this, I believe that it may be true that part of the body's immune response is activated; that is, antibodies are produced to counteract the invaders — this time, ingestants or inhalants that are upsetting the pH balance. It is a known fact that many people develop allergies or full-blown autoimmune diseases which are relieved or go into remission when they adhere to a special diet which restricts the intake of these substances. When their bodies return to a healthy state again, they may be able to tolerate some of the originally offending foods or substances. Many allergenic substances are acid forming — e.g. animal products and refined sugar. Some foods are extremely alkaloid, such as the "nightshade" family of potatoes, tomatoes, and eggplant. Both categories of acid and alkaline foods contain many known allergens. Hypothetically, I believe there could be a relationship!

The Balancing Act Of Acid And Alkaline

Life is possible and maintained as the result of the acid and alkaline balance in the body. The existence and proper action of the cells is possible if there is not a significant variation, either in the acid or the alkaline direction. Acids are chemical compounds containing hydrogen, which are necessary for a chemical reaction to take place. Alkalies are also compounds, which neutralize acids and form salts. Our body fluids, both blood and cell, change from one to another, to maintain a constant condition. They are "two sides of the same coin" — a chemical property.

Any solution is either more acid or more alkaline. An acid solution always contains some alkaline, and an alkaline solution always contains some acid. The pH scale ranges from 0.0 to 14.0. Most biological systems, including man's, have a pH value near neutrality (pH 7). Most cells are slightly acidic, about 6.8; and most body fluids, including the blood, are slightly alkaline (pH 7.4). The stomach, with a high content of gastric juice (hydrochloric acid) has a pH of about 1.0.

Depending on diet and other factors, urine may be as acidic as pH 4.0.   What we eat or drink is always more acid or more alkaline. However, as was mentioned earlier, blood buffers keep the pH under control. These buffers are actually mixtures of weak acids and salts, of strong bases. They are sodium bicarbonate, alkaline sodium phosphate, calcium, and potassium. These are non-volatile, in that they cannot be breathed away. Therefore, the kidneys play a role.

If large amounts of acid appear in the blood, there is a danger that the two sodiums, calcium, and potassium, will be lost through the kidneys. Therefore, these buffers are lost as ammonium salts are formed, circulated in the blood, and filtered out through the kidneys. This is how the stress response upsets the pH balance. It seems plausible that further inhalation and ingestion of either acid or alkaline substances could expedite the destructive process.

Obviously, stress can either decrease or increase the activity of the CNS (Central Nervous System) by upsetting the acid-alkaline balance. On one side of the "scales" is acid. It is a fact that the alarm or shock reaction causes the blood to have more acid. The "scales" are tipped! This can happen for a number of reasons, but what we are concerned about here is the effect of stress on acidosis. Hydrogen ions build up in the bloodstream. This causes depression of the central nervous system. The heart relaxes and may cease to beat. This can lead to coma and death if the pH of the blood falls below 7.0.

Fortunately, this reaction is rare. However, in less extreme circumstances, there are definite problems. There is either rapid breathing, which is called hyperventilation, or extremely slow breathing, which causes a build-up of carbonic acid in the blood. Animal source food and refined sugar are two examples of additional stressors, in that they cause increased acidity in the blood.

Drugs also increase the acid content of the blood. They, as well as certain foods, are carriers of acid or alkaline, which in turn affects our cells, our muscles, our nerves, hormones, enzymes, genes, organs, and yes, our thoughts! It seems the psychedelic drugs have both strong acid and alkaline forming elements. The acid, in particular, affects the brain, and the alkalines circulate in the bloodstream to other parts of the body. The alkalinity excites the nervous system, but the brain is inhibited by the acid, which renders it incapable of organizing messages.

This disequilibrium can bring on the "bad trips" or the "good trips," known as hallucinations. A high concentration of acid can eventually cause brain damage.

Refined sugar and animal source foods have some of this same potential. In fact, all so-called "uppers," including sugar, have both the "upping" and "downing" effects — the "roller coaster" ride! In many people, sugar brings on a 20 minute "high" and a two hour "crash." This can be the result of over-stimulation of the pancreas, which brings the blood sugar down too low. However, many people still go for the "sugar fix!"

A great deal of acid an be produced by stimulation of the organs, either through the alarm reaction, intake of energizing drugs, or consuming too much meat, dairy products, or sugar. Many times, it is the combination of all of them that "does one in!"

Physical and emotional stress, drugs, sugar, meat, and dairy products stimulate the adrenal glands to release cortisone and adrenalin. Some chemical additives can do the same thing. These "juices" cause the burning of glucose, as well as the storage of fat. Glucose burning results in a greater amount of acid production. The body needs an abundant supply of minerals to maintain the blood in a slightly alkaline state; but a mineral imbalance may develop. This can lead to a sensitivity to salt intake. For instance, there's not enough potassium, but too much salt. The blood may also be low in calcium and magnesium.

Tiredness, lethargy, and fatigue are the result of acidity. Stress of all kinds causes a build-up of carbon dioxide in the blood, which increases the blood acidity. Then the respiratory center in the brain is hampered, and reduced breathing is the result. Less oxygen is taken in; and this results in less cell metabolism — *low* metabolism — which leads to fatigue. Since over-acidity inhibits nerve action, a person in this condition cannot think well or act quickly. One lacks the ability to think clearly or be decisive — one's mental awareness is not up to par.

There is a cancer connection! First of all, when we are tired, we are likely to catch colds — our immune systems are not functioning properly. We have more discomforts and pains of all kinds and descriptions, such as headaches, chest pains, and stomach aches, to name a few. Acid-forming substances may accumulate in some parts of the body, as the blood attempts to keep a bit alkaline. The acid in these areas can then damage or kill some cells. In an adaptation process, some other cells may mutate or become abnormal, in order to survive the acid condition. They become malignant!

They can't communicate with the control center or memory code (DNA), and so they grow profusely and wildly — this is cancer. The more sensitive nerve cells which connect with the brain are killed; and the nuclei or centers of the body cells are damaged, so that there's no control over their growth rate. Cancer cells grow well in a culture solution of metabolic wastes, which are produced as the result of normal cell activity. The metabolic wastes are definitely acidic.

Therefore, it behooves us to control stress and its effects on the body, in order to prevent cancer. Learn to relax (the opposite of stress), avoid too much protein, because not only is it acid forming, it provides the where-with-all to make new cells — yes, cancer cells! When sugar and animal foods are consumed together, there is a greater incidence of cancer. Eskimos have few cases of cancer; they consume high amounts of meat, but little or no sugar. It is interesting at this point to note that neither do they have atherosclerosis, because they eat large amounts of fish oil, which apparently prevents the build-up of cholesterol.

Nonetheless, they do have osteoporosis, because their high consumption of protein draws the calcium right out of their bones! In India, cancer is rare; however, they consume great amounts of sugar. In short, it appears that the human body may be able to withstand one insult, but not two, three, four, or more! These are all effects of the alarm or shock reaction on the body.

Now, let's consider what happens when the scales are tipped the other way — more alkaline. Alkalosis is the opposite of acidosis. Keep in mind that slight alkalinity is desirable and that alkalosis does not occur nearly as often as acidosis. However, if there is too much alkalosis (not enough hydrogen ions), the nervous system is overexcited, the peripheral being affected first. The nerves fire automatically and repetitiously even when they are not receiving usual stimulation. The muscles go into a state of tonic spasm — the arms, the face, and the legs. If the respiratory muscles are affected, the individual may die.

Sometimes, effects on the CNS may cause extreme nervousness or even convulsions. This is the sympathetic function of the stress reaction, which is seen as one approaches and enters into Selye's third stage of exhaustion.[16] In other words, as one lives with unresolved stress, day after day, first:

one is "shot down" (alarm or shock), then, weakened but determined, one gets on "one's own two feet" again (resistance), but keeps doing all the "wrong things," until finally one wears down, and nears "check out time," which is the exhaustion phase.

Besides insurmountable physical or emotional stress, there are psychedelic drugs, with their alkaline properties, as mentioned earlier. These excite the nervous system and can cause hallucinations. This is true of all the "uppers," some of which are LSD, "pot," heroin, cocaine, amphetamines (speed), nicotine, caffeine, alcohol, and yes, refined sugar!

The body reacts to alcohol as it does sugar, particularly in regards to the effects on the pancreas. Sugar over-stimulates the pancreas to produce insulin (a high), that is followed by a "lull" in performance which brings on low blood sugar — a depressed state like that of acidosis.

Therefore, sugar is like a "double-edged sword!" It can kill you one way or the other, or both! This is why some consider sugar to be a "drug," and a drug it is! Furthermore, sugar has no nutritive value — no vitamins, no minerals — just calories! The term "empty calories" is an appropriate one.

In order to effect digestion, important vitamins and minerals are drawn from the body to get the job done. This is how vitamin and mineral depletion can occur. Sugar and alcohol are both "leaches," as they leach out valuable vitamins and minerals. They're both dehydrators, as the body tries to rid itself of toxins. The "cotton mouth" and frequent urination are signs of this process.

Medications such as narcotics, analgesics, antimalarials, local anesthetics, stimulants, blood pressure elevators, pupil dilators, or muscle relaxants are composed of alkaloids. They cause vaso-constriction in certain parts of the body and vaso-dilation in other parts, to get the energy and power where it is needed most — to defend one's self!

These changes should only last for a very brief period of time, or damage will occur. In reality, the muscle is not contracting; it is expanding inwardly to hold or prevent the blood from getting through, so the result is constricted space! Overuse or improper use of the above named medications can be extremely hazardous because of the over-energizing effect that high alkalinity has on the body.

Foods also play a role in alkalinity. Certain plant foods coming from the Solanaceae family (such as potato, tomato, eggplant, henbane, thorn apple, and nightshade) are all alkaloids. Ergots are alkaloid. They are produced by a fungus or ergot that grows on cereal grains and caused much illness, until man learned not to eat moldy grains. Basically, ergot causes constriction of blood vessels, a stress response. Good health foods — such as fruits, most vegetables, spices, and honey — stimulate the sympathetic nerves. However, this does not mean that they are bad, when eaten properly.

Most certainly, for the get-up-and-go necessary for today's living, carbohydrates should comprise at least 60 to 65 percent or more of our daily calories. They should be eaten in smaller amounts six times a day, in their natural form — unprocessed. The fiber content insures a slower and more steady absorption rate — more energy continuously. The gastro-intestinal tract and body are not stressed as when attempting to digest three large meals per day, plus the other assaults many make on it every day.

Even though honey is a simple sugar, it may not be absorbed as rapidly as refined sugar, because its molecules are larger than those of refined sugar. Honey is a monosaccharide, containing both glucose and fructose. Sugar, on the other hand, is disaccharide, but it also contains glucose and fructose; however, its molecules are smaller. This may account for the fact that some individuals cannot tolerate table sugar, but seem relatively safe with a small amount of honey.

The prefix mono means one, and di means double or containing two molecules. On Carlton Fredericks' glycemic scale, fructose rates a 20, sugar rates a 59, and honey rates an 87![17] Honey is much sweeter, but apparently is slower to be digested. "A little dab will do it" because of its sweetness intensity and its molecular structure.

So, since foods are the carriers of acid and alkaline, it seems only prudent to maintain a diet balanced along these lines. It also seems feasible to counteract genetic and/or environmentally induced states of imbalance (illness) with food in order to attain wellness. In this way, we can move from "illth" to health! All bacteria or microorganisms harmful to the body grow in an alkaline soil, and likewise, in the over-alkaline chemistry of the body. This explains why bacterial diseases are so common among the over-stressed. Some of the more common disease states are due to the proliferation of staphylococcus, streptococcus, and influenza microorganisms. Therefore, when we are "stressed-out," we are more vulnerable to the onslaught of bacterial infections.

It should now be understandable why many nutrition-conscious people recommend no sugar, no meat, no additives, no salt, no refined foods, and no drugs! Then there are the vitamin and mineral "pushers," the AA's (acid-alkaline) balancers, the "folks" with their medicinal (vinegar and honey) solution, and many more. By the same token, one can better understand the concerns evidenced by "fitness freaks," in terms of their "exercise craze," and the many varied "shrinks," for their advocacy of biofeedback, progressive relaxation, desensitization, increased awareness, gathering of information, problem-solving, and understanding.

Newer on the scene are those who emphasize adjusting subluxations of the spine, acupuncture, acupressure, touch, muscle testing, and the strengthening of vital organs.

Last, but not least, are the "amalgam mongers," who advocate no silver amalgam fillings in teeth, because of the toxicity of mercury and the increased electrical activity generated by dissimilar metals in the acid-containing mouth — a battery!

In summary, all of these positions have something to offer. With knowledge and understanding can come the skills necessary for control of our lives for increased well-being and longevity — quality and quantity of life. May we not have to sacrifice one for the other. That's what this book is all about!

4.

FROM BAD STRESS TO GOOD STRESS

The Loss Of Adaptive Energy And How To Conserve It

Continued activation of the "fight or flight" and its effect response on human beings were first described and explained by Dr. Hans Selye, from Montreal, Canada, in the early 1950's. His General Adaptation Syndrome of the mind-body connection is made up of three stages.[1]

As one continues to be fearful, anxious, tense, and worried, one progresses through the alarm, resistance, and exhaustion stages. During this long-term stress, produced by threatening or anxiety-arousing experiences, the individuals' physical and psychological reserves are used up. He or she becomes more prone to illness, has greater difficulty recovering, and the quality of life is diminished. If the syndrome is not halted or reversed early, then one reaches the later stages where permanent damage occurs. Chronic activation of the "fight or flight" response leads to irreversible damage.

Dr. Selye coined the term adaptation energy to mean how well the human organism can adapt to change. Each individual is endowed with a limited amount of adaptation energy, from the moment of conception, to enable that person to cope with physical and psychological stress. The greater the stress, the faster it is used up. When one runs "out of gas," one can die an early death. One's adaptation energy has been used up. There is not enough energy left to fight a virus or bacterium, to detect and eliminate cancer cells, or to foster a healing process. Illness does not kill, *unless there is a depletion of energy.* Premature aging is the result of unnecessary depletion of adaptation energy.[2]

As we already know, during the alarm phase the catecholamines are poured into the bloodstream, which leads to a number of physical changes in the body. There is an increase in blood pressure which may, over time, become chronic hypertension. This then increases the risk of stroke and heart attack, as the result of increased pressure in the blood vessels, which can dislodge cholesterol plaques and blood clots.

If this happens, arteries in the heart or brain may become blocked which results in immediate damage to the cells. Increased blood pressure can also cause a blood vessel, particularly in the brain, to burst — an aneurysm — with subsequent damage. The heart rate increases, which puts great strain on the heart and blood vessels. Fatty acids are released into the bloodstream, which increases the chances of cholesterol deposits on the walls of the arteries. Sugars are released into the bloodstream, that can trigger the pancreas to overproduce insulin, which can bring on hypoglycemia or diabetes, when the pancreas falters or "gives out." Muscle tensions increase, which leads to aches and spasms, headaches, and asthma. Metabolism is raised, which can cause shaking, tremors, and fatigue. All digestive processes are curtailed, which leads to indigestion, diarrhea, acidity, and flatulence. The increase of sugar, oxygen, and epinephrine in the brain may increase anxiety, anger, and mood swing. Some even become incoherent and panic stricken.

If one has enough adaptive energy and resilience to survive the alarm stage, then one enters the resistance stage. Here, as we know, the adrenal glands are stimulated to produce high levels of the corticoids. Hence, the blood pressure can stay high with a greater risk of kidney disease and cardiovascular irregularities. An imbalance in hydrochloric acid and bicarbonate of soda in the stomach can lead to ulcers. The immune system is suppressed, decreasing the number of white blood cells, which lowers resistance to disease, including diabetes. The lymph nodes actually shrink in size. The pituitary gland stimulates the thyroid gland to produce thyroxine, which increases the metabolic rate.

If high enough, it can produce loss of appetite, hyperactivity, insomnia, chronic fatigue, and possibly goiters. However, individuals may remain overweight, because the body stores more fat during stress — the famine adaptation mechanism. Sex and growth hormones are in scarce supply, leading to actual shrinking of the sex glands, less desire for sex, lowered sperm count, irregular menstruation, and spontaneous abortions. Lack of growth hormones delays normal growth patterns and puberty.

Finally, unless some of the stress is abated, there is exhaustion in every sense of the term. Any organ system that has been over-stressed becomes fragile, thus leading to organ-specific disease, as the result of energy depletion. As a "last ditch" attempt to survive, the catecholamines are poured into the system again. This leads to rapid consumption of what little energy is left. The immune system is weak, which leads to a greater likelihood of infectious diseases, cancer, and autoimmune diseases, such as rheumatoid arthritis. The brain is deprived of an energy supply and, as we know, it requires a great deal.

At the same time, there is less waste disposal which leads to toxicity of the brain. There are fewer neurotransmitters within the brain, which creates imbalances such as memory loss, confusion, incoherence, speech difficulties, and loss of judgment. Personality disorders, with inattentiveness and emotional extremes, are common in this state of exhaustion. Many symptoms of senility are produced, which seem to have no connection to other disease states.

When the adaptation system breaks down, the individual is no longer able to maintain internal body balances or to fight off disease. In spite of "heroic" treatment measures, the individual succumbs due to depletion of adaptation energy. Death is the final adaptation on this earth.

There are at least eight major factors that increase premature aging or the unnecessary depletion of adaptation energy, which, in turn, increases the probability of debilitating our abilities and subsequent death. The first two are, for the most part, unchangeable as far as improvements are concerned. The other six are modifiable.

The two "fixed" components consist of our inheritance and time. They are rather impervious to alteration. Information carried within the genetic composition of the body's cells determines the amount of adaptation energy and, subsequently, how long that body can function. The variation in longevity is due, in part, to the fact that no one gets half of their characteristics from their mother and half from their father. A quarter of the genetic traits come from each parent and the rest from earlier ancestors. From each of our four grandparents, comes a sixteenth. These cells do deteriorate as the result of such factors as X-ray, radiation (including that from the sun), some toxic chemicals, and some viruses.

By minimizing exposure to these agents, genetic breakdown can be limited. However, genetic material is not subject to any great improvement at this point in time, at least, through any changes in lifestyle or medications.

Neither is the element of time. The unavoidable truth is that adaptation energy does diminish over time. The only recourse we have is to use it as slowly, effectively, and enjoyably as possible. Many negative factors can be limited or avoided, in order to enhance our energy for living long and well.

Fortunately, there are six factors over which we can exert some control.

First, let's take a look at distress. We already know the ramifications of stress on the body, with its greater and greater demands on the body's resources. These levels of distress can be broken through relaxation and good stress. Intervention in this area is what this whole book is about.

Secondly, all major illness and disease put extra strain on one's system. Preventative medicine is the "state of the art." This can be accomplished by learning to live a better lifestyle, through proper exercise, relaxation, and nutrition. This most certainly minimizes energy depletion.

A third consideration is that of iatrogenic diseases, which are the result of improper medical and psychological treatment, such as unnecessary surgery, risks of hospitalization, errors made by physicians and other medical personnel, and improper or detrimental counseling and therapy. Intense surveillance on the part of the patient-doctor team is mandatory, in order to avoid iatrogenic diseases.

Exposure to toxic substances is our number four concern. We are exposed to as many as 600,000 chemical compounds, most of which have not been adequately tested for their effects. However, the three common social habits of smoking, drinking, and drug abuse also introduce toxic substances into our bodies. Moreover, certain food additives, air and water pollution, and occupational hazards cause toxic substances to permeate our bodies. All of these effect adaptation energy either by altering genetic material, producing disease, or damaging body tissue. Our culture presupposes a certain amount of exposure to these deleterious substances, but many can be avoided in the best interests of conserving adaptation energy.

Perhaps the factors over which we can exercise the most control are sedentariness and diet. The human biosystem becomes less efficient through the continual habits of sitting and lack of dynamic movement. "Use it or lose it" is the motto here! The less you use yourself, the less effective you are. Disuse is definitely a pre-disease state. Low impact aerobic exercise, active involvement in life's experiences, and creative endeavor generate reserves.

Eustress, or positive stress, is probably the greatest energy producer. Likewise, what we eat absolutely enhances or degrades our performance. In brief, far too many of our people consume too much salt, which puts a strain on the heart and kidneys and raises blood pressure. Sugar consumption has doubled during this century. We already know how it increases one's stress reactivity by disturbing the blood-sugar balance and pushing individuals toward hypoglycemia and diabetes.

Caffeine activates the sympathetic nervous system, and is now implicated as a factor in stress-related disorders such as cardiovascular diseases.

Certainly, we can observe many people who are nervous, "jittery," anxious, or depressed after consuming large amounts of coffee in scientifically controlled studies. Excessive consumption of fats, both saturated and unsaturated, are now implicated as causes of diseases, such as cardiovascular, cancer, and autoimmune. The scientific evidence seems to be nearing confirmation levels.

Over-eating over-taxes the body and depletes energy at a very rapid rate. The additional problem of becoming overweight is that it places a great strain on the physical and psychological systems. There are fewer and fewer overweight people in the progressively older-age categories. One simply needs to visit a retirement home or shelter-care facility to make these observations. Past the age of 80, there are very few people who are overweight. "Fat people" do not survive that long!

"Diet is probably the most accessible aspect of unnecessary adaptation depletion and can, with some assistance and a good deal of willpower, be altered so as to enhance your energy reserves, instead of draining them," says Sigmund Stephen Miller in his book, *Life Span Plus*.[3]

According to Hans Selye, you have just so much adaptation energy. "If you use too much of your energy in resisting the stresses and strains of life, it's like running your car through the streets and keeping your brakes on at the same time. You will wear it out more rapidly." He goes on to say, "The real crises in our civilization are not recognized as being psychosomatic, and psychosomatic diseases are essentially diseases of stress.

"If you get a gastric ulcer, doctors say you have a psychosomatic ulcer. But the trouble is not the ulcer; it is your boss or your child or your spouse. With our contemporary medical methods, it is relatively easy to teat the ulcer. But even if you cure the ulcer, the patient still comes back, because he continues to have what caused it in the first place."[4]

The key to handling stress is to know yourself and your stress level, according to Selye. With every threat to your well-being, you have to decide whether to put up a "fight," or take "flight," or try to "flow" gracefully. Many who do the latter wind up in the "gutter!" Perhaps it would be better to simply "step aside."

Selye believed that it was important to learn to live with the increased demands of modern society by following a code of behavior based on natural law. Selye's code was one of altruistic egoism — helping yourself by helping others. He believed that the way to help others was to make them happy by giving them "...ideas, motivation, something to do, work that is pleasant. Apart from drug therapy or surgery, which have already been well established in treating many diseases, there is a much more important way to make people healthy, and that is to make them happy."[5]

Stress Is Not Always Bad

It seems everyone rushes, rushes, rushes, in all directions! Visualize or picture in your mind for a moment the subway screeching to a stop and busy people rushing onto the platform. Hundreds more throng into the train, as it takes off for the next stop, where people race up wide stairs to the street level and hurry to their places of employment. On the street, children carry armloads of books and run to school. Shop owners scurry to open their establishments for quick morning service. Truck drivers sling bundles of newspapers onto the cement sidewalk, where speedy hands quickly ready them for rapid distribution. All of this is a virtual "anthill" of activity.

Today, all life seems to be running at high speed. We rush to lunch; we rush back to work; we rush home only to rush to the store, to our sports, and to our evening's activities. We even rush through our vacations. In this quick flight, life yields less and less meaning. Lost in a world of rapid transit, instant foods, and quick-thinking computers, life to thousands has lost its joys and reality, to be replaced by a gnawing sense of emptiness, loneliness, and frustration. People can become too exhausted to seek the real meaning and purpose of life.

However, stress doesn't have to be bad. With the right attitude, it can be the best thing that could ever happen. Even though the heart pounds, blood pressure rises, and the adrenal hormones are produced whether you're glad, sad, or mad, there still is a profound difference in the effects on the body. The stress response is activated, but there's a curious dichotomy of stress, according to those who study humor psychology. One might die from being frightened, but it's not likely that anyone would die from laughing! The first one constitutes bad stress; the second one is good stress.

Researchers have conducted laboratory studies where the physiological responses of groups of subjects were compared. Some were exposed to fear conditions, while others watched Abbott and

Costello films. They were all attached to electronic devices and IV's. The subjects who experienced mirth produced an increase in blood pressure, heart rate, and the secretion of catecholamines, particularly that of adrenalin — as did those subjects who experienced fear. However, a profound difference showed up in the actual hormone profile. With fear, there was a surge of adrenalin, but with mirth there was a much more conservative amount. Another phenomenal finding was that heart rate and blood pressure of those who laughed eventually dropped down below the original levels. This was very beneficial. What a marvelous way to relax and allow the body to restore itself. However, those who experienced fear, continued to also experience the damaging effects of distress on the body.

There are other kinds of "good stress" that produce the same beneficial results. Paul J. Rasch, M.D., president of the American Institute of Stress, reports that symphony conductors who work long hours, travel frequently, and deal with prima donnas and sensitive artists, live long and productive lives. They have some very good things going for themselves! These include enjoyment of what they're doing, pride of accomplishment, approval of their peers, and the applause of the audiences.[7] These are all positive "vibes" or positive stresses.

Whether or not stress is good or bad for you is a matter of how you look at it. All of life's challenges are like a roller coaster ride. Either you can stiffen your back, clench your knuckles until they're white, shut your eyes, lock your jaws, and just wait for it to be over, or you can be a wide-eyed thrill seeker, relishing every plunge and ready to do it again!

Kobassa and Maddi studied the personality differences between those executives who stand up to the turmoil of organizational change and those who do not. Those who saw the company and themselves in a positive light, saw their work load as challenging, were more involved, and were able to be more independent. They had a sense of commitment, control, and challenge — they were hardy. They had fewer illnesses and lower blood pressures than their more vulnerable counterparts. All psychological signs of anxiety, depression, and suspiciousness (paranoia) were also lower. What was stress to the others was not stress for them!

Surprisingly, hardiness does not seem to be a genetic trait. That is, one is not born with it as a mental counterpart of a strong constitution. Dr. Maddi says, "Rather, hardiness is a set of beliefs about the world and themselves and the interaction between the two."[8] Hardy people have neither better genes nor happier childhoods. What they do have are better attitudes. They are higher in self-esteem and think of themselves and the world as worthwhile. They have confidence that they can influence events around them and see change, even though painful, as an opportunity to learn and grow. These kinds of people do not eliminate stress, but they are able to keep it from reaching explosive levels. They actually enjoy it!

Attitudes can be adjusted. Drs. Maddi and Kobassa have a hardiness intervention program funded by the National Institute of Mental Health. Through a counseling program, hardiness increased. Dr. Maddi states, "There was a measurable decrease in mental and physical strain, anxiety, depression, suspicion, and blood pressure. We also found that there was an increase in immunoglobulin A, a marker of immune response in the upper respiratory area, suggesting a strengthening of the immune system."[9]

The program involves only 15 hours of hardiness intervention, consisting of several relatively easy-to-learn psychological techniques. For example, participants learn to distinguish between what is stressful and what is not. This is accomplished by keying in on feelings of fear, that may be buried in the unconscious. Even though one might complain about "never having enough time to do anything," it may be that past experiences of failure may have conditioned them for a "fear of failure" syndrome, and so deadlines are not met. Procrastination is the result. This protects the self-image. The threatened individual comes to believe that it wasn't his or her own fault that they didn't have enough time! Once a person comes to realize that fear of failure is hampering his or her performance, then that person can gain a new sense of control.

However, a tendency to procrastinate is common. It causes much stress and suffering, as procrastinators put off work until the last possible moment. There is an old adage that "There wouldn't be much done if it weren't for the last minute." Nonetheless, this is a very expensive practice, as those who practice it usually feel very ashamed of their last-minute efforts. Those who work only under pressure, skip school or work, and/or give false reasons (rationalizations) for being late, are placing a great deal of stress on themselves. Psychologists Jane Burka and Lenora Yuen studied students who procrastinated. They found that many of these students seemed to equate performance in school with their personal worth.[10] I have observed this same phenomena. By procrastinating, it is possible to blame poor performance on a late start, rather than on a lack of ability. This is much less threatening to the individual.

In addition, there are people with very high expectations for themselves, known as perfectionists. They, too, may find it difficult to start on a project. If they are unrealistic enough to expect the impossible from themselves, they end up with all-or-nothing work habits. I have seen this so many times. Many students actually "drop out" if they can't be assured of an "A" grade. This is really a form of neuroticism where otherwise capable human beings are "frozen" with fear.

In order to overcome these problems, procrastinators must face the self-worth conflict. They can start to make progress by learning better study or work skills and more effective time management. One should know how to do his or her job well. This provides a feeling of satisfaction and pride, that pays big dividends on one's investments of time and energy.

In addition, a formal time schedule can help prevent procrastination and insure motivation. To prepare a time schedule, one should start with a chart showing all the hours in every day of the week. All committed times should be filled in first. These would include such commitments as work, meals, appointments, sleep, and so on. Then "open" or "free" times are observable. If there are none, make some! "All work and no play makes Jack a dull boy." Then schedule in the times when you are going to work on your project. The "bottom line" is then to do it!

Keeping a schedule causes one to feel positive because of the honest effort being made to do well. More is accomplished as the result of not thinking about playing while working, and not worrying about working while playing! One can avoid the feeling that he or she is working all the time, when in fact one is worrying all the time — profoundly stressed and accomplishing little, if anything! So, there is a cure for procrastination. Give it a try — you will like it!

Any of us can transform stress. This is actually our only hope, when we realize that we can't avoid it. You can also learn to ask yourself how something could have been worse and how it could have been better. In this way, you will begin to realize that you do have some skills. Any time you understand how much worse something could have been, you know you didn't "mess up" as badly as you might have! This is a real consolation, and your self-image improves. Always remember that if a situation is unchangeable, such as the personality or ill-health of another significant person, then you can do other things that will give you a sense of commitment, such as your job. "God grant me the power to change the things I can, the serenity to accept the things I cannot change, and the wisdom to know the difference" is the Alcoholics Anonymous prayer, and one that is appropriate for all of us in difficult situations.

However, failure may be your best route to success, so says Robert G. Allen in his book, *The Challenge.* The single greatest obstacle blocking success is the fear of failure. Many people fear failure more than they want to succeed. Procrastination, perfectionism, and anxiety are all symptoms of this malady, even though most will not admit to "fear." Robert Allen says that "If you can handle the fear of failure and rejection, you can have just about anything you want in life — even success." To "rise to the challenge," he suggests five steps. The first two are of paramount importance. Number one is to "have a dream worth failing for." We all have goals we want to reach and things we want to do, but sometimes they are weak and afraid to come out. Dreams need to be big and real, to counteract the fear.[11]

Secondly, we need to "view success as something we fail into, not something we fall into." Failure is not the opposite of success; they go hand in hand. In fact, people who are successful have failed many times; they are the most persistent failers on the face of the earth.[12] Many famous people have been told, many times, that they couldn't sing, couldn't write, couldn't paint, couldn't dance, or couldn't, period!

However, these same people weren't afraid to fail and persevered because they believed they had a dream that was worth "failing for." Each failure also taught them, by providing feedback. Their roads to success were paved with failures! These failures were the "stepping stones" to success.[13]

Next is to learn to fail in the right places. Don't try to improve your financial situation by staying in a dead-end or minimum-wage job. No one in his right mind would dig for gold in a salt mine! Dig in a place where there's a chance of "striking pay dirt." In addition, "learn to see the good in every failure or setback." Make the best of the way things turn out, and things will turn out better. Many setbacks in life turn out to be blessings in disguise. Failures that cause pain can be guideposts to success. Failure is necessary! It teaches valuable lessons that lead to success.[14]

"Jump!" Allen says. "Fear is like a chasm, separating you from what you really want from life," he continues. If you don't make it the first time, try again, but no one can take that jump for you. Faith precedes a miracle. If you believe in something strongly enough and jump when challenged, success can eventually be yours.[15]

Of course, you should look before you leap, but you'll never land if you don't first jump![16]

Therefore, stress is not always bad. In fact, it can be the best thing that ever happened. There is such a thing as "good stress!" Anytime we feel good about something or make the best of a bad situation, there is only a moderate amount of adrenalin produced; and all the physiological responses of stress drop below their original levels — reflecting true relaxation and peace of mind.

Napoleon Bonaparte said, "The best cure for the body is to quiet the mind."

Norman Cousins — A Case In Point

Norman Cousins is first remembered for his visits in Africa with the remarkable Dr. Albert Schweitzer, who had a tremendous influence on him. In 1964, Cousins contracted an extremely serious illness and used humor as an essential part of his miraculous recovery. He attributed his recovery to an active partnership with his physician, large doses of love, hope, faith, laughter, confidence, and the will to live.

Then again on December 22, 1980, he suffered a heart attack from which he also recovered. He has spent many years as adjunct professor in the Program of Medicine, Law, and Human Values, at the UCLA School of Medicine. He died in December, 1990.

According to Cousins, there are two systems necessary for the normal functioning of the body that need to be understood and emphasized. They are the healing system and the belief system, which work together. "The healing system is the way the body mobilizes all its resources to combat disease. The belief system is often the activator of the healing system. The belief system represents the unique element in human beings that makes it possible for the human mind to affect the working of the body," says Cousins.[17]

"All things center around belief, which is a prime physiological reality. Expectations cause physiological change. Our thoughts, hopes, ideas, attitudes, and desire do become chemical substances. Confidence in the prospects of recovery, plus competent medical attention, are essential. One cannot substitute for the other. What we believe, however, is the most powerful option we have for the life force."

What the patient actually *thinks* will happen is a strong activator of the biochemical processes — in terms of life or death. Research goes back to as early as 1938, as to the importance of the patient's faith in the physician.

In 1960, Dr. A.K. Shapiro documented this fact.[18] Those who have strong confidence, versus those who are sad and giving up, tend to have a better outcome. "The fighting spirit" is far more conducive to recovery than are feelings of helplessness and hopelessness. We must never underestimate the power to regenerate and live within self-imposed limits. The body has a natural drive toward perfectibility, which can be enhanced through the "will to live." Let us not forget that!

When a patient goes to a doctor, that patient wants more than anything else to know that he or she matters. All patients expect sensitivity and tenderness. They do not want impersonal and "cold" scientists, who attach "absoluteness" to their findings. They become concerned if they are deprived of access to their physicians. There needs to be a deeply human response by the physician, when the patient asks him or her for some help. In the majority of cases, the physician should reassure the patient that he or she has a healing system systematically designed to take care of most problems. "Reverence for life" is essential in the doctor-patient relationship.

Pain certainly puts limitations on one's activities, but it is not always an indication of poor health, according to Cousins. It is more often the result of such factors as tension, stress, worry, inactivity, boredom, frustration, suppressed anger, inadequate sleep, an imbalanced diet, use of drugs, or other abuses of our modern society. All of these states, nonetheless, can lead to poor health. Many patients need a considerate and tactful explanation that illness can be the result of "wear and tear" on the body and mind. All of the factors mentioned above certainly do contribute to illness, especially when they occur in combination and/or without respite. However, laughing can help an illness. Cousins says that laughing enhances respiration, but we also know that it calms the mind, reduces the stress hormones, and so benefits the body. Cousins' good emotions of "love," "faith," and "grace" are so necessary, because they are so regenerative![19]

5.

EUSTRESS

Dr. Hans Selye termed the kinds of stress that are beneficial or therapeutic as eustress.[1] They are health-promoting, rather than harmful or in distress. All mirthful activities such as laughing, loving, singing, dancing, or exercising are health-enhancing experiences. The initial "high" is not as great as one of distress, and then the physiological stress levels fall *below* those of the pre-eustress state of the organism. The production of endorphins gives the pleasurable sensations as any pains or discomforts are reduced, and joy is the outcome.

We need to make sure that we are getting enough eustress in our lives, to offset the effects of distress or bad stress. Positive, pleasurable, and life-enhancing experiences make living worthwhile. Hiking up a mountain on a clear, crisp day, or playing a musical instrument, or writing a story, or just sitting quietly, taking in the surrounding environmental stimuli, are all examples of positive, curative, and enjoyable stress.

Eustress increases stimulation and improved memory by enhancing both awareness and motivation. As one becomes almost totally immersed in his or her pleasurable activities, there is less interference with the perception of that experience. This leads to better coding of the information in the brain and, therefore, better memory. One cannot remember what one has not clearly perceived. Eustress improves alertness and desire by making the immediate surroundings "upbeat" and something worth remembering. The recall or review of pleasurable memories serves to help people gain a better understanding of what they have accomplished. If not used excessively (living in the past), this reverie can have beneficial results to individuals, as they continue to move on down life's pathways, with optimism and hope. Eustress, along with a positive and flexible self-image, improves the ability to store and then retrieve information in one's best interests, at later dates. If we are flexible, and not too demanding and rigid, we actually can laugh about our idiosyncracies and shortcomings. Then, we are better able to cope as imperfect humans in an imperfect society.

Consequently, anything you do that you enjoy and that makes you feel good about yourself is eustressful. Laughter has the potential of literally performing miracles. There can be no depreciation when there is appreciation. Never a day should go by, but what we smile and laugh about something. There is no better medicine! Many have espoused its benefits, particularly Norman Cousins who, for many years, was living proof of its benefits.

We should seek out any experiences, activities, or people that make us feel good. "Go out around" or "step aside" from those who do not. This practice is mutually satisfying to both parties. Of course, this does not mean to shirk one's responsibilities in marriage, parenting, or on the work scene. *There* is nothing that gives me any more eustress than to "look before I leap" — but then jump into a situation "with both feet," when I think something really needs to be changed. If improvements occur, that's extremely rewarding. If they don't, it's still satisfying to know that I did my best, according to my beliefs.

We can't control all the variables, and we don't win them all! "Good" stress is well worth the price, but "bad" stress is not. Therefore, let's work for the positive rewards of living.

Eustress is a positive and helpful form of adaptation which, in itself, means adjusting to change. These changes may be the result of your efforts, or they may be due to variables over which you have had no control. Nonetheless, a change which is new and different occurs, to which you must adapt physically and psychologically. This should be done in a way that is least harmful and the most beneficial.

Our perceptions, or how our brain interprets new experiences, determine for the most part the amount of stress or eustress that we feel. The way anyone responds to a particular event, at a particular time, is the result of that person's personality (the sum total of one's typical ways of responding) and state of mind — a very personal matter. They are *subjective* (personal reactions,) rather than *objective* (applying to all).

Some enjoy music — others do not; some are verbal — others are not; some are social — others are not; and on and on! Therefore, optimal adaptation is possible if each individual can find the lifestyle that is most conducive to his or her emotional health. Styles need to change as individuals grow and develop. Some of the needs of older people are not the same as when they were younger. However, many remain virtually unchanged, because personalities may remain intact, for the most part.

After early childhood, certain modifications of overt behaviors — due to personality structure — may occur; but massive changeovers in underlying structure are rare, indeed!

From the time of your conception, and certainly your birth, you have experienced stress and eustress. Hopefully, there has been enough of the latter to give you a pleasant personality. Everything you have ever experienced in the past has had effects in both directions. Whether you had a difficult or easy birth, whether you received adequate or inadequate care, whether you received affectionate stimulation or not, and whether you learned to feel good or bad about yourself, all have determined the way you respond.

A past history of enjoyment creates the expectation of the same; and if we expect enjoyment, that's usually what we get, at least in some measure. Good experiences in the past beget or guarantee a willingness to engage in more of the same as we go along. If not, then there is too much fear or anger, very potent stressors, which do the opposite of what we want — i.e., eustress. Some help is available to these people in overcoming their fears if they have the personal motivation to do so. No one can do it for them!

However, many people are so distressed, so much of the time, that they are unable to experience eustress. This happens because they are tense, nervous, anxious, or depressed, which inhibits and suppresses their ability to know or to remember what it feels like to be happy. They forget what it means to really be joyful, creative, and energized. Distress and eustress are two opposite forces. However, any person can learn to *increase* the pleasurable and *decrease* the unpleasant — accentuate the positive and eliminate the negative! Relaxation is the key. Individuals who can relax fully and deeply for a few minutes a day are known to be happier and healthier than those who do not. One can think more clearly, and feel more invigorated, and good when relaxing. A low-stress diet is very beneficial and helps the body to relax. Relaxation should be the counterpart of exercise; a happy balance of the two is what is needed. Once the body is in a relaxed state — parasympathetic function — it is receptive to change in the positive direction.

Techniques for learning to relax are many. As mentioned earlier, Napoleon Bonaparte contended that "The way to quiet the body is to quiet the mind." Several good mental techniques rely on imaging. This is a process of creative thinking that is positive in nature and accomplished during a relaxed state. It involves "seeing" or "visualizing" hoped-for goals with tremendous intensity.

For some people, prayer is also used, whereby confidence or faith is placed in a power outside of themselves. By seeking this help outside of self, the "self" can then "sit back and take it easy." This, then, is a form of relaxation that gives one's own inner healing resources or restorative powers a chance to work. Positive affirmations like "I am feeling better" or "My body is growing stronger each day" help insure that the health-promoting effects of relaxation continue.

Research shows these techniques to be helpful supplements in treating gastrointestinal disorders, high blood pressure, chronic headaches, coronary bypass surgery, and cancer.

The Menninger Foundation in Topeka, Kansas is well known for its work in biofeedback research. Essentially, biofeedback is a way of monitoring the physiological changes as a result of stress. By placing electrodes on the surface of the skin, at various body locations, the biofeedback machines are designed to pick up electrical activity in the body and give an audible or visual signal whenever there is a change in the body's physiological activity.

Measurable changes include temperature, muscle tension, blood pressure, and brainwave activity. The machines are battery operated and considered completely safe, as no electrical current is ever administered. Once patients can actually see (through feedback of their biological responses (biofeedback)) what their bodies are doing after activation of the autonomic nervous system, they can learn to control these responses. They do it through relaxation training. The greatest successes have been in treating high blood pressure and migraine headaches, both the result of vaso-constriction of the peripheral arteries, during the stress "fight or flight" response.

More blood is pushed to the center of the body; the heart then works harder to get the increased blood supply to the large muscles, for strength, and to the lungs, for oxygenation. It is entirely feasible that this increased blood pressure, increased heart rate, increased blood clotting, and increased heart contractions can be reduced through the relaxing effects of eustress.

The next time somebody tries to tell you that "It's all in your head." Please realize that it's probably not in your head, but the power to get rid of it may well be.

Many people mistakenly believe that they can simply "put their worries aside" for an hour or so, or maybe a weekend, and then automatically return to stress-free living. This is just not true! The human body does not work that way. The only way to handle excessive levels of stress is through ongoing *stress management:* plenty of relaxation, eustress, exercise, good nutrition, and other anti-stress behavior, on a daily basis. Do not stagnate! Don't repeat the same old patterns and stay in the same old "ruts." Human beings have the potential to adapt. We are made to solve problems, to learn new things every day of our lives, to change ourselves for the better, and to improve the world around us. New stimulation, new ideas, new places, new people, and new experiences are all necessary to keep us feeling worthwhile and competent. This is what makes us feel good about ourselves — the ultimate eustress that we all need.

Of course, changes should not be so massive and different as to cause one to feel a loss of one's identity. A sense of coherence is also very necessary for that good feeling. Some folks are more fearful and some more fearless because of their personality makeup. The extent to which one explores the uncharted areas in one's life, in discovering and rediscovering the vast range of his or her talents and capabilities, is a very personal matter. It cannot be forced, but it can be encouraged.

Eustress improves the functioning of the immune system. Just as negative emotions can make you sick, positive ones can make you better. We now have concrete, scientifically verifiable explanations of the mind-body connection, particularly the one between the mind and the immune system. The body's immune system is far more able to fight off disease when it is involved with more positive and eustressful experiences.

The new area of psychoneuroimmunology has confirmed what orthodox and Eastern traditions have maintained for a long time. That is, that how we think and feel has a profound effect on our bodies and determines the degree to which we can resist disease. Research confirms that all kinds of stress, both external and internal, effect the immune system. Stress, attitudes, and emotions either enhance or suppress your chances of getting cancer. What applies to the treatment of the disease is even more relevant to its prevention.

Certain guidelines have emerged with respect to enhancing the functions of the immune system. They, of course, propose the inclusion of eustressful experiences about which we have learned. These include reducing stress levels to the point where they are not a daily occurrence, learning to express (not repress) all human emotions, (including anger and frustration) in appropriate ways, maintaining a positive and optimistic outlook on life and perception of one's self, and promoting supportive and loving relationships with family and friends.

Newer on the scene, particularly since the 1970's, are the benefits of regular exercise. It is not known whether exercise works directly on the immune system or indirectly. Nonetheless, it is true that regular and appropriate exercise does enhance immune system function and aid in the prevention of cancer and infectious diseases. It also relieves stress and improves nutrient circulation.

Aerobic exercise which is sustained, moderate activity that requires the heart to pump more blood throughout the entire body and the lungs to take in more oxygen, is the method of choice. This kind of exercise should be maintained for approximately 20 to 30 minutes, at least three times a week. There are many options available to almost everyone. These include walking, swimming, dancing, jogging, hiking, rowing, bicycling, and cross-country skiing. Some of these might be more suitable than others depending on health conditions and personal preference. Nonetheless, they are all good kinds of eustress.

Newer on the scene yet and still in the area of controversy is that of nutrition, a component of stress and eustress. We do know that poor nutrition weakens the immune system; but we don't know — 100 percent — the benefits or dangers of supplementation, for example. However, a conservative course between medical orthodoxy and radical "megadoses" would seem prudent, according to recent evidence.

According to this position, which is endorsed by both progressive biomedical scientists and many holistic practitioners, the typical American diet is probably deficient in micronutrients, such as vitamins and minerals. This is said to be the result of over-refining and over-processing of our foods. There are also increased needs for certain nutrients, as the result of stress or toxic agents in our air, food, and water. The aging process and disease also change the body's requirements.

Dr. Michael Colgan of New Zealand, who studied at Rockefeller University and is now head of a nutritional institute in California, says that without vitamin and mineral supplements, there is no way to get adequate nutrition. Dr. Colgan believes that doses which are tailored to any individual's biochemical needs do improve physical and mental performance, control of pain and depression, and do slow down the aging process, with its accompanying disease states. He claims that the government's RDA's of the 48 essential nutrients are totally inadequate for optimum health — the immune system is hampered![2]

The two vitamins which have been specifically linked to immune system enhancement are A, along with beta-carotene, which is its dietary precursor, and C. Vitamin A/beta-carotene is absorbed by the body better from dietary sources, such as carrots, dark green leafy vegetable, yams, sweet potatoes, and the like. In order to get enough vitamin C supplementation is necessary. Therefore, the scales are now tipped in favor of intelligent supplementation, another form of eustress.

However, there is a great deal of concern. The little plastic packets of vitamins and minerals, once found only in health food stores but now available in mainstream convenience markets, such as AM-PM, 7-11, and Stop'n Go, are a waste of money! The Super-Energy Pack (cost: $0.99) contains 5,000 percent of the U.S. RDA for vitamin B6 and more than 1,500 times the U.S. RDA for B12. It is now known that these levels are an almost toxic dose. It is believed that what our bodies cannot use, we simply urinate away. However, it does not appear that we can be so sure of that! At one time that was said of protein, and now we have evidence that too much of it can damage our kidneys, and draw calcium out of the bones, among other stress-related effects.

Some claim that there's no evidence that vitamins can help alleviate emotional stress! That's true! However, certain vitamins help our bodies handle physical stress, such as surgery, burns, smoking, or excessive drinking. With our present knowledge and understanding from the fields of psychology and physiology, about what emotional stress also does to the body, it would appear that a balanced diet with adequate vitamins, minerals, and low-stress foods are a necessity. Otherwise, more distress — not eustress. Vitamins may not alleviate the emotional stress itself, but they can help the body to withstand that stress. This will be explained further as we go along.

Furthermore, there is abundant evidence that many balanced diets are nutritionally deficient. It has also been shown that larger quantities of certain nutrients are needed, in order to offset the effects of stress, including those of pollution and chemical additives. Both emotional stress and smoking deplete the body's store of vitamin C. Animals can synthesize vitamin C under stress, but human beings cannot. However, no responsible authority recommends taking supplements in place of food or adopting a "more is better" attitude — both are unhealthy and not conducive to a state of eustress and good health.

Know You Can With Tryptophan

Judith J. Wurtman, a research scientist in the Department of Nutrition and Food Science at the Massachusetts Institute of Technology, wrote a book called *The Carbohydrate Craver's Diet*. She says, "The manufacture of a brain chemical, serotonin, is influenced by the amount of carbohydrate-rich foods an animal or a human eats."[3]

Serotonin, one of a class of brain chemicals known as neurotransmitters, is made from tryptophan, an amino acid (amino acids are the components of protein). When carbohydrate foods are eaten, insulin is released into the blood. Insulin increases the amount of tryptophan that gets into the brain and, subsequently, the level and activity of serotonin. Serotonin controls our level of awareness; it is what makes you feel relaxed and puts you to sleep at night. "So when you are upset, tense, anxious, nervous, or frustrated, eating carbohydrate will calm you down and make it easier to cope with the stress that is producing these unpleasant emotions," says Wurtman. However, there is no direct and non-invasive way to measure serotonin in the brain. The effects tell the story! One can be grumpy and irritable, but become normal and placid after eating carbohydrate. In addition, one's carbohydrate hunger is shut off when enough serotonin has been produced.[4]

Tryptophan is an amino acid found in protein-rich foods such as meat or fish. However, eating protein does not have the same effect. In order to enter the brain, tryptophan has to compete with the other more plentiful amino acids; it has a difficult time getting into the brain. Some words of caution are in order: Do not take tryptophan in concentrated form (pills) — too much can cause extreme drowsiness or dizziness, as well as block the entry of the other four essential amino acids needed for good health. In other words, too much tryptophan would constitute a profound level of stress! Also there were reports that some imported tryptophan was contaminated. It has been withdrawn from the market — tryptophan, in pill form, is no longer available.

Therefore, protein does not increase tryptophan nor serotonin! Eating carbohydrate foods which are starchy and/or sweet causes insulin to be secreted into the blood. The blood always contains amino acids that are moving from the blood to the cells. When insulin comes in, the amino acids leave the blood very rapidly and enter the cells of the body — except for tryptophan. It remains in the blood until the other amino acids are out of the way, and then enters the brain easily — serotonin is increased and carbohydrate hunger is shut off!

However, in order to facilitate this feat, the carbohydrate must be eaten alone — not with protein! Otherwise, the amino acids from the protein will hamper the tryptophan from entering the brain. Eating carbohydrates alone causes brain tryptophan and brain serotonin to be increased. The only emotions that can be experienced are relaxation and calmness! Taking tryptophan alone will not do it.

People can actually lose weight without suffering an insatiable craving for sweets by sticking to a low-calorie diet that contains enough carbohydrate during and between meals, to stimulate the production of serotonin, which shuts off the carbohydrate hunger. The small amount in fruit and vegetables may not be enough to accomplish this. Also, the fructose in fruit releases less insulin than sucrose or starch. Therefore, more fruit may need to be eaten. A piece of candy may be better!

Consuming normal amounts of carbohydrates always insures an increased sense of well-being. I have learned from personal experience that when I feel "uptight" and tense, a snack does the trick! I can then relax and focus on what I have to do, without being irritable! Everybody should snack once or twice a day when the carbohydrate hunger is most intense.

Deprivation causes overeating, not the snacking! Moderate amounts will control the appetite and bring on a feeling of satisfaction. High-protein-low-carbohydrate diets fail because not enough serotonin is produced to control the appetite.

Don't eat a carbohydrate snack (200 calories) within an hour after finishing a meal. This is too soon after eating protein. However, a very small amount of sugar, up to two teaspoons (which is 32 calories) or a piece of hard candy (which is about 20 calories) could be eaten *with* a meal, to make you feel satisfied, says Wurtman.[5] The serotonin will relax us when we're "uptight" and make us sleep when we are tired. What more could we ask for? I say, "Nothing!"

"At times when you must stay awake and you need to eat, try an egg or cheese for a snack," says Wurtman.[6] However, if you need to sleep, then stick with carbohydrates.

A food that has a minimum of 25 grams up to 60 or slightly over of carbohydrate is necessary to activate the insulin-tryptophan-serotonin connection. It is important to keep one's caloric intake within the limits. Therefore, a snack should not contain more than 200 calories. Snacks must be eaten in order to achieve a state of contentment and relaxation! One loses any feeling of guilt when one learns what the rewards can be! Yes, even a one-ounce candy bar, a one-ounce bag of chips, a plain doughnut, a muffin, a slice of cake, a brownie, a cookie, a hot drink with two to three teaspoons of sugar, or a cracker with jam or jelly would not hurt anyone's diet — if only used occasionally. Any one of these would satisfy one's urge to eat sweets. It takes 20 minutes to a half-hour for the carbohydrate-serotonin connection to take place. Take ten minutes to eat the snack, and then stop! No more! As your stomach takes in sweets, so, too, is your disposition becoming sweeter — more relaxed, calm, and tranquil. Be nice to yourself, and be nice to others!

Stress is the most common cause of overeating. Even though a few lose their appetites when stressed (probably as the result of exhaustion), the great majority overeat. The unsightly and bulging stomach is no comfort, even though eating may have helped temporarily. However, acute stress can be helped with a "coping food" These should contain 25 to 60 grams of carbohydrates and be pleasurable to eat. Indulge yourself! You will become relaxed! You will calm down and be better able to cope and deal with the cause of your stress. Above all, don't feel guilty! That would counteract the wonderful feeling of tranquility.

If one does "fall off the wagon" and consume too many calories one day, a reduction in calories for three or four succeeding days will balance things out. Eat your pie or hot biscuits and feel better. Then you can go out and "slay the monster!" However, don't overdose. Take one serving and stop! Coping food is a tranquilizer, and a much more reliable one than Valium or "booze," on which many people OD (overdose).

Many people also know the rules of stress management, but resort to eating too much, instead. Stress has a way of doing this, so identify the stresses that lead to overeating. Then remove yourself from the stressful situations, psychologically, if not physically. Talk over your problems with significant others. This usually will lead to some viable alternatives. However, some avoid doing unpleasant chores by eating instead — procrastination. Still others eat as a break from work or school — diversion. If the food consumed at these times is a snack of 25 to 60 grams of carbohydrates of not more than 200 calories, then eustress is the result!

Exercise is a must, according to Wurtman. She says, "The more calories you use up in activity, the less guilty you have to feel about dessert." When dieting, which is eating fewer calories, the body slows down metabolically. This necessitates speeding up muscularly, to increase the rate at which calories are burned.[7] However, if one does not increase energy expenditure through exercise, then the famine adaptation reflex which causes the body to conserve and store calories (fat) takes over. This mechanism "kicks in" immediately, if one eats less than 800 calories a day or goes for 18 hours without eating. When on any diet with decreased calorie intake, the body will use less and less energy for its basic metabolic functions, after six to eight weeks. Eventually, though, the body does adapt and so starts to "cannibalize" its fat stores — weight loss! Exercise does assist in increasing calorie use. "The more frequently you move those muscles, the more rapidly the weight will come off," states Wurtman.[8]

Calorie use can be increased through active sports, running, walking, or hiking. For those who have been rather sedentary or in ill-health, it is necessary to do only what is compatible with their hearts, lungs, backs, and knees! Athletic skill, time, money, and climate also play a role. Increasing the amount of moving done during the day is also very beneficial. It is well to incorporate more physical activities into your time at home, at work, or anytime, anywhere — "boogie your buns!"

When the fat in your fat cells is burned, it turns into water and carbon dioxide. Therefore, we breathe out and urinate out our fat stores. What a way to go! It is when we lose the water that our weight goes down. Cutting down on the amount of salt we ingest also helps, and caffeine can be used as a diuretic by some people. However, be patient! No one is a camel, and so cannot hold the water forever!

Implications are, then, that eating a meal high in carbohydrates and low in protein causes a neurochemical change, that is, increased serotonin, that brings about a reduction in intake of carbohydrate, but not protein. This is a biologically evolved phenomena that helps to maintain nutritional balance. It should prevent animal and man from consuming too many sweets and becoming inactive and/or lethargic.

However, this delicate balance seems to be very vulnerable to excesses, and under such conditions, does not seem to function adequately. Consuming too much protein is also very stressful. There are many stresses inflicted on the body by the typical American diet — high in refined sugar, salt, fat, and yes, protein. Protein, in general, has an energizing effect on the mind and body. Excesses are believed to be responsible for putting excess strain on the kidneys, drawing calcium out of the bones (as does a typical stress reaction), and other detrimental effects.

It is also true that some people may suffer some kind of a deficiency in the nutritional, metabolic, neurochemical, and behavioral feedback loop that predisposes them to obesity; but this does not negate the fact that they (probably more than any other) can profit from understanding and observing the carbohydrate-tryptophan-serotonin connection. We need to get "in tune" and "mesh" with our biological inheritance for optimal eustress — not overwhelming *distress*. We need to be "at-ease" to prevent "dis-ease."

Do Not Lean On Tyrosine

Protein foods which contain only small amounts of fat and/or carbohydrates contribute to a more alert, energetic, and motivated state of mind, according to Wurtman.[9] However, extremes of these states constitute the stress response, as we already know. It only takes three or four ounces of protein food to insure that there is enough tyrosine to stimulate the production of dopamine and norepinephrine — the alertness chemicals. These keep us mentally "up!" We can think quickly and accurately as we tackle challenges.

If the brain already has an ample supply of the alertness chemicals, eating more protein won't help matters any and could have deleterious effects. In fact, excessive amounts of concentrated tyrosine can cause undesirable changes in blood pressure. For this reason, do not take it in pill form! This also holds true for tryptophan, discussed earlier. Too much tryptophan, in concentrated form, can cause extreme drowsiness or dizziness. Either of these amino acids, in excessive amounts, can block the entry of the other four essential ones needed for good health.

There is also an indirect effect of the protein-tyrosine-norepinephrine and dopamine connection, where the stress response is concerned. We must realize that by eating protein, the amount of tyrosine is increased. This prevents tryptophan from getting into the brain, and the brain then cannot manufacture serotonin, which is the calming chemical. Therefore, one would remain "up" — sympathetic nervous system functioning. One would not be able to experience parasympathetic functioning because of the inability of the brain to manufacture serotonin. In other words, there would be little opportunity for the relaxation response, and the system could "burn out" all too soon.

So, although protein is very necessary for maintenance of life itself, massive amounts do constitute undesirable stress responses in the body! Too much protein, then, with too little carbohydrate, would do the same thing as any other stress response — increase catecholamines and steroids that, over time, cause the serious physiological changes discussed in the chapter on stress. Interestingly, serotonin is not classified as a catecholamine, but as an indoleamine, necessary for relaxation, the counterpart of stress!

Protein Should Be Lean

Fat also influences the mind in negative ways by interfering with the rate of absorption of protein, as well as of carbohydrate. Blood is diverted away from the brain during the digestive process. Fat increases this effect, and the mind is dulled. One tends to want to "curl up like a pig" (in more ways than one) and go to sleep. Fats are also high calorie foods — gram for gram more than twice as high as protein or carbohydrate. Fat takes longer to digest, and so it effects your mood and mind negatively. Therefore, high fat protein foods do not accomplish the desired results. Killer diseases are linked to high dietary fat consumption and to body fat which can also be the result of consuming too many calories of any food group, including that of refined sugar, which is a simple carbohydrate!

Acupress For Eustress

Frank R. Bahr, M.D. in Munich, Germany established the German Academy for Acupuncture and the German Academy for Auricular Medicine, in 1974. In his book, Dr. Bahr's Acu-Diet, he explains that by massaging specific acupressure points, one can influence the eating center to reduce the appetite.[10] This is the same center that responds to stress and can be manipulated for a relaxation response. We have known for some time that acupuncture and acupressure can successfully release the reflexes and bring about suppression of pain or compulsion.

One of the main research centers is the medical school in Peking, China. There in 1974 and 1975, Dr. Han Chisheng demonstrated that reflexes in the brains of rabbits could be released by means of acupressure. The subsequent changes in neurotransmitters influenced pain sensitivity and eating compulsion. Dr. Sebastian P. Grossman, of the University of Chicago, also has reported that by interfering with the neurotransmitter, serotonin, overeating could be induced.[11]

The production of serotonin can be influenced by acupressure. "What particular effect is to be achieved, whether it is pain suppression or of eating compulsion, depends solely on the choice of the point to be stimulated," says Dr. Bahr.[12] Strong pressure on muscles and tendons inhibits the neural action in the thalamus of the brain and reticular activating system of the brain stem.

According to Dr. Bahr, it is extremely important to control stress-related eating because of the dangers involved. People who are overweight by 10 percent or more are overburdening their hearts, jeopardizing fat and carbohydrate metabolism, and increasing the risk of high blood pressure and gallstones. Liver damage is increased in those who also consume large amounts of alcohol. The heart has to pump up to forty more quarts of blood per hour! The blood may also be too high in cholesterol. This increases the danger of cardiac infarction two-fold.[13]

In the obese, diabetes and other metabolic disorders are four times greater. High blood pressure (with the corresponding headaches, decreased energy, sleep disturbance, heart cramps, and cardiac infarcts) is three times greater, as is the liklihood of gallstones. Altogether, this constitutes a drastic reduction in life expectancy for the overweight, both in terms of quality of life and quantity of life! In fact, every two pounds of excess weight takes approximately four months from one's life. One should also be cognizant of the pain and misery involved, subsequent to death itself. Yet, the average weight for American men and women continues to climb. This is a dangerous epidemic and one that cries for relief.

That relief can come from first understanding how our bodies are programmed to store energy in the form of fat, just the same as any other species of life. Before the refrigerator was invented, our ancestors were hunters, who stored nutrition in their own bodies. They needed this capacity because it was a long time between feasts. They took the energy from the environment and stored it to maintain body temperature, functions, and the ability to move. They nourished themselves from *within,* by breaking down stored fats. In times of famine, they usually survived. However, in extreme cases their muscle and tissue could also be used up and they would starve to death. One positive note is that this capacity for internal nourishment gives us, their descendants, the precious where-with-all to get rid of piled-on weight. This should be done sensibly, of course, lest we use up our vital muscles by converting protein (amino acids) into energy, as did our ancestors, during famines, when they starved. The recent starvation in Ethiopia is a case in point!

We have also inherited a "lust for eating" which has both positive and negative aspects. Nature has purposefully coupled perpetuation (sex) and preservation (food) of the species with pleasurable sensations — the more essential the function, the more intense the pleasure! So, eating shares in common with reproduction — eat, drink, and be merry! They are lustful pursuits. In these ways, we are innately predisposed to preserve and perpetuate our species.

In years gone by, as history tells us, most people worked very hard physically. Builders lugged stones and cement, miners hacked coal, diary barns were mucked out with a pitchfork, and farmers walked behind the plow pushing it into the furrow as they went. These activities all called for a great deal of food and, yes, a great deal of fat for energy! There are only a few who do these kinds of jobs today, and they are the only ones who should consume energy-rich heavy diets.

Most men today probably consume 3,600 or more calories per day, instead of the recommended 2,700 or less. Most women probably consume 3,000 or more calories per day, instead of the necessary 2,000 or less. On the average, both men and women consume too much fat! If one consumes two ounces of fat per day over the necessary requirements, one can gain four pounds of fat in a month. According to the American Heart Association and the National Academy of Science, one's consumption of fat should not be over 30 percent of the total caloric intake. Many authorities recommend a far less amount.

Environmental conditions further the consumption of food, in addition to the genetic survival reflexes. For instance, when a baby cries because it needs attention and affection, it gets a bottle instead! The baby then becomes conditioned and demands the bottle when it needs love. This "substitute" gratification is then generalized to the cookie jar, candy box, or bottle, whenever the individual experiences anger, tension, or frustration.

In this way, we are no different that Pavlov's dogs! This phenomenon constitutes the "nervous eating" about which we hear so much. Our fat can actually be the result of grieving, because we do not have the love and affection that we need so desperately.

Although the ability to unerringly react to stress was a dire necessity for our strong ancestors, it has been passed on to our weaker pencil-pushers of today. It is still necessary in order to prepare us to avoid real and immediate physical danger. However, it is unfortunate that today so many stress reactions are triggered by inconsequential irritants. Disagreements at work or home are not usually life or death matters, but our systems respond as if they were! Unfortunately, there are no feasible ways of working off these tensions, as there were in earlier times. We cannot throw our desks out the window, or run and scream, or rearrange someone's face! "The little man in the white coat" would incarcerate us rather quickly! So what do we do? We eat! It is as if the organism mistakenly believes that it has to replace the energy which hasn't been used up in the first place. "Be that as it may, with many people stress is certainly the reason for their eating more than is good for them," says Dr. Bahr.[14] This can be a fatal scenario in our society, where food is, for the most part, continuously available.

With our programming for "eat-when-you-can-so-you-won't-want-later" mentality, unless we use some restraints, we become fat and consequently ill. The "feeding center" becomes an "addiction center."

However, it is this addiction of compulsive eating that can't be broken! Other habits, such as smoking or drinking, can be broken, if the object of craving is strictly withheld from the addict. But, compulsive eating cannot be stopped that way, for obvious reasons — everyone has to eat! Otherwise, we would starve to death. Therefore, it is mandatory that something be done to control the midbrain, where the impulses to eat originate.

Judith Wurtman explained how to do this by eating carbohydrate without protein, to increase the production of serotonin in the brain, which brings about relaxation and cessation of appetite.[15] However, Dr. Bahr explained (almost a decade earlier) how to accomplish the same thing with acupressure.[16] There may be "different strokes for different folks," but perhaps a combination of the two would be in order!

Researchers in Austria, Germany, China, Canada, and our Untied States have confirmed that acupuncture works. There are free nerve endings located under the skin, at specific points on the body. Stimulation of these points, along directional energy routes or meridians, results in release of neural impulses that travel via the nerve pathways through the spine and into the brain stem and then to the midbrain. It is here, in the nonspecific nuclei of the midbrain, that the impulses are processed and reflexively release neurochemical substances to transmit information. In the case of acupressure, fingertip pressure is exerted to massage the same points that are used for acupuncture. The absolutely harmless procedure can be self-administered and used for curbing the compulsive-eating center.

In order to accomplish this, progressive conditioning is necessary. Eventually, only ten seconds of acupressure will be enough to suppress the appetite. In order to release a reflex, free nerve endings must be stimulated. Therefore, pressure definitely has to be felt; but too much could injure the skin or cause bruising. There are nine acupressure points that can be massaged for the release of serotonin, the neurotransmitter that reduces appetite and gives a sense of well-being. (See Figure B, "Acupress for Eustress," Appendix, p. 189.) The spots to be located are more sensitive to pressure than the surrounding area. In other words, pressure will be felt more strongly when you are right on! This is known as pressure sensitive identification. Dr. Bahr has identified the nine acupressure points for the control of appetite and a sense of well-being.

The first acupressure point is one which Dr. Bahr himself found, not the Chinese. The point is located exactly midway between the nose and the upper lip on the inside. The trick is to massage the lip in an upward direction by about one-eighth of an inch. The point itself, which is on the inside of the lip, will be massaged downward by the counterpressure of the upper jaw. A finger and thumb, if clean and sanitary, or the rounded end of a pencil or ballpoint pen may also be used. The neat thing is that one can practice this overeater's acupressure inconspicuously, anywhere and anytime. Keep in mind that this technique only curbs compulsive eating. A low calorie diet is also necessary, if one wishes to lose weight.

The second point, also discovered by Dr. Bahr,[17] is important for conditioning the stomach muscles, which have become stretched through gluttony. The stretch receptors have become habituated and fail to respond. Through stimulation of these, and eating less, the stomach receptors will again become effective, and the hollow feeling in the stomach will disappear. The stomach actually goes back to its normal size.

This acupressure point lies exactly halfway between your navel and your breastbone. This point should be massaged upward with the thumbnail in approximately one inch strokes three or more times a day, following the massage of point number one.

Points number three through nine are those which were discovered by the Chinese. Point number three, which is called shao-chong (turbulence center of the wave), is used to stimulate heart and psyche in treating stress and depression. This point is located close to the root of the nail, on the ring finger side of the little finger. It should be massaged toward the outside. Do this on both sides of the body.

Also good for treating depression is point number four, which is called tung-li (connection with the inner life). It is located one and one-half to two fingers above the wrist, and it should be acupressured in the direction of the inside of the little finger and on both sides of the body.

Point number five, which is called shao-hai (small dewey sea of energy) and also known as the "point of vivaciousness," is found on the inner end of the elbow fold, when the elbow is bent. Use of this point is beneficial for energy and it is also an appetite depressant. Personally, this is one of my favorite spots — it seems to keep me endlessly writing and typing!Complete lack of vitality is also alleviated through pressure on point number six. It is known as ch'i-hai, and it lies two or three finger widths below the navel. It should be massaged upward.

Point number seven is used for treating the restlessness of depression and for exhaustion. It is known as tsu-san-li (Asiatic calm or heavenly equanimity). It is located directly under the kneecap and under the tip of the ring finger, when the palm of the hand is placed across the kneecap. Use on both sides of the body.

Point number eight is called ho-hu, and it is useful in treating exhaustion. It is two finger widths below the knuckle at the base of the index finger and half a finger toward the thumb. It should be massaged in the direction of the elbow. Use both sides of the body.

Point number nine, called lieh-ch'ueh (past the straits), is used to counteract the feeling of feebleness. It is located on the underside of the arm, two finger widths from the hand. Here is where the pulse is easily felt. It should be acupressed in the direction of the thumb.

In summary, each of these points should be massaged one to three times daily, for about ten seconds, which amounts to 30 or more strokes per point. All the anti-stress acupressure points are used after the overeater's one on the inside of the lip. We all have reflexes that can be overridden. In this case, tension and appetite can be restrained by correctly using acupressure. Some may need to apply it more frequently and longer, to condition the reflexes — maybe several days.

However, the daily acupressure can habituate (no longer respond) the reflex pathways, and you can cut down on the number and frequency of applications — eustress has been accomplished! Acupressure frees you from compulsion, but it should not be used with extreme or fad diets. You will not suffer if you phase out your craving for food with acupressure. Brute force is not necessary. It is very important to adhere to a well-balanced, gentle diet (low in calories), that causes the body to break down its fat. Acupress — eat less — eustress!

Adaptation energy can be conserved through proper management. The advantages of eustress far outweigh those of stress. Manipulating the intake of carbohydrate and protein, to achieve an energy-relaxation balance in the body, offers great promise. Acupressure offers a viable means of control. So do other variations of the same basic principle. The next chapter is devoted to an introduction of the exciting new fields of *Touch for Health* and *Biokinesiology*.

6.

BIOKINESIOLOGY

Touch Gives Us Much

In addition to acupuncture and acupressure, touch is a wonderful generator of well-being, as well as well-feeling. Over the last 25 years, the chiropractic profession has developed safe, simple, and easy-to-use techniques, from ancient disciplines and Oriental health practices, that enable people to be more creative with their own lives.

"The methods are so simple and so rewarding to use that we believe nearly everyone will want to use or be helped with these techniques when they seem appropriate," says John F. Thie, D.C., in his book *Touch For Health*. He also states, "We know these methods of health enhancement are not harmful, and that people can use them to help each other, without endangering themselves or others." [1]

These methods and techniques are no longer the province of the chiropractic profession and they should become a part of all health care and physical fitness programs. This knowledge is now available to anyone who wants to use it. I am most certainly one of those people! "We should be concentrating on man's health and how to maintain it, rather than on illness and how to cure it.... This must start in the home environment, with all persons caring for each other," says Dr. Thie[2] — and I agree!

Chiropractors who have had *Touch for Health* training now successfully treat all kinds of organ ailments, using applied kinesiology, which is the science of muscle activation. This is possible because organs share lymph and acupressure meridians. As we know, meridians are the channels along which energy flows within us — electro-magnetic transmission of information throughout the entire body. Life systems are energized by this flow of energy. Meridians contain a free-flowing, colorless, noncellular liquid, according to Oriental philosophy. The science of anatomy and physiology explains this phenomenon in terms of the nerve impulses, which are responsible for carrying out the many functions of the body. Meridians have been measured and mapped by modern technological methods. Acupressure points (which are electro-magnetic in character and have free nerve endings) are located in the capillaries of the skin, in blood vessels, and in organs of the body. There are some 500 of these points which can be used, usually in a definite sequence, to accomplish a specific action.

It is necessary to understand how the muscles perform in order to see the efficacy of this approach. Normally, the body is in a steady state of contraction, in order to maintain posture-muscle tone. That is, when one muscle is *contracting* to move, the opposite muscle relaxes until time to return to the original position. At that time, the process is reversed. Energy must flow freely, in order for the muscles to perform in this way. If tension or stress cuts off or inhibits the flow of energy, then the muscle becomes weak — it fails to respond to the message to *contract*. We know that this happens to certain parts of the body during the "fight" or "flight" response to stress.

With the use of kinesiology, energy flow can be restored through reflex action — turning on energies to the muscles. Muscle weaknesses can be detected and treated! When muscles are improved through restoration of energy flow, the organs of the body that share the same system are given relief. The whole person is helped! Activation of skin areas with deep massage or light touch can actually cause the muscles to move bones which have previously been misaligned by muscle tension and/or muscle weakness — the "new wave" orthopedic and chiropractic manipulations! Muscle balance is necessary for good posture and good health.

All muscles should be operating at maximum strength, and there should not be more than 15 percent difference between the two sides of the body. However, if the energy flow is restricted as a result of stress, certain muscles will become weak. Strength can be restored to these muscles and to the organs which share the same circuit by pressing or holding certain spots on the body to stimulate the flow of energy in that system.

However, in cases of muscle tension or spasms in certain parts of the body, muscles may need to be weakened or sedated or relaxed. Over-energized muscles cause spasticity, while under-energized ones cause flaccidity. Kinesiology assists the "balancing act!"

When stress is intense or constant, as is typical in our society, it is as if the circuit is "overloaded," and the "circuit breaker" pops — no flow of energy! If muscles are weak, this is undoubtedly what has happened. It appears to be the result of an over-reaction to stress when the parasympathetic system "kicks in" to "pull us down" — a safety valve!

An extreme reaction of this type is known as shock. Many experience semi-shock reactions. These have short-term advantages, but continued reactions of this type are deleterious, as they impair physical and mental functioning. The "circuit breaker" needs to be reset before energy can flow properly. By going to certain parts of the body and pressing or holding certain points, proper flow of energy can be restored. When this occurs, the muscles are strong and the related body organs are strengthened.

Stress Release In Action

Wayne W. Topping, with a Ph.D. in Geology and additional training in *Touch for Health* as well as nutrition, herbology, massage, anatomy, physiology, and organic chemistry practiced during the 80s at his Stress Release Center in Bellingham, Washington. One of his books is called *Stress Release: Identifying and Releasing Stress Through the Use of Muscle Testing.*[3]

In his book, he explains how the use of the Emotional Stress Release (ESR) is being used in conjunction with other techniques to successfully treat many problems. He reports that people are breaking themselves of negative dietary and thought patterns, reducing their emotional stress load, relieving themselves of pain from old accidents, overcoming learning disabilities, and more! All these are possible as a result of Applied Kinesiology or muscle-testing.

However, before one can reduce his or her stress level, he or she needs to have some understanding of stress, its purpose, and how it accumulates. Then should come prevention of the buildup of stress and the reduction of what already exists.

Dr. Hans Selye, himself a biologist, defined stress as "The non-specific response of the body to any demand made upon it."[4] For instance, cold temperatures make us shiver and hot temperatures cause us to perspire, in order to keep the body in a homeostatic state — a non-specific response. The greatest stressors, however, are psyche related — unpleasant emotions and the things that are done in response to nervous tension, such as smoking, drinking, improper eating, and inadequate exercise.

No stress would mean no life — death! The goal is to minimize the stress and maximize the benefits. Under normal conditions, the body is capable of keeping itself in balance. However, life today poses many problems which literally push the body out of balance.

We are well aware of Selye's three separate stages of the stress cycle — the alarm, resistance, and exhaustion — the General Adaptation Syndrome (GAS). Selye likened this process to the three stages of man's life when he said, "...childhood (with its characteristic low resistance and excessive responses to any kind of stimulus), adulthood (during which adaptation to most commonly encountered agents has occurred and resistance is increased) and finally, senility (characterized by irreversible loss of adaptability and eventual exhaustion) ending with death."[5]

The reality of the matter is that genetically predetermined adaptation energy is used up at a normal rate. However, under the conditions with which we live today, this whole process is "telescoped" or "speeded-up." The increased wear and tear on the body leads to premature accumulation of waste products, such as calcium in the arteries, joints, and lens of the eye — i.e., premature aging! Too many life changes, too quickly, bring on illnesses.

We know that the hypothalamus in the brain is the first to be impacted by stress. Dr. Topping states, "In our biokinesiology work, we find an imbalanced hypothalamus to be associated with cravings and addictions to sweets, alcohol, drugs, and sex."[6] The hormones secreted by the endocrine glands resulting from activation of the hypothalamus, cause the arteries to constrict and the heart to beat faster to send blood rushing to the muscles and the lower brain. Blood clotting time is increased, for protection during injury. The white blood count is raised to fight possible infection. The red blood cells increase in number, to carry more oxygen to burn the sugar and thereby provide more energy. The bronchial tubes are dilated to maximize the intake of oxygen. Blood flow is diverted from the periphery of the body to the vital organs — cold hands and warm heart! Even though the skin can be red when angry, it goes white when afraid. The digestive processes slow down; but the pupils of the eyes dilate, in order to see a wider range, for possible danger. More sugar is released into the blood from storage in the liver and the muscles. Pro-inflammatory and anti-inflammatory corticoids are released into the bloodstream. These corticoids cause the thymus gland to shrink and the lymph nodes to atrophy.

There is an accompanying inhibition of the inflammatory reactions and production of sugar for energy. The corticoids are also responsible for ulcers of the stomach and small intestines, formerly said to be the result of too much hydrochloric acid or a deficiency of sodium bicarbonate. Small wonder the body breaks down and craves "junk food" — fuel for the fire!

Different organs start to fail in different people, as each individual has his or her own "weak link in the chain." Some may be inherited, some are due to accident or injury, and some are the result of psychological trauma. Over time, all negative emotions have an adverse effect on the organs of the body.

For instance, the emotion of disgust can cause a contraction of the stomach violent enough to cause vomiting. Many of us have felt "sick to the stomach!"

Jealousy is another major negative emotion that affects the parathyroid, according to biokinesiologists, who use muscle testing to detect body imbalances. They also use positive emotions, good nutrition, acupressure, and "low-impact" or proper exercise to restore the body to balance.

One function of the parathyroid is to regulate the calcium level in the bloodstream by dissolving calcium from the bones. Yes, calcium is stored in the bones to be withdrawn and facilitate the relaxation counterpart of muscle contraction. It is entirely feasible that if the parathyroid gland were out of balance, the bones could actually dissolve in space — osteoporosis.

Open Up The Gates

Of extreme importance to the understanding of "nervous tension" and its control is to realize what is happening to the blood supply — the supplier of energy. This information is paramount to muscle testing and restoration of balance. There are four stages which the biokinesiologists find valuable in explaining this phenomenon:

The first one is called the Alert stage, much like Selye's Alarm stage. Here, as we know, the hypothalamus directs the thyroid and adrenal glands to release hormones into the bloodstream. There is significant increase in energy. We are prepared for action; but more times than not, we do not take action! The stress hormones accrue and the body goes out of balance.

During the second stage of Response, the blood supply to the muscles is increased to carry sugar for fuel in the "fight" or "flight" response. In order to do this, the stomach is deprived of blood. First order of importance is survival. If you survive, you can digest your food later! The frontal lobes of the cerebral cortex are also deprived of blood, so conscious decision making is out! Survival situations demand immediate, short-term, and automatic reactions, based on past experience; so the blood is sent to the lower brain centers and reflexive brain stem. Time is of the essence! There simply is not enough time to allow for conscious thinking and still survive.

In both the Alert and Response stages, the muscles are strong because of the optimal amount of blood supplied to them. However, thinking or conscious problem solving capacity is diminished. We are programmed to respond much like a cat does, when approached by a dog. If the cat has kittens (assets to be protected), it is likely to arch its back, its hair stands on end, it raises a paw, and hisses — a "fight" option. If no kitten is present, it streaks down the alley and up a tree, with the dog in hot pursuit. Their stress hormones are burned up, and their systems go back into balance.

The striking difference between the cat and a man is that the man is not likely to burn up the stress hormones. In our society, the same options are not available, as they are for the cat; and human beings generally do not participate in enough stress release alternatives. They "bottle things up" and "stew on things!" This is how they become overwhelmed.

The third stage is that of Overwhelm. Here, the body takes on the task of detoxifying or breaking down the stress hormones. Blood leaves the muscles and goes to the liver, kidneys, and lungs for this complex task — another reflex action. Note that no more blood is sent to the frontal lobes of the cerebral cortex. We're still in the "fog!" We're less coordinated and more accident prone, because our muscles are weak. We can't recall names or where we placed things, because our brains are weak! Our minds can "go blank," and we "freak out!" How many times have you "blanked-out" on a test, turned in an incomplete paper, walked out of the classroom, and then remembered everything? The ideas come flooding to your brain, once the blood supply is restored to the frontal lobes of the brain. Even though knowledge may be stored in the brain, recall is impossible during the "overwhelm" state. Soon, we will learn to correct this unfortunate occurrence in the "nick of time."

Overwhelm is comparable to alarm or shock reaction. The parasympathetic nervous system is slowing us down for very good reasons. For every "up," there is a "down." Let's hope that the "ups" are not too high and the "downs" are not too low — otherwise fainting, or coma, or death!

Therefore, if you feel like sitting or lying down, do it, and don't fight it! Your body is giving you a message, and it tells you no lies! At this time, you are very vulnerable and need to rest or relax, which gives your body time to break down the stress hormones.

Joeckel says, "In a way, overwhelm is like getting drunk and passing out. Passing out keeps you from drinking too much and possibly killing yourself. It also gives your liver, lungs, and kidneys time to clear the alcohol from your system. Likewise, overwhelm is a natural safeguard. As much as we dislike how out of control it makes us feel, without this protective device we'd die trying to respond to intense pressure. (It functions like the circuit breakers in your fuse box.)"[7]

During the final stage of the stress cycle, called Recovery (hopefully) the body is returning to normal function. One of three things is happening. Either you are burning up the stress hormones through actual physical "fight or flight," or cleaning house or doing aerobic exercise, to deliberately break down the stress hormones, or else your body "punches overload"; and in the overwhelm stage, it's doing for you what you weren't doing for yourself! Now we are ready to learn an effective method of *decreasing* the overwhelm and *increasing* the recovery through muscle testing and touch — it is incredibly simple!

The Science Of Muscle Testing

Although there are 42 different Touch-for-Health muscle tests for massage treatment points, relative to all parts of the body and every organ, we will concentrate on those which are the most important to checking for intense emotional strain (distress). They are the pectoralis major clavicular/stomach and digestive functions and the supraspinatus/brain and thinking functions.

First, we'll take a look at the pectoralis major clavicular/stomach and digestive functions. This chest muscle helps bend and turn the arm at the shoulder. Stimulating the reflexes for this muscle affects both the stomach and the emotional centers in the brain. This connection may explain the digestive disturbances that are brought on by emotional stress, which then disturbs the hydrochloric acid balance.

Dr. Thie says that to test for possible weakness of this muscle, the subject can sit, stand, or lie down (face up) with the arms held straight forward or slightly to the side and level with the shoulder. The palms should be held out, with thumbs toward the feet. Pressure is then applied on the forearm, to pull the arm down and away from the body. If the muscle proves weak, there is obviously a lack of blood flow which indicates an overwhelm state of the body.[8]

To strengthen or treat the pectoralis, have the subject continue to think about some aspect of his or her life which is causing stress, and touch the neurovascular holding points on the forehead, for up to 10 minutes. These points are called the frontal eminences, and can be felt as a slight bulge on each side of the forehead between the eyebrows and the hairline. Hold these repeatedly until the emotional stress no longer affects the muscle. Touch stimulates vaso-dilation of the blood vessels in this region. The muscle becomes strong, the subject is no longer overwhelmed; and he or she can no longer think "bad thoughts" — a well-nourished brain is incompatible with stress! I told you that it was incredibly simple!

Allergies are often linked with emotions, and can also be tested with this method. After chewing a suspected food for a few moments, if an allergy exists, this same muscle will go weak. It is, in fact, over-stimulation of the stress response (overwhelm or shock) that brings about this reaction. Therefore, I believe that any food or substance which has this over-energizing effect on the body (causing it to push "overload" and become weak) is an allergen, in a very real sense. It is also undoubtedly affecting the immune system. Under normal conditions, this would probably hold true; but the corticoids produced by the extreme stress response impair the immune system; and the individual is more susceptible to infections and/or inflammation.

Kinesiologists have found that people with allergy-related problems can be helped with Vitamin B found in wheat germ, whole grains, liver, and brewers yeast. The hydrochloric acid balance can be improved by eating tripe (part of stomach of the cud-chewing animals) and rare meat; and by chewing foods well. Avoiding sugars and sweets, especially before meals, is beneficial. This is due to the fact that stress foods impair the production of hydrochloric acid in the stomach, and this leads to fermentation.

The problems associated with fermentation were discussed by Hubert O. Swartout, M.D., in his *Guide To Health* in 1938. These can take the form of belching, bloating, or diarrhea, with accompanying headache and a feeling of mental dullness. Fermentation occurs wherever and whenever there is organic matter, combined with heat and moisture. Digestive juices usually hold this process in check, but absence of acid in the stomach (Achylia), due to stress, can decrease the efficiency; and fermentation is the result.[9]

There are other conditions that hinder the digestive processes. Too much water-drinking with meals, which dilutes the acid; overeating beyond the capacity of the digestive juices; and rapid eating before enough acid can be produced, all may increase fermentation. A diet too high in carbohydrates (sugar), tea, coffee, and condiments (like mustard and pepper) further the fermentation. The "sour stomach" may not be due to too much hydrochloric acid, but instead to a lack of it!

We many times treat ourselves with anti-acids, when we would do better to actually take hydrochloric acid! However, this would usually constitute only a temporary measure, until the stress-producing problems can be resolved. Taking hydrochloric acid is simply supplying of the natural secretions that the stressed stomach glands are not able to produce. It also enables the stomach enzymes (digestive ferments) to act, since they require the presence of acid to work properly.

Without acid stimulation, food goes rapidly into the duodenum, whether sufficiently digested or not. The individual is likely to have bad breath and a poor appetite. A heavy feeling in the stomach, distress, and sometimes pain are also common. One always feels better when the stomach is empty. These are all conditions of overwhelm, when the person begins to lose weight, rather than gain, as in the earlier stages of stress. Malnourishment — even anorexia — may result.

The kinesiologists now offer us much — practically a miracle — almost 50 years after Dr. Swartout!

In muscle testing, a specific muscle is placed in its contracted position, isolated as much as possible from its neighboring muscles. Then an attempt is made to extend the muscle, to see whether it is strong or weak in comparison to the usual overall strength of the individual. It is a way of testing the energy circuits of the muscle, to determine if they are turned on or off. In addition to emotional stress, the muscles may be weak because of such things as nutritional deficiencies, sensitivity to metals, colors, perfumes, or vertebrae that are out of alignment.

The supraspinatus/brain and thinking is the second muscle which is affected by emotional stress. This muscle helps in moving the arm away from the body, as well as to hold the arm into the shoulder socket. Those who do a great deal of thinking, working at a desk, or driving are likely to suffer brain fatigue that affects the supraspinatus. Anxiety and emotional stress can then result from the mental strain.

To test for this possible weakness, the subject should stand or lie down, with the arm held about 15 degrees away from the body — the elbows straight. Pressure is applied against the forearm, to push it toward the groin. The neurovascular holding points are the frontal eminences, between the eyebrows and the hairline, and the anterior fontanel — the baby's soft spot on the top of the head.

These points are to be held, especially the ones on the forehead, until the muscle is not affected by thinking about the problem, if there is emotional stress. Blood has then reached the frontal lobes of the cerebral cortex. The touch has stimulated vaso-dilation of this area. Children who are slow learners, because of emotional stress, can be helped with this technique.

Hands On

As we now know, during the initial phase of the stress response, the physiology of the body changes, so as to alter the blood flow. It gets shunted from certain parts of the body (such as the cerebral cortex and skin) and sent to other parts, such as the muscles, organs, and endocrine glands involved in immediate survival. If the individual cannot release the stress through channels such as fighting, fleeing, or some other physical means, the neurochemicals rise to an extremely high level and are very toxic. The body becomes weak, and the cerebral cortex of the brain is shut down — the stress mess!

To alleviate this, relocation of blood is necessary. It must leave the liver, kidneys, and lungs, where it has been "pooled" in the center of the body, and go to the periphery. Before this happens, the blood pressure may also be high, as the heart is pumping hard in an attempt to send the blood through the narrow capillaries. The opening up or closing down of the capillaries seems to constitute the change in blood flow. The face flushes when we are angry in the initial phase of the stress response; but the color diminishes when we enter the overwhelm — we are scared, but actually too paralyzed to do anything about it! We have long known about the surge of adrenalin when the sympathetic nervous system prepares us for action, but what we haven't understood is what happens when we don't take action!

Terrance Bennett, D.C., first discovered the neurovascular holding points, which when held, redirect the blood flow. He did this by watching the internal effects through a giant X-ray unit — called fluoroscope. He died an early death from radiation poisoning![10] George Goodheart, D.C., further studied this phenomenon of touch, to send messages by way of the nervous system to alter the vascular blood flow.[11] This is done by holding or touching neurovascular holding points, of which there are many. However, the frontal eminences, which are two slightly prominent bumps on each side of the face, are most useful. When one touches these two points, with enough pressure to slightly stretch the skin, one can feel a slight pulse from 70 to 74 beats per minute. Surprisingly, when under stress, these are not synchronized! When thoughts are no longer stressful, the two pulses become synchronized. Blood has moved back into the two hemispheres of the brain, equally, allowing proper control over the nervous system. One is no longer "stressed-out," "spaced-out," or "pooped-out!"

Now let's see how you can achieve this marvelous release of tension very quickly. It's best to lie down on your back, but you can also sit in a chair. Place your hands or fingers on the frontal eminences. Think of a minor stressful event first, until you feel at ease with the technique. Guide your thinking from the beginning of the stressful scene and proceed through it, in sequence, until you come to the end of it. Always dwell on the negative aspects such as "ugly and nasty" feelings that might be fear, anger, jealousy, hate, remorse, or grief.

Concentrate also on "bad" thoughts, sights, sounds, odors, or pains. This is different from the directions given in biofeedback training, where you are instructed to think good, relaxing thoughts!

From personal experience, I know that biokinesiology can be learned very quickly and is a good adjunct for biofeedback. It is so difficult to clear one's mind of negative thoughts in biofeedback. However, it can be accomplished through the relaxation response which alters blood flow. The "neat thing" about kinesiology is that this occurs automatically from *touch*. In either case, however, one must be consciously aware enough to make a voluntary response to do something: either consciously put the negative out of one's mind, through relaxing and thinking positively; or put your hands on your head and thinking negatively!

During the process of visualizing a painful event through biokinesiology, do not judge your feelings as good or bad or try to forget or suppress them. This is a real plus! Visualize everything as clearly and distinctly as possible, while holding your head at the same time. The mind is actually desensitized — a clearing-house approach.

As a psychologist, I have always been for dealing with reality. However, reality is sometimes too painful and the very where-with-all to deal with it eludes us! This technique counteracts the overwhelm response, and we can get back in control. Anything — no matter how terrible — can be handled, if there is blood to the brain! If our nervous systems do not allow us to remain calm through "storms on the sea of life," then this simple stress release technique is a life saver! A chiropractor in Moscow, Idaho taught me this most valuable technique, for which I am very appreciative.

While visualizing a painful situation, one might ask oneself questions, such as the following: Where am I? What do the people look like? What is being said to me? What might I say in response? How am I feeling at this time? Perhaps you cannot consciously visualize everything, because of the difficulties you feel. However, your own brain has the capacity to create images beyond the wildest imagination, as it also does during your sleeping and dreaming! Just cover as many elements as you possibly can. Stimulate your sense. If it concerns a person, visualize and hear that individual.

Whatever your concern, confront it. Do all of this from one to two times or more, until the pulses on the frontal eminences are synchronized. However, you will know anyway — a great weight has been lifted! The mountain of a problem has shrunk down to a mole hill! You can no longer think about the negative situation. It is impossible, because it no longer overwhelms you and you'll be "going on with living." It is as if the image or scene dissolved or became clouded.

Whatever the case, you will be relaxed and back in control, happily pursuing your greatest interests and exemplifying zest for life. What more could anyone ask? As a country girl, I learned long ago that "one can lead a horse to water, but one cannot make him drink." So the rest is up to you!

To verify the physical changes that have occurred, you need a friend who agrees to work with you, to test your pectoralis major clavicular muscles as earlier described. If your self-treatment has been successful, your muscles will be strong.

Next, think of a stressful situation — the muscles will go weak! Ask your friend to place his or her fingers over the frontal eminences and go through the procedure again. I tell my students to think of "ugly, mean, nasty" thoughts! It works every time. There is no exception! When you feel you have completed the procedure, let your friend know and have him/her re-test the pectoralis major clavicular muscles. Presto! They will be strong! The thoughts are no longer overwhelming you. Of course, on occasion, it may be necessary to go through the cycle more than once. Whenever the muscles test strong, you have finished. You no longer have restricted breathing — you take a deep breath and give a sigh of relief. Besides that, your friend may now be a new convert! He/she too, can be helped through bad times! All this can be completed in as short a time as 20 seconds and no longer than 10 minutes, in most cases.

There are many life situations for which this technique is applicable. Life deals us many "wicked blows" — traumatic experiences. Personal and interpersonal problems should not go unresolved day after day, week after week, and year after year — that constitutes overwhelm and exhaustion. The worry about forthcoming events can also be released with this technique.

For example, if you have an exam coming up, visualize yourself fearfully sitting in the classroom while putting your hands on your forehead. This will release the stress, and you will be less likely to "blank out" during the actual exam. It will not store information in your brain, but it certainly will make that easier for you, as well as put you in a better position to recall what you have learned. Most of all us know more than we actually put down on a test. This is because of stress that interferes with the blood flow to the cerebral cortex. You may be wondering where it was when you needed it most!

Several other practical applications have been demonstrated. Parents can use this technique to quiet a child who wakes up screaming, because of a terrifying nightmare. The child will calm down and go back to sleep again. Many parents seem to "instinctively" do this, whenever a child is sick or crying. Perhaps some of us have lost a basic reflex, because we are self-conscious, afraid to be seen in this position, fearful of smearing our make-up, or messing up our hair! We are somewhat of a "no touch" society. However, decision makers have been known to do this since history began.

I can recall my father saying, "Damn my fool head!" as he would bend over with his head in his hands. Soon he would be up and going "full speed ahead!" We all should learn to consciously use biokinesiology and make it a habit. However, there may be times or occasions when it would not be appropriate to have your hands over your frontal eminences. In this case, either place the thumbs lightly over the opposing thumb pads, or imagine that the fingertips are being held lightly over the frontal eminences. Either will work, to some degree.

At the very time when we need it most, the blood may be away from our cerebral cortex. Thus, the probability of our remembering to use this technique is reduced. The only way to counteract this is to have it become a habit — sort of a conditioned response! We know from behavioral psychology that any consequences following a response that is rewarding, increases the probability of the reoccurrence of that same response.

In this case, the pleasure and sense of well-being brought about by the release of stress is so rewarding that the human organism will continue to behave in such a way as to insure its continuance — that's a habit! For that matter, I have also found that it works wonders with my cat and our dogs! Students of all ages — grade school, high school, and college — should learn to push their "magic buttons." How much more positive and worthwhile they could feel! Their enthusiasm would be contagious, and this would work wonders for the "mass hysteria" that seems to prevail.

For example, one of my former college students said, in a paper written for a Psychology class, "I had always wanted to be an elementary teacher and decided to register for college. I was so excited — school would be like a vacation from Safeway. The first two weeks were great, but I soon found myself jumping back on the road to success. If I was to be a successful student, I must succeed with a 4.0 GPA! My perfectionistic tendencies toward success were again taking over my life. I became physically sick. I could feel my breakfast elevating to my throat. My skin turned a putrid white, and was cool and clammy to the touch. My hands began to tremble, and the thoughts in my mind became fuzzy. I was perspiring heavily and, as usual, nervousness caused me to get diarrhea.

No, I was not on drugs! I was simply scared! Have you ever prepared for a test in college, did everything you were supposed to do, and flunked it anyway? That's what happened to me. It was my first test in college. Although I just loved my instructor and felt she had given me adequate material, along with ample time to succeed, the minute I began the test I knew I would fail! What I had experienced is commonly called test anxiety. Evidently, I was not the only one in class to experience this trauma, as our following lecture was devoted purely to stress and hypertension, and a new holistic way to cope with them. Kinesiology and Acutouch have helped me through each test I have taken since. By practicing what I learned that day, I've been able to maintain a 3.5 GPA, and I attribute this to my studies in the field of Acutouch, along with the professional theories of my instructor, Dr. Sarah (Mom) Culton, Spokane Falls Community College."

The Things That We Don't Want To Think About

Thinking about difficult situations can again bring on the overwhelm response, even after one has learned the technique with more simple and non-threatening stress visualization. It may be necessary to take a break and use a key word or phrase that has positive connotations. If this isn't done, anyone could become hysterical, have headaches or other pains in the body, have allergic reactions such as asthma, increased blood pressure, or a rise in blood sugar!

Therefore, it is paramount to use caution and not punish yourself. This treatment of choice should be most pleasurable. Heavy and traumatic situations take more time. Be patient with yourself! If you feel that you are not able to handle these on your own, do seek the help of a trained Touch-For-Health professional to assist you.

If headaches or other discomforts occur instead of subsiding, switch to your key word or phrase. Then revert back to focusing in on the negative situation. By all means, don't forget to hold the frontal eminences! This is the only way to release the stress. I believe that this would be truly facing up to reality, with enough blood to the cerebral cortex, instead of the reflexive brain stem, to keep from over-emotionalizing.

Of course, I believe that to be emotional is to be human! Human emotions can be beautiful. They show love, care, and concern. Sometimes, we do temporarily "go weak." That's perfectly normal! This is the way the body shifts its energy to "take care of business." Furthermore, the body has the natural capacity to regain its balance on its own! I think that it would be a mistake to view all muscle weakness as an indication of long-term, unresolved emotional problems (a pseudo-Freudian approach). If we were to desensitize all our emotions, we would be "cold-hearted" creatures, indeed; with little, if any, empathy for other people. We could become so preoccupied with self that we would not be effective as social human beings.

Some stress or negative emotions is the price we pay for a social conscience; that is, care and concern for the welfare of others, as well as ourselves! Whatever you do, do not allow ill-informed or misguided individuals (who are in it for a "buck") convince you that you need long-term therapy to "clear" your "deep-seated" emotions, that go back to your childhood. Of course, we are "what we are because of where we were when"; but the stress comes from dealing with the "here and now!" that needs to be released!

However, just because stress is released through visualization and touching of the frontal eminences, does not mean that it is resolved "forever and a day!" Revisualization of any stressful situation will cause the stress response to reoccur with possible overwhelm. Chiropractors were very gracious in sharing their new-found techniques, but perhaps they may now be in the wrong hands!

As a licensed School Psychologist, as well as a College Professor of Psychology, I can agree with Gordon Stokes and Daniel Whiteside that the problems of the disabled learner may be based on failure to learn how to learn.[12] Stress can get locked into the system when there is fear of failure, fear of teachers, fear of peers, resentment, or boredom. This condition then brings on the overwhelm response, and students do fail to learn; not that there's an abnormality in basic genetic and biological ability, but lack of blood flow to the brain, due to the over-emotionalizing!

The area of the stress can be identified by testing the pectoralis major clavicular muscles before and after certain affirmations, such as "I want to read well," "I want to write well," " I want to speak well," or "I want to do well in arithmetic." If the muscles go weak on any one or more of these, that's evidence that there's an extreme reaction associated with each skill. The next step is to hold the fingers over the frontal eminences, while the student repeats the affirmations either orally or silently. Whatever the origin of the stress, it can be released with the ESR method. Whenever the stress has been released, the muscles will become strong, and the brain is ready to go to work! Success will be very rewarding.

Some interesting ramifications have become apparent. Through the identification process (child becoming like the parents), very young children pick up stress patterns from their parents, particularly the one who spends the most time with them or provides the greatest emotional support. This also holds true for allergies.

Sometimes, when the parent changes, so does the child. It is also true, according to Topping, that when the ESR technique seems not to have worked a hundred percent, it may be because not all the senses related to the anxiety were cleared. One may need to think of the visual, the auditory, or the tactile to completely erase the stress of a situation which is being visualized at any given point in time.

Topping claims that eye movements correspond with stress.[13] He says that eye movements in the same direction as those of the actual stress-arousing encounter access the part of the brain where the awareness of that particular situation is located. Doing ESR with the eyes held in the same position as those of the actual experience eliminates stress very quickly. However, we may not be aware of these positions.

Topping claims that rotating the eyes in a large circle will pick up all of the possible positions. It is not necessary to recall and stress release previous events that involve the same emotions, because the present situation will "push the same buttons." The current ones should be stress-released as the person holds the frontal eminences and rotates the eyes. Do not move the eyes too fast.[14]

Topping wrote that foil placed on the center of the forehead, over the reflex to the pineal gland and under both heels (when doing ESR with eye rotations), quickly facilitates the release of stress. It must be that this procedure may alter the electro-magnetic flow of energy.[15] At a recent workshop, I understood Topping to say that he now recommends touching the thumb and ring finger while the pointer and middle fingers touch the frontal eminences! He claims that this works better!

Affirmations and Self-Fulfilling Prophesies

Many of us have been programmed or conditioned not to think well of ourselves; and we make every attempt to hide it — this is defensive behavior. During our growing-up years, we may have been told or made to feel dumb, stupid, ugly, clumsy, or "no good." Over time, these repetitious admonitions do become our reality, and we become what we think — a self-fulfilling prophesy!

Affirmations, which are positive thoughts that we can cause to become our consciousness, can offset beliefs that are not appropriate for us. However, there are negative affirmations, like "I've always hated arithmetic," "I'm a lousy student," or "I never was good at that." It is such a tragedy, as negative self-talk reinforces the buildup of negative emotions that make people feel defeated.

Some individuals get like an animal which stays tied with a small rope or no rope at all. The animal didn't start out that way. When it was young, it tried with all its might to break loose from a big rope, but couldn't; so it gave up. So do we! We start out on a course of self put-down and never even attempt new things. We're in a rut, and we tend to stay there, because that's our safety zone.

However, we can choose to make life more exciting, if we desire. The first step is to release the current stress, set goals, and then back them up with positive affirmations. These can be verbal and/or visual. It's very good medicine for the "blues" to stress-release, and then accentuate the positive!

Choose your positive affirmation and write it down twenty times — then it's reality to you. Put it in the present tense, because if it's in the future tense, you might procrastinate! For instance, do not say, "I'm not going to be fat" — that creates a negative picture in your mind. Instead say, "I will eat less today." Two good times to work on these affirmations are the first thing in the morning and before going to bed at night. This is when we are less bombarded by stimuli. It's great to get off on a positive note, and positive thoughts are processed while you are sleeping and dreaming. That's a lot better than going to bed worrying and waking up the next morning tired. It is true that our subconscious mind (not consciously aware) can work for our benefit — not (we hope) to our detriment. This has been confirmed in recent research on sleeping and dreaming.

This whole process is one of a very personal nature. If you are too open and joyous about your venture, others may accuse you of "ramming it down their throats." Perhaps it would be better to "do your own thing" quietly. Then, perhaps, your true friends will see some positive changes in you. This may "rattle their cages" a little, and they will be curious enough to try to find out what you've "been up to!"

It is also true that one can notice a negative reaction coming from one's own subconscious (that part of the nervous system where memory of the past has been stored). Sometimes the discrepancy between what you *want to be* and what you *have been* is great enough to trigger the fear response. Everyone has a certain fear of the unknown, and this is no exception. Realize this and don't give up! Whatever your negative reactions to the affirmation are, express them one by one. In this way, tension is gradually reduced, and the "old you" is ready for the "new you." Holding the frontal eminences while doing this is not required, but it might be very helpful. Do not dwell on them or rehearse them — release them one by one — that's it!

Psychologically, this process is known as extinction of an old response to further the learning of a new — operant conditioning. "All good things come to those who love the Lord," "If at first you don't succeed, try, try again," "All things go well when the Lord is on your side," "Keep smiling," "Nothing accomplished without great labor," and "It is better to have loved and lost than never to have loved at all" are positive affirmations with Biblical and/or historical significance, that have been used for many years.

Let's all choose affirmations that are appropriate for us; write them; post them, repeat them, but by all means, carry them out. The rewards will be so great that you will never go back — this is behavior modification in action!

There's another astonishing technique called the "temporal tap," because its application requires tapping over the temporal bone around the upper part of the ear while using verbal or visual stimulation. In this way, the sensory input of the brain can be alerted to the importance of any particular stimulation. Hypothetically, the area around the ears has the greatest concentration of nerves anywhere in the body. This is part of our genetic programming for self-preservation. It acts as a filter system for sensory input.

Some incoming stimuli need to be acted upon — some do not. To those which do not need our attention, our nervous system habituates (fails to respond). Examples of these might be the whirring fan, the droning speaker, the yelling parent, or the blaring TV — all incessant. We "tune out!" These are all non-threatening. They are not important for our survival or well being. Therefore, we phase them out of our awareness, and so pay little or no attention. Then we wonder what has happened to our communication!

This reminds me of an old story about the farmer who hit his horse over the head and knocked him out. His neighbor came along and wanted to know what had happened. The farmer responded, "Well, I had to get his attention before I could teach him anything!" So it may also be with the temporal tap, but just a tap will do it! A demonstration convinced me of this!

The self-protective mechanism allows you to not notice the buzzing confusion of a crowd; but let someone call your name and immediately you are wide awake and alert, because there may be some concern about your safety. Your filter system alerts you to the most relevant incoming data. How fortunate this is, indeed! Without it, we would be totally overwhelmed.

The problem arises when we become impervious to the things that are in our best interests, and this does happen. Our society and our lifestyles are so stimulating that they are conducive to over-filtering, in order to survive — again our nervous systems "punch overload." Researchers in the field of Applied Kinesiology have found the temporal tap, while making a verbal suggestion, appears to alert the respective hemisphere of the importance of what is being said — it wakes up the sleepy brain!

Physiological research in the field of psychology has verified that the right and left sides of the brain are programmed for different functions. Basically, the left hemisphere is the logic brain that takes care of analytical, verbal, and writing skills, and processes input linearly, like a computer. The right brain is the gestalt brain, that is artistic and takes care of our appreciation of rhythms and shapes. It receives information simultaneously. Here is a fantastic contribution made by the Biokinesiologists! The logic brain acts on a positive suggestion, but not on a negative one! Could this be why so many people, probably over 90 percent, who are left brain dominant have a difficult time taking negative criticism? I think so!

For this reason, it would be much more profitable to offer a positive suggestion, such as "You'll get along fine," rather than "Do not worry" — the positive one will be accepted — the negative one will not! It will only get your defenses up! These are our self-protection and self-preservation mechanisms at work. There's nothing wrong with a person who can't take criticism. He or she is a perfectly normal human being. The fault lies in what goes in! However, since we cannot control this, we can learn to direct the positive to the left hemisphere and the negative to the right hemisphere. Try tapping the left temporal lobe while giving positive suggestions — it will make a "whale" of a difference.

At this point in time, I am telling my husband what a wonderful thing I have learned! I'm sure that he will be grateful for this! I may not tap him on the head, or again, I may! There is one thing for sure — I'll endeavor to always be positive in what I say. "Aha!" — the light has dawned — insight! Now, if he will just do the same for me. I'm sure he will, because there will no longer be any motivation to "strike back" in self-defense.

When something is negative, tap the right side of the head! Perhaps we should have a discipline called Kinesio-psychology. I thought of Psycho-kinesiology, but many would not be able to accept the negative connotation of Psycho! The few who could, would have more right-brain function. They would be less likely to be "psycho," in fact, because they would see the whole big picture of things — the gestalt. They are more relaxed, are less likely to "take offense," and are just more "gracious" people! Many of us would do well to develop our right brain functions to greater capacity. I believe that this is happening when the pulses on both frontal eminences are synchronized — indicating an equal supply of blood to both sides of the brain. The primitive capillary network is responsible for distributing a fresh supply of blood that carries oxygen and nutrients to the brain.

However, when under stress, there's no time to be creative, and more blood is sent to the left hemisphere (even though restricted) than to the right. The brain says "I can run or I can fight!" However, if too much fear or negative affirmations exist, then the nervous system becomes overwhelmed, and no physical action is taken. Blood is instead sent to the internal organs (liver, kidneys, and lungs) to detoxify or break down the over supply of stress hormones, which were secreted as a result of the stress response. We are then weak and confused!

The whole concept here is not to be "locked into" either the left or the right hemisphere of the brain, but to have both working together — coherence, as the Transcendental Meditation people call it.

Biokinesiology can be a "means to an end" — electrical balance equals tranquility and peace of mind. When this occurs, we can more successfully deal with the realities of "negativism." We'll always be faced with it as long as we live, and we need a way to deal with it — and here it is! When the right brain is accessed in some way, it will respond positively to a negative statement — logic doesn't get in the way! It transcends reason and, therefore, does not see reality as an assault or a threat to the "ego" or conscious self. It is not judgmental! This may be the "heart" of consciousness expansion. If you don't like it, but have to live with it, tap your head on the right side. This way you can tap your way to success without dancing!

Knock, Knock — No Answer

If by chance, these techniques don't seem to be working, it may be that you are "wired" differently or have crossed dominance — your "doorbell" may not be working! If you have a dominant right eye, with a dominant left hand, or the reverse, the electro-chemical impulses may be reaching over to the opposite side of the brain, unintentionally, and possibly even making matters worse. It is easy to know which is your dominant hand, but many do not know which one of their eyes is dominant. To test for this, simply look at an object with both eyes open. Then close one eye at a time. If the object seems to jump in space when the eye is alternately opened and closed, then that is your dominant eye. If it is not on the same side of the body as your dominant hand, then you have crossed dominance. When tapped on the side of the head, there probably would not be a sufficient increase in neurological activity on the desired side to make a significant difference.

At any rate, we do know that this kind of neurological disorganization can impair learning function, and the temporal tap may not work. However, I believe that the anxiety created in the individual with this condition accounts for more of the handicap than does the condition itself. This anxiety can be treated with the ESR technique of applying touch to the frontal eminences. In this case, blood is equally supplied to both sides of the brain, and there is a calming effect, not an energizing one, as with the temporal tap. Certainly, this is worth a try!

Many individuals have difficulty in school because of the fine visual- motor control necessary and the need to sequence information linearly, like a computer. They are handicapped in areas such as reading, writing, and arithmetic, but do well in activities that do not require this degree of coordination and linear processing. Therefore, they may be more creative, if given the opportunity and encouragement — positive affirmations.

Some individuals with so-called learning disabilities show brilliance, if emotions do not become a problem. I see a real need for kinesiology to be added to our psychological "bag of tricks."

There are other times that the technique may not work. The body may be out of balance electrically, as the result of extreme stress overload. In this case, a neutralization process may help. Remove all jewelry, as metals may adversely effect the electrical system.

Some practitioners recommend firmly massaging the hollows just below and slightly to the side of the inner ends of the collar bones, for 20-30 seconds; then the mastoids (the rounded bones behind the ear lobes), for about 20 seconds; and then pressing the mastoid bones six times, in rapid succession, using about three pounds of pressure.

This process seems to equally divide the nerve supply to both sides of the brain. To do the actual tapping, you can stand up or lie down and extend your arm out in front of you, at a 90-degree angle, with the palm down and the thumb pointing down. Your partner then tries to push your arm down and out, at about a 45-degree angle. Do so with both arms. When there is weakness shown during a time of about two seconds, your partner should use the right hand to tap over the left temple, and vice versa — so that you won't find an arm in your face!

The three middle fingers (with the thumb holding back the little finger) are used, with a firm, rapid rhythm of two beats a second, up and over the bony ridge around your ear, from the front to back. For reasons given earlier, a positive statement should be tapped into the left brain and a negative statement tapped into the right brain. Then, if the person is accepting (not fighting) the suggestion, the muscles should become strong. For some people, it's just harder to get it through their heads!

The temporal tap is a boon, indeed. If it "wears off," so to speak, because of the amount of stress you are dealing with, then do it again! It is preferable to verbalize your statements out loud; but if you are not comfortable with that, just think them — it's a very private matter. Once learned, use the technique on yourself, there's no danger of anyone else poking an arm in your face — you simply use your right hand on the right side of your head and the left hand on the left side of your head! Hands were made for touching! Do it for yourself!

As improbable as it may sound at first, the two sides of the brain may be in opposition to a given point of view! The logic brain may have valid reasons for a certain course of action — getting a degree or marrying a particular individual — while the gestalt brain may have other reasons for not continuing the action. The result is inaction! No progress can lead to feelings of failure and frustration — low self-esteem.

Supportive evidence for this concept comes from research on one form of stuttering, which is caused by an unusual ability to construct speech from both the right and the left hemispheres (usually it's the left). The two sides are in competition. If either side is anesthetized by injecting an anesthetic into the carotid artery, there is no stuttering!

Because of the criss-crossing of impulses, the left brain controls the right side of the body, and the right brain controls the left side of the body. If both pectoralis muscles are strong, but one goes weak when a goal is stated, the side of the brain opposite that muscle is not accepting it. There would be conflict between the two! Keep in mind that the right arm gives the logical viewpoint (objective), and the left arm gives the emotional response (subjective). They need to work together — both are important. There needs to be interaction or coherence of the two in order for there to be agreement. However, this may take "some doing" — compromising, if you will!

In the process, this problem-solving behavior may generate even more stress. The ESR technique is a must for this. Decision — not indecision — is the result. There is no vacillation. Make up your mind and do it! The only voluntary decision needed is the one to use the technique. The rest takes care of itself.

In conclusion, the biokinesiologists offer many techniques for releasing stress, some of which I have described in this chapter. They are well worth your time and consideration. For more information and/or help, I suggest that you contact a qualified Touch-For-Health professional or Biokinesiologist. They are most likely to be found among duly-licensed health care professionals, such as chiropractic, osteopathic, naturopathic, medical, dental, optometric, or psychological practitioners.

What I have reported in this chapter is solely for educational purposes. Persons using these ideas and correction procedures which I have discussed, do so entirely at their own risk. However, the only possible risks that I am aware of are those of allowing oneself to be "brain-washed" by unscrupulous individuals who are in it for their own selfish interests, not *your* best interests! Some may not have adequate knowledge of psychology, nutrition, or exercise to insure a well-balanced approach. Therefore, choose your practitioners wisely. The techniques can have a powerful influence in changing your life for the better! They are tools to be shared with others — the essence of true happiness! Happiness enhances the immune system.

7.

THE IMMENSE IMMUNE SYSTEM

The immune system is designed to keep us alive and well. In order to do this, it is necessary for the body to know the difference between itself and anything else that might invade it. This internal intelligence usually allows it to protect itself by destroying the intruder. This monumental task is accomplished through recognition and differentiation of different shapes among the large molecules on the surface of the cells.

The body "looks," so to speak, at these molecules after one is conceived and the new life begins. It instinctively knows what is not itself. In other words, the body accepts itself. It is a unique masterpiece different from anyone else. Your proteins are different from mine and from every other human being who has ever lived! This uniqueness is what causes problems with organ transplants, not excluding bone marrow transplants. The body says, "That's not mine," and it goes about trying to get rid of it through a process called rejection.

The protein of an organ from a donor has different markings, and so it is recognized as an invader to be destroyed. The body says, "It doesn't belong," as it also does with bacteria, a germ, a virus, a fungus, or a cancer cell. A healthy body can declare and win the war, but a weak one may not. The only reasons that transplants last as long as they do is because of massive doses of Prednisone (synthetic cortisone) to control the inflammation and potent immune suppressant drugs, to "down" the body's defenses. The body is actually weakened, and it is very vulnerable to infections of all kinds. We already know what cortisone in large amounts can do, and without a strong immune system, we do not have the where-with-all to fight off the invaders. How much better *prevention* would be — the control and/or release of all forms of stress!

Immunology is no longer science fiction. Powerful microscopes and new laboratory techniques have given us "action shots" of both the offense and the defense. The internal battles are no longer in the realm of "Star Wars," but have been photographed as actual "Cell Wars." To see these actual pictures, refer to the June, 1986 issue of *National Geographic,* "Our Immune System: the Wars Within." These pictures show an army of special cells on continuous search-and-destroy missions, guarding the body against disease. However, cancer, rheumatoid arthritis, and the deadly AIDS virus prove to be mighty enemies.[1]

The "Cell Wars" within the body are vicious, indeed. First of all, along comes the marauders — sleazy, formidable, and hungry characters known as invaders (viruses). They are little more than bundles of genes that must get into someone else's territory in order to find the resources for growth (host cells). When this happens, the fight is on! The body's guards (macrophages) see them break in, start to destroy them (consume), and seize their guns (antigens). This is a signal for help. Some of the backup crew (helper T cells) recognize these weapons, join (bind to) the guards (macrophages), and start fighting. They take over, become the "commander in chief," give orders to the armed services headquarters (spleen and lymph nodes) to draft and train more soldiers (killer T cells).

The defense plants or arms and munitions factories are strategically located in the same area (spleen and lymph). Defense plant workers (B cells) manufacture weapons (antibodies) which are rushed to the battlefield, where they either annihilate the enemy (viruses) or capture them for attack by other soldiers (cells and chemicals).

After the enemy (viruses) has been conquered, leaders (suppressor T cells) cut down on the production by the defense plants (B cells) and curtail the destructive activity of the soldiers (T cells). The attack is called off! However, the national Guard or Armed Forces Reserves (memory T and B cells) are kept at home (blood and lymphatic system), ready to move quickly, should the same foe (viruses) once again invade the country (body).

Memory cells are stimulated into action by man-made vaccines, which are made of weakened or dead germs. These can "fool" the memory cells into thinking that a live virus has attacked. They go into action, and the body does not experience the actual disease. Peaceful co-existence is more of a myth than a reality!

If the defenses (immune system) are strong, one can win again and again. However, if they have been weakened by the effects of internal strife (stress) such as famine (poor diet) and/or emotional upheaval (chemical warfare), then our chances for survival, or well-being, or quality of life have been diminished. Macrophage cells (which are the housekeepers and frontline defenders) engulf and digest debris that accumulates in the bloodstream. They are the ones that summon the helper T cells when encountering a foreign organism. They are part of a vast communications system that connects the immune system, hormone producing cells, nerve cells, and brain cells. They receive and respond to electrical-chemical messages from the brain. In fact, they manufacture many of the same chemicals. This constitutes the talking back and forth between the brain and the immune system. So it should come as no surprise that this is how the brain can make us sick or make us well.

Negative emotions tear down the immune system, but positive emotions build it up. An optimistic outlook can help one recover from a serious illness, but a pessimistic outlook can plummet one in the other direction. This is the whole crux of the mechanisms of psychosomatic disease. During strong emotional stress, we know that the body releases extremely large amounts of cortisone, which incapacitate the macrophage cells and they cannot respond normally to infection.

So do excessive exercise and overeating, that are forms of physical stress and cause the overproduction of cortisone, to which the macrophage and T cells succumb. However, mild or moderate exercise (80 percent of maximum heart rate) — not stressful — can actually strengthen the immune system by stimulating the replacement of macrophages and the T cells that have been destroyed. The slight increase in endorphins can also reduce anxiety and bring about a feeling of well-being, thus reducing the ravages of stress.

Proper exercise may also bring about an increase in the production of interleukin and interferon, both of which strengthen the immune system. Interleukin is one of several chemicals with which immune cells communicate during battle. It causes lymphocytes to multiply in number. Interferon is a protein produced by virus-infected cells that stops the growth of the virus. The word means to interfere plus on. It is the body's natural defense against infection. Interferon is a class of protective proteins produced by the white cells and fibroblasts (connective tissue cells) which not only prevent viruses from penetrating body cells, but may also regulate cell development.

Interferon is now used to treat one rare kind of leukemia, and may in the future be used in the treatment of chronic leukemia, kidney cancer, sarcoma (cancer) in AIDS patients, and even the common cold. Now, another newly identified chemical called tumor necrosis factor seems to destroy malignant cells without affecting normal cells. The immune system is being strengthened to attack its foes.

All of these chemicals are now manufactured or grown in bacteria or yeast cultures. Today, genetic engineers can take a gene for interleukin from a human cell, put it in a germ, and the germ makes interleukin! Insulin can also be produced. Monoclonal antibodies are produced by the fusing of two cells — say a B cell and a white-cell cancer. This hybrid produces antibodies against the cancer, and it can live indefinitely. Other monoclonal antibodies have been produced to use in colon and pancreatic cancers. Each one is specific to one particular germ or cancer. It is hoped that these new discoveries will help in man's struggle against disease. However, we do not yet know what problems may be encountered. It seems that certain freedoms from the ravages of stress might, indeed, cut down on the necessity for this type of treatment, which is, again, after the fact. The mind and body have already suffered much pain and are weakened in the process.

Support Your Local Defense Plant

Both interleukin and interferon are destroyed through the stress response; but proper exercise can stimulate the production of both, and thus strengthen the immune system. The damage can be reversed! Another way to weaken or strengthen the immune system is through nutrition. It is absolutely essential that our bodies get the necessary nutrients they need, in order to be prepared at all times. The millions of immune cells that we have are manufactured out of the food we eat — the amino acids, proteins, vitamins, and minerals. Vitamin A deficiency lowers the number of T cells; vitamin B6 and B12 deficiency decreases the number of antibodies; and vitamin C deficiency lowers macrophage activity, as Stuart Berger explains.

Minerals are extremely important for the proper functioning of the immune system. Without zinc, lymph system tissues and the thymus actually shrink — no development and no storage facilities! Zinc is needed to stimulate the macrophages, and without it, T cells are reduced in number. An inadequate intake of selenium cuts down on the number of antibodies. Heavy metals, such as copper, cadmium, and lead weaken T cells, further explains Stuart Berger.[2]

There are about 22 amino acids that, linked together, form protein in the body. Body cells can make many of these; but eight of them (for adults) and nine of them (for children) including histidine, must come from the food we eat. So these nine are called essential amino acids. Four of them are known as lysine, methionine, phenylalanine, and tryptophan — and all are necessary in the production of T cells to fight off invading germs and cancer.

Quite ironically, the above named amino acids are the very same vital elements that are destroyed by stress, through the overproduction of cortisone by the adrenal glands. The immuno-nutrition link should now be clear.

It is absolutely crucial that your body gets the necessary nutrients to create the 200,000 new immune cells and the thousands of antibody molecules every second of your life. Every day, the body must rebuild millions of cells if over-all health is to be maintained.

There have been several significant findings. First, the types of foods that build a healthy body also build a healthy immune system, but more urgent stress needs are taken care of before those of the immune system. For instance, proteins first feed the brain and nervous system, then the vital organs, and then the muscles and skin. Whatever is left goes to the leukocytes, macrophages, and antibodies. The immune system is slowed down, or shut down, if the diet is deficient in any way.

Therefore, it is very important to eat the right nutrients in sufficient quantities. Fats should be kept low, but vegetables, fruits, high fiber foods, and complex carbohydrates — such as whole wheat bread, whole grains, and cereals — should be kept high. Breakfast is the most important meal of the day.

However, there is merit in earning one's breakfast *first* with some kind of physical activity — thus increasing the metabolic rate. Exercise is very important for healthy circulation of the blood and for lymph vessels, which are the main avenues of travel for the antibodies. Exercise insures body tone, which reduces the breakdown of cells during the aging process. Autoimmune diseases partly result from a lack of exercise, that leads to cellular deterioration, which, however, can be controlled through exercise, as well as nutrition.

Furthermore, sleep is a time of restoration for the immune system, as protein, necessary vitamins, and minerals are assimilated. Heavy meals just before bedtime are stress inducing and therefore are not recommended. Stimulants and alcohol before retiring are also stress inducing and detrimental. Last but not least, all drugs have deleterious effects on the immune system.

Medications for colds suppress the localized immune response. Marijuana constricts the production of interferon, delays the response of white blood cells, and slows the production of antibodies. Tobacco suppresses the immune system, and heavy alcohol use is associated with increased risk of cancer, tuberculosis, and other infections.

For reasons not clearly established but supported by numerous studies, a smile and sunshine in your heart will cause your immune system to produce more white blood cells. I say, "Control stress before it controls you!"

Major Diseases of the Immune System

Our immune systems are being seen as more vulnerable and more important than ever before. It is our first and sometimes *only* line of defense. Auto-immune deficiency disease or AIDS, as tragic as it is, is teaching us this lesson. The virus, carried only in semen and blood, apparently only strikes those people whose immune systems are weakened in some way. For instance, drug abusers certainly do have weakened immune systems. The results of stress are everywhere!

Of the leading developed countries in Europe and North America, the U.S. now ranks first in both the number of AIDS cases reported and the rate per 100,000 people afflicted. *The London Sunday Observer* (*Parade Magazine*, Dec. 21, 1986) reported 24,491 cases. That is about 10.50 cases per 100,000 people! Next in order is Canada, with about one-fifth as many. All other countries are lower! In some, the incidence is rare.

Obviously, many of our life-styles in the United States are not conducive to healthy immune systems. Education is our only hope. A new, virulent scourge that relentlessly disarms the immune system is AIDS. It probably began with the green monkey of Central Africa, which harbored a harmless virus in its bloodstream. Then, about 15 years ago, nature probably altered the genetic code of the virus through a kind of random mutation it uses to evolve all species. As with the influenza virus, the new virus crossed the boundary from animal to man. In 1981, it started attacking — seemingly — otherwise healthy and young homosexual men. There appeared many bizarre infections and cancer. It is still running rampant. Most die, as there is no cure, as yet. The warriors within are decimated — the immune system fails to function.

Bacteria, protozoa, fungi, and viruses stalk us in countless forms. Streptococci and staphlococci continually swarm over our skin, seeking access. The bacterium, clostridium botulinum, which causes botulism, is a single cell that can release a toxin so potent that a minute amount can kill thousands. Plasmodium malariae, a single-celled parasite transmitted by a mosquito, destroys red blood cells and causes chills, high fever, and weakness, for millions of people.

Any virus is the simplest and yet the most devious enemy to the body. A virus is a protein-coated bundle of genes, containing instructions for making identical copies of itself. However, it lacks the basic ability for reproduction — technically, it is not alive! In order to reproduce itself, it has to get inside one of our living cells. There it works like our cells DNA, issuing its own instructions — the cell becomes a virus factory. The cell eventually ruptures, and viral clones invade nearby cells. Thousands of copies are made very quickly, as with Rhinovirus 14, one of the causes of the common cold. Its surface is rough and ridged, with peaks that allow it to grab and hang on to the cell it will invade. Then war is declared on the immune system.

The immune system, with its phagocytes and lymphocytes (T and B cells), starts the defense. Of the one hundred trillion cells that make up the human body, one in every hundred is a defense cell. In a healthy system, the phagocytes or scavengers of the system engulf and consume anything that seems out of place in the bloodstream, tissues, and lympathic systems.

For example, they consume particles of dust and other pollutants that enter with each breath; and, up to a certain point, they can cleanse blackened lungs! However, over too long a time, smoking destroys phagocytes faster than they can be replenished. Other pollutants, such as silica and asbestos, overwhelm them — thus, diseases like cancer.

When the skin is injured, the ever-swarming bacteria and micro-organisms invade. Immediately, the blood vessels dilate which enables the phagocytes to flow freely and devour the invaders. This causes the usual swelling and reddening. Fibrin is woven across the wound, to restore the skin's barrier. However, if the phagocytes cannot destroy the foes fast enough, nearby cells are invaded, and infection occurs. One type of phagocyte, called a macrophage, takes a piece of an invader, called an antigen, and carries it on its own surface. It alerts a highly specialized class of lymphocytes (called the T cells) to recognize a particular virus.

The thymus gland, that lies behind the breastbone and above the heart, produces the T cells — T stands for thymus derived. As the T cells mature in the thymus, they learn to identify and tell the difference between the antigens of different kinds of viruses — an almost infinite variety. They are even so diligent they destroy organ transplants that are recognized as foreign — a process known as rejection.

The T cells that detect antigens actually do no killing, but they summon the killer T cells to do the job — trained killers. They produce a chemical that kills bacteria or destroys infected cells before viruses have time to multiply. More phagocytes can be called into action, and the spleen and lymph nodes are stimulated to produce B cells. These are the antibodies which slow down, capture — and/or kill unwelcome cells. Locking together, they form substances in the bloodstream called complement. It blows up like a bomb, blasting the invader. Then the peacemaker comes in, the suppressor T cells, to turn off the B cells and the helper T cells. The battle is won, but not forgotten! Memory cells will live a long time and protect one from any particular virus which has been defeated — this is called immunity!

Why then, AIDS? What goes wrong? We don't know all the answers. However, AIDS, as well as hepatitis B, must get into the blood stream quickly to survive. If exposed to air, they die. Therefore, it would be extremely difficult to contract except through the exchange of blood or semen. Nonetheless, stress of any kind — physical, emotional, and/or nutritional — could weaken the immune system and make the body much more vulnerable. The presence of other microbes could also cause greater vulnerability.

We also know that AIDS continues to kill, despite the most concentrated research efforts against a single disease! In San Francisco alone, the disease claims the lives of two people per day. Nationwide, 20 people per day die of it! One simple reason why the AIDS virus is so deadly is that it kills the one lymphocyte most critical to the immune response — the helper T cell.

The AIDS virus was isolated in 1983. It enters the body concealed inside a helper T cell from an infected host, usually in blood or semen, and overpowers the defending T cells. Here it can lie dormant for months or years. Then when another infection triggers the invalid T cells to divide, the AIDS virus also divides. The multiplied clones infect nearby T cells, and the body loses the very sentinels that should be alerting the rest of the immune system — there is no defense, and the enemy runs free! A healthier life-style that protects one from exposure and is conducive to a healthy immune system is the best insurance against this scourge.

Cancer

With cancer, the body becomes its own worst enemy. It is too alive! It just keeps multiplying, and it can't control itself. Probably, all of us have potential cancer cells within us. As they turn cancerous, the antigens on their surfaces change enough to alert the vigilant T cells. In a healthy body, the immune system seeks out and destroys the abnormal cells. Sometimes, though, the cancer cells overwhelm the immune system, and cancer is the result.

Those whose personalities incapacitate them into seemingly sureptitious "flight" seem more prone to infections and cancer. They appear to withdraw from situations and have difficulty interacting with others. They also appear to have difficulty dealing with the reality of their own experiences. In contrast with the auto-immune personality, that seems to have too much "fight" or "shot-gun" approach which destroys healthy tissue, the cancer prone personality is lacking in "fight" or has no fight at all, inside or out. There is, indeed, a parallel between personality and disease. There is the auto-immune personality, as well as the cancer prone personality.

However, according to Goodskin, there is evidence that there are different cancer profiles. For example, women likely to develop cervical cancer show a different profile than those with other forms of cancer. Karl Goodwin and his co-workers studied 73 women who were awaiting results of abnormal Pap smears or biopsies of the cervix, to see which ones would actually develop cancer. The composite cancer personality is known to be one which is cooperative, self-sacrificing, overly optimistic, and socially inclined.[3]

However, the women who did develop cervical cancer were hostile, seemingly fearless, hard-headed, punitive toward others, and blunt in social situations. They tended to have trouble coping with stressful life situations. I personally know several individuals who seem to be socially alienated, particularly from close relatives or past friends, and do nothing about it! It's a sort of "giving-up" on what could be mutually satisfying relationships with those with whom one would ordinarily expect warm reciprocation. They display symptoms of anxiety, hopelessness, and despair about the future — and it can become a "self-fulfilling prophesy!"

Cervical cancer is an "epidemic illness." Preventive measures should be based on change of attitude and coping style. Any therapy that would offer self-help in increasing social support and decreasing alienation would be a step in the right direction. However, each lady with cervical cancer is her own worst enemy! I have found that it is very difficult to help these individuals to help themselves, because they view others as a threat to their well-being. They are not just defensive but offend others, all as a result of the faulty perception of threat to self. They seem to believe that they are right and everybody else is wrong!

People who are "too nice" are also vulnerable to cancer, according to Henry Dreher in his book, *The Complete Guide to Cancer Prevention*. There is now the "Type C" personality, reflecting characteristics associated with cancer; in much the same that "Type A" has been used to describe personality factors associated with heart disease. The "Type C" person is the one who has a strong desire to please others. He or she will go to great lengths to be overly concerned about the welfare of others, to the detriment of his or her own personal needs or desires. Frustration and anger are repressed or held in, which cause a "bottling-up" of stress, with subsequent chemical changes in the body.[4]

Most of the individuals who possess these personality traits probably suffer from lack of self-esteem. They try to cover up or compensate for their feelings of inadequacy. They can and do make themselves feel better, but what a price to pay!

The history of this research goes back to the 1970s, in London, where Dr. Steven Greer and his research teams conducted psychological studies on women with breast lumps. It was found that the women with malignant lumps suppressed anger more often than the ones with benign tumors.[5] Then in the 1980s, Lydia Temorshok, a psychologist at the University of California. in San Francisco, performed assessments of 150 melanoma patients. She found that a large number of them did not express negative emotions. Even in cases of known cancer, they still would almost never vent their anger, sadness, or fear. Each of them maintained an outward manifestation of an even temperament. These individuals with Type C patterns relapsed more often and were more severely ill than those who could express their emotions. Their immune systems were weaker.[6] The point is that the emotions were always there, but found no expression. Therefore, their bodies could find no relief from the onslaught!

The good news is that Type C behavior can be modified or changed in one's own best interests. Psychotherapist Stepanie Simonton-Atchley, an instructor at the University of Arkansas for Medical Sciences, believes that acute stress must be monitored. She recommends

(1) Be aware of what you are feeling in response to stress and find appropriate ways to express it, rather than trying to force yourself to be optimistic;

(2) Routinely practice a relaxation technique, such as meditation. Exercise regularly — an excellent antidepressant, and

(3) Maintain a social support group.[7]

In contrast, individuals with auto-immune personalities tend to have deep-seated feelings of rejection, or feel that they are viewed as inadequate or inferior by other significant persons. Therefore, these individuals may exhaust themselves in trying to be "all things to all people." They expect the impossible from themselves, as if they were possessed with some super-human abilities and stamina. It is as if nature is trying to "pull them down." The body seemingly turns on itself in another very direct way.

Suicidal Assault

Immunological theory maintains that the immune system may be weakened in a very direct way and cause trouble. "Sometimes the white cells attack normal body cells."[8] Rheumatic fever, fibromyalgia, rheumatoid arthritis, systemic lupus erythematosus, diabetes, pernicious anemia, and even multiple sclerosis can be caused this way.

Medicine sometimes attempts to slow down the immune system, but this could result in an increase in the incidence of infectious diseases, including cancer. Methotrexate and cyclosporine are two such drugs; they are powerful immunosuppressants, capable of "turning off" the white blood cells. If this happens, the whole immune system is severly weakened in the process of reducing the body's production of antibodies against itself. Along with the good comes the bad! These are, at best, "stop gap" measures, which are "after the fact."[9]

The reasons for the body's attack on itself are not clear. It does seem that long-term chronic stress does influence the immune response in this way. Quite interestingly, a woman's white blood cells may destroy a man's sperm, leading to infertility. An expectant mother's white cells may also reject the baby! What remains a mystery is why one's own body attacks its own self, causing such diseases as arthritis.

Attention is now turning to the role of chronic stress in seemingly "overactivating" the immune system; but in reality, it is "messing up" its basic intelligence — that of distinguishing friend from foe. It may be possible that the suppressor T cells have difficulty in discerning the different markings on protein. Their recognition and discriminating powers may be faulty. Therefore, the immune system in this situation could be weakened, but in a different way than that of cancer. It can't do its job properly. It has gone berserk and is shooting down fellow comrades!

Quite ironically, it does seem from observation that those whose personalities propel them to "fight" in response to stress, are more aggressive, and even "hard to get along with," are more likely to fall victims to auto-immune diseases. It may be that the suppressor T cells, which help protect the body's tissues from being attacked by its own antibodies, break down under stress. When this happens, they can no longer prevent the B cells from making antibodies, even if they are no longer needed. Thus, such diseases as rheumatoid arthritis, where healthy tissue is ravaged, do occur. If the kidneys and lungs are damaged, the disease is known as systemic lupus erythematosis.

When the immune system mounts battles against imaginary enemies, allergic reactions result. Some are mild — some can kill! Thousands of harmless substances — such as pollen, animal dander, dust, foods, and chemicals — can cause allergic reactions. There is nothing wrong with the substance itself — it is simply that individuals can have antibodies which mistakenly recognize a particular substance as an enemy! In the case of hay fever, antibodies recognize pollen as an enemy. Cells in the body spill out potent chemicals (such as histamine), that lead to allergic symptoms. T cells can order B cells to make even more antibodies, as if matters aren't bad enough! The sniffles and runny nose of hay fever, the rash and itch of poison ivy, the aches and pains of arthritis, the wheezing and choking of asthma, or the irregular gate and trembling of multiple sclerosis, may all be the sound and fury of an over-reacting immune system!

Some allergies appear to be inherited — others do not. In any case, a healthy immune system is one's best assurance against allergies of any kind or description. A great deal more will undoubtedly be known in the near future. Scientists didn't even know how antibodies were produced until the late 1950s; and the distinction between T and B cells wasn't clear until the 1960s. More is now being revealed about the role of macrophages. Someday, man-made antibodies may be used to destroy unwanted cells, such as cancer cells, B cells involved in allergic reactions, or T cells that turn against our own tissue in auto-immune responses.

Until that time our best hope is to insure a healthy immune system. Hall and Goldstein state that, "We are witnessing the birth of a new integrative science, psychoneuroimmunology, which begins with the premise that neither the brain nor the immune system can be excluded from our scheme that proposes to account for the onset and course of human disease. ...the first, and, in the long run, the most valuable, clinical spinoffs of psychoneuroimmunology will be in disease prevention, in the development of ways to manage stress."[10]

Psychology and the Immune System

There are new links being discovered between the brain and the immune system, and how they interact to influence our susceptibility to disease. A new and exciting field of research, known as psychoimmunology, is rapidly developing and should provide us with many more answers in the near future. At this point in time, we are aware that the immune system recognizes and fights foreign materials within the body. We have seen how it is involved in the body's response to cancer and autoimmune diseases. The degree of susceptibility to any disease depends on how well the immune system is working. Moreover, the brain, which is subject to psychological and emotional factors, can affect the integrity of the immune system and influence whether or not one becomes ill!

Nonetheless, orthodox medicine and biology have long neglected psychological influences on disease. This has been due to the fact that we didn't understand the brain and the immune system — there simply were no obvious and plausible mechanisms that could account for any such phenomena! Now, we are starting to see some results of systematic investigations. Clinicians and epidemiologists have long known that there are actual links between stress and disease. They believe that psychoimmunology is more than psychosomatic medicine, in that the new field includes the recognition that diseases are caused by organic as well as psychological factors — what is psychological affects the brain, which in turn affects the immune system, which determines the degree to which one is or is not resistant to disease!

Several studies have found statistically significant correlations between high life-event scores and subsequent illnesses. One was done to investigate whether stress affected the incidence of a glandular fever known as infectious mononucleosis, a disease caused by Epstein-Barr virus (EBV).

It was found that about 20 percent of those who originally had no antibodies did indeed develop antibodies to the virus, and one-fourth of these actually "came down" with the disease. This same group (five percent of the original group) were the ones who suffered most from academic pressures. They had fathers who were "over-achievers," and they, themselves, were highly motivated, but poor achievers.

So, here we see an example of a direct link between emotional states and susceptibility to illness. In another study, researchers found that out of a group of student nurses who carried antibodies for herpes simplex virus I (HSU-I), those who actually had more cold sores, were those who described themselves as typically unhappy. Yet another area of research, although controversial, showed an association between "life events," such as bereavement, marriage, loss or change of job, or the birth of a baby, and illness. These associations are now thought to be significant, but weak, and more direct evidence is needed — here enter the psychoimmunologists!

One study took blood samples from bereaved subjects and isolated the lymphocytes to see how well the subject's immune systems were functioning, the lymphocytes were exposed to a "mitogen," a chemical that stimulated them to divide and proliferate — to increase in number in order to fight off the enemy! The lymphocytes from the bereaved subjects were significantly less responsive as long as two months after bereavement! This serves as definite evidence that extreme psychological and emotional stress damages this one important part of the immune system.

The same results have been found true for men whose wives have had terminal breast cancer. The depressed immune system functioning continued for up to a year after the death of their wives! However, it is well to realize that the bereavement also caused loss of sleep, poor eating habits, and greater consumption of alcohol, tobacco, caffeine, and drugs — all stressors which can also affect the immune system.

Even everyday social stresses debilitate the immune system. For instance, students have been found to have fewer "natural killer cells" on exam days — they actually secrete fewer antibodies in their saliva during times of academic pressure. I say that there is no wonder that attendance goes down after an exam! All of the above are examples of actual organic changes.

However, all data from human research is limited. In the first place, ethical considerations prevent scientists from subjecting people to stress in order to see what it does to their immune systems; and secondly, what data we do have is (many times) ambiguous and difficult to interpret. Controlled studies in which the impact or effect of one causal factor or independent variable can be studied are almost impossible. The only option remaining, in order to have truly controlled experiments, is to use animals, even though some of these tests may be ethically disturbing. The "rule of thumb" is this: If there is the probability of helping the "human condition," then animal research is considered legitimate.

Quite surprisingly, it has been found that psychological stress does not always cause trouble. In fact, stress can sometimes increase an animal's resistance to disease. If they can control or alter the stress by behaving in some different way, stress then seems to increase their resistance to disease.

Groups of animals that could turn off electric shock by pressing a lever had more resistance to disease than those whose levers were inoperable. Both groups received identical shocks at precisely the same times — the only difference was psychological; that is, whether or not they were in control! Uncontrolled shock caused more ulcers and faulty immune system functioning. The researchers measured the responsiveness of the rats' lymphocytes and found them to be decreased.

Uncontrolled shock induces a psychological state known as "learned helplessness" in animals. In humans, one kind of depression is very similar, wherein the individual "gives up" and stops trying to better himself or herself. Severe depression is also associated with an impaired immune system and subsequent illness. However, the duration of stress is also a contributing factor.

For instance, acute stress sometimes has the opposite effect — even in the same subjects! With research on mice, conducted at Johns Hopkins University in Baltimore, loud, uncontrollable noise initially reduced the responsiveness of their lymphocytes; but if the stress lasted for more than approximately a week, their lymphocytes became more active than those of the unstressed mice! It appears that if one can "weather the storm," one becomes stronger — the story of all truly successful people!

There are now indications, at the animal level, that immune responses can be Pavlovian or classically conditioned. In other words, at the autonomic nervous system level, an organism can learn to respond to a second stimulus, if it is presented at about the same time as the original stimulus — at least for a limited period of time.

At the Univeristy of Rochester in New York state, Robert Ader and his colleagues conditioned rats to suppress their immune systems by pairing flavored water with the drug called cyclophosphamide. When the rats were initially injected with red blood cells from sheep, they produced antibodies. With the drug and then with the flavored water, their production of antibodies subsided[11] — association learning had occurred!

From these findings, it appears possible to condition a lowered immune response in humans suffering from autoimmune diseases, such as rheumatoid arthritis, pernicious anemia, or thyroid disease. However, lowering the immune response can have deleterious effects and lead to infections and cancer! If the decision is made to undergo this type of therapy, it may be possible (through conditioning) to reduce the amount of the drug needed — flavored water might become a partial substitute for the drug. At this point, however, immune conditioning remains, unfortunately, a hotly disputed issue!

If, indeed, immune system conditioning is a reality, as I'm certain it is, the explanation would seem to be in how the autonomic nervous system responds — this appears to be the crux of the matter! We already know that when the autonomic system is activated, certain hormones are secreted to prepare us for action — self-protection and self-preservation. The hypothalamus in the brain responds to sensory stimulation and/or perceived threat to self. It sends chemical messages to the adrenals, which in turn secrete corticosteroids to reduce inflammation in damaged or infected tissue and to mobilize the body's energy reserves. These "stress hormones" provide the where-with-all to cope with short-term physical and psychological demands.

However, they also affect the immune system in undesirable ways. We have seen how corticosteroids decrease the number of antibodies produced. The lymph nodes (which are the sources of the lymphocytes) decrease in size or atrophy. The number and responsiveness of lymphocytes, which are already circulating in the blood, are reduced, thereby impairing the ability of the immune system to resist infection.

Corticosteroids, however, cannot be the only link between stress and the immune system. Evidence for this was provided by reasearchers when they found that stress can reduce the number of lymphocytes in rats, even after their adrenal glands had been removed!

Psychological stress brings about changes in many different hormones, neurotransmitters and neuromodulators, which also affect the immune system. Some of these substances are growth hormones, insulin, vasopressin, testosterone, prolactin, adrenalin, noradrenalin, endorphins, and enkephalins.

In addition, there is increasing evidence that cells of the immune system carry receptors on their surfaces that recognize and draw to themselves various transmitters and hormones — binding. This internal intelligence can alter the activity of the lymphocytes. It is no secret, then, that psychological factors can influence the immune system via any number of chemical messengers, in addition to the corticosteroids. Our nervous systems include many "messengers" doing a great deal of "talking!"

For example, the opiate-like substances which control pain and give a sense of euphoria are chemical messengers known as neuropeptides or endorphins and enkephalins. They are manufactured throughout the body in response to stress, particularly that which is uncontrollable. Researchers have found receptors for these neuropeptides on the surfaces of white blood cells. Therefore, there is no doubt that the activity of the lymphocytes and the natural killer cells can be altered by the presence of neuropeptides that are released during times of stress!

8.

ALLERGIES — ALIENS AGAINST SELF

Allergies can be thought of as a form of metabolic rejection, in that there is something atypical about a person's chemistry that is sensitive to (and rejects) substances that are not offensive to the normal body. Obviously, a component of the immune system has gone astray, causing the person's body to make a special type of allergic antibody against the offending substance (allergen). Whenever the person comes in contact with that particular allergen, whether it be an inhalant or food, the allergen reacts with the antibody that has become attached to the connective cells—known as mast cells. The result is an allergic reaction. An allergy is a sensitivity to some particular substance known as an allergen. This state can become a form of chronic stress on the body, that can predispose it to other disease states.

Almost any food, as well as inhalants and chemicals, can be an allergen to some people. Some allergic reactions may take the form of hay fever, asthma, hives, high blood pressure, severe fatigue, constipation, ulcers, dizziness, headache, mental disorders, hyperactivity, or hypoglycemia. One may feel excessively tired, bloated, have palpitations, perspire profusely, or feel mentally "fuzzy" after eating.

Other complications may range from listlessness, insomnia, irritability, migraine headaches, depression, poor memory, violent outbursts, or hallucinations. One may be addicted to the very same substance that is an allergen. This happens if the allergic substance also stimulates the release of adrenalin — the quick "high!" The body "craves" the substance to relieve the misery which, in turn, creates more misery — a vicious cycle!

Food allergies may be illusive creatures that are difficult to track! Many have transitory effects — they are felt at some times and not at others. Any substance may cause a reaction when one is upset emotionally, but not show up when one is tranquil. Heredity plays a role, but unusually high amounts of one or more nutrients would be necessary to trigger such a response. Stress of any kind — such as poor diet, insufficient sleep, emotional trauma, or infections — can predispose the body to an allergic reaction. This is due to the damaging effects on the immune system. A healthy body can resist allergens, but one that has been ravaged by stress has a difficult time. Either the lack of proper nutrients or the ingestion of improper substances can increase cell permeability, allowing easy access by incompatible substances. This, then, sets off the immune response — its job is to exterminate or eradicate the invader. Sometimes it responds intelligently — sometimes it does not! The body must be properly nourished to do its job well. Any serious stress can render this impossible.

Candida Albicans

One result of immune system malfunction that has received recent consideration is called *Candida Albicans*. It is a strain of yeast that is a member of a broader classification of organisms, known as fungi. They contain no chlorophyl, cannot make their own food, and prefer to live in people. Usually, the yeast is kept in check by the immune system. In infants, where the immune system does not accomplish this, a condition known as oral thrush occurs.

Virtually all humans harbor this yeast in their gastrointestinal and genitourinary tracts. With a healthy immune system, its proliferation is kept to a minimum, and all is silent. Given a self-destructive life style, Candida growth can proceed unchecked — defenses have been weakened. The immune system has become sluggish and weakened. Toxins produced by Candida move, via the bloodstream, to all parts of the body.

However, there is no medical test to diagnose the problem, because we all have it, to some degree. The only alternative is to examine the lifestyle of the patient.

Candida prefers chocolate, sweets, grains, dairy products, fruit juices, and nuts. These are the very same foods to which many people become addicted — have a craving for them, because of their energizing effect on the nervous system, albeit, short term. Many people with this condition lose their appetitie for vegetables and animal protein. Candida overgrowth often produces a sensitivity to most other molds and yeasts — thus, a craving for fermented, pickled, smoked, or dried foods. This just adds more fuel to the fire!

Certain drugs can upset the ecological balance of the intestinal flora and suppress the immune system. They include antibiotics such as penicillin, ampicillin, tetracyclin, erythromycin, amoxicillin, and Keflex. Immuno-suppressants, which are chemicals that reduce inflammation by paralyzing our defense mechanisms, are also faulted. They include cortisone, prednisone, and other steroid-like treatments, such as the birth control pill, that contributes to Candidiasis by upsetting the hormone balance. Hormone changes during the ovarian cycle and pregnancy can also contribute to Candida growth.

Our early warning system gives us signals when drugs, foods, or other forms of distress have weakened our defenses. It is much like a smoke detector, burglar alarm, or seat belt buzzer that enables us to avoid disaster. We should be in control of our health. We are not innocent victims of disease. Every symptom is a signal that gives us an important message that something in our health-style needs to be altered.

When we make the proper changes, our self-healing mechanisms will co-exist with Candida Albicans, as well as with other inhabitants of our bodies.

When Allies Become Aliens — Allergies

If one is suspect for an allergy problem, the first thing to do is to avoid the substances (whether inhalants or foods) to which one reacts. It may be possible to determine the foods to which one's immune system is sensitive through cytotoxic testing, RAST testing, or fasting. However, as is the case with all allergies, a healthy body is capable of neutralizing toxic substances; and a body with malfunctioning defense mechanisms cannot. It only makes sense that the offending substances should be eliminated; but if the body is not strengthened, the individual will become allergic to other entities, according to Donsback, in his book, *Allergies,* published in 1980.[1]

There isn't a more frustrating experience than to go through any form of allergy testing, eliminate all the offending foods, find the old allergies are no more, but consent to an additional test that reveals a whole new set! It seems like one never gets well — just changes allergies! One still catches everything that comes along, has low resistance, and a low energy level.

Let's consider for a time how stress effects the gastrointestinal tract, and how this can subsequently lead to allergies. Stress inhibits digestion — digestive functions slow down, almost to a stop! The production of hydrochloric acid and digestive enzymes is curtailed, as the important, immediate functions for survival receive attention. Blood flow is routed to the reflex centers of the brain, heart, lungs, and large muscles, for fight or flight. Without the proper supply of "digestive juices," the digestive tract cannot function normally. Many things can, and do, go wrong!

The digestive tract is actually a tube, from the outside world or environment which passes through our bodies. It begins at the lips and ends with the anus. It is designed to provide for the intake and digestion of food, absorption of nutrients, and the removal of waste products. In the mouth, complex starches are broken down by Ptyalin and enzymes, in the saliva. Rapid chewing during stress interferes with this first action — eating slowly and chewing ones' food well, while calm, facilitates this action.

In the stomach, proteins start to be digested by action of the hydrochloric acid and the enzyme called pepsin. While experiencing stress, proteins may not undergo proper breakdown before entering the small intestine. It is in the small intestine that proteins should complete their digestive change into amino acids. Food allergies can often be treated by taking additional digestive enzymes that break down the protein into amino acids. Also, it is in the small intestines that carbohydrates are broken down to simple sugars, and fats are digested — that is, if there is adequate pancreatin and bile.

Carbohydrates are not acted upon by any juices in the stomach; only the mouth and small intestine. Therefore, normally, any carbohydrate eaten arrives in the small intestine three to fifteen minutes after eating. However, concentrated or refined carbohydrates can get trapped with proteins (such as meat, fish, eggs, or cheese) that may take up to five hours to digest. Some fats are also broken down in the stomach, which further inhibits the production of hydrochloric acid. The climate is right for fermentation — heat, sugar, and bacteria! There's not enough hydrochloric acid to take care of bacteria normally associated with protein.

For best nutrition, all concentrated sweets should be eaten on an empty stomach. If not, burping and belching are the body's normal reflexes to relieve the distress. In addition to this problem caused by ingesting concentrated or refined sugars with protein, there is also the reality of not enough hydrochloric acid, caused by the stress reaction. In addition, it should be noted that after the age of 35, hydrochloric acid production becomes less and less. It may be necessary and feasible to take hydrochloric acid and pepsin tablets. Simply eating less and not exceeding the body's requirements for nutrition could solve many problems! If a decision is made to take hydrochloric acid and pepsin tablets, again, take no more than necessary, as ulcers may be the result!

Here is an explanation of how stress can cause ulcers. In the first place, there is not enough hydrochloric acid in the stomach, and the emptying time is delayed. Then some bile is regurgitated or backed up from the duodenum into the stomach. Bile is very caustic and can cause the stomach lining to become irritated — even ulcerated! The alkalinity of the bile causes reflex secretion of hydrochloric acid — now there's too much instead of too little!

The irritation to the stomach lining by the bile and acid secretion causes contraction of the small arteries in the stomach wall — arteriolar spasm. This can produce gastritis or even an ulcer. Here, it would be well to avoid substances which stimulate hydrochloric acid secretion such as coffee, tea, cola drinks, alcohol, or cigarettes.

While all the above described discomforts are being experienced, something else is likely to be happening. Normally, amino acids from digested protein are absorbed through the intestinal mucosa. However, in an allergic reaction, the tissues lose their natural selective absorption powers, and crude or undigested protein can be absorbed. These more complex structures create more allergic reactions — a vicious cycle!

Here is an interesting scientific explanation presented by Chuck Bates: "Long protein molecules called macromolecules are among the products of digestion in the gut. Dairy and wheat products produce large quantities of the molecules during digestion. If receptor sites in the membranes of the intestine absorb these molecules improperly, they get into the bloodstream. The next step would be for an over-ambitious immune system to attack these molecules as enemy invaders."[2] Thus, an allergic reaction is set off. This macromolecule gut absorption theory was first published in 1974, but has generated renewed interest.

The use of alcohol increases and prolongs hypersensitivity, indefinitely. This is because ethanol greatly increases the permeability of intestinal membranes. This makes it more likely that macromolecules will be absorbed into the bloodstream. Alcohol also contributes to immune system hypersensitivity by creating a PGE1 deficiency. PGE1 is a substance made from EFA (essential fatty acids) which has a profound influence on the nervous, cardiovascular, and immune systems. It regulates calcium uptake in the neurons and influences the behavior of many neuro-transmitters. The source of EFA in our diets is cold-pressed or unprocessed vegetable oil. PGE1 deficiency lowers the activity of the T suppressor cells that cool off immune system activity.

Many gastro-intestinal problems take months to quiet down. Until they do, the inflammation will cause "leaky bowels," where macromolecules are readily absorbed. I believe it is possible that one of the curses of sugar is that in the fermentation process, alcohol is manufactured which causes abnormal permeability of the intestinal wall — thus, allergic reactions to substances which get through!

EPA and PGE1 Deficiencies

Some fascinating research has been conducted in British Columbia (of Canada) and Washington State Indian Reservations. Chuck Bates reports that, "It is hypothesized that essential fatty acids (EFA) called eicosapentaenoic (EPA), and prostoglandin E1 (PGE1) deficiencies predispose Coastal Indians to food allergies which in turn predispose them to autoimmune, inflammatory, and psychiatric disorders."[3]

EPA and PGE1 are both essential fatty acids, that are manufactured in the body by enzymes. EPA inhibits inflammatory PGE2. Its inflammatory properties are due to its ability to inhibit inflammatory leukotrienes. PGE1 regulates T suppressor cell activity. Thus, people deficient in these two EFA's could be predisposed to autoimmune disease or hyperallergic states.

Bates, a clinical psychologist in B.C., Canada says, "Indians are especially hard hit by diabetes, arthritis, arthralgias, lupus erythematosus, obesity, alcoholism, depression and suicide, GI tract inflammatory disease, migraine, asthma, eczema, gallstones, and essential hypertension. The children suffer from high rates of chronic bronchitis, obitis media, and allergies." Bates says that schizophrenic rates are three times higher in Coastal Indians than in North American Indians, with no traditional access to seafoods! Arthritis rates are three to four times higher![4]

It is possible that the Coastals have a racially deprived PGE1 and EPA deficiency because of inherited enzyme inactivity. They didn't need this function, because they subsided for 20,000 years on a traditional seashore diet, mainly composed of salmon rich in EFA that didn't require enzyme action. This also gave them high doses of lithium, which gave them stability. They were healthy and strong!

Today, however, with reliance on Caucasian foods, rather than traditional foods, this requirement is not being met. This predisposes them to gastric inflammatory states, that, in turn, increases the permeability of gut membranes and the probability that macromolecules will be absorbed. When in the bloodstream, these could trigger the immune response. Lack of PGE1 would cause the activity of the immune T suppressor cells to be lowered — a hyperimmune situation, in which inflammation would be the result. Then the fires would burn out of control, because of over-active PGE2 and leukotrienes. It looks as if the gastric membranes are the first line of defense.

Bates says,

> Every Indian patient I have treated suffers from chronic GI tract inflammatory problems. These will be exacerbated by alcohol use, creating a chemically induced PGE1 deficiency in the gut which may make worse a condition already there for genetic reasons. Alcohol freezes the activity of the enzymes needed. The resulting inflammation may create or exacerbate food intolerances and stimulation of the immune system through macromolecule absorption. Finally, circulating immune complexes would trigger autoimmune damage to healthy tissue or an insult to the brain.[5]

Some Indians are violently allergic to salmon! Why would this occur after all the years of reliance on this food for survival! It seems reasonable that GI tract membrane damage, allowing production of salmon digestion into the bloodstream, would account for this triggering of the immune system and subsequent inflammation.

The Brain and Depression

There is no reason to believe that the brain is not also affected by allergies. The brain receives the same blood supply, and so is influenced by the immune system — and depression is the result. However, the depression is usually not the commonly thought of vegetative type, where the individual becomes lethargic, withdrawn, or gives up. Instead, it is characterized by behaviors such as agitation, restlessness, irritability, and a hair-trigger temper.

Speculatively, these states could involve synaptic disinhibition, which could bring on epileptic seizures. Many depressed patients show food sensitivities with PGE1 and EFA deficiencies.

Dr. Gislason of Vancouver, who works in the area of food allergies, says that major depression usually accompanies other disorders, and that it improves as other health problems improve. Gut revision therapy often outperforms the antidepressant drugs.[6]

Bates says, "The biochemistry of depression is not well understood by medical science." However, he say, "Indications are that depression may be the result of EFA deficiencies. If by chance, you are feeling "out of sorts," you may want to try some diet modifications. There may be an incredible change in your outlook on life! First of all, increase your intake of EFA's, to aid the activity of the enzymes that manufacture them in your body.[7]

Two of these are needed. One is called GLA or gammalinolenic acid. The only source of GLA (after breast feeding) is the oil of the evening primrose seed. We normally manufacture our own after infancy. EPA is available in salmon and other marine oils. Both of the EFA's can be purchased in health food stores and in some drug stores in the U.S.

However, EPA is not available in Canada because it is considered a "new drug" by Canadian federal authorities. In contrast, insurance companies do not cover the cost of these in the U.S., because they are considered "foods"! Primrose oil is very expensive. However, when taken with EPA, there is better utilization of it, and you get more for your money! There are some cautions about its use. Too much can interfere with normal blood clotting or cause insomnia — obviously, it's a blood thinner! Native Indians can't tolerate it, but they do very well with EPA — that's much more natural for them!

A deficiency of the enzyme called D6D or delta-6-desaturase enzyme hampers the manufacture of proper levels of EFA's. Those with 25 percent or higher ancestry that is Celtic Irish (usually Catholic), Scandinavian, Native Indian, Welsh, or Scottish are suspect for this deficiency by virtue of their genetic background, according to Bates.[8]

Some other correlative factors are alcohol problems, followed by anxiety or depression, teetotalling, religious fanaticism, mental illness, gastro-intestinal diseases, cystic fibrosis, or diabetes, personally, or among relatives. Emotional "uplifts" from certain foods and winter "depressions" are also indicative of possible D6D deficiency.

If one has a significant number of the above afflictions, then one's D6D enzyme is probably in need of help. It needs zinc, magnesium, pyridoxine, vitamin C, and the B vitamins. Alcohol should be avoided, because it stops the activity of the enzyme. Saturated fats in red meats and dairy products counteract D6D activity. So do the trans-fatty acids of margarine. A good substitute for butter is cold pressed safflower oil, mixed with just a little butter. It would be even better to mix the safflower oil with mayonnaise!

Most cooking oils contain trans-fatty acids, except for cold pressed safflower oil. Therefore, deep fried fast foods and pastries containing trans-fatty acids should be avoided. It is possible to use cold pressed safflower oils and have a wonderful home-made pie crust! Dietary lithium from sea salt, kelp tablets, seaweed, and other seafoods is a real stabilizer. In summary, primrose oil, EPA in marine oils, and the above detailed modifications will correct any EFA deficiencies you may have — no more depression! A local physician involved in research and treatment is Dean Patterson, D.O., at Coulee Dam, Washington.

Another EFA that cannot be manufactured in the body like other EFA's is Cis-LA or cis-linoleic acid — it must come from food! It is the stuff of which brain cells are made! It is present in dairy products and seed oils, such as sunflower, corn, and soy. Safflower oil is by far the richest source.

Keep in mind that all of these fats are liquid at room temperature. That's why they are called unsaturated. Animal fats are solid at room temperature, and so they are called saturated. Cis-LA and GLA were undoubtedly plentiful in the diet of early man who had, hunting and gathering economies, but today's feedlot animals are low in EFA's. Foraging wild game is a rich source.

Organ meats are high in EFA — our ancestors loved them! In today's commercial vegetable oils, most Cis-LA is destroyed by processing. Is it any wonder that today's typical American diet is deficient in EFA's? No! EFA's are our most important brain food, not protein, which has more to do with brawn. In order to survive in today's times, we need to be more intelligent, not bigger and stronger!

Washout

Warning! The technique I am about to describe should not be undertaken without medical supervision. The purpose of the "washout" is to clear from the body every possible macro-protein molecule that may have triggered an allergic reaction of any kind. In order to do this, a synthetic food called Vivonex (which contains everything the body needs, in order to live) is consumed for a week. It is a powder that is blended with distilled or spring water and sipped slowly through a straw for a half hour per packet. In order to receive an adequate intake of all nutrients, about five packets a day are necessary. It is quite expensive — about four dollars a packet in 1987. Health insurance companies do not cover the cost, as it is a food, not a drug! Washout is no easy task, and not everybody can do it. As for me, I fell short of reaching the goal!

The experience can be very painful, as one goes into the third or fourth day. All symptoms are more severe, whether they be inflammatory and/or emotional. The severity of the withdrawal effects is in direct proportion to the severity of the food sensitivity. If there's no pain, there were no food insensitivities in the first place. However, if one has had addictions, there will be cravings, as well as the "blues!"

As for me, I experienced no particular trauma. My so-called arthritis gave me more discomfort; but by the end of the fifth day, I was beginning to feel just "super!" I was clearheaded and full of vim, vigor, and vitality. I didn't know whether to continue or not, but I did — for a while!

Then came the challenge for me — that of introducing foods. The idea is to introduce one simple, pure version of a food each day. It was suggested that one take primrose oil the first day and EPA oil the second day, but I neglected to do this. One is to start with the least allergenic foods and work up to the most allergenic one, adding a new one each day, while taking a multivitamin. This I tried!

Day one — Uncle Ben's Converted Rice; day two — canned sugar-free pears; day three — carrots; day four — cauliflower; day five — wheat free tamari sauce; day six — broccoli; day seven — lettuce; day eight — turkey; and day nine — chicken.

Then vegetables are to be introduced, with the exception of potatoes, tomatoes, and peppers — no oils or butter! Then the ones with a higher probability of causing trouble — tuna, canned in water; cold pressed safflower oil, cod, salmon, beef, tomatoes, potatoes, green peppers, other fish, and grains, except for wheat.

The very last foods are almost sure to give a reaction. In order, they are wheat products, products containing yeast, prepared meats, and finally, dairy products and the complicated group of sauces, dressings, and spices that are very difficult to track. If one has a reaction to any food, then one eliminates that from the diet. Well, this whole scenario takes a considerable length of time. I "fell off the wagon" sometime before the first week was over! I had a voracious appetite, many social commitments, and I didn't get back on!

However, I do believe that this technique has merit, even though it is highly controversial among health care practitioners. I concluded that I probably had some problems of this nature, and proceeded to make recommended nutritional modifications for proper digestion and assimilation. I have continued to take Basic Preventive tablets and Omega-3 marine Fish Oil Concentrate, which are manufactured and distributed by Advanced Medical Nutrition, Inc., located in Hayward, California.

In addition to these, I have continued to take Dolobid, a nonsteroid anti-inflammatory drug. The collagen-vascular disease, with which I was once diagnosed as having, now seems to be in remission. However, I do live with the prior damage, which occurred when the disease was running rampant — hip degeneration.

Adrenals and Allergies

There is no doubt that mental and emotional stress and/or poor diet can lead to allergies. There is a tie between our emotions and chemical balance in the allergic reaction. As we know, the sympathetic nervous system responds to any stimulus and activates the adrenal glands — the sympatho-adrenal system. Stimulation such as fear, anger, temperature change, or even an overactive imagination causes the autonomic nervous system to speed up. This leads to increased heart rate and higher blood pressure because of vaso-constriction in all parts of the body except the heart, lungs, large muscles, and the brain stem. Breathing rate increases, and all digestive functions come to a virtual halt.

All of this action is possible because of the hormones which are released from the adrenal — all in split seconds! The same things happen when drugs or toxins are taken into the body. These reactions are our physical defense mechanisms that accommodate our psychological defense mechanisms.

Research using cats, and removing their adrenal nerve supplies, produced some significant changes, physically. Their capacity for muscular activity decreased by 35 percent; they did not respond to cold by erection of hair and vaso-constriction of blood vessels of the skin; and they could not control their body temperature. Emotionally, they went into shock when excited. This shows the absolute necessity for higher blood pressure, higher blood sugar, and more oxygen, in order to respond to the stress of life. If we cannot accommodate to the demands placed on our bodies, we are in serious trouble! However, constant and incessant stress can eventually weaken the body's capacity in this respect.

Besides the changes noted above, all the cats developed allergic reactions to many foods and chemicals that previously were neutral! Of course, these were the result of no adrenal function; but decreased function would also cause conditions such as decreased energy, allergies, and temperature adaptation irregularities.

If a foreign protein enters the bloodstream in an undenaturated condition, signals are immediately sent out for antibodies to attack and destroy the foreign organism. Most of the hormones necessary for this task originate in the adrenal glands.

For instance, when the antibodies attack any foreign protein, it is denatured by chemical action which produces a by-product knows as histamine. This is a tissue toxin that causes vaso-dilation or blood vessel enlargement, that results in flushing sensations and redness of the skin — just the opposite of vaso-constriction! There is increased permeability of the blood vessel wall, which allows fluids to escape, causing swelling or edema. Thus, the allergic response!

It can manifest itself as congestion in the respiratory tract (asthma), bumps on the skin (eczema), or itching (dermatitis) anywhere in the body. Other internal effects may occur, such as mental instability, headaches, gastro-intestinal upsets, diarrhea, or sinusitis — too much vaso-dilation, in all the wrong places! Because of the curtailment of digestive functions necessary to break down raw proteins into amino acids, which is caused by stress — not enough digestive enzymes — supplementation may help for a time, until the body is able to cope with the stress or the stress is eliminated altogether!

Under normal conditions, histamine is neutralized with anti-histamine, which is produced by the liver. However, if the liver is busy neutralizing too much fat and toxins to keep them out of general circulation, it may not be able to secrete an adequate supply of anti-histamine — and allergies result! Allergies do clear up after rest and fasting — all kinds and descriptions! This may be due to the fact that the liver has time to detoxify. A load would also be taken off the adrenal glands, so that they would be more capable of producing an anti-histamine — a backup mechanism.

The use of the adrenal hormone ACTH and cortisone have been used to temporarily alleviate allergic symptoms. Therefore, this testifies as to the involvement of the adrenals in allergies. Continued use of these hormones constitutes a terrific and continued stress reaction in the body.

The overuse creates a chemical imbalance, in which white blood cells are destroyed, calcium is drawn out of the bones, cataracts appear, and a multitude of other problems — horror stories, yes, but true!

The use of Prednisone, synthetic but powerful, is now questioned. However, some holistic physicians are administering ACE (Adrenal Cortical Extract), a natural and weaker solution, with measured successes. This seems to bolster a weakened adrenal system, and allergies of all kinds subside.

Proper nutrition can definitely bolster the system to better deal with allergies. Research indicates that many have improved on diets that are lower in fat and concentrated carbohydrates, but ample in protein. The addition of B-complex vitamins brings about improvement. The adrenal glands cannot produce an adequate supply of pantothenic acid in the system. Allergies are reduced with injections of cortisone (dangerous), but they are also relieved with daily supplements of pantothenic acid, for a period of time — from 250-2000 mg. daily! Some can do well with as low as 100 mg. daily, while others may need 3000 mg. to affect a change!

Other nutrients are tantamount! Vitamin B-6 can boost anti-histamine. Magnesium (which "spares" B-6) is helpful and safe. Vitamin C has anti-histamine properties. Since we cannot manufacture vitamin C, as other animals can, it is suggested that we take an equivalent amount — 3,000 to 5,000 mg. daily! Even small amounts have been found to be effective. Vitamin C also protects cell membrane permeability, to keep out foreign proteins. So does vitamin E — 400 IU daily. Vitamin A protects and strengthens the skin and mucous membranes of the respiratory and genitourinary tract. Diets basically low in concentrated or refined carbohydrates, with adrenal support, are recommended for allergies, as well as for hypoglycemia. Both are the result of overworked and/or malfunctioning adrenals. If a biochemical balance is maintained in the body, then the stage is never set up for disease entities of any kind or description!

In summary, feed your adrenals properly. The greater the stress, the more certain nutrients are needed. Consider the use of digestive enzymes, possible adrenal nucleoprotein or DNA, get adequate rest and relaxation, control and/or release your stress, go on a cleansing fast (not just water) such as the Vivonex (insures all valuable nutrients), and by all means, follow a good diet, that is as close to nature as possible — no refined, over- cooked, processed, or preserved foods! This insures the intake of all necessary nutrients, including fiber.

Essential fatty acid intake is essential. Do not mix concentrated carbohydrates with protein or fat — fermentation! For the very same reason, eat all sweets on an empty stomach. Have you even wondered what went wrong when you ate eggs with orange juice? This is it — fermentation! However, natural foods that contain both carbohydrates and protein seem to give no trouble. Restrict salt intake, because it causes potassium to be excreted (stress response).

Avoid alcohol, because it has been scientifically established that it destroys brain and liver cells, as well as increasing permeability of the gut! Do not smoke anything — tobacco or "pot" — they have the potential for destroying vitamin C and are carcinogenic, as they weaken the immune system.

Coffee and tea are habit-forming drugs, because they stimulate the production of adrenalin. Thus, they are deleterious to the central and autonomic nervous systems, especially when over-consumed. There are safe and tasty herbal teas and cereal beverages, available as alternatives. Now, "the ball is in your court!" You can control your allergies!

The first study of its kind with human subjects, conducted by the American Health Foundation in New York City, showed that a lowfat diet boosted immunity — there was a rise in the activity of the natural killer cells by 49 percent. The men in the study followed a diet with less than 25 percent of its calories from fat — for three months. They also consumed 300 fewer calories a day. The lower the fat intake, the higher the health benefits — fewer viral infections, such as "colds," and less cancer![9]

Some tumor cells produce a chemical messenger (called prostaglandin E2) that suppresses the immune system and allows the growth to spread. Reducing total fat intake, particularly the polyunsaturated fats, can also decrease the production of this prostaglandin — improving the immune response. The next chapter is devoted to the sad story on fats!

9.

FAT'S THE ENEMY — NOT CALORIES

Unsaturated Fat — A Wolf In Sheep's Clothing

A severe threat to the immune system is that of free radical damage, brought about by stress, as it increases the basic metabolic functions of the body. Fats are adding fuel to the fire! What are free radicals? They sound like a "left-wing political group," out to get us. Well, in essence, they are!

According to Dr. Harman, Professor of Medicine and Biochemistry at the University of Nebraska College of Medicine, free radicals are produced during normal metabolism by the breakdown of peroxidized (rancid) fat, by whole blood cells, and by radiation. They cause mayhem in our bodies! They have an unpaired electron, are chemically reactive and destructive, and have been found to be causative agents in the aging process and in degenerative diseases.[1]

Oils and fats, particularly *polyunsaturated* fats, become rancid when they are exposed to oxygen or air pollutants, such as nitrogen oxide and ozone. These rancid fats inhibit immune function. As they break down, they release more free radicals, that further impair immune function. Research studies described by Pearson and Shaw verified the harmful effects of rancid fats and the release of free radicals on the immune system — the macrophages were greatly inhibited.[2] Infectious diseases or cancer can be the result. I personally know a lady who, when she learned that her husband had high cholesterol, proceeded to cook and bake everything with massive amounts of unsaturated fats — he died of cancer! Peroxidized lipids are also linked to abnormal blood clotting and atherosclerosis. A healthy immune system can handle some clots and lesions, but a damaged one cannot.

Overweight people are more susceptible to diseases of all kinds. The reason may be that they are full of peroxidized fat! However, we do not go totally rancid, until rigor mortis sets in. This is because living cells produce enzymes, such as superoxide dismutase and catalase, that "scavenge" or break down the free radicals. They deter the auto-oxidation or anti-self reaction occurring in our own bodily "butter," in much the same way as the healthy immune system handles a virus.

Free radicals do originate from the environment; but more often than not, they are produced spontaneously, like fire from the spark plugs in our automobile motors. Scavengers keep us alive! If it were not for them, the unsaturated fats and oils in our cells would mix with the iron and other minerals and become saturated. At that time, we would get solid or plasticize. Interestingly enough, free radical technology is the foundation for the plastic industry! Normal weight people can also be at risk, if they eat significant quantities of polyunsaturated fats. In this case, antioxidant nutrients are a safeguard. Haas says, "You literally can tie the hands of time with my high antioxidant peak performance program."[3]

Let's take a further look at the damage wreaked by free radicals. These sinister substances destroy healthy tissue, including the deoxyribonucleic acid (DNA) or genetic material, that is our memory from the past — and tells us what we are to be. Their unpaired electrons allow them to electrocute our cells!

Some free radicals may actually serve a useful purpose, but too many cause harm, when there are not enough antioxidants to protect our cells. They enter our bodies through food, smoke, air, and water, but are also created through cellular metabolism. Actually, this is the same process through which radiation damages the body. Remember Hiroshima and Nagasaki! The very oxygen we breathe is implicated in the formation of free radicals, but let's not try to live without it! What we can live without is a great deal less fat!

A high-fat diet, especially the unsaturated kind, increases the probability of high free radical potential in the body. High-fat diets are related to slow healing rates. They contribute to the pain of arthritis. Haas believes that "Serum iron accumulates in the membranes and fluids surrounding affected joints and interacts with oxygen to form free radicals." A chain reaction occurs, whereby the protective fluid breaks down; and protein- dissolving enzymes leak into the area. The more damage, the more stiffness and pain.

Haas definitely believes that diet has a great deal to do with the effective treatment of arthritis and related diseases.[4] As people age, so do their joints. High-fat and high-cholesterol diets are disastrous, particularly if they are low in natural antioxidants needed to offset the effects of oxygen and other free radical stimulants. This brings us to the crux of the matter — what are antioxidents, how do they work, and where do we get them?

Perhaps the best antioxidants are in our available foods — vitamin E, C, beta carotene (pro-vitamin A, which is safer than vitamin A, because it is transformed by the body into active Vitamin A, at a safe rate, when it is needed); the B complex vitamins thiamine (B-1); pyrodoxine (B-6); pantothenic acid (B-5); sulfur containing cysteine and methionine, which are amino acids; and BHT (butylated hydroxytoluene). These are all chemicals that combine with free radicals and prevent them from attacking molecules in the body — they oxidize them!

The most susceptible molecules are DNA (deoxyribolucleic acid — our genetic memory), lipids (fats), and proteins. The antioxidants react with the oxidants and oxidize them — the dangerous "buggers" are "zapped!" The greater the psychological and/or physical stress, which brings on heightened metabolism, the heavier the exposure to pollutants, the greater the use of any drugs, and the higher the intake of fats (especially the unsaturates), the greater the need for antioxidants!

To make sure that we understand free radical reaction, let's consider what happens when an apple is cut in half, and the two halves are exposed to air — they turn dark! When butter is not refrigerated and exposed to air, it turns rancid. Wet iron rusts and rubber becomes hard, all because of free radicals, through the process of oxidation. This occurs anytime there is an interaction between matter and oxygen, which is a regular occurrence in our bodies. Antioxidant preparations keep cars from rusting, paper from turning yellow, and leather and rubber products from disintegrating. What about living organisms?

Dr. Harman and his colleagues studied mice. They wanted to find out if mice could live longer if they received antioxidants in their diets. BHT (butylated hydroxytoluene) and vitamin E made up the independent variable. The dependent variable? The mice lived longer. Adding a level one percent or less of total food intake increased their life expectancy by 15 to 44 percent![5]

Dr. Harman also fed mice and rats diets containing fats as high as 20 percent of the weight of the total diet.[6] It is interesting to note that this percentage may be similar to the 42 percent of total caloric fat intake in the typical American diet, in 1977. The U.S. Senate Select Committee on Nutrition and Human Needs, in a report that same year, called *Dietary Goals for the United States* recommended that the amount be reduced to 30 percent total calories from fat.

Since that time, Covert Bailey says, the figure should be reduced to 23 percent,[7] and Pritikin advocated a lowly 10 percent.[8] During the last few years, Americans may have decreased their intake of fats by about 4 percent — a good sign; but we would still be very high! Harman's diets for the mice and rats were high in fat content — the animals which ate the most unsaturated fat, had the highest death rates; and so do humans!

What has happened to many Americans is this: Because of the publicity concerning the fact that *saturated* fats create a buildup of cholesterol that leads to atherosclerosis, they have switched to *unsaturated* fats. Many reputable medical doctors have recommended that vegetable oils that are polyunsaturated be used for cooking. This seemed logical; but many people misunderstood and overdid it, adding oil to everything and deep-fat frying! The natural oils found in raw nuts and seeds, whole grains, avocados, and vegetables would be preferable. Unrefined vegetable oils provide vitamin E, which is a very good antioxidant and provides essential fatty acids. These cannot be produced by the body, but are necessary for normal healthy skin, arteries, blood, glands, and nerves, as well as for breaking down cholesterol.

Linoleic acid is the most commonly found essential fatty acid; but it can be destroyed by processing of oils or by exposure to heat, light, or air. Processing known as hydrogenation not only destroys linoleic acid, but alters some of the components into "unnatural" arrangements. This abnormal type of fatty acid has been shown to collect in the heart. They are products like margarine or Crisco!

Manufacturers turn vegetable oil (which is liquid) into a solid, by adding a chemical known as hydrogen. Brenton explains that the process hydrogenates the oil in varying degrees and changes it into a semi-solid fat.[9] Then it is no different than animal fat, except that there is no linoleic acid, which the body needs so desperately. For this reason, it would be far wiser to consume a small amount of butter than margarine!

In summary, concentrated and man-altered fats, such as modified vegetable oils, should not be used! This finding comes from the research on free radicals and the need for essential fatty acids.

Contrary to public opinion, as the result of massive advertising, a high level of *any kind* of fat is not conducive to good health. The concern with large amounts of unsaturated fats lies with the known fact that they increase oxidation reactions in the cells. This is exactly the same thing that emotional and physiological stress does to the body, through increased metabolic rate! Free radicals are produced during normal metabolism, and a healthy immune system can cope. However, when an already over-stressed body is "put upon" to handle massive numbers of free radicals, as the result of increased oxidation reactions in the cells, we age much faster!

Aging is defined as "the decline of physiological functions which occurs with time, accompanied by a falling probability or survival," according to Pearson and Shaw.[10] Blood cells of older people are "popcorn" shaped or "budded. This is, theoritically, the result of oxidation damage to the cell membrane. When normal cells are exposed to light and oxygen, they do the same thing!

In spite of our preoccupation with fat and overconsumption of it, a fat-soluble vitamin, E, has been found to inhibit the oxidizing effects of unsaturated fats — a "rustproofing" effect. Dr. Harman fed 20 International Units (I.U.) of vitamin E per three and one-half ounces of food to mice whose diets were relatively high in unsaturated fats. It was successful! Breast tumors were significantly reduced, and they were resistant to disease — an improved immune system response.[11]

Although the above findings are very encouraging, it should be emphasized that there was not a complete reversal of the ill effects. It would seem wise to control the amount of fat consumption in the first place, and then to insure an adequate intake of vitamin E, for insurance purposes. According to the latest research findings, daily requirements for children are 3-10 milligrams; men,

10; women, 8; and 10 during pregnancy. In addition to acting as antioxidant against free radicals, these amounts insure red blood cell formation, and prevent the destruction (by oxygen) of vitamin A and essential fatty acids. Vitamin E also has been reported to relieve breast disease (chronic cystic mastitis), leg cramps on walking (intermittent claudation), and protect against the formation in the body of cancer-causing nitrosamines.

Scientists are hoping to find a way to completely stop the production of free radicals by preventing oxidation in the first place, where an organic compound meets with an oxygen molecule. This radical reaction releases a free electron that damages healthy cells — the aging process! As yet, the prevention of oxidation remains in the realm of science fiction. In the meantime, control of fat intake and ingestion of adequate amounts of vitamin E and other known antioxidants would seem prudent.

Hans Selye, told us that simply living uses much energy. He said that stress is the "nonspecific response of the body to any demand made upon it." It is the interaction between a force and the resistance to it. He said further, "Stress is just like energy." So it is with the force of free radical damage to our bodies. Selye also contended that, "If you use too much of your energy in resisting the stresses of life, it's like running your car and keeping the brakes on at the same time. You'll wear out more rapidly." This is the aging process — but accelerated![12]

Another important contributor to this area of study is Dr. Roy L. Walford, who heads the UCLA Research Laboratory for the Study of Immunology and the Aging Process, is a member of the White House Conference on Aging, is chairman of The National Institute on Aging Task Force on Immunology, and is a member of the National Academy of Science Committee on Aging.

In his 1984 book entitled *Maximum Life Span,* he admits that deciding what to take to increase one's chances for survival requires transposing evidence from rodents to humans, which amounts to "informed guesswork."[13] However, that's no different than what happened back in the 1950s when advocates started clamoring for diets high in polyunsaturated fats, to decrease serum cholesterol levels. It was accepted on incomplete evidence. True, it has helped one problem, but aggravated another. It now seems time to go on another "hunch" and reduce the polyunsaturates as well. We have animal research evidence that polyunsaturated fats increase free radicals, that can have a very deleterious effect on the body, including a higher incidence of cancer.

Walford explains that free radicals are like sharks that attack polyunsaturated fats, which in turn yield lipid peroxides. These break down to form "chemicals known as aldehydes, which crosslink proteins, lipids, and DNA," says Walford. His definition states, "A cross-linking agent is a chemical with two reactive groups with which it seizes hold of two otherwise separate molecules or parts of the same molecule and binds them firmly together."[14]

We first learned about the cross-linking theory from those who tanned hides! Normal metabolism turns out cross-linkers, perhaps "cross-clinkers," which cause rigidity and immobilization of our cells and connective tissue. The symptoms are similar to those of the autoimmune collagen diseases or rheumatoid arthritis. These diseases could be the result of this cross-linking process. At any rate, as a sufferer of this very same malady, I do many times feel as if I were being cross-linked!

The very oxygen we breathe is a very poisonous gas and does trigger the response of producing free radicals. Outer terrestrial beings from methane planets would choke and die from the stuff, yet we live and fight for it! How do we take it? Well, life on earth has been programmed with certain enzymes to destroy the "little devils." Some of these by name are superoxide dismatase (SOD), catalase, and glutathione peroxidase, which are free radical "scavengers," produced naturally in the body. The species with longer life-spans have more scavengers, but these can be depleted through physical abuse — stress! Once damage occurs, it's irreparable. That's why we are many times exhorted to learn to "live with it," even if we are a bit "stiffer" in the morning and a bit "foggier" in the afternoon!

The antioxidants (such as vitamin E, selenium, vitamin C, and BHT) added to the diet can help in the battle; but there's not enough research yet to recommend megadoses, according to Walford. He says, extrapolating from animal research findings, that adequate quantities would be 600 I.U. of vitamin E, 160 micrograms of selenium, 250 milligrams of BHT, 300 milligrams of cysteine, 120 milligrams of methionine, 600 milligrams of ascorbyl palmitate, 1000 milligrams of vitamin C, and 300 milligrams of bioflavinoids.[15]

The first six are to be taken before eating and the last two after or between meals. Vitamin C is an acid, so it should not be taken on a completely empty stomach. Since it is water-soluble, it is rapidly excreted. For this reason, it should be taken at regular intervals.

However, Walford points out that the only sure way to control free radical damage and thus extend the maximum life span is through caloric undernutrition without malnutrition. From 1500- 2000 calories per day should do the job, but any reduction would have to be done gradually, in order to allow the body time to metabolically adapt and prevent "shock" damage. The rule is not to lose more than one-half to one pound per month. Lose 20-25 percent of body weight over four to six years to increase life span![16]

So, if I weigh 150 pounds and want to lose 20 of this, I should do it over a period of about one and one-half years. Of course, that's not easy for those of us who want what we want when we want it — preferably now!

Nonetheless, rapid weight loss would not increase my life span — quite the contrary! To be successful in this program, the foods must be extremely high in nutrition — no empty calories of sugar, honey, alcohol, and non-essential fat. Incidentally, there is some indication that the FDA may approve a sugar that tastes sweet and a synthetic oil, neither of which can be digested or absorbed. What a way to "eat your cake and not have it too!" We really have no idea what the consequences of this might be!

It may seem paradoxical that underweight people actually do have shorter life spans than the slightly overweight. This can be explained by the fact that people can be underweight, because they are not eating the right things. On the everyday careless diet of the typical American, many overeat in order to get the necessary nutrients — they store too much and become fat! In this case, overnutrition would be better than malnutrition. Undernutrition without malnutrition is a far better choice for longevity.

To lose weight too rapidly is not good, because it does not allow for metabolic adaptation, and malnutrition can occur. Total fasting also can be detrimental, but occasionally not eating, particularly when one does not feel well, does no harm. Skipping meals or intermittent fasting can actually create a natural "high."

As a psychologist, I can tell you that this could be used as a reward for controlling food intake — a behavior modification technique that could bring about changes in life-style. The pleasure of physical well-being and clearer thought would be very rewarding, in my mind! Hesoid, an ancient Greek poet, wrote, "Fools not to know that half exceeds the whole, How blest the sparing meal and temperate bowl."

For people in mid-life (age 30-40), fat content should be reduced to even less than 10-15 percent, protein 20-25 percent (and less as the person gets older), leaving the rest of the percentage to complex carbohydrates that should range from 60-70 percent or more. Fat content can go as low as two to five percent, before any essential fatty acid deficiency would occur. A fairly safe rule of thumb is not to use over two tablespoons of fat per day, if we wish to stay under 30 percent fat; less than one tablespoon, for 15 percent fat, and only one teaspoon of fat, such as safflower oil, for meeting the essential fatty acid requirement of two to five percent fat.

At this point, each individual needs to use his or her own judgment; but where there is a steady supply of available food, massive storage of it in the body is not necessary for survival. Even if it were, there would always be the "trade-off" to be considered. The cost of carrying it around is formidable! After age 50, the protein content should be reduced to 10-15 percent. "Oldsters" might as well join the "rabbit brigade," because the optimum diet should be made up of over 80 percent complex carbohydrates.

This wonderful diet of Walford's must be low in sodium — no added salt in cooking or at the table![17] The great creator built us to use about 250 milligrams, which is equivalent to about one-twentieth of a teaspoon — just a mere pinch! We're actually consuming twenty times this amount. For instance, Walford points out that eight ounces of pork and beans can contain almost 1000 milligrams of sodium; a hamburger, over 1500; one tablespoon of salad dressing, over 300; one ounce of low fat cottage cheese, 400; a dill pickle, over 1100; tuna, over 600; a cheese sandwich, over 1500.[18] No wonder, one in every six Americans has hypertension! We already know that stress causes the body to retain salt — our diet is insult added to injury!

Let's talk about refined sugar for a moment. The average American consumes a whopping 128 pounds of sugar per year, where none is needed! A twelve-ounce can of Coca-Cola has nine teaspoons of sugar. It's added to peanut butter, tomato sauce, salad dressing, and chili — anything processed! Excess sugar can be stored as fat! We are presented with a "synthetic feast of prefabricated foods." This could be the result of more than 60 food lobbyists in Washington, D.C.

One example given for cutting down on consumption of meat, with its fat content, is to eat beans and rice together — the beans supply the essential amino acid called lysine and the rice supplies another called methionine. In fact, all grains (such as rice, oats, wheat, and corn) balance with legumes (beans), lentils, and peas to provide a nearly complete protein source. Milk and soybeans are the only two foods which contain a nearly balanced protein source, with the exception of meat. The fat content in all animal source foods causes the problems. My Adventist friends have a greater longevity than my "meat-eating" family, but so do Mormons, and they eat meat! Obviously, other variables are involved.

Well, what remains for the future is mostly fantasy for everyone; but I'm counting on life-extension brought about by calorie restriction — particularly fat! We know it works impressively and consistently. Cross-linking slows down, and free radicals are halted. I predict that we'll know a great deal more by the year 2000. In the meantime, I'm going to make every effort to have less stress with less fat!

Percentages of Calories From Fat

In a Special Supplement to *The Spokesman-Review Spokane Chronicle*, Sunday, March 11, 1990, these facts were presented:

> 1) Only 3 percent of the fat you eat is used by your body in the process of digestion, transport, and storage,
>
> 2) That which isn't converted to energy by strenuous exercise heads for your hips, and

3) Fat also is associated with heart disease, stroke, hypertension, diabetes and some cancers.[19]

The fat we eat is the fat we wear! In fact, the fatty tissue in the body looks like the fat from which it came. Autopsies have shown that the fat of an Eskimo resembles the fat of a whale, the fat of a Mediterranean looks like olive oil, and the fat of the typical American looks like that of cows, pigs, and chickens! Studies confirm that one can become fat on 1500 calories a day, if half of those calories are fat. Since we do consume an average of 42 percent of our calories from fat, it's easy to see why we have such a problem. In fact, the consumption of ice cream has doubled and that of cakes and cookies has gone up 56 percent.

Old fashioned dieting is out — the practice encourages the production of more fat! Remember the famine adaptation syndrome? The body actually stores more fat to prepare for an emergency and slows down its metabolism, at the same time, to conserve energy! Now, it is being explained that the only way to go is to combine the reduction of fat with moderate exercise. Unfortunately, we are consuming 42 percent of our calories from fat, while the medical profession is recommending 30 percent. However, the truth of the matter is that our bodies require less than ten percent!

Dr. Robert Stark, in his book, *Controlling Fat For Life*, says that "Unless a person is starving, it's impossible not to get enough fat." He states that the fat content of foods, as a percent of total calories, is a far more useful measure than grams of fat, as a percent of the food's total serving weight.[20]

For example, low-fat milk is a seemingly low 2 percent fat by weight, which accounts for the massive consumption of it by people who think that they are doing the right thing! However, its percentage of calories from fat is 35! By comparison, the percentage of calories from fat in non-fat milk is only 2 — incredible, but true. All fats and oils provide 100 percent of their calories from fat: mayonnaise - 99.8 percent; tartar sauce - 95 percent; bacon - 94 percent; cream cheese - 90 percent; and peanut butter - 75 percent.

In addition to these, avocados are 88 percent fat, olives are 96 percent fat, and both margarine and butter are 100 percent fat!

Fortunately, the more fat one resists, the easier it becomes! When one eats a high-carbohydrate, high fiber diet that's low in fat, no conscious effort is necessary — it becomes automatic! Our tastes change. For example, whole milk is no longer acceptable to our taste buds. What a way to cut calories!

Fat Calories in Common Foods

Less than 10 percent:

Skim milk, dry cereal, uncreamed cottage cheese, dried beans and peas, baked or broiled potatoes, most breads, fruits and vegetables (except avocados and olives), egg whites, water-packed tuna, angel food cake, pretzels.

10 to 20 percent:

Roasted chicken (white meat, no skin), broiled fish, sherbet.

20 to 30 percent:

Creamed cottage cheese, granola, 2 percent milk, low-fat yogurt, most cookies, white and yellow cake (no icing), breaded and fried seafood, broiled chicken with skin, fruit pie, brownies.

40 to 50 percent:

Chocolate cake, fried chicken, regular ice cream, donuts, waffles, pecan pie, whole milk, canned salmon, whole milk yogurt, tortilla chips.

50 to 65 percent:

Eggs, potato chips, cheesecake, most candy bars, broiled beef loin.

65 to 80 percent:

Cheese, cold cuts, dry roasted peanuts, ham, bacon, peanut butter, pork chops, cashews, sunflower seeds.

80 to 90 percent:

Sausages, salad dressing, cream cheese, sour and light cream, hot dogs.

More than 90 percent:

Mayonnaise, butter, margarine, oil, shortening, salt pork.

It is very important to know how to calculate your fat/calorie ratio, because food labels usually do not provide this information. The standard formula for doing this is: Grams of fat (found on ingredient list) X 9 = fat calories. Fat calories divided by total calories X 100 = percentage of fat. This should help clear up the common misunderstanding that exists.

For example, a food item that claims to be 98 percent fat-free is still 2 percent fat by weight. Remember that fat contains more than twice the calories for its weight than does either protein or carbohydrates.

An excellent guide for controlling fat content in foods, as well as providing extensive information concerning the nutritive value of virtually all foods, is *Nutritive Value of Foods* issued by Cooperative Extension, College of Agriculture and Home Economics, Washington State University, Pullman, Washington in April of 1989.[21] I consider this publication, or one of its kind, to be an absolute must for anyone who's taking this matter seriously! (See Appendix)

The first thing that one needs to do is to determine the RDA for calories needed per day; then determine the amount of fat (in grams) that provides 10, 20, or 30 percent of those calories, and then stay within that limit!

For example, if you are consuming 1,500 calories per day, the 30 percent limit of grams of fat places you at 50; 2,000 calories - 67 grams of fat; 2,500 calories - 83 grams of fat; and 3,000 calories - 100 grams of fat.

In other words, it is the total caloric intake and the number of allowable grams of fat, according to your level of fat consumption, that you have selected as being right for you. There is more and more indication that nobody needs more than 10 percent fat in his or her diet, unless of course, the person is doing extremely strenuous physical labor. Even then, increasing the total caloric intake might be a better way to go.

Subsequently, if one needs an 1,800 maintenance diet and desires to stay within the 10 percent allowance for fat, then 20 grams of fat per day would be the maximum! This is actually simple to accomplish, if one eats plenty of unrefined carbohydrates and adequate protein. If you get your protein from vegetable or animal source, you get enough fat! For this same 1,800 calorie food plan, the RDA for protein is 44 grams, for a female over 50 years of age and weighing 120 pounds. I hope that I haven't confused you with numbers — the very best thing to do is to refer to a guide for the nutritive value of foods — determine what is right for you!

Weight Reduction

Basically, what one needs to do in order to lose unwanted weight is to reduce caloric intake (primarily fats), and engage in moderate exercise. First, let's take a look at caloric reduction.

Think of that same example (given earlier) of the female over 50 years of age, who weighs 120 pounds — she needs 1,800 calories per day, with 10 percent fat of 20 grams, and 44 grams of protein. If, however, this same woman has gained, say 20-50 pounds over the course of the last decade or two, "creeping obesity," then, by all means, she should consider caloric reduction! Generally speaking, the less calories one consumes, the more weight is lost. However, this process requires the use of good judgment and discretion. One cannot proceed too rapidly for the following reasons.

First of all, the body can only lose 2-4 pounds per week, without sacrificing lean body mass or muscle. With a stringent diet, the amount lost during the first week may be 70 percent water! When one dramatically cuts calories, or goes too long without eating at all, the body responds by slowing down its metabolism by as much as 15 percent, in just a few days — famine adaptation. In this survival mode, the body resists burning fat tissue, because it's perceived as potential fuel. One also feels tired and lethargic — the body's way of conserving for a potential famine (no available food). If one is "foolhardy" and insists on starving one's self, then lean body mass is lost — health deteriorates as the body is damaged!

When one loses weight in this drastic manner, one still stays in the survival mode. That is, the body says, "I've got to keep saving for bad times ahead!" If you try to eat normally, the fat comes right back on, faster than ever before! That's because you lost fat, not fat cells — they just fill right back up again! It is for this very same reason that total fasting is dangerous — it brings about the "shock" reaction of stress in full force! It is possible, but much more difficult, to rebuild muscle (lean mass) than fat. Therefore, in this situation, one gains more fat than lean mass (muscle). This is why "chronic" dieters wind up heavier than before the first diet

Another sensible way to break this vicious cycle is to shift the fat-to-muscle ratio through exercise. Weight-loss programs should include slow weight loss, modified eating habits, and exercise. Not always, but sometimes a support group or counseling is necessary. Anyway, the ultimate goal should be to balance "intake" with "outgo" of energy units, in such a way as to eliminate the body's instinct to store unnecessary fat. This can be achieved as "Grandma" said: "Eat right, get plenty of rest, and exercise" — stress control!

Therefore, in order for the "over-fifty lady" to lose the 20-50 pounds which crept up on her, she needs to likewise do so gradually, over a period of no less than 5 to 10 weeks, for every 20 pounds of desired loss — the same applies for anyone! I would say that a good rule of thumb is not to go below 800 calories per day or go without eating for over 18 hours (don't skip breakfast), to prevent the body from going into the conservative survival mode (famine adaptation).

For over-all stress prevention, it would be better not to consume less than 1200 calories per day — the time lost is safety gained! Since there is variation from one individual to another in BMR (basic metabolic rate), the point at which one starts to become lethargic with loss of energy is the point in time that one should "up the calories" — immediately, but moderately! "Listen" to your body — it can tell you much!

With a short trial period, one should be able to determine the appropriate level of caloric intake to stay in the "burning mode" — weight loss.

In summary, high fat is high risk! We have known for some time that fatty food is a causative agent in heart disease, and that it is the major producer of body fat. We now realize that fatty food is also associated with both the cause and growth of cancer. These cancers may be of the colon, rectum, prostate, or breast. Some cancers are caused or initiated by fat, and others seem to feed on it. Whether it's saturated, monosaturated, polyunsaturated, or cholesterol, *it's the total fat intake that's the major factor*. High fat diets are high-calorie diets. The result is weight gain, if not accompanied with sufficient exercise — and a greater probability of illnesses of every description. To eat fewer high-fat foods is the only way to reduce fat intake.

Fat should account for 30 percent or less of the total daily calories. It now seems wise to go much less than the 30 percent! We have seen that as little as one teaspoon a day can supply the essential fatty acids. However, dairy products, meat, nuts, and seeds supply vital nutrients and need not be totally eliminated.

For example, if you consume 2,000 calories a day, and 40 percent of them are from fat, you can cut your fat intake to 30 by lowering your diet by 200 calories, which is 22 grams of fat — the amount contained in a tablespoon of butter or mayonnaise. Only lean meat should be served, in two- to three-ounce portions with all visible fat trimmed off. Herbs and spices can flavor meats and vegetables in place of fat.

Do not fry foods — steam, poach, broil, microwave, bake, or stir-fry. Vegetable cooking sprays should replace fat, if you insist on frying your food. Eliminate fatty sauces and gravies. Fruit and low-fat frozen or unfrozen yogurt make acceptable and enjoyable desserts. A nice trim figure, with vim, vigor, and vitality, is the reward — one would not choose to ever be fat again!

10.
THE BALANCED DIET — STRESS CONTROL

Which Foods and Why

In order to get all the nutrients your body needs, it is necessary to eat many different foods each day — how you feel and function is closely related to what you eat. Weight Watchers provide the following information to help us learn how to plan a balanced diet; equally important whether we are losing weight or keeping it off:[1]

Protein

found in fish, poultry, lean meat, eggs, cheese, milk, legumes, and peanut butter helps build and repair all body tissue, assists in forming antibodies that fight infection, and supplies energy.

Carbohydrates

found in whole grains, breads, cereals, legumes, pasta, rice, vegetables (including starchy vegetables), and fruits supply the most efficient source of energy and adds fiber to the diet.

Fats

found in vegetable oils, margarine, and mayonnaise supply essential fatty acids and carry fat-soluble vitamins.

Vitamin A

found in sweet potatoes, carrots, pumpkin, spinach, greens, winter squash, broccoli, cantaloupe, apricots, peaches, milk, and liver helps keep the skin clear and smooth, helps keep mucous membranes and inner linings of the body healthy and resistant to infection, and is important for good vision and helps eyes adjust to dim light.

Vitamin C (Ascorbic Acid)

found in oranges, grapefruit, strawberries, cantaloupe, kiwi fruit, papaya, mango, honeydew, green peppers, brussels sprouts, broccoli, potatoes, tomato juice, and mixed vegetable juice gives strength to body tissues, especially walls of blood vessels and gums, helps in formation of bones and teeth, promotes healing of wounds, and enhances the absorption of iron.

Thiamine (B1)

found in lean meat (especially pork), liver, lima beans, grains, peas, pasta, breads, and soybeans helps body cells convert carbohydrates into energy, is important in maintaining normal appetite and good digestion, and helps keep nervous system and gastrointestinal tract functioning well.

Riboflavin (B2)

found in milk, yogurt, cheese, poultry, fish, liver, kidneys, grains, cereals, breads, and pasta assists cells in using oxygen, is important for healthy eyes and good vision, helps keep skin smooth and healthy, and maintains normal function of nervous system.

Niacin

found in grains, breads, cereals, peanut butter, fish, poultry, lean meat, liver, and kidney aids in normal growth and development and maintains normal function of nervous system and gastrointestinal tract.

Calcium

found in milk, cheese, yogurt, salmon with bones, sardines with bones, spinach, and broccoli aids in the formation and maintenance of strong bones and teeth, and permits healthy nerve functioning and normal blood clotting.

Iron

iron found in lean meat, poultry, clams, shrimp, liver, tofu, legumes, grains, eggs, lima beans, dried fruit, and leafy green vegetables helps build red blood cells that carry oxygen from lungs to all parts of the body, helps body cells change food into energy, and increases resistance to infection.

Fiber

found in bran products, whole grains, fruits, legumes, and vegetables (including starchy vegetables) aids elimination, may lower blood cholesterol levels, and may control blood glucose levels.

Food Groups

An excellent food guide comes from MineraLab, Inc., 3501 Breakwater Ave., Hayward, CA 94545.[2] It is a modification of the traditional basic four group guide, which has long been used to help plan adequate diets. However, recent research indicates that menus planned from the simplistic basic four are inadequate, and that more than half of the nutrients do not meet even RDA. Only foods that contribute positively to adequate diets are tabulated in this food guide. For example, whole grain bread is included, but white bread is not, because it is not a good nutrient source. The eight groups of foods from which all the necessary nutrients can be obtained are as follows:

1) Dairy products

One serving equals one cup milk, yogurt, buttermilk, kefir, cottage cheese, etc.; two ounces cheese or cream cheese. If available, certified raw, unpasteurized dairy products are preferable to pasteurized, homogenized types. Unprocessed, natural cheeses (Jack, Gouda, etc.) should be used instead of processed, chemicalized varieties (American, Velveeta, etc.). Skim milk cheeses may be a preferable alternative.

2) *Animal source protein*

One serving equals three ounces meat, fish, or poultry, including liver or other organ meats. Lean varieties of meat are preferable and visible fat should be trimmed. Processed or packaged meats (hot dogs, salami, lunchmeat) contain much fat and chemicals and should be avoided. Two eggs can substitute for one serving in this group.

3) *Legumes and Nuts*

One serving equals one ounce nuts or seeds, ¾ cup cooked legumes (dry beans, lentils, split peas, etc.), ¾ cup tofu, or two tablespoons nut butter. Nuts and seeds should be whole, fresh unsalted varieties such as raw sunflower or pumpkin seeds, sesame seeds, raw almonds, fresh walnuts, etc. Cracked nuts or broken pieces are often rancid and should not be purchased. Peanut butter should be the nonhydrogenated types, without additives. It is often advisable to pour off the excess oil from the top of nut butters, so as to obtain a lower fat content.

4) *Vitamin C-rich fruits and vegetables*

One serving equals one orange, grapefruit, or other citrus fruit; one cup citrus juice; one-half papaya or cantaloupe; one cup strawberries; ½ - ¾ cup broccoli or sweet pepper. Other fruits and vegetables contain vitamin C (tomatoes, potatoes, asparagus, etc.), but in lesser quantities.

5) *Dark-green vegetables and fruits*

One serving equals 3/4 cup cooked leafy greens or one cup raw; ½ - ¾ cup carrots, squash, sweet potato, asparagus; three apricots or one peach; or, other deep green or orange colored varieties. Foods in this group are rich in vitamin A, folic acid, and magnesium.

6) *Other fruits and vegetables*

One serving equals one apple, banana, pear, etc.; ¾ - 1 cup berries, grapes, cherries, or other fruit; ½ cup other vegetable, such as cabbage, green beans, eggplant, beets; fresh fruits and vegetables are preferable to frozen types and canned varieties should be avoided.

7) *Whole grain cereal products*

One serving equals ¾ cup whole grain cereal or pasta; one slice whole grain bread; two corn tortillas; 6-8 whole grain crackers; one ounce dry whole grain cereal; or, two tablespoons wheat germ. Only whole grain products are credited; enriched, refined grain products do not qualify, as they are inadequate in many nutrients and would detract, rather than contribute, to optimum health. Brown rice, 100% whole wheat and rye products, yellow corn meal products, buckwheat, millet, and oats are examples to choose from. Whole grain flours should be freshly ground and used quickly, to maintain freshness. Only freshly milled wheat germ should be used, as it quickly turns rancid only seven days after milling. Unfortunately, most commercial types are not suitable.

One serving equals one tablespoon unrefined vegetable oil or butter. Unrefined oils provide vitamin E and essential fatty acids. Oils, if used, should be protected from light (dark bottles), air, and heat, before and after purchase. Additional servings from the nut and seed group can substitute for this category. It is preferable to avoid the concentrated fats and oils, such as vegetable oils, and obtain fatty acids from the nut and seed group instead.

The recommended adequate number of daily servings for food groups need to be adjusted to accommodate special dietary needs. For instance, children, teens, and pregnant or lactating women should increase dairy consumption by one to two servings or obtain adequate protein and calcium from alternative sources. For example, an active over-fifty female, who is 5'2" and who weighs 130 pounds, needs a maintenance diet of about 1700 calories. In order to meet the caloric requirements, as well as basic nutritional needs, she should increase the consumption of dairy products to 2 servings, the animal source protein foods to 2 servings, the legumes and nuts to 2 servings, the other fruits and vegetables to 2 servings, and whole grain cereals products to 4 servings. This would constitute a completely balanced diet, with absolutely everything needed, and no more!

If, however, this same over-fifty female weighs 157 pounds, 27 pounds over her desired weight, then she should reduce her caloric intake by approximately 500 (preferably fat calories) per day and stay active. This should constitute a loss of 1/2 to 2 pounds per week or the 27 pounds in about 15 weeks! She should also remember not to go over 18 hours without eating or go under a minimum of 1200 calories per day!

A Reminder About Sugar

Please remember that sugar and starch are carbohydrates that are used by the body as fuel. They also can be used with the amino acid, tryptophan, to bring about the relaxation response. However, in excess consumption, they are implicated in low and high blood sugar and in hypoactivity, as well as hyperactivity — the "roller-coaster" effect (the 20-minute high and the two-hour crash)!

If consumed in calorically dense forms, such as beer or dried fruits, they add weight to your torso! However, when consumed in natural, complex carbohydrates, the calories are low, and the fat content is very low. Athletes can pump up their metabolism by 10 percent for as long as two or three hours with starches and the sugar in fruit. Sugar is not a prime factor in unwanted fat.

The reason for associating sugar and starch consumption with dangerous weight gain is the fact that they are usually consumed with fat, such as in pastries, candies, pies, cakes, and on and on! The sugars in these combination foods are burned up, but the fat is stored — it does nothing for your energy level, but increases your weight! At the same time, you will probably suffer indigestion and "sour stomach," because the fast digesting carbohydrates are caught up and trapped by the slow digesting fat which causes fermentation and gas. Malabsorption problems may also occur, as discussed earlier. It is worth repeating that you can become obese on just 1,500 calories a day, if half of those calories come from fat! Only 3 percent of fat intake is used by the body as fuel — the rest is potential flab!

Although sugar and starch are not exactly innocent in the "battle of the bulge," neither are they the true villains. They do represent potential danger, but neither is a prime contributor to body fat. Sugar and starch are victims, primarily, through "guilt by association," say the experts. Watch out for that piece of fudge — your body would burn the sugar, but the fat would hang around — the same goes for sauce-laden pastas! Please don't laugh now, but you might try substituting raw or steamed "veggies" — such as broccoli, spinach, brussel sprouts, lima beans, peas, asparagus, artichokes, cauliflower, sweet potatoes, or carrots — the ten most healthful vegetables, in order! You could even use a little sugar to improve the flavor, if that is what it would take! Be a Jack Sprat — he could eat no fat!

The Grand Finale

Susan E. Gebhardt and Ruth Matthews, in their Nutritive Value of Foods, have tabulated the total information necessary to plan nutritionally adequate diets by nutritionists, dieticians, physicians, and consumers like you and me! With their "blessings," you can find a copy of it in the Appendix.

11.

CONCLUSIONS & IMPLICATIONS

Well, hopefully, I have taken you through the basic considerations of better health through stress control, with an emphasis on an improved understanding of exercise, relaxation, and nutrition. I have shown you how stress can *predispose* us, but, at the same time, how it need not predestine our future. There are ways to cope — recognition comes first! Next, we saw how stress can actually work for us — *eustress*. Basic relaxation, through biokinesiology, was an eye-opener! We can now see how to have a healthier immune system with fewer allergies and sensitivities.

It should be clear that underlying most of our problems may be the basic problem of poor nutrition — not enough "good input" for the necessary "energy output!" Many of us can now say "scat" to fat! We have the where-with-all to balance our diets and control the "stress monster." We can avoid contributing to the nation's $33 billion weight-loss industry, with its exploitation of the wallets — and health — of millions of overweight Americans. If you take seriously the findings which I have reported to you, you will be able to sensibly and safely control your weight without getting "sucked-in" to the recent and zealous marketing of various formula products — you will not succumb to the risk of possible complications and/or fatalities.

I realize that, as the old saying goes, "No good deed goes unpunished." Marilyn vos Savant stated in the March 18, 1990 *Parade Magazine*, that she finds that saying more accurate than inaccurate. She says, "There seems to be little in life that someone, somewhere, cannot and does not condemn. The courageous criticize the bad; the cowardly criticize the good."[1] My writing may not be perfect, but it is my sincere hope that there are, out there, somewhere, enough concerned and/or sincere individuals to see the "good," maximize the "good," and at the same time critique any possible "bad" for future improvement. May there be more courageous souls than cowards! I would like to end with this quote from Sharon Timmons, a former student in one of my Psychology of Adjustment classes, at Spokane Falls Community college:

What This Class has Meant to Me

To say this class has changed my life is a great deal like saying Albert Einstein was "pretty smart." It would be a profound understatement, if ever there was one! And it wasn't simply MY life that was changed; my family was able to benefit immensely, as well. To elaborate on all the many changes would take forever, but I would like to highlight some of the more vital changes that have affected me, my husband, and our children.

For as long as I can remember, it seems as though I've been weak, tired, irritable, and out-of-sorts with the entire world — in short, sick, and miserable. After Dr. Culton introduced me to biokinesiology, the initial results were slightly less than astounding! I was admittedly skeptical, at first, but that changed quickly — very quickly! I found myself able to relax, feel refreshed, and experience an abundance of energy — without taking a single pill! And the feeling lasted, without diminishing, except for common, ordinary, garden-variety FATIGUE that comes at the end of the day: after going to school, driving 120 miles round trip, taking care of 4 young children, doing homework, and sharing life with a very helpful, wonderful man. If it hadn't happened to me first-hand, I never would have believed it was possible.

I wasn't the only member of my family to be helped by this wonderful relaxation and rejuvenating exercise — my husband has been helped immeasurably, as well. He has suffered from both petit mal and grand mal epilepsy, since he was 14 years of age. It resulted from a serious head injury, and has never been completely controlled. He has always had seizures — some of them very, very severe. After learning biokinesiology and applying it to our lives here at home, we have gained a measure of control over his seizures, for the very first time in 10 years! Since I've known my husband, this is the FIRST TIME the seizures haven't controlled HIM!

Visual imagery and biokinesiology aren't the only tools we've acquired, to change our lives. We've also acquired a very healthy respect for sane, healthful, intelligent nutrition. We have, to the best of our ability, vastly reduced our intake of salt and fat, and virtually eliminated processed sugars and simple carbohydrates from our diet. It's amazing how cleaning all that sticky sludge out of your system tones your body and sharpens your brain!

Our children have benefitted immensely, as well. We have had a variety of problems with our four girls — endless ear infections, colds, flu, behavior problems, and, with our second, slight obesity. These have all but disappeared since changing our diet for the better. Except for our 7-year-old's slight chubbiness, the changes are miraculous.

Even our 8-year-old, who is retarded, has improved enormously. She has even learned to read, which, for her, is the grandest miracle of all! I can't believe it's a mere coincidence that it happened 2 short months after altering our diet! This little girl believes so whole-heartedly that sugar is bad for her that she WILL NOT eat it, period! Even when her beloved grandmother offered her a piece of candy, she refused. She said "It's bad, Nanny; it's sugar." Guess who ELSE is changing the way she eats now? 'From the mouths of babes,' huh?

My one deep regret concerning this class is that it's ending. It seems like we've only just started, and now it's already over, unfortunately. That's the one thing about it I would change: It's ending far, far too soon.

You've been my mentor and you've been my friend; and I'm going to miss you a great deal, Dr. Sarah A. Culton. I'm also going to miss our conversations and the fun we had. I'll always remember the special time we had in this class, and the things you taught me. Thank you for everything — from all of us. This family will always owe you an enormous debt, for all you've done for us.[2]

Appendix
NUTRITIVE VALUE OF FOODS

A table of the nutritive values for household measures comprises the greater part of this appendix. This will prove to be a great asset in learning more about nutrition and food. This knowledge will help you attain a proper diet which is, it is worth repeating, one key to reducing stress in your life.

Nutritive Value of Foods

A glass of milk...a slice of cooked meat...an apple...a slice of bread...What food values does each contain? How much cooked meat will a pound of raw meat yield? How much daily protein is recommended for a healthy 14-year-old boy?

Ready answers to questions like these are helpful to homemakers who need the information to plan nutritionally adequate diets and to nutritionists, dietitians, physicians, and other consumers.

The answers will be found in the tables in this publication.

Explanation of the Tables

Some helpful volume and weight equivalents are shown in table 1.

Table 1.— Equivalents by Volume and Weight

Volume

Level measure	Equivalent
1 gallon	4 quarts
(3.786 liters; 3,786 milliliters)	
1 quart	4 cups
(0.946 liter; 946 milliliters)	2 pints
1 cup	8 fluid ounces
(237 milliliters)	1/2 pint
	16 tablespoons
2 tablespoons	1 fluid ounce
(30 milliliters)	
1 tablespoon	3 teaspoons
(15 milliliters)	

Weight

Avoirdupois weight	Equivalent
1 pound (16 ounces)	453.6 grams
1 ounce	28.35 grams
3-1/2 ounces	100 grams

Nutritive Value of Foods (Table 2)

Table 2 shows the nutritive values of 908 common foods.

Foods listed.—Foods are grouped under the following main headings:

    Beverages
    Dairy products
    Eggs
    Fats and oils
    Fish and shellfish
    Fruits and fruit juices
    Grain products
    Legumes, nuts, and seeds
    Meat and meat products
    Mixed dishes and fast foods
    Poultry and poultry products
    Soups, sauces, and gravies
    Sugars and sweets
    Vegetables and vegetable products
    Miscellaneous items

Most of the foods listed are in ready-to-eat form. Some are basic products widely used in food preparation, such as flour, fat, and cornmeal.

The approximate measure shown for each food is in cups, ounces, pounds, some other well-known unit, or a piece of a certain size. The measures shown do not necessarily represent a serving, but the unit given may be used to calculate a variety of serving sizes. For example, values are given for 1 cup of applesauce. If a serving is 1/2 cup, divide the values by 2 or multiply by 0.5; for a 2/3 cup serving multiply values by 0.67. The cup measure refers to the standard measuring cup of 8 fluid ounces. The ounce is one-sixteenth of a pound avoirdupois, unless "fluid ounce" is indicated. The weight of a fluid ounce varies according to the food measured. If the household measure of a food is listed as 1 ounce, the nutrients are based on a weight of 28.35 grams, although only 28 grams is shown in the table. All other measures are based on the actual weight shown.

The weight in grams for an approximate measure of each food is shown. The weight applies to only the edible portion of the food, such as the banana pulp without the peel. For fruits and vegetables, whenever possible a market unit and its weight are given in the food description to indicate the weight of an item as purchased including the inedible parts that will be removed.

Food values.—Table 2 also shows values for water; food energy; protein; fat; total saturated, mono-unsaturated, and polyunsaturated fatty acids; cholesterol; carbohydrate; five minerals (calcium, phosphorus, iron, potassium, and sodium); and five vitamins (vitamin A, thiamin, riboflavin, niacin, and ascorbic acid or vitamin C). Water content is included because the percentage of moisture present is needed for identification and comparison of many food items. Values are in grams or milligrams except for food energy and vitamin A.

Food energy is reported in calories. The calorie is the unit of measurement of the energy furnished the body by protein, fat, and carbohydrate. Alcohol also contributes to the calorie content of alcoholic beverages. Calorie values have been rounded to the nearest 5 calories. Vitamin A is reported in two different units: International Units (IU), used in the past for expressing vitamin A activity, and Retinol Equivalents (RE), the units currently used by the Food and Nutrition Board for expressing the Recommended Daily Dietary Allowances for vitamin A. International Units are rounded to the nearest 10 IU.

Nutrient data are from revised sections 1 through 12 of Agriculture Handbook No. 8. Values for foods not in the published AH-8 sections have been reviewed and updated as necessary using information currently available in the National Nutrient Data Bank. Most differences in this bulletin from values in the published sections of AH-8 are due to rounding.

Values for food energy (calories) and nutrients shown in table 2 are the amounts present in the part of the item that is customarily eaten—corn without cob, meat without bone, peaches without skin, European-type grapes without seeds. If additional parts are eaten—the peach skin, for example—amounts of some nutrients obtained will be somewhat greater than those shown.

Thiamin, riboflavin, niacin, and iron values in enriched white flours, white bread and rolls, cornmeals, pastas, farina, and rice are based on the current enrichment levels established for those products by the Food and Drug Administration. (Enrichment levels for riboflavin in rice have not been put into effect and are not used in table 2.) Enriched flour is used in most home-prepared and commercially prepared baked goods.

Niacin values are for preformed niacin occurring naturally in foods. The values do not include additional niacin that may be formed in the body from tryptophan, an essential amino acid in the protein of most foods. Among the better sources of tryptophan are milk, meats, eggs, legumes, and nuts.

Values for many prepared items have been calculated from the ingredients in typical recipes. Examples are biscuits, corn muffins, macaroni and cheese, custard, and many dessert-type items. Adjustments were made for nutrient losses during cooking.

Values for toast and cooked vegetables are without fat added, either during preparation or at the table. Values for cooked vegetables, dry beans, pasta, noodles, rice, meat, poultry, and fish are without salt added. Cutting or shredding vegetables may destroy a portion of some vitamins, especially ascorbic acid. Since such losses are variable, no deduction has been made.

The mineral contribution of water was not considered for coffee, tea, soups, sauces, or concentrated fruit juices prepared with water. Sweetened items contain sugar unless identified as artifically sweetened.

Several manufactured items—including some milk products, ready-to-eat breakfast cereals, imitation cream products, fruit drinks, and various mixes—are included in table 2. Such foods may be fortified with one or more nutrients; the label will describe any fortification. Values shown here for these foods may be based on products from several manufacturers and, therefore, may differ somewhat from the values provided by any one source.

For meat, values describe it after it has been cooked and drained of the drippings. For many cuts, two sets of values are shown: meat including lean and fat parts, and lean meat from which the fat has been removed either before or after cooking.

Yield of Cooked Meat (Table 3)

Meat undergoes certain losses from the time it is purchased to the time it is eaten. Among these are losses during cooking from evaporation of moisture, loss of fat in the drippings, and removal of parts such as bone, gristle, and fat before or after cooking.

Table 3 shows, for several retail cuts, the yield of cooked meat from 1 pound of raw meat. Yield is given as ounces of:

> Cooked meat with bone and fat
>
> Cooked lean and fat
>
> Cooked lean only

Among the factors influencing the yield of meat is the proportion of fat and lean. Many cuts have an outside layer of fat extending all or part way around. The thickness of this fat layer varies depending on the cutting and trimming practices in the market. The information on yield in table 3 and on nutritive value in table 2 applies to retail cuts trimmed according to typical market practices. Deposits of fat within a cut (marbling) may be extensive. They usually are not affected by retail trimming but may be discarded at the table.

Recommended Daily Dietary Allowances (Table 4)

Table 4 shows Recommended Daily Dietary Allowances (RDA) for calories and for several nutrients essential for maintenance of good nutrition in healthy, normally active persons. This table is adapted from a more extensive table published by the Food and Nutrition Board of the National Academy of Sciences, National Research Council, in 1980.

Nutrients not shown in tables 2 and 4 but for which the Food and Nutrition Board published RDA in 1980 are vitamin B_6, vitamin B_{12}, folacin, vitamin D, vitamin E, magnesium, iodine, and zinc. More detailed information about RDA's may be obtained from the publication from which table 4 is adapted.

Food Sources of Additional Nutrients (Table 5)

Table 5 lists foods that are of special value in supplying the eight nutrients not shown in tables 2 and 4. Foods are considered to be of special value as a source of a nutrient if a serving of the food is relatively high in the nutrient.

The RDA for one nutrient shown in tables 2 and 4 is notably difficult to achieve by some individuals. Iron allowances are not met in diets for many preschool-age children and females of childbearing age. Choosing foods rich in iron—lean meats, shellfish, liver, heart, kidney, dry beans and peas, dark-green vegetables, dried fruit, and cereals with added iron—can help in meeting iron allowances. Iron supplements, in addition to a varied diet, are recommended for pregnant and lactating women.

Fat That Provides 30 and 35 Percent of Calories (Table 6)

Several scientific groups suggest that Americans moderate the amount of fat in their diets. Some recommend that fat be limited to amounts that will provide no more than 30 to 35 percent of calories. Table 6 shows the amount of fat that provides 30 and 35 percent of calories for diets of several total daily calorie intakes. For example, a woman wishing to moderate her fat intake to 35 percent of her 2,000-calorie diet should select foods that total no more than 78 grams of fat per day. She can estimate the grams of fat in the foods she eats from table 2.

A number of other publications of the Human Nutrition Information Service, U.S. Department of Agriculture, give helpful information about nutrients and which foods they are found in.

Agriculture Handbook No. 8, "Composition of Foods...Raw, Processed, Prepared," is a more technical publication with data for a much more extensive list of foods. It is being revised in sections. The revised sections now available are:

No. 8-1 Dairy and Egg Products
8-2 Spices and Herbs
8-3 Baby Foods
8-4 Fats and Oils
8-5 Poultry Products
8-6 Soups, Sauces, and Gravies
8-7 Sausages and Luncheon Meats
8-8 Breakfast Cereals
8-9 Fruits and Fruit Juices
8-10 Pork Products
8-11 Vegetables and Vegetable Products
8-12 Nut and Seed Products

Other publications containing information on a specific nutrient are "The Sodium Content of Your Food," Home and Garden Bulletin No. 233, and "Calories and Weight," Agriculture Information Bulletin No. 364. Additional information on evaluating and planning diets is available from "The Hassle Free Guide to a Better Diet," L-567, and "Nutrition and Your Health: Dietary Guidelines for Americans," Home and Garden Bulletin No. 232.

These publications may be purchased from the Superintendent of Documents, U.S. Government Printing Office, Washington, DC 20401, or any U.S. Government Printing Office bookstore.

Table 2. Nutritive Value of the Edible Part of Food

(Tr indicates nutrient present in trace amount.)

Item No.	Foods, approximate measures, units, and weight (weight of edible portion only)			Water	Food energy	Pro-tein	Fat	Fatty acids		
								Satu-rated	Mono-unsatu-rated	Poly-unsatu-rated
	Beverages		Grams	Per-cent	Cal-ories	Grams	Grams	Grams	Grams	Grams
	Alcoholic:									
	Beer:									
1	Regular	12 fl oz	360	92	150	1	0	0.0	0.0	0.0
2	Light	12 fl oz	355	95	95	1	0	0.0	0.0	0.0
	Gin, rum, vodka, whiskey:									
3	80-proof	1-1/2 fl oz	42	67	95	0	0	0.0	0.0	0.0
4	86-proof	1-1/2 fl oz	42	64	105	0	0	0.0	0.0	0.0
5	90-proof	1-1/2 fl oz	42	62	110	0	0	0.0	0.0	0.0
	Wines:									
6	Dessert	3-1/2 fl oz	103	77	140	Tr	0	0.0	0.0	0.0
	Table:									
7	Red	3-1/2 fl oz	102	88	75	Tr	0	0.0	0.0	0.0
8	White	3-1/2 fl oz	102	87	80	Tr	0	0.0	0.0	0.0
	Carbonated:[2]									
9	Club soda	12 fl oz	355	100	0	0	0	0.0	0.0	0.0
	Cola type:									
10	Regular	12 fl oz	369	89	160	0	0	0.0	0.0	0.0
11	Diet, artificially sweetened	12 fl oz	355	100	Tr	0	0	0.0	0.0	0.0
12	Ginger ale	12 fl oz	366	91	125	0	0	0.0	0.0	0.0
13	Grape	12 fl oz	372	88	180	0	0	0.0	0.0	0.0
14	Lemon-lime	12 fl oz	372	89	155	0	0	0.0	0.0	0.0
15	Orange	12 fl oz	372	88	180	0	0	0.0	0.0	0.0
16	Pepper type	12 fl oz	369	89	160	0	0	0.0	0.0	0.0
17	Root beer	12 fl oz	370	89	165	0	0	0.0	0.0	0.0
	Cocoa and chocolate-flavored beverages. See Dairy Products (items 95-98).									
	Coffee:									
18	Brewed	6 fl oz	180	100	Tr	Tr	Tr	Tr	Tr	Tr
19	Instant, prepared (2 tsp powder plus 6 fl oz water)	6 fl oz	182	99	Tr	Tr	Tr	Tr	Tr	Tr
	Fruit drinks, noncarbonated:									
	Canned:									
20	Fruit punch drink	6 fl oz	190	88	85	Tr	0	0.0	0.0	0.0
21	Grape drink	6 fl oz	187	86	100	Tr	0	0.0	0.0	0.0
22	Pineapple-grapefruit juice drink	6 fl oz	187	87	90	Tr	Tr	Tr	Tr	Tr
	Frozen:									
	Lemonade concentrate:									
23	Undiluted	6-fl-oz can	219	49	425	Tr	Tr	Tr	Tr	Tr
24	Diluted with 4-1/3 parts water by volume	6 fl oz	185	89	80	Tr	Tr	Tr	Tr	Tr
	Limeade concentrate:									
25	Undiluted	6-fl-oz can	218	50	410	Tr	Tr	Tr	Tr	Tr
26	Diluted with 4-1/3 parts water by volume	6 fl oz	185	89	75	Tr	Tr	Tr	Tr	Tr
	Fruit juices. See type under Fruits and Fruit Juices.									
	Milk beverages. See Dairy Products (items 92-105).									
	Tea:									
27	Brewed	8 fl oz	240	100	Tr	Tr	Tr	Tr	Tr	Tr
	Instant, powder, prepared:									
28	Unsweetened (1 tsp powder plus 8 fl oz water)	8 fl oz	241	100	Tr	Tr	Tr	Tr	Tr	Tr
29	Sweetened (3 tsp powder plus 8 fl oz water)	8 fl oz	262	91	85	Tr	Tr	Tr	Tr	Tr

[1] Value not determined.
[2] Mineral content varies depending on water source.

	Nutrients in Indicated Quantity												
Cholesterol	Carbohydrate	Calcium	Phosphorus	Iron	Potassium	Sodium	Vitamin A value (IU)	Vitamin A value (RE)	Thiamin	Riboflavin	Niacin	Ascorbic acid	Item No.
Milligrams	Grams	Milligrams	Milligrams	Milligrams	Milligrams	Milligrams	International units	Retinol equivalents	Milligrams	Milligrams	Milligrams	Milligrams	
0	13	14	50	0.1	115	18	0	0	0.02	0.09	1.8	0	1
0	5	14	43	0.1	64	11	0	0	0.03	0.11	1.4	0	2
0	Tr	Tr	Tr	Tr	1	Tr	0	0	Tr	Tr	Tr	0	3
0	Tr	Tr	Tr	Tr	1	Tr	0	0	Tr	Tr	Tr	0	4
0	Tr	Tr	Tr	Tr	1	Tr	0	0	Tr	Tr	Tr	0	5
0	8	8	9	0.2	95	9	(1)	(1)	0.01	0.02	0.2	0	6
0	3	8	18	0.4	113	5	(1)	(1)	0.00	0.03	0.1	0	7
0	3	9	14	0.3	83	5	(1)	(1)	0.00	0.01	0.1	0	8
0	0	18	0	Tr	0	78	0	0	0.00	0.00	0.0	0	9
0	41	11	52	0.2	7	18	0	0	0.00	0.00	0.0	0	10
0	Tr	14	39	0.2	7	[3]32	0	0	0.00	0.00	0.0	0	11
0	32	11	0	0.1	4	29	0	0	0.00	0.00	0.0	0	12
0	46	15	0	0.4	4	48	0	0	0.00	0.00	0.0	0	13
0	39	7	0	0.4	4	33	0	0	0.00	0.00	0.0	0	14
0	46	15	4	0.3	7	52	0	0	0.00	0.00	0.0	0	15
0	41	11	41	0.1	4	37	0	0	0.00	0.00	0.0	0	16
0	42	15	0	0.2	4	48	0	0	0.00	0.00	0.0	0	17
0	Tr	4	2	Tr	124	2	0	0	0.00	0.02	0.4	0	18
0	1	2	6	0.1	71	Tr	0	0	0.00	0.03	0.6	0	19
0	22	15	2	0.4	48	15	20	2	0.03	0.04	Tr	[4]61	20
0	26	2	2	0.3	9	11	Tr	Tr	0.01	0.01	Tr	[4]64	21
0	23	13	7	0.9	97	24	60	6	0.06	0.04	0.5	[4]110	22
0	112	9	13	0.4	153	4	40	4	0.04	0.07	0.7	66	23
0	21	2	2	0.1	30	1	10	1	0.01	0.02	0.2	13	24
0	108	11	13	0.2	129	Tr	Tr	Tr	0.02	0.02	0.2	26	25
0	20	2	2	Tr	24	Tr	Tr	Tr	Tr	Tr	Tr	4	26
0	Tr	0	2	Tr	36	1	0	0	0.00	0.03	Tr	0	27
0	1	1	4	Tr	61	1	0	0	0.00	0.02	0.1	0	28
0	22	1	3	Tr	49	Tr	0	0	0.00	0.04	0.1	0	29

[3]Blend of aspartame and saccharin; if only sodium saccharin is used, sodium is 75 mg; if only aspartame is used, sodium is 23 mg.
[4]With added ascorbic acid.

Item No.	Foods, approximate measures, units, and weight (weight of edible portion only)			Water	Food energy	Pro-tein	Fat	Fatty acids		
								Satu-rated	Mono-unsatu-rated	Poly-unsatu-rated
	Dairy Products		Grams	Per-cent	Cal-ories	Grams	Grams	Grams	Grams	Grams
	Butter. See Fats and Oils (items 128-130).									
	Cheese:									
	Natural:									
30	Blue-------------------	1 oz------------	28	42	100	6	8	5.3	2.2	0.2
31	Camembert (3 wedges per 4-oz container)-------------	1 wedge---------	38	52	115	8	9	5.8	2.7	0.3
	Cheddar:									
32	Cut pieces------------	1 oz------------	28	37	115	7	9	6.0	2.7	0.3
33		1 in³----------	17	37	70	4	6	3.6	1.6	0.2
34	Shredded--------------	1 cup----------	113	37	455	28	37	23.8	10.6	1.1
	Cottage (curd not pressed down):									
	Creamed (cottage cheese, 4% fat):									
35	Large curd--------	1 cup----------	225	79	235	28	10	6.4	2.9	0.3
36	Small curd--------	1 cup----------	210	79	215	26	9	6.0	2.7	0.3
37	With fruit--------	1 cup----------	226	72	280	22	8	4.9	2.2	0.2
38	Lowfat (2%)--------	1 cup----------	226	79	205	31	4	2.8	1.2	0.1
39	Uncreamed (cottage cheese dry curd, less than 1/2% fat)-----------------	1 cup----------	145	80	125	25	1	0.4	0.2	Tr
40	Cream---------------	1 oz------------	28	54	100	2	10	6.2	2.8	0.4
41	Feta----------------	1 oz------------	28	55	75	4	6	4.2	1.3	0.2
	Mozzarella, made with:									
42	Whole milk------------	1 oz------------	28	54	80	6	6	3.7	1.9	0.2
43	Part skim milk (low moisture)-----------	1 oz------------	28	49	80	8	5	3.1	1.4	0.1
44	Muenster-------------	1 oz------------	28	42	105	7	9	5.4	2.5	0.2
	Parmesan, grated:									
45	Cup, not pressed down------	1 cup----------	100	18	455	42	30	19.1	8.7	0.7
46	Tablespoon------------	1 tbsp----------	5	18	25	2	2	1.0	0.4	Tr
47	Ounce---------------	1 oz------------	28	18	130	12	9	5.4	2.5	0.2
48	Provolone-------------	1 oz------------	28	41	100	7	8	4.8	2.1	0.2
	Ricotta, made with:									
49	Whole milk------------	1 cup----------	246	72	430	28	32	20.4	8.9	0.9
50	Part skim milk--------	1 cup----------	246	74	340	28	19	12.1	5.7	0.6
51	Swiss---------------	1 oz------------	28	37	105	8	8	5.0	2.1	0.3
	Pasteurized process cheese:									
52	American-------------	1 oz------------	28	39	105	6	9	5.6	2.5	0.3
53	Swiss---------------	1 oz------------	28	42	95	7	7	4.5	2.0	0.2
54	Pasteurized process cheese food, American -------------	1 oz------------	28	43	95	6	7	4.4	2.0	0.2
55	Pasteurized process cheese spread, American------------	1 oz------------	28	48	80	5	6	3.8	1.8	0.2
	Cream, sweet:									
56	Half-and-half (cream and milk)	1 cup----------	242	81	315	7	28	17.3	8.0	1.0
57		1 tbsp----------	15	81	20	Tr	2	1.1	0.5	0.1
58	Light, coffee, or table-------	1 cup----------	240	74	470	6	46	28.8	13.4	1.7
59		1 tbsp----------	15	74	30	Tr	3	1.8	0.8	0.1
	Whipping, unwhipped (volume about double when whipped):									
60	Light-----------------	1 cup----------	239	64	700	5	74	46.2	21.7	2.1
61		1 tbsp----------	15	64	45	Tr	5	2.9	1.4	0.1
62	Heavy---------------	1 cup----------	238	58	820	5	88	54.8	25.4	3.3
63		1 tbsp----------	15	58	50	Tr	6	3.5	1.6	0.2
64	Whipped topping, (pressurized)	1 cup----------	60	61	155	2	13	8.3	3.9	0.5
65		1 tbsp----------	3	61	10	Tr	1	0.4	0.2	Tr
66	Cream, sour-------------	1 cup----------	230	71	495	7	48	30.0	13.9	1.8
67		1 tbsp----------	12	71	25	Tr	3	1.6	0.7	0.1

Nutrients in Indicated Quantity

Cholesterol	Carbohydrate	Calcium	Phosphorus	Iron	Potassium	Sodium	Vitamin A value (IU)	Vitamin A value (RE)	Thiamin	Riboflavin	Niacin	Ascorbic acid	Item No.
Milligrams	Grams	Milligrams	Milligrams	Milligrams	Milligrams	Milligrams	International units	Retinol equivalents	Milligrams	Milligrams	Milligrams	Milligrams	
21	1	150	110	0.1	73	396	200	65	0.01	0.11	0.3	0	30
27	Tr	147	132	0.1	71	320	350	96	0.01	0.19	0.2	0	31
30	Tr	204	145	0.2	28	176	300	86	0.01	0.11	Tr	0	32
18	Tr	123	87	0.1	17	105	180	52	Tr	0.06	Tr	0	33
119	1	815	579	0.8	111	701	1,200	342	0.03	0.42	0.1	0	34
34	6	135	297	0.3	190	911	370	108	0.05	0.37	0.3	Tr	35
31	6	126	277	0.3	177	850	340	101	0.04	0.34	0.3	Tr	36
25	30	108	236	0.2	151	915	280	81	0.04	0.29	0.2	Tr	37
19	8	155	340	0.4	217	918	160	45	0.05	0.42	0.3	Tr	38
10	3	46	151	0.3	47	19	40	12	0.04	0.21	0.2	0	39
31	1	23	30	0.3	34	84	400	124	Tr	0.06	Tr	0	40
25	1	140	96	0.2	18	316	130	36	0.04	0.24	0.3	0	41
22	1	147	105	0.1	19	106	220	68	Tr	0.07	Tr	0	42
15	1	207	149	0.1	27	150	180	54	0.01	0.10	Tr	0	43
27	Tr	203	133	0.1	38	178	320	90	Tr	0.09	Tr	0	44
79	4	1,376	807	1.0	107	1,861	700	173	0.05	0.39	0.3	0	45
4	Tr	69	40	Tr	5	93	40	9	Tr	0.02	Tr	0	46
22	1	390	229	0.3	30	528	200	49	0.01	0.11	0.1	0	47
20	1	214	141	0.1	39	248	230	75	0.01	0.09	Tr	0	48
124	7	509	389	0.9	257	207	1,210	330	0.03	0.48	0.3	0	49
76	13	669	449	1.1	307	307	1,060	278	0.05	0.46	0.2	0	50
26	1	272	171	Tr	31	74	240	72	0.01	0.10	Tr	0	51
27	Tr	174	211	0.1	46	406	340	82	0.01	0.10	Tr	0	52
24	1	219	216	0.2	61	388	230	65	Tr	0.08	Tr	0	53
18	2	163	130	0.2	79	337	260	62	0.01	0.13	Tr	0	54
16	2	159	202	0.1	69	381	220	54	0.01	0.12	Tr	0	55
89	10	254	230	0.2	314	98	1,050	259	0.08	0.36	0.2	2	56
6	1	16	14	Tr	19	6	70	16	0.01	0.02	Tr	Tr	57
159	9	231	192	0.1	292	95	1,730	437	0.08	0.36	0.1	2	58
10	1	14	12	Tr	18	6	110	27	Tr	0.02	Tr	Tr	59
265	7	166	146	0.1	231	82	2,690	705	0.06	0.30	0.1	1	60
17	Tr	10	9	Tr	15	5	170	44	Tr	0.02	Tr	Tr	61
326	7	154	149	0.1	179	89	3,500	1,002	0.05	0.26	0.1	1	62
21	Tr	10	9	Tr	11	6	220	63	Tr	0.02	Tr	Tr	63
46	7	61	54	Tr	88	78	550	124	0.02	0.04	Tr	0	64
2	Tr	3	3	Tr	4	4	30	6	Tr	Tr	Tr	0	65
102	10	268	195	0.1	331	123	1,820	448	0.08	0.34	0.2	2	66
5	1	14	10	Tr	17	6	90	23	Tr	0.02	Tr	Tr	67

Item No.	Foods, approximate measures, units, and weight (weight of edible portion only)		Grams	Water	Food energy	Pro-tein	Fat	Fatty acids		
								Satu-rated	Mono-unsatu-rated	Poly-unsatu-rated
	Dairy Products—Con.		Grams	Per-cent	Cal-ories	Grams	Grams	Grams	Grams	Grams
	Cream products, imitation (made with vegetable fat):									
	Sweet:									
	Creamers:									
68	Liquid (frozen)	1 tbsp	15	77	20	Tr	1	1.4	Tr	Tr
69	Powdered	1 tsp	2	2	10	Tr	1	0.7	Tr	Tr
	Whipped topping:									
70	Frozen	1 cup	75	50	240	1	19	16.3	1.2	0.4
71		1 tbsp	4	50	15	Tr	1	0.9	0.1	Tr
	Powdered, made with whole									
72	milk	1 cup	80	67	150	3	10	8.5	0.7	0.2
73		1 tbsp	4	67	10	Tr	Tr	0.4	Tr	Tr
74	Pressurized	1 cup	70	60	185	1	16	13.2	1.3	0.2
75		1 tbsp	4	60	10	Tr	1	0.8	0.1	Tr
76	Sour dressing (filled cream type product, nonbutterfat)--	1 cup	235	75	415	8	39	31.2	4.6	1.1
77		1 tbsp	12	75	20	Tr	2	1.6	0.2	0.1
	Ice cream. See Milk desserts, frozen (items 106-111).									
	Ice milk. See Milk desserts, frozen (items 112-114).									
	Milk:									
	Fluid:									
78	Whole (3.3% fat)	1 cup	244	88	150	8	8	5.1	2.4	0.3
	Lowfat (2%):									
79	No milk solids added	1 cup	244	89	120	8	5	2.9	1.4	0.2
80	Milk solids added, label claim less than 10 g of protein per cup	1 cup	245	89	125	9	5	2.9	1.4	0.2
	Lowfat (1%):									
81	No milk solids added	1 cup	244	90	100	8	3	1.6	0.7	0.1
82	Milk solids added, label claim less than 10 g of protein per cup	1 cup	245	90	105	9	2	1.5	0.7	0.1
	Nonfat (skim):									
83	No milk solids added	1 cup	245	91	85	8	Tr	0.3	0.1	Tr
84	Milk solids added, label claim less than 10 g of protein per cup	1 cup	245	90	90	9	1	0.4	0.2	Tr
85	Buttermilk	1 cup	245	90	100	8	2	1.3	0.6	0.1
	Canned:									
86	Condensed, sweetened	1 cup	306	27	980	24	27	16.8	7.4	1.0
	Evaporated:									
87	Whole milk	1 cup	252	74	340	17	19	11.6	5.9	0.6
88	Skim milk	1 cup	255	79	200	19	1	0.3	0.2	Tr
	Dried:									
89	Buttermilk	1 cup	120	3	465	41	7	4.3	2.0	0.3
	Nonfat, instantized:									
90	Envelope, 3.2 oz, net wt.[6]	1 envelope	91	4	325	32	1	0.4	0.2	Tr
91	Cup	1 cup	68	4	245	24	Tr	0.3	0.1	Tr
	Milk beverages:									
	Chocolate milk (commercial):									
92	Regular	1 cup	250	82	210	8	8	5.3	2.5	0.3
93	Lowfat (2%)	1 cup	250	84	180	8	5	3.1	1.5	0.2
94	Lowfat (1%)	1 cup	250	85	160	8	3	1.5	0.8	0.1

[5] Vitamin A value is largely from beta-carotene used for coloring.
[6] Yields 1 qt of fluid milk when reconstituted according to package directions.

Cholesterol	Carbohydrate	Calcium	Phosphorus	Iron	Potassium	Sodium	Vitamin A value (IU)	(RE)	Thiamin	Riboflavin	Niacin	Ascorbic acid	Item No.
Milligrams	Grams	Milligrams	Milligrams	Milligrams	Milligrams	Milligrams	International units	Retinol equivalents	Milligrams	Milligrams	Milligrams	Milligrams	
0	2	1	10	Tr	29	12	[5]10	[5]1	0.00	0.00	0.0	0	68
0	1	Tr	8	Tr	16	4	Tr	Tr	0.00	Tr	0.0	0	69
0	17	5	6	0.1	14	19	[5]650	[5]65	0.00	0.00	0.0	0	70
0	1	Tr	Tr	Tr	1	1	[5]30	[5]3	0.00	0.00	0.0	0	71
8	13	72	69	Tr	121	53	[5]290	[5]39	0.02	0.09	Tr	1	72
Tr	1	4	3	Tr	6	3	[5]10	[5]2	Tr	Tr	Tr	Tr	73
0	11	4	13	Tr	13	43	[5]330	[5]33	0.00	0.00	0.0	0	74
0	1	Tr	1	Tr	1	2	[5]20	[5]2	0.00	0.00	0.0	0	75
13	11	266	205	0.1	380	113	20	5	0.09	0.38	0.2	2	76
1	1	14	10	Tr	19	6	Tr	Tr	Tr	0.02	Tr	Tr	77
33	11	291	228	0.1	370	120	310	76	0.09	0.40	0.2	2	78
18	12	297	232	0.1	377	122	500	139	0.10	0.40	0.2	2	79
18	12	313	245	0.1	397	128	500	140	0.10	0.42	0.2	2	80
10	12	300	235	0.1	381	123	500	144	0.10	0.41	0.2	2	81
10	12	313	245	0.1	397	128	500	145	0.10	0.42	0.2	2	82
4	12	302	247	0.1	406	126	500	149	0.09	0.34	0.2	2	83
5	12	316	255	0.1	418	130	500	149	0.10	0.43	0.2	2	84
9	12	285	219	0.1	371	257	80	20	0.08	0.38	0.1	2	85
104	166	868	775	0.6	1,136	389	1,000	248	0.28	1.27	0.6	8	86
74	25	657	510	0.5	764	267	610	136	0.12	0.80	0.5	5	87
9	29	738	497	0.7	845	293	1,000	298	0.11	0.79	0.4	3	88
83	59	1,421	1,119	0.4	1,910	621	260	65	0.47	1.89	1.1	7	89
17	47	1,120	896	0.3	1,552	499	[7]2,160	[7]646	0.38	1.59	0.8	5	90
12	35	837	670	0.2	1,160	373	[7]1,610	[7]483	0.28	1.19	0.6	4	91
31	26	280	251	0.6	417	149	300	73	0.09	0.41	0.3	2	92
17	26	284	254	0.6	422	151	500	143	0.09	0.41	0.3	2	93
7	26	287	256	0.6	425	152	500	148	0.10	0.42	0.3	2	94

[7]With added vitamin A.

Item No.	Foods, approximate measures, units, and weight (weight of edible portion only)			Water	Food energy	Pro-tein	Fat	Fatty acids		
								Satu-rated	Mono-unsatu-rated	Poly-unsatu-rated
	Dairy Products—Con.		Grams	Per-cent	Cal-ories	Grams	Grams	Grams	Grams	Grams
	Milk beverages:									
	Cocoa and chocolate-flavored beverages:									
95	Powder containing nonfat dry milk	1 oz	28	1	100	3	1	0.6	0.3	Tr
96	Prepared (6 oz water plus 1 oz powder)	1 serving	206	86	100	3	1	0.6	0.3	Tr
97	Powder without nonfat dry milk	3/4 oz	21	1	75	1	1	0.3	0.2	Tr
98	Prepared (8 oz whole milk plus 3/4 oz powder)	1 serving	265	81	225	9	9	5.4	2.5	0.3
99	Eggnog (commercial)	1 cup	254	74	340	10	19	11.3	5.7	0.9
	Malted milk:									
	Chocolate:									
100	Powder	3/4 oz	21	2	85	1	1	0.5	0.3	0.1
101	Prepared (8 oz whole milk plus 3/4 oz powder)	1 serving	265	81	235	9	9	5.5	2.7	0.4
	Natural:									
102	Powder	3/4 oz	21	3	85	3	2	0.9	0.5	0.3
103	Prepared (8 oz whole milk plus 3/4 oz powder)	1 serving	265	81	235	11	10	6.0	2.9	0.6
	Shakes, thick:									
104	Chocolate	10-oz container	283	72	335	9	8	4.8	2.2	0.3
105	Vanilla	10-oz container	283	74	315	11	9	5.3	2.5	0.3
	Milk desserts, frozen:									
	Ice cream, vanilla:									
	Regular (about 11% fat):									
106	Hardened	1/2 gal	1,064	61	2,155	38	115	71.3	33.1	4.3
107		1 cup	133	61	270	5	14	8.9	4.1	0.5
108		3 fl oz	50	61	100	2	5	3.4	1.6	0.2
109	Soft serve (frozen custard)	1 cup	173	60	375	7	23	13.5	6.7	1.0
110	Rich (about 16% fat), hardened	1/2 gal	1,188	59	2,805	33	190	118.3	54.9	7.1
111		1 cup	148	59	350	4	24	14.7	6.8	0.9
	Ice milk, vanilla:									
112	Hardened (about 4% fat)	1/2 gal	1,048	69	1,470	41	45	28.1	13.0	1.7
113		1 cup	131	69	185	5	6	3.5	1.6	0.2
114	Soft serve (about 3% fat)	1 cup	175	70	225	8	5	2.9	1.3	0.2
115	Sherbet (about 2% fat)	1/2 gal	1,542	66	2,160	17	31	19.0	8.8	1.1
116		1 cup	193	66	270	2	4	2.4	1.1	0.1
	Yogurt:									
	With added milk solids:									
	Made with lowfat milk:									
117	Fruit-flavored[8]	8-oz container	227	74	230	10	2	1.6	0.7	0.1
118	Plain	8-oz container	227	85	145	12	4	2.3	1.0	0.1
119	Made with nonfat milk	8-oz container	227	85	125	13	Tr	0.3	0.1	Tr
	Without added milk solids:									
120	Made with whole milk	8-oz container	227	88	140	8	7	4.8	2.0	0.2
	Eggs									
	Eggs, large (24 oz per dozen):									
	Raw:									
121	Whole, without shell	1 egg	50	75	80	6	6	1.7	2.2	0.7
122	White	1 white	33	88	15	3	Tr	0.0	0.0	0.0
123	Yolk	1 yolk	17	49	65	3	6	1.7	2.2	0.7
	Cooked:									
124	Fried in butter	1 egg	46	68	95	6	7	2.7	2.7	0.8
125	Hard-cooked, shell removed	1 egg	50	75	80	6	6	1.7	2.2	0.7
126	Poached	1 egg	50	74	80	6	6	1.7	2.2	0.7
127	Scrambled (milk added) in butter. Also omelet	1 egg	64	73	110	7	8	3.2	2.9	0.8

[8]Carbohydrate content varies widely because of amount of sugar added and amount and solids content of added flavoring. Consult the label if more precise values for carbohydrate and calories are needed.

Nutrients in Indicated Quantity

Cho-les-terol	Carbo-hydrate	Calcium	Phos-phorus	Iron	Potas-sium	Sodium	Vitamin A value		Thiamin	Ribo-flavin	Niacin	Ascorbic acid	Item No.
							(IU)	(RE)					
Milli-grams	Grams	Milli-grams	Milli-grams	Milli-grams	Milli-grams	Milli-grams	Inter-national units	Retinol equiva-lents	Milli-grams	Milli-grams	Milli-grams	Milli-grams	
1	22	90	88	0.3	223	139	Tr	Tr	0.03	0.17	0.2	Tr	95
1	22	90	88	0.3	223	139	Tr	Tr	0.03	0.17	0.2	Tr	96
0	19	7	26	0.7	136	56	Tr	Tr	Tr	0.03	0.1	Tr	97
33	30	298	254	0.9	508	176	310	76	0.10	0.43	0.3	3	98
149	34	330	278	0.5	420	138	890	203	0.09	0.48	0.3	4	99
1	18	13	37	0.4	130	49	20	5	0.04	0.04	0.4	0	100
34	29	304	265	0.5	500	168	330	80	0.14	0.43	0.7	2	101
4	15	56	79	0.2	159	96	70	17	0.11	0.14	1.1	0	102
37	27	347	307	0.3	529	215	380	93	0.20	0.54	1.3	2	103
30	60	374	357	0.9	634	314	240	59	0.13	0.63	0.4	0	104
33	50	413	326	0.3	517	270	320	79	0.08	0.55	0.4	0	105
476	254	1,406	1,075	1.0	2,052	929	4,340	1,064	0.42	2.63	1.1	6	106
59	32	176	134	0.1	257	116	540	133	0.05	0.33	0.1	1	107
22	12	66	51	Tr	96	44	200	50	0.02	0.12	0.1	Tr	108
153	38	236	199	0.4	338	153	790	199	0.08	0.45	0.2	1	109
703	256	1,213	927	0.8	1,771	868	7,200	1,758	0.36	2.27	0.9	5	110
88	32	151	115	0.1	221	108	900	219	0.04	0.28	0.1	1	111
146	232	1,409	1,035	1.5	2,117	836	1,710	419	0.61	2.78	0.9	6	112
18	29	176	129	0.2	265	105	210	52	0.08	0.35	0.1	1	113
13	38	274	202	0.3	412	163	175	44	0.12	0.54	0.2	1	114
113	469	827	594	2.5	1,585	706	1,480	308	0.26	0.71	1.0	31	115
14	59	103	74	0.3	198	88	190	39	0.03	0.09	0.1	4	116
10	43	345	271	0.2	442	133	100	25	0.08	0.40	0.2	1	117
14	16	415	326	0.2	531	159	150	36	0.10	0.49	0.3	2	118
4	17	452	355	0.2	579	174	20	5	0.11	0.53	0.3	2	119
29	11	274	215	0.1	351	105	280	68	0.07	0.32	0.2	1	120
274	1	28	90	1.0	65	69	260	78	0.04	0.15	Tr	0	121
0	Tr	4	4	Tr	45	50	0	0	Tr	0.09	Tr	0	122
272	Tr	26	86	0.9	15	8	310	94	0.04	0.07	Tr	0	123
278	1	29	91	1.1	66	162	320	94	0.04	0.14	Tr	0	124
274	1	28	90	1.0	65	69	260	78	0.04	0.14	Tr	0	125
273	1	28	90	1.0	65	146	260	78	0.03	0.13	Tr	0	126
282	2	54	109	1.0	97	176	350	102	0.04	0.18	Tr	Tr	127

Item No.	Foods, approximate measures, units, and weight (weight of edible portion only)			Water	Food energy	Pro-tein	Fat	Fatty acids		
								Satu-rated	Mono-unsatu-rated	Poly-unsatu-rated
	Fats and Oils		Grams	Per-cent	Cal-ories	Grams	Grams	Grams	Grams	Grams
	Butter (4 sticks per lb):									
128	Stick	1/2 cup	113	16	810	1	92	57.1	26.4	3.4
129	Tablespoon (1/8 stick)	1 tbsp	14	16	100	Tr	11	7.1	3.3	0.4
130	Pat (1 in square, 1/3 in high; 90 per lb)	1 pat	5	16	35	Tr	4	2.5	1.2	0.2
131	Fats, cooking (vegetable shortenings)	1 cup	205	0	1,810	0	205	51.3	91.2	53.5
132		1 tbsp	13	0	115	0	13	3.3	5.8	3.4
133	Lard	1 cup	205	0	1,850	0	205	80.4	92.5	23.0
134		1 tbsp	13	0	115	0	13	5.1	5.9	1.5
	Margarine:									
135	Imitation (about 40% fat), soft	8-oz container	227	58	785	1	88	17.5	35.6	31.3
136		1 tbsp	14	58	50	Tr	5	1.1	2.2	1.9
	Regular (about 80% fat): Hard (4 sticks per lb):									
137	Stick	1/2 cup	113	16	810	1	91	17.9	40.5	28.7
138	Tablespoon (1/8 stick)	1 tbsp	14	16	100	Tr	11	2.2	5.0	3.6
139	Pat (1 in square, 1/3 in high; 90 per lb)	1 pat	5	16	35	Tr	4	0.8	1.8	1.3
140	Soft	8-oz container	227	16	1,625	2	183	31.3	64.7	78.5
141		1 tbsp	14	16	100	Tr	11	1.9	4.0	4.8
	Spread (about 60% fat): Hard (4 sticks per lb):									
142	Stick	1/2 cup	113	37	610	1	69	15.9	29.4	20.5
143	Tablespoon (1/8 stick)	1 tbsp	14	37	75	Tr	9	2.0	3.6	2.5
144	Pat (1 in square, 1/3 in high; 90 per lb)	1 pat	5	37	25	Tr	3	0.7	1.3	0.9
145	Soft	8-oz container	227	37	1,225	1	138	29.1	71.5	31.3
146		1 tbsp	14	37	75	Tr	9	1.8	4.4	1.9
	Oils, salad or cooking:									
147	Corn	1 cup	218	0	1,925	0	218	27.7	52.8	128.0
148		1 tbsp	14	0	125	0	14	1.8	3.4	8.2
149	Olive	1 cup	216	0	1,910	0	216	29.2	159.2	18.1
150		1 tbsp	14	0	125	0	14	1.9	10.3	1.2
151	Peanut	1 cup	216	0	1,910	0	216	36.5	99.8	69.1
152		1 tbsp	14	0	125	0	14	2.4	6.5	4.5
153	Safflower	1 cup	218	0	1,925	0	218	19.8	26.4	162.4
154		1 tbsp	14	0	125	0	14	1.3	1.7	10.4
155	Soybean oil, hydrogenated (partially hardened)	1 cup	218	0	1,925	0	218	32.5	93.7	82.0
156		1 tbsp	14	0	125	0	14	2.1	6.0	5.3
157	Soybean-cottonseed oil blend, hydrogenated	1 cup	218	0	1,925	0	218	39.2	64.3	104.9
158		1 tbsp	14	0	125	0	14	2.5	4.1	6.7
159	Sunflower	1 cup	218	0	1,925	0	218	22.5	42.5	143.2
160		1 tbsp	14	0	125	0	14	1.4	2.7	9.2
	Salad dressings: Commercial:									
161	Blue cheese	1 tbsp	15	32	75	1	8	1.5	1.8	4.2
	French:									
162	Regular	1 tbsp	16	35	85	Tr	9	1.4	4.0	3.5
163	Low calorie	1 tbsp	16	75	25	Tr	2	0.2	0.3	1.0
	Italian:									
164	Regular	1 tbsp	15	34	80	Tr	9	1.3	3.7	3.2
165	Low calorie	1 tbsp	15	86	5	Tr	Tr	Tr	Tr	Tr
	Mayonnaise:									
166	Regular	1 tbsp	14	15	100	Tr	11	1.7	3.2	5.8
167	Imitation	1 tbsp	15	63	35	Tr	3	0.5	0.7	1.6
168	Mayonnaise type	1 tbsp	15	40	60	Tr	5	0.7	1.4	2.7
169	Tartar sauce	1 tbsp	14	34	75	Tr	8	1.2	2.6	3.9
	Thousand island:									
170	Regular	1 tbsp	16	46	60	Tr	6	1.0	1.3	3.2
171	Low calorie	1 tbsp	15	69	25	Tr	2	0.2	0.4	0.9

[9] For salted butter; unsalted butter contains 12 mg sodium per stick, 2 mg per tbsp, or 1 mg per pat.
[10] Values for vitamin A are year-round average.

Cho-les-terol	Carbo-hydrate	Calcium	Phos-phorus	Iron	Potas-sium	Sodium	Vitamin A value (IU)	Vitamin A value (RE)	Thiamin	Ribo-flavin	Niacin	Ascorbic acid	Item No.
Milli-grams	Grams	Milli-grams	Milli-grams	Milli-grams	Milli-grams	Milli-grams	Inter-national units	Retinol equiva-lents	Milli-grams	Milli-grams	Milli-grams	Milli-grams	
247	Tr	27	26	0.2	29	[9]933	[10]3,460	[10]852	0.01	0.04	Tr	0	128
31	Tr	3	3	Tr	4	[9]116	[10]430	[10]106	Tr	Tr	Tr	0	129
11	Tr	1	1	Tr	1	[9]41	[10]150	[10]38	Tr	Tr	Tr	0	130
0	0	0	0	0.0	0	0	0	0	0.00	0.00	0.0	0	131
0	0	0	0	0.0	0	0	0	0	0.00	0.00	0.0	0	132
195	0	0	0	0.0	0	0	0	0	0.00	0.00	0.0	0	133
12	0	0	0	0.0	0	0	0	0	0.00	0.00	0.0	0	134
0	1	40	31	0.0	57	[11]2,178	[12]7,510	[12]2,254	0.01	0.05	Tr	Tr	135
0	Tr	2	2	0.0	4	[11]134	[12]460	[12]139	Tr	Tr	Tr	Tr	136
0	1	34	26	0.1	48	[11]1,066	[12]3,740	[12]1,122	0.01	0.04	Tr	Tr	137
0	Tr	4	3	Tr	6	[11]132	[12]460	[12]139	Tr	0.01	Tr	Tr	138
0	Tr	1	1	Tr	2	[11]47	[12]170	[12]50	Tr	Tr	Tr	Tr	139
0	1	60	46	0.0	86	[11]2,449	[12]7,510	[12]2,254	0.02	0.07	Tr	Tr	140
0	Tr	4	3	0.0	5	[11]151	[12]460	[12]139	Tr	Tr	Tr	Tr	141
0	0	24	18	0.0	34	[11]1,123	[12]3,740	[12]1,122	0.01	0.03	Tr	Tr	142
0	0	3	2	0.0	4	[11]139	[12]460	[12]139	Tr	Tr	Tr	Tr	143
0	0	1	1	0.0	1	[11]50	[12]170	[12]50	Tr	Tr	Tr	Tr	144
0	0	47	37	0.0	68	[11]2,256	[12]7,510	[12]2,254	0.02	0.06	Tr	Tr	145
0	0	3	2	0.0	4	[11]139	[12]460	[12]139	Tr	Tr	Tr	Tr	146
0	0	0	0	0.0	0	0	0	0	0.00	0.00	0.0	0	147
0	0	0	0	0.0	0	0	0	0	0.00	0.00	0.0	0	148
0	0	0	0	0.0	0	0	0	0	0.00	0.00	0.0	0	149
0	0	0	0	0.0	0	0	0	0	0.00	0.00	0.0	0	150
0	0	0	0	0.0	0	0	0	0	0.00	0.00	0.0	0	151
0	0	0	0	0.0	0	0	0	0	0.00	0.00	0.0	0	152
0	0	0	0	0.0	0	0	0	0	0.00	0.00	0.0	0	153
0	0	0	0	0.0	0	0	0	0	0.00	0.00	0.0	0	154
0	0	0	0	0.0	0	0	0	0	0.00	0.00	0.0	0	155
0	0	0	0	0.0	0	0	0	0	0.00	0.00	0.0	0	156
0	0	0	0	0.0	0	0	0	0	0.00	0.00	0.0	0	157
0	0	0	0	0.0	0	0	0	0	0.00	0.00	0.0	0	158
0	0	0	0	0.0	0	0	0	0	0.00	0.00	0.0	0	159
0	0	0	0	0.0	0	0	0	0	0.00	0.00	0.0	0	160
3	1	12	11	Tr	6	164	30	10	Tr	0.02	Tr	Tr	161
0	1	2	1	Tr	2	188	Tr	Tr	Tr	Tr	Tr	Tr	162
0	2	6	5	Tr	3	306	Tr	Tr	Tr	Tr	Tr	Tr	163
0	1	1	1	Tr	5	162	30	3	Tr	Tr	Tr	Tr	164
0	2	1	1	Tr	4	136	Tr	Tr	Tr	Tr	Tr	Tr	165
8	Tr	3	4	0.1	5	80	40	12	0.00	0.00	Tr	0	166
4	2	Tr	Tr	0.0	2	75	0	0	0.00	0.00	0.0	0	167
4	4	2	4	Tr	1	107	30	13	Tr	Tr	Tr	0	168
4	1	3	4	0.1	11	182	30	9	Tr	Tr	0.0	Tr	169
4	2	2	3	0.1	18	112	50	15	Tr	Tr	Tr	0	170
2	2	2	3	0.1	17	150	50	14	Tr	Tr	Tr	0	171

[11]For salted margarine.
[12]Based on average vitamin A content of fortified margarine. Federal specifications for fortified margarine require a minimum of 15,000 IU per pound.

Item No.	Foods, approximate measures, units, and weight (weight of edible portion only)		Water	Food energy	Protein	Fat	Fatty acids		
							Saturated	Monounsaturated	Polyunsaturated
		Grams	Percent	Calories	Grams	Grams	Grams	Grams	Grams
	Fats and Oils—Con.								
	Salad dressings:								
	Prepared from home recipe:								
172	Cooked type[13]	1 tbsp	16	69	25	1	2	0.5	0.6	0.3
173	Vinegar and oil	1 tbsp	16	47	70	0	8	1.5	2.4	3.9
	Fish and Shellfish								
	Clams:								
174	Raw, meat only	3 oz	85	82	65	11	1	0.3	0.3	0.3
175	Canned, drained solids	3 oz	85	77	85	13	2	0.5	0.5	0.4
176	Crabmeat, canned	1 cup	135	77	135	23	3	0.5	0.8	1.4
177	Fish sticks, frozen, reheated, (stick, 4 by 1 by 1/2 in)	1 fish stick	28	52	70	6	3	0.8	1.4	0.8
	Flounder or Sole, baked, with lemon juice:								
178	With butter	3 oz	85	73	120	16	6	3.2	1.5	0.5
179	With margarine	3 oz	85	73	120	16	6	1.2	2.3	1.9
180	Without added fat	3 oz	85	78	80	17	1	0.3	0.2	0.4
181	Haddock, breaded, fried[14]	3 oz	85	61	175	17	9	2.4	3.9	2.4
182	Halibut, broiled, with butter and lemon juice	3 oz	85	67	140	20	6	3.3	1.6	0.7
183	Herring, pickled	3 oz	85	59	190	17	13	4.3	4.6	3.1
184	Ocean perch, breaded, fried[14]	1 fillet	85	59	185	16	11	2.6	4.6	2.8
	Oysters:								
185	Raw, meat only (13-19 medium Selects)	1 cup	240	85	160	20	4	1.4	0.5	1.4
186	Breaded, fried[14]	1 oyster	45	65	90	5	5	1.4	2.1	1.4
	Salmon:								
187	Canned (pink), solids and liquid	3 oz	85	71	120	17	5	0.9	1.5	2.1
188	Baked (red)	3 oz	85	67	140	21	5	1.2	2.4	1.4
189	Smoked	3 oz	85	59	150	18	8	2.6	3.9	0.7
190	Sardines, Atlantic, canned in oil, drained solids	3 oz	85	62	175	20	9	2.1	3.7	2.9
191	Scallops, breaded, frozen, reheated	6 scallops	90	59	195	15	10	2.5	4.1	2.5
	Shrimp:								
192	Canned, drained solids	3 oz	85	70	100	21	1	0.2	0.2	0.4
193	French fried (7 medium)[16]	3 oz	85	55	200	16	10	2.5	4.1	2.6
194	Trout, broiled, with butter and lemon juice	3 oz	85	63	175	21	9	4.1	2.9	1.6
	Tuna, canned, drained solids:								
195	Oil pack, chunk light	3 oz	85	61	165	24	7	1.4	1.9	3.1
196	Water pack, solid white	3 oz	85	63	135	30	1	0.3	0.2	0.3
197	Tuna salad[17]	1 cup	205	63	375	33	19	3.3	4.9	9.2
	Fruits and Fruit Juices								
	Apples:								
	Raw:								
	Unpeeled, without cores:								
198	2-3/4-in diam. (about 3 per lb with cores)	1 apple	138	84	80	Tr	Tr	0.1	Tr	0.1
199	3-1/4-in diam. (about 2 per lb with cores)	1 apple	212	84	125	Tr	1	0.1	Tr	0.2
200	Peeled, sliced	1 cup	110	84	65	Tr	Tr	0.1	Tr	0.1
201	Dried, sulfured	10 rings	64	32	155	1	Tr	Tr	Tr	0.1
202	Apple juice, bottled or canned[19]	1 cup	248	88	115	Tr	Tr	Tr	Tr	0.1
	Applesauce, canned:								
203	Sweetened	1 cup	255	80	195	Tr	Tr	0.1	Tr	0.1
204	Unsweetened	1 cup	244	88	105	Tr	Tr	Tr	Tr	Tr

[13] Fatty acid values apply to product made with regular margarine.
[14] Dipped in egg, milk, and breadcrumbs; fried in vegetable shortening.
[15] If bones are discarded, value for calcium will be greatly reduced.
[16] Dipped in egg, breadcrumbs, and flour; fried in vegetable shortening.

Cholesterol	Carbohydrate	Calcium	Phosphorus	Iron	Potassium	Sodium	Vitamin A value (IU)	Vitamin A value (RE)	Thiamin	Riboflavin	Niacin	Ascorbic acid	Item No.
Milligrams	Grams	Milligrams	Milligrams	Milligrams	Milligrams	Milligrams	International units	Retinol equivalents	Milligrams	Milligrams	Milligrams	Milligrams	
9	2	13	14	0.1	19	117	70	20	0.01	0.02	Tr	Tr	172
0	Tr	0	0	0.0	1	Tr	0	0	0.00	0.00	0.0	0	173
43	2	59	138	2.6	154	102	90	26	0.09	0.15	1.1	9	174
54	2	47	116	3.5	119	102	90	26	0.01	0.09	0.9	3	175
135	1	61	246	1.1	149	1,350	50	14	0.11	0.11	2.6	0	176
26	4	11	58	0.3	94	53	20	5	0.03	0.05	0.6	0	177
68	Tr	13	187	0.3	272	145	210	54	0.05	0.08	1.6	1	178
55	Tr	14	187	0.3	273	151	230	69	0.05	0.08	1.6	1	179
59	Tr	13	197	0.3	286	101	30	10	0.05	0.08	1.7	1	180
75	7	34	183	1.0	270	123	70	20	0.06	0.10	2.9	0	181
62	Tr	14	206	0.7	441	103	610	174	0.06	0.07	7.7	1	182
85	0	29	128	0.9	85	850	110	33	0.04	0.18	2.8	0	183
66	7	31	191	1.2	241	138	70	20	0.10	0.11	2.0	0	184
120	8	226	343	15.6	290	175	740	223	0.34	0.43	6.0	24	185
35	5	49	73	3.0	64	70	150	44	0.07	0.10	1.3	4	186
34	0	[15]167	243	0.7	307	443	60	18	0.03	0.15	6.8	0	187
60	0	26	269	0.5	305	55	290	87	0.18	0.14	5.5	0	188
51	0	12	208	0.8	327	1,700	260	77	0.17	0.17	6.8	0	189
85	0	[15]371	424	2.6	349	425	190	56	0.03	0.17	4.6	0	190
70	10	39	203	2.0	369	298	70	21	0.11	0.11	1.6	0	191
128	1	98	224	1.4	104	1,955	50	15	0.01	0.03	1.5	0	192
168	11	61	154	2.0	189	384	90	26	0.06	0.09	2.8	0	193
71	Tr	26	259	1.0	297	122	230	60	0.07	0.07	2.3	1	194
55	0	7	199	1.6	298	303	70	20	0.04	0.09	10.1	0	195
48	0	17	202	0.6	255	468	110	32	0.03	0.10	13.4	0	196
80	19	31	281	2.5	531	877	230	53	0.06	0.14	13.3	6	197
0	21	10	10	0.2	159	Tr	70	7	0.02	0.02	0.1	8	198
0	32	15	15	0.4	244	Tr	110	11	0.04	0.03	0.2	12	199
0	16	4	8	0.1	124	Tr	50	5	0.02	0.01	0.1	4	200
0	42	9	24	0.9	288	[18]56	0	0	0.00	0.10	0.6	2	201
0	29	17	17	0.9	295	7	Tr	Tr	0.05	0.04	0.2	[20]2	202
0	51	10	18	0.9	156	8	30	3	0.03	0.07	0.5	[20]4	203
0	28	7	17	0.3	183	5	70	7	0.03	0.06	0.5	[20]3	204

[17] Made with drained chunk light tuna, celery, onion, pickle relish, and mayonnaise-type salad dressing.
[18] Sodium bisulfite used to preserve color; unsulfited product would contain less sodium.
[19] Also applies to pasteurized apple cider.
[20] Without added ascorbic acid. For value with added ascorbic acid, refer to label.

Table 2. Nutritive Value of the Edible Part of Food (Continued)

(Tr indicates nutrient present in trace amount.)

Item No.	Foods, approximate measures, units, and weight (weight of edible portion only)		Water	Food energy	Pro-tein	Fat	Fatty acids		
							Satu-rated	Mono-unsatu-rated	Poly-unsatu-rated
		Grams	Per-cent	Cal-ories	Grams	Grams	Grams	Grams	Grams
	Fruits and Fruit Juices—Con.								
	Apricots:								
205	Raw, without pits (about 12 per lb with pits)----------------- 3 apricots------	106	86	50	1	Tr	Tr	0.2	0.1
	Canned (fruit and liquid):								
206	Heavy syrup pack------------- 1 cup-----------	258	78	215	1	Tr	Tr	0.1	Tr
207	3 halves--------	85	78	70	Tr	Tr	Tr	Tr	Tr
208	Juice pack------------------- 1 cup-----------	248	87	120	2	Tr	Tr	Tr	Tr
209	3 halves--------	84	87	40	1	Tr	Tr	Tr	Tr
	Dried:								
210	Uncooked (28 large or 37 medium halves per cup)----- 1 cup-----------	130	31	310	5	1	Tr	0.3	0.1
211	Cooked, unsweetened, fruit and liquid---------------- 1 cup-----------	250	76	210	3	Tr	Tr	0.2	0.1
212	Apricot nectar, canned----------- 1 cup-----------	251	85	140	1	Tr	Tr	0.1	Tr
	Avocados, raw, whole, without skin and seed:								
213	California (about 2 per lb with skin and seed)-------------- 1 avocado-------	173	73	305	4	30	4.5	19.4	3.5
214	Florida (about 1 per lb with skin and seed)-------------- 1 avocado-------	304	80	340	5	27	5.3	14.8	4.5
	Bananas, raw, without peel:								
215	Whole (about 2-1/2 per lb with peel)----------------------- 1 banana--------	114	74	105	1	1	0.2	Tr	0.1
216	Sliced------------------------- 1 cup-----------	150	74	140	2	1	0.3	0.1	0.1
217	Blackberries, raw--------------- 1 cup-----------	144	86	75	1	1	0.2	0.1	0.1
	Blueberries:								
218	Raw-------------------------- 1 cup-----------	145	85	80	1	1	Tr	0.1	0.3
219	Frozen, sweetened------------- 10-oz container	284	77	230	1	Tr	Tr	0.1	0.2
220	1 cup-----------	230	77	185	1	Tr	Tr	Tr	0.1
	Cantaloup. See Melons (item 251).								
	Cherries:								
221	Sour, red, pitted, canned, water pack------------------ 1 cup-----------	244	90	90	2	Tr	0.1	0.1	0.1
222	Sweet, raw, without pits and stems---------------------- 10 cherries-----	68	81	50	1	1	0.1	0.2	0.2
223	Cranberry juice cocktail, bottled, sweetened---------- 1 cup-----------	253	85	145	Tr	Tr	Tr	Tr	0.1
224	Cranberry sauce, sweetened, canned, strained-------------- 1 cup-----------	277	61	420	1	Tr	Tr	0.1	0.2
	Dates:								
225	Whole, without pits------------ 10 dates--------	83	23	230	2	Tr	0.1	0.1	Tr
226	Chopped---------------------- 1 cup-----------	178	23	490	4	1	0.3	0.2	Tr
227	Figs, dried--------------------- 10 figs---------	187	28	475	6	2	0.4	0.5	1.0
	Fruit cocktail, canned, fruit and liquid:								
228	Heavy syrup pack--------------- 1 cup-----------	255	80	185	1	Tr	Tr	Tr	0.1
229	Juice pack-------------------- 1 cup-----------	248	87	115	1	Tr	Tr	Tr	Tr
	Grapefruit:								
230	Raw, without peel, membrane and seeds (3-3/4-in diam., 1 lb 1 oz, whole, with refuse)---- 1/2 grapefruit--	120	91	40	1	Tr	Tr	Tr	Tr
231	Canned, sections with syrup---- 1 cup-----------	254	84	150	1	Tr	Tr	Tr	0.1
	Grapefruit juice:								
232	Raw-------------------------- 1 cup-----------	247	90	95	1	Tr	Tr	Tr	0.1
	Canned:								
233	Unsweetened----------------- 1 cup-----------	247	90	95	1	Tr	Tr	Tr	0.1
234	Sweetened------------------- 1 cup-----------	250	87	115	1	Tr	Tr	Tr	0.1
	Frozen concentrate, unsweetened								
235	Undiluted-------------------- 6-fl-oz can-----	207	62	300	4	1	0.1	0.1	0.2
236	Diluted with 3 parts water by volume------------------- 1 cup-----------	247	89	100	1	Tr	Tr	Tr	0.1

[20] Without added ascorbic acid. For value with added ascorbic acid, refer to label.
[21] With added ascorbic acid.

Cho-les-terol	Carbo-hydrate	Calcium	Phos-phorus	Iron	Potas-sium	Sodium	Vitamin A value		Thiamin	Ribo-flavin	Niacin	Ascorbic acid	Item No.
							(IU)	(RE)					
Milli-grams	Grams	Milli-grams	Milli-grams	Milli-grams	Milli-grams	Milli-grams	Inter-national units	Retinol equiva-lents	Milli-grams	Milli-grams	Milli-grams	Milli-grams	
0	12	15	20	0.6	314	1	2,770	277	0.03	0.04	0.6	11	205
0	55	23	31	0.8	361	10	3,170	317	0.05	0.06	1.0	8	206
0	18	8	10	0.3	119	3	1,050	105	0.02	0.02	0.3	3	207
0	31	30	50	0.7	409	10	4,190	419	0.04	0.05	0.9	12	208
0	10	10	17	0.3	139	3	1,420	142	0.02	0.02	0.3	4	209
0	80	59	152	6.1	1,791	13	9,410	941	0.01	0.20	3.9	3	210
0	55	40	103	4.2	1,222	8	5,910	591	0.02	0.08	2.4	4	211
0	36	18	23	1.0	286	8	3,300	330	0.02	0.04	0.7	[20]2	212
0	12	19	73	2.0	1,097	21	1,060	106	0.19	0.21	3.3	14	213
0	27	33	119	1.6	1,484	15	1,860	186	0.33	0.37	5.8	24	214
0	27	7	23	0.4	451	1	90	9	0.05	0.11	0.6	10	215
0	35	9	30	0.5	594	2	120	12	0.07	0.15	0.8	14	216
0	18	46	30	0.8	282	Tr	240	24	0.04	0.06	0.6	30	217
0	20	9	15	0.2	129	9	150	15	0.07	0.07	0.5	19	218
0	62	17	20	1.1	170	3	120	12	0.06	0.15	0.7	3	219
0	50	14	16	0.9	138	2	100	10	0.05	0.12	0.6	2	220
0	22	27	24	3.3	239	17	1,840	184	0.04	0.10	0.4	5	221
0	11	10	13	0.3	152	Tr	150	15	0.03	0.04	0.3	5	222
0	38	8	3	0.4	61	10	10	1	0.01	0.04	0.1	[21]108	223
0	108	11	17	0.6	72	80	60	6	0.04	0.06	0.3	6	224
0	61	27	33	1.0	541	2	40	4	0.07	0.08	1.8	0	225
0	131	57	71	2.0	1,161	5	90	9	0.16	0.18	3.9	0	226
0	122	269	127	4.2	1,331	21	250	25	0.13	0.16	1.3	1	227
0	48	15	28	0.7	224	15	520	52	0.05	0.05	1.0	5	228
0	29	20	35	0.5	236	10	760	76	0.03	0.04	1.0	7	229
0	10	14	10	0.1	167	Tr	[22]10	[22]1	0.04	0.02	0.3	41	230
0	39	36	25	1.0	328	5	Tr	Tr	0.10	0.05	0.6	54	231
0	23	22	37	0.5	400	2	20	2	0.10	0.05	0.5	94	232
0	22	17	27	0.5	378	2	20	2	0.10	0.05	0.6	72	233
0	28	20	28	0.9	405	5	20	2	0.10	0.06	0.8	67	234
0	72	56	101	1.0	1,002	6	60	6	0.30	0.16	1.6	248	235
0	24	20	35	0.3	336	2	20	2	0.10	0.05	0.5	83	236

[22] For white grapefruit; pink grapefruit have about 310 IU or 31 RE.

Table 2. Nutritive Value of the Edible Part of Food (Continued)

(Tr indicates nutrient present in trace amount.)

Item No.	Foods, approximate measures, units, and weight (weight of edible portion only)		Water	Food energy	Pro-tein	Fat	Fatty acids Satu-rated	Fatty acids Mono-unsatu-rated	Fatty acids Poly-unsatu-rated
	Fruits and Fruit Juices—Con.	Grams	Per-cent	Cal-ories	Grams	Grams	Grams	Grams	Grams
	Grapes, European type (adherent skin), raw:									
237	Thompson Seedless--------------	10 grapes-------	50	81	35	Tr	Tr	0.1	Tr	0.1
238	Tokay and Emperor, seeded types	10 grapes-------	57	81	40	Tr	Tr	0.1	Tr	0.1
	Grape juice:									
239	Canned or bottled--------------	1 cup-----------	253	84	155	1	Tr	0.1	Tr	0.1
	Frozen concentrate, sweetened:									
240	Undiluted-------------------	6-fl-oz can-----	216	54	385	1	1	0.2	Tr	0.2
241	Diluted with 3 parts water by volume-------------------	1 cup-----------	250	87	125	Tr	Tr	0.1	Tr	0.1
242	Kiwifruit, raw, without skin (about 5 per lb with skin)-----	1 kiwifruit-----	76	83	45	1	Tr	Tr	0.1	0.1
243	Lemons, raw, without peel and seeds (about 4 per lb with peel and seeds)---------------------	1 lemon---------	58	89	15	1	Tr	Tr	Tr	0.1
	Lemon juice:									
244	Raw-------------------------	1 cup-----------	244	91	60	1	Tr	Tr	Tr	Tr
245	Canned or bottled, unsweetened	1 cup-----------	244	92	50	1	1	0.1	Tr	0.2
246		1 tbsp----------	15	92	5	Tr	Tr	Tr	Tr	Tr
247	Frozen, single-strength, unsweetened------------------	6-fl-oz can-----	244	92	55	1	1	0.1	Tr	0.2
	Lime juice:									
248	Raw-------------------------	1 cup-----------	246	90	65	1	Tr	Tr	Tr	0.1
249	Canned, unsweetened-----------	1 cup-----------	246	93	50	1	1	0.1	0.1	0.2
250	Mangos, raw, without skin and seed (about 1-1/2 per lb with skin and seed)------------------	1 mango---------	207	82	135	1	1	0.1	0.2	0.1
	Melons, raw, without rind and cavity contents:									
251	Cantaloup, orange-fleshed (5-in diam., 2-1/3 lb, whole, with rind and cavity contents)----	1/2 melon-------	267	90	95	2	1	0.1	0.1	0.3
252	Honeydew (6-1/2-in diam., 5-1/4 lb, whole, with rind and cavity contents)----------------	1/10 melon------	129	90	45	1	Tr	Tr	Tr	0.1
253	Nectarines, raw, without pits (about 3 per lb with pits)-----	1 nectarine-----	136	86	65	1	1	0.1	0.2	0.3
	Oranges, raw:									
254	Whole, without peel and seeds (2-5/8-in diam., about 2-1/2 per lb, with peel and seeds)	1 orange--------	131	87	60	1	Tr	Tr	Tr	Tr
255	Sections without membranes-----	1 cup-----------	180	87	85	2	Tr	Tr	Tr	Tr
	Orange juice:									
256	Raw, all varieties-------------	1 cup-----------	248	88	110	2	Tr	0.1	0.1	0.1
257	Canned, unsweetened------------	1 cup-----------	249	89	105	1	Tr	Tr	0.1	0.1
258	Chilled------------------------	1 cup-----------	249	88	110	2	1	0.1	0.1	0.2
	Frozen concentrate:									
259	Undiluted--------------------	6-fl-oz can-----	213	58	340	5	Tr	0.1	0.1	0.1
260	Diluted with 3 parts water by volume--------------------	1 cup-----------	249	88	110	2	Tr	Tr	Tr	Tr
261	Orange and grapefruit juice, canned-------------------------	1 cup-----------	247	89	105	1	Tr	Tr	Tr	Tr
262	Papayas, raw, 1/2-in cubes-------	1 cup-----------	140	86	65	1	Tr	0.1	0.1	Tr
	Peaches:									
	Raw:									
263	Whole, 2-1/2-in diam., peeled, pitted (about 4 per lb with peels and pits)----	1 peach---------	87	88	35	1	Tr	Tr	Tr	Tr
264	Sliced----------------------	1 cup-----------	170	88	75	1	Tr	Tr	0.1	0.1
	Canned, fruit and liquid:									
265	Heavy syrup pack-------------	1 cup-----------	256	79	190	1	Tr	Tr	0.1	0.1
266		1 half----------	81	79	60	Tr	Tr	Tr	Tr	Tr
267	Juice pack-------------------	1 cup-----------	248	87	110	2	Tr	Tr	Tr	Tr
268		1 half----------	77	87	35	Tr	Tr	Tr	Tr	Tr

[20]Without added ascorbic acid. For value with added ascorbic acid, refer to label.
[21]With added ascorbic acid.

Nutrients in Indicated Quantity

Cho-les-terol	Carbo-hydrate	Calcium	Phos-phorus	Iron	Potas-sium	Sodium	Vitamin A value (IU)	Vitamin A value (RE)	Thiamin	Ribo-flavin	Niacin	Ascorbic acid	Item No.
Milli-grams	Grams	Milli-grams	Milli-grams	Milli-grams	Milli-grams	Milli-grams	Inter-national units	Retinol equiva-lents	Milli-grams	Milli-grams	Milli-grams	Milli-grams	
0	9	6	7	0.1	93	1	40	4	0.05	0.03	0.2	5	237
0	10	6	7	0.1	105	1	40	4	0.05	0.03	0.2	6	238
0	38	23	28	0.6	334	8	20	2	0.07	0.09	0.7	[20]Tr	239
0	96	28	32	0.8	160	15	60	6	0.11	0.20	0.9	[21]179	240
0	32	10	10	0.3	53	5	20	2	0.04	0.07	0.3	[21]60	241
0	11	20	30	0.3	252	4	130	13	0.02	0.04	0.4	74	242
0	5	15	9	0.3	80	1	20	2	0.02	0.01	0.1	31	243
0	21	17	15	0.1	303	2	50	5	0.07	0.02	0.2	112	244
0	16	27	22	0.3	249	[23]51	40	4	0.10	0.02	0.5	61	245
0	1	2	1	Tr	15	[23]3	Tr	Tr	0.01	Tr	Tr	4	246
0	16	20	20	0.3	217	2	30	3	0.14	0.03	0.3	77	247
0	22	22	17	0.1	268	2	20	2	0.05	0.02	0.2	72	248
0	16	30	25	0.6	185	[23]39	40	4	0.08	0.01	0.4	16	249
0	35	21	23	0.3	323	4	8,060	806	0.12	0.12	1.2	57	250
0	22	29	45	0.6	825	24	8,610	861	0.10	0.06	1.5	113	251
0	12	8	13	0.1	350	13	50	5	0.10	0.02	0.8	32	252
0	16	7	22	0.2	288	Tr	1,000	100	0.02	0.06	1.3	7	253
0	15	52	18	0.1	237	Tr	270	27	0.11	0.05	0.4	70	254
0	21	72	25	0.2	326	Tr	370	37	0.16	0.07	0.5	96	255
0	26	27	42	0.5	496	2	500	50	0.22	0.07	1.0	124	256
0	25	20	35	1.1	436	5	440	44	0.15	0.07	0.8	86	257
0	25	25	27	0.4	473	2	190	19	0.28	0.05	0.7	82	258
0	81	68	121	0.7	1,436	6	590	59	0.60	0.14	1.5	294	259
0	27	22	40	0.2	473	2	190	19	0.20	0.04	0.5	97	260
0	25	20	35	1.1	390	7	290	29	0.14	0.07	0.8	72	261
0	17	35	12	0.3	247	9	400	40	0.04	0.04	0.5	92	262
0	10	4	10	0.1	171	Tr	470	47	0.01	0.04	0.9	6	263
0	19	9	20	0.2	335	Tr	910	91	0.03	0.07	1.7	11	264
0	51	8	28	0.7	236	15	850	85	0.03	0.06	1.6	7	265
0	16	2	9	0.2	75	5	270	27	0.01	0.02	0.5	2	266
0	29	15	42	0.7	317	10	940	94	0.02	0.04	1.4	9	267
0	9	5	13	0.2	99	3	290	29	0.01	0.01	0.4	3	268

[23]Sodium benzoate and sodium bisulfite added as preservatives.

Item No.	Foods, approximate measures, units, and weight (weight of edible portion only)		Water	Food energy	Pro-tein	Fat	Fatty acids		
							Satu-rated	Mono-unsatu-rated	Poly-unsatu-rated
		Grams	Per-cent	Cal-ories	Grams	Grams	Grams	Grams	Grams
	Fruits and Fruit Juices—Con.								
	Peaches:								
	Dried:								
269	Uncooked-------------------- 1 cup----------	160	32	380	6	1	0.1	0.4	0.6
270	Cooked, unsweetened, fruit and liquid---------------- 1 cup----------	258	78	200	3	1	0.1	0.2	0.3
271	Frozen, sliced, sweetened------ 10-oz container	284	75	265	2	Tr	Tr	0.1	0.2
272	1 cup----------	250	75	235	2	Tr	Tr	0.1	0.2
	Pears:								
	Raw, with skin, cored:								
273	Bartlett, 2-1/2-in diam. (about 2-1/2 per lb with cores and stems)----------- 1 pear----------	166	84	100	1	1	Tr	0.1	0.2
274	Bosc, 2-1/2-in diam. (about 3 per lb with cores and stems)---------------- 1 pear----------	141	84	85	1	1	Tr	0.1	0.1
275	D'Anjou, 3-in diam. (about 2 per lb with cores and stems)----------------- 1 pear----------	200	84	120	1	1	Tr	0.2	0.2
	Canned, fruit and liquid:								
276	Heavy syrup pack------------- 1 cup----------	255	80	190	1	Tr	Tr	0.1	0.1
277	1 half----------	79	80	60	Tr	Tr	Tr	Tr	Tr
278	Juice pack------------------ 1 cup----------	248	86	125	1	Tr	Tr	Tr	Tr
279	1 half----------	77	86	40	Tr	Tr	Tr	Tr	Tr
	Pineapple:								
280	Raw, diced--------------------- 1 cup----------	155	87	75	1	1	Tr	0.1	0.2
	Canned, fruit and liquid:								
	Heavy syrup pack:								
281	Crushed, chunks, tidbits--- 1 cup----------	255	79	200	1	Tr	Tr	Tr	0.1
282	Slices------------------- 1 slice--------	58	79	45	Tr	Tr	Tr	Tr	Tr
	Juice pack:								
283	Chunks or tidbits---------- 1 cup----------	250	84	150	1	Tr	Tr	Tr	0.1
284	Slices-------------------- 1 slice--------	58	84	35	Tr	Tr	Tr	Tr	Tr
285	Pineapple juice, unsweetened, canned--------------------- 1 cup----------	250	86	140	1	Tr	Tr	Tr	0.1
	Plantains, without peel:								
286	Raw------------------------- 1 plantain------	179	65	220	2	1	0.3	0.1	0.1
287	Cooked, boiled, sliced--------- 1 cup----------	154	67	180	1	Tr	0.1	Tr	0.1
	Plums, without pits:								
	Raw:								
288	2-1/8-in diam. (about 6-1/2 per lb with pits)---------- 1 plum----------	66	85	35	1	Tr	Tr	0.3	0.1
289	1-1/2-in diam. (about 15 per lb with pits)-------------- 1 plum----------	28	85	15	Tr	Tr	Tr	0.1	Tr
	Canned, purple, fruit and liquid:								
290	Heavy syrup pack------------- 1 cup----------	258	76	230	1	Tr	Tr	0.2	0.1
291	3 plums---------	133	76	120	Tr	Tr	Tr	0.1	Tr
292	Juice pack------------------ 1 cup----------	252	84	145	1	Tr	Tr	Tr	Tr
293	3 plums---------	95	84	55	Tr	Tr	Tr	Tr	Tr
	Prunes, dried:								
294	Uncooked---------------------- 4 extra large or 5 large prunes	49	32	115	1	Tr	Tr	0.2	0.1
295	Cooked, unsweetened, fruit and liquid---------------------- 1 cup----------	212	70	225	2	Tr	Tr	0.3	0.1
296	Prune juice, canned or bottled--- 1 cup----------	256	81	180	2	Tr	Tr	0.1	Tr
	Raisins, seedless:								
297	Cup, not pressed down---------- 1 cup----------	145	15	435	5	1	0.2	Tr	0.2
298	Packet, 1/2 oz (1-1/2 tbsp)---- 1 packet-------	14	15	40	Tr	Tr	Tr	Tr	Tr
	Raspberries:								
299	Raw-------------------------- 1 cup----------	123	87	60	1	1	Tr	0.1	0.4
300	Frozen, sweetened-------------- 10-oz container	284	73	295	2	Tr	Tr	Tr	0.3
301	1 cup----------	250	73	255	2	Tr	Tr	Tr	0.2

[21] With added ascorbic acid.

Nutrients in Indicated Quantity

Cholesterol	Carbohydrate	Calcium	Phosphorus	Iron	Potassium	Sodium	Vitamin A value		Thiamin	Riboflavin	Niacin	Ascorbic acid	Item No.
							(IU)	(RE)					
Milligrams	Grams	Milligrams	Milligrams	Milligrams	Milligrams	Milligrams	International units	Retinol equivalents	Milligrams	Milligrams	Milligrams	Milligrams	
0	98	45	190	6.5	1,594	11	3,460	346	Tr	0.34	7.0	8	269
0	51	23	98	3.4	826	5	510	51	0.01	0.05	3.9	10	270
0	68	9	31	1.1	369	17	810	81	0.04	0.10	1.9	[21]268	271
0	60	8	28	0.9	325	15	710	71	0.03	0.09	1.6	[21]236	272
0	25	18	18	0.4	208	Tr	30	3	0.03	0.07	0.2	7	273
0	21	16	16	0.4	176	Tr	30	3	0.03	0.06	0.1	6	274
0	30	22	22	0.5	250	Tr	40	4	0.04	0.08	0.2	8	275
0	49	13	18	0.6	166	13	10	1	0.03	0.06	0.6	3	276
0	15	4	6	0.2	51	4	Tr	Tr	0.01	0.02	0.2	1	277
0	32	22	30	0.7	238	10	10	1	0.03	0.03	0.5	4	278
0	10	7	9	0.2	74	3	Tr	Tr	0.01	0.01	0.2	1	279
0	19	11	11	0.6	175	2	40	4	0.14	0.06	0.7	24	280
0	52	36	18	1.0	265	3	40	4	0.23	0.06	0.7	19	281
0	12	8	4	0.2	60	1	10	1	0.05	0.01	0.2	4	282
0	39	35	15	0.7	305	3	100	10	0.24	0.05	0.7	24	283
0	9	8	3	0.2	71	1	20	2	0.06	0.01	0.2	6	284
0	34	43	20	0.7	335	3	10	1	0.14	0.06	0.6	27	285
0	57	5	61	1.1	893	7	2,020	202	0.09	0.10	1.2	33	286
0	48	3	43	0.9	716	8	1,400	140	0.07	0.08	1.2	17	287
0	9	3	7	0.1	114	Tr	210	21	0.03	0.06	0.3	6	288
0	4	1	3	Tr	48	Tr	90	9	0.01	0.03	0.1	3	289
0	60	23	34	2.2	235	49	670	67	0.04	0.10	0.8	1	290
0	31	12	17	1.1	121	25	340	34	0.02	0.05	0.4	1	291
0	38	25	38	0.9	388	3	2,540	254	0.06	0.15	1.2	7	292
0	14	10	14	0.3	146	1	960	96	0.02	0.06	0.4	3	293
0	31	25	39	1.2	365	2	970	97	0.04	0.08	1.0	2	294
0	60	49	74	2.4	708	4	650	65	0.05	0.21	1.5	6	295
0	45	31	64	3.0	707	10	10	1	0.04	0.18	2.0	10	296
0	115	71	141	3.0	1,089	17	10	1	0.23	0.13	1.2	5	297
0	11	7	14	0.3	105	2	Tr	Tr	0.02	0.01	0.1	Tr	298
0	14	27	15	0.7	187	Tr	160	16	0.04	0.11	1.1	31	299
0	74	43	48	1.8	324	3	170	17	0.05	0.13	0.7	47	300
0	65	38	43	1.6	285	3	150	15	0.05	0.11	0.6	41	301

Item No.	Foods, approximate measures, units, and weight (weight of edible portion only)		Water	Food energy	Pro-tein	Fat	Fatty acids		
							Satu-rated	Mono-unsatu-rated	Poly-unsatu-rated
		Grams	Per-cent	Cal-ories	Grams	Grams	Grams	Grams	Grams
	Fruits and Fruit Juices—Con.								
302	Rhubarb, cooked, added sugar----- 1 cup-----------	240	68	280	1	Tr	Tr	Tr	0.1
	Strawberries:								
303	Raw, capped, whole------------- 1 cup-----------	149	92	45	1	1	Tr	0.1	0.3
304	Frozen, sweetened, sliced------ 10-oz container	284	73	275	2	Tr	Tr	0.1	0.2
305	1 cup-----------	255	73	245	1	Tr	Tr	Tr	0.2
	Tangerines:								
306	Raw, without peel and seeds (2-3/8-in diam., about 4 per lb, with peel and seeds)----- 1 tangerine-----	84	88	35	1	Tr	Tr	Tr	Tr
307	Canned, light syrup, fruit and liquid---------------------- 1 cup-----------	252	83	155	1	Tr	Tr	Tr	0.1
308	Tangerine juice, canned, sweet-ened---------------------- 1 cup-----------	249	87	125	1	Tr	Tr	Tr	0.1
	Watermelon, raw, without rind and seeds:								
309	Piece (4 by 8 in wedge with rind and seeds; 1/16 of 32-2/3-lb melon, 10 by 16 in) 1 piece--------	482	92	155	3	2	0.3	0.2	1.0
310	Diced------------------------ 1 cup-----------	160	92	50	1	1	0.1	0.1	0.3
	Grain Products								
311	Bagels, plain or water, enriched, 3-1/2-in diam.[24] --------------- 1 bagel---------	68	29	200	7	2	0.3	0.5	0.7
312	Barley, pearled, light, uncooked 1 cup-----------	200	11	700	16	2	0.3	0.2	0.9
	Biscuits, baking powder, 2-in diam. (enriched flour, vege-table shortening):								
313	From home recipe--------------- 1 biscuit-------	28	28	100	2	5	1.2	2.0	1.3
314	From mix--------------------- 1 biscuit-------	28	29	95	2	3	0.8	1.4	0.9
315	From refrigerated dough-------- 1 biscuit-------	20	30	65	1	2	0.6	0.9	0.6
	Breadcrumbs, enriched:								
316	Dry, grated----------------- 1 cup-----------	100	7	390	13	5	1.5	1.6	1.0
	Soft. See White bread (item 351).								
	Breads:								
317	Boston brown bread, canned, slice, 3-1/4 in by 1/2 in[25] -- 1 slice---------	45	45	95	2	1	0.3	0.1	0.1
	Cracked-wheat bread (3/4 en-riched wheat flour, 1/4 cracked wheat flour):[25]								
318	Loaf, 1 lb---------------- 1 loaf----------	454	35	1,190	42	16	3.1	4.3	5.7
319	Slice (18 per loaf)--------- 1 slice---------	25	35	65	2	1	0.2	0.2	0.3
320	Toasted------------------- 1 slice---------	21	26	65	2	1	0.2	0.2	0.3
	French or vienna bread, en-riched:[25]								
321	Loaf, 1 lb---------------- 1 loaf----------	454	34	1,270	43	18	3.8	5.7	5.9
	Slice:								
322	French, 5 by 2-1/2 by 1 in 1 slice---------	35	34	100	3	1	0.3	0.4	0.5
323	Vienna, 4-3/4 by 4 by 1/2 in---------------------- 1 slice---------	25	34	70	2	1	0.2	0.3	0.3
	Italian bread, enriched:								
324	Loaf, 1 lb---------------- 1 loaf----------	454	32	1,255	41	4	0.6	0.3	1.6
325	Slice, 4-1/2 by 3-1/4 by 3/4 in---------------------- 1 slice---------	30	32	85	3	Tr	Tr	Tr	0.1
	Mixed grain bread, enriched:[25]								
326	Loaf, 1 lb---------------- 1 loaf----------	454	37	1,165	45	17	3.2	4.1	6.5
327	Slice (18 per loaf)--------- 1 slice---------	25	37	65	2	1	0.2	0.2	0.4
328	Toasted------------------- 1 slice---------	23	27	65	2	1	0.2	0.2	0.4

[24] Egg bagels have 44 mg cholesterol and 22 IU or 7 RE vitamin A per bagel.
[25] Made with vegetable shortening.

Cholesterol	Carbohydrate	Calcium	Phosphorus	Iron	Potassium	Sodium	Vitamin A value (IU)	Vitamin A value (RE)	Thiamin	Riboflavin	Niacin	Ascorbic acid	Item No.
Milligrams	Grams	Milligrams	Milligrams	Milligrams	Milligrams	Milligrams	International units	Retinol equivalents	Milligrams	Milligrams	Milligrams	Milligrams	
0	75	348	19	0.5	230	2	170	17	0.04	0.06	0.5	8	302
0	10	21	28	0.6	247	1	40	4	0.03	0.10	0.3	84	303
0	74	31	37	1.7	278	9	70	7	0.05	0.14	1.1	118	304
0	66	28	33	1.5	250	8	60	6	0.04	0.13	1.0	106	305
0	9	12	8	0.1	132	1	770	77	0.09	0.02	0.1	26	306
0	41	18	25	0.9	197	15	2,120	212	0.13	0.11	1.1	50	307
0	30	45	35	0.5	443	2	1,050	105	0.15	0.05	0.2	55	308
0	35	39	43	0.8	559	10	1,760	176	0.39	0.10	1.0	46	309
0	11	13	14	0.3	186	3	590	59	0.13	0.03	0.3	15	310
0	38	29	46	1.8	50	245	0	0	0.26	0.20	2.4	0	311
0	158	32	378	4.2	320	6	0	0	0.24	0.10	6.2	0	312
Tr	13	47	36	0.7	32	195	10	3	0.08	0.08	0.8	Tr	313
Tr	14	58	128	0.7	56	262	20	4	0.12	0.11	0.8	Tr	314
1	10	4	79	0.5	18	249	0	0	0.08	0.05	0.7	0	315
5	73	122	141	4.1	152	736	0	0	0.35	0.35	4.8	0	316
3	21	41	72	0.9	131	113	[26]0	[26]0	0.06	0.04	0.7	0	317
0	227	295	581	12.1	608	1,966	Tr	Tr	1.73	1.73	15.3	Tr	318
0	12	16	32	0.7	34	106	Tr	Tr	0.10	0.09	0.8	Tr	319
0	12	16	32	0.7	34	106	Tr	Tr	0.07	0.09	0.8	Tr	320
0	230	499	386	14.0	409	2,633	Tr	Tr	2.09	1.59	18.2	Tr	321
0	18	39	30	1.1	32	203	Tr	Tr	0.16	0.12	1.4	Tr	322
0	13	28	21	0.8	23	145	Tr	Tr	0.12	0.09	1.0	Tr	323
0	256	77	350	12.7	336	2,656	0	0	1.80	1.10	15.0	0	324
0	17	5	23	0.8	22	176	0	0	0.12	0.07	1.0	0	325
0	212	472	962	14.8	990	1,870	Tr	Tr	1.77	1.73	18.9	Tr	326
0	12	27	55	0.8	56	106	Tr	Tr	0.10	0.10	1.1	Tr	327
0	12	27	55	0.8	56	106	Tr	Tr	0.08	0.10	1.1	Tr	328

[26] Made with white cornmeal. If made with yellow cornmeal, value is 32 IU or 3 RE.

Item No.	Foods, approximate measures, units, and weight (weight of edible portion only)			Water	Food energy	Pro-tein	Fat	Fatty acids		
								Satu-rated	Mono-unsatu-rated	Poly-unsatu-rated
			Grams	Per-cent	Cal-ories	Grams	Grams	Grams	Grams	Grams
	Grain Products—Con.									
	Breads:									
	Oatmeal bread, enriched:[25]									
329	Loaf, 1 lb	1 loaf	454	37	1,145	38	20	3.7	7.1	8.2
330	Slice (18 per loaf)	1 slice	25	37	65	2	1	0.2	0.4	0.5
331	Toasted	1 slice	23	30	65	2	1	0.2	0.4	0.5
332	Pita bread, enriched, white, 6-1/2-in diam.	1 pita	60	31	165	6	1	0.1	0.1	0.4
	Pumpernickel (2/3 rye flour, 1/3 enriched wheat flour):[25]									
333	Loaf, 1 lb	1 loaf	454	37	1,160	42	16	2.6	3.6	6.4
334	Slice, 5 by 4 by 3/8 in	1 slice	32	37	80	3	1	0.2	0.3	0.5
335	Toasted	1 slice	29	28	80	3	1	0.2	0.3	0.5
	Raisin bread, enriched:[25]									
336	Loaf, 1 lb	1 loaf	454	33	1,260	37	18	4.1	6.5	6.7
337	Slice (18 per loaf)	1 slice	25	33	65	2	1	0.2	0.3	0.4
338	Toasted	1 slice	21	24	65	2	1	0.2	0.3	0.4
	Rye bread, light (2/3 enriched wheat flour, 1/3 rye flour):[25]									
339	Loaf, 1 lb	1 loaf	454	37	1,190	38	17	3.3	5.2	5.5
340	Slice, 4-3/4 by 3-3/4 by 7/16 in	1 slice	25	37	65	2	1	0.2	0.3	0.3
341	Toasted	1 slice	22	28	65	2	1	0.2	0.3	0.3
	Wheat bread, enriched:[25]									
342	Loaf, 1 lb	1 loaf	454	37	1,160	43	19	3.9	7.3	4.5
343	Slice (18 per loaf)	1 slice	25	37	65	2	1	0.2	0.4	0.3
344	Toasted	1 slice	23	28	65	3	1	0.2	0.4	0.3
	White bread, enriched:[25]									
345	Loaf, 1 lb	1 loaf	454	37	1,210	38	18	5.6	6.5	4.2
346	Slice (18 per loaf)	1 slice	25	37	65	2	1	0.3	0.4	0.2
347	Toasted	1 slice	22	28	65	2	1	0.3	0.4	0.2
348	Slice (22 per loaf)	1 slice	20	37	55	2	1	0.2	0.3	0.2
349	Toasted	1 slice	17	28	55	2	1	0.2	0.3	0.2
350	Cubes	1 cup	30	37	80	2	1	0.4	0.4	0.3
351	Crumbs, soft	1 cup	45	37	120	4	2	0.6	0.6	0.4
	Whole-wheat bread:[25]									
352	Loaf, 1 lb	1 loaf	454	38	1,110	44	20	5.8	6.8	5.2
353	Slice (16 per loaf)	1 slice	28	38	70	3	1	0.4	0.4	0.3
354	Toasted	1 slice	25	29	70	3	1	0.4	0.4	0.3
	Bread stuffing (from enriched bread), prepared from mix:									
355	Dry type	1 cup	140	33	500	9	31	6.1	13.3	9.6
356	Moist type	1 cup	203	61	420	9	26	5.3	11.3	8.0
	Breakfast cereals:									
	Hot type, cooked:									
	Corn (hominy) grits:									
357	Regular and quick, enriched	1 cup	242	85	145	3	Tr	Tr	0.1	0.2
358	Instant, plain	1 pkt	137	85	80	2	Tr	Tr	Tr	0.1
	Cream of Wheat®:									
359	Regular, quick, instant	1 cup	244	86	140	4	Tr	0.1	Tr	0.2
360	Mix'n Eat, plain	1 pkt	142	82	100	3	Tr	Tr	Tr	0.1
361	Malt-O-Meal®	1 cup	240	88	120	4	Tr	Tr	Tr	0.1
	Oatmeal or rolled oats:									
362	Regular, quick, instant, nonfortified	1 cup	234	85	145	6	2	0.4	0.8	1.0
	Instant, fortified:									
363	Plain	1 pkt	177	86	105	4	2	0.3	0.6	0.7
364	Flavored	1 pkt	164	76	160	5	2	0.3	0.7	0.8

[25] Made with vegetable shortening.
[27] Nutrient added.
[28] Cooked without salt. If salt is added according to label recommendations, sodium content is 540 mg.
[29] For white corn grits. Cooked yellow grits contain 145 IU or 14 RE.
[30] Value based on label declaration for added nutrients.

Nutrients in Indicated Quantity

Cho-les-terol	Carbo-hydrate	Calcium	Phos-phorus	Iron	Potas-sium	Sodium	Vitamin A value (IU)	(RE)	Thiamin	Ribo-flavin	Niacin	Ascorbic acid	Item No.
Milli-grams	Grams	Milli-grams	Milli-grams	Milli-grams	Milli-grams	Milli-grams	Inter-national units	Retinol equiva-lents	Milli-grams	Milli-grams	Milli-grams	Milli-grams	
0	212	267	563	12.0	707	2,231	0	0	2.09	1.20	15.4	0	329
0	12	15	31	0.7	39	124	0	0	0.12	0.07	0.9	0	330
0	12	15	31	0.7	39	124	0	0	0.09	0.07	0.9	0	331
0	33	49	60	1.4	71	339	0	0	0.27	0.12	2.2	0	332
0	218	322	990	12.4	1,966	2,461	0	0	1.54	2.36	15.0	0	333
0	16	23	71	0.9	141	177	0	0	0.11	0.17	1.1	0	334
0	16	23	71	0.9	141	177	0	0	0.09	0.17	1.1	0	335
0	239	463	395	14.1	1,058	1,657	Tr	Tr	1.50	2.81	18.6	Tr	336
0	13	25	22	0.8	59	92	Tr	Tr	0.08	0.15	1.0	Tr	337
0	13	25	22	0.8	59	92	Tr	Tr	0.06	0.15	1.0	Tr	338
0	218	363	658	12.3	926	3,164	0	0	1.86	1.45	15.0	0	339
0	12	20	36	0.7	51	175	0	0	0.10	0.08	0.8	0	340
0	12	20	36	0.7	51	175	0	0	0.08	0.08	0.8	0	341
0	213	572	835	15.8	627	2,447	Tr	Tr	2.09	1.45	20.5	Tr	342
0	12	32	47	0.9	35	138	Tr	Tr	0.12	0.08	1.2	Tr	343
0	12	32	47	0.9	35	138	Tr	Tr	0.10	0.08	1.2	Tr	344
0	222	572	490	12.9	508	2,334	Tr	Tr	2.13	1.41	17.0	Tr	345
0	12	32	27	0.7	28	129	Tr	Tr	0.12	0.08	0.9	Tr	346
0	12	32	27	0.7	28	129	Tr	Tr	0.09	0.08	0.9	Tr	347
0	10	25	21	0.6	22	101	Tr	Tr	0.09	0.06	0.7	Tr	348
0	10	25	21	0.6	22	101	Tr	Tr	0.07	0.06	0.7	Tr	349
0	15	38	32	0.9	34	154	Tr	Tr	0.14	0.09	1.1	Tr	350
0	22	57	49	1.3	50	231	Tr	Tr	0.21	0.14	1.7	Tr	351
0	206	327	1,180	15.5	799	2,887	Tr	Tr	1.59	0.95	17.4	Tr	352
0	13	20	74	1.0	50	180	Tr	Tr	0.10	0.06	1.1	Tr	353
0	13	20	74	1.0	50	180	Tr	Tr	0.08	0.06	1.1	Tr	354
0	50	92	136	2.2	126	1,254	910	273	0.17	0.20	2.5	0	355
67	40	81	134	2.0	118	1,023	850	256	0.10	0.18	1.6	0	356
0	31	0	29	[27]1.5	53	[28]0	[29]0	[29]0	[27]0.24	[27]0.15	[27]2.0	0	357
0	18	7	16	[27]1.0	29	343	0	0	[27]0.18	[27]0.08	[27]1.3	0	358
0	29	[30]54	[31]43	[30]10.9	46	[31,32]5	0	0	[30]0.24	[30]0.07	[30]1.5	0	359
0	21	[30]20	[30]20	[30]8.1	38	241	[30]1,250	[30]376	[30]0.43	[30]0.28	[30]5.0	0	360
0	26	5	[30]24	[30]9.6	31	[33]2	0	0	[30]0.48	[30]0.24	[30]5.8	0	361
0	25	19	178	1.6	131	[34]2	40	4	0.26	0.05	0.3	0	362
0	18	[27]163	133	[27]6.3	99	[27]285	[27]1,510	[27]453	[27]0.53	[27]0.28	[27]5.5	0	363
0	31	[27]168	148	[27]6.7	137	[27]254	[27]1,530	[27]460	[27]0.53	[27]0.38	[27]5.9	Tr	364

[31] For regular and instant cereal. For quick cereal, phosphorus is 102 mg and sodium is 142 mg.
[32] Cooked without salt. If salt is added according to label recommendations, sodium content is 390 mg.
[33] Cooked without salt. If salt is added according to label recommendations, sodium content is 324 mg.
[34] Cooked without salt. If salt is added according to label recommendations, sodium content is 374 mg.

Item No.	Foods, approximate measures, units, and weight (weight of edible portion only)		Grams	Water (Percent)	Food energy (Calories)	Protein (Grams)	Fat (Grams)	Fatty acids Saturated (Grams)	Fatty acids Mono-unsaturated (Grams)	Fatty acids Poly-unsaturated (Grams)
	Grain Products—Con.									
	Breakfast cereals:									
	Ready to eat:									
365	All-Bran® (about 1/3 cup)	1 oz	28	3	70	4	1	0.1	0.1	0.3
366	Cap'n Crunch® (about 3/4 cup)	1 oz	28	3	120	1	3	1.7	0.3	0.4
367	Cheerios® (about 1-1/4 cup)	1 oz	28	5	110	4	2	0.3	0.6	0.7
	Corn Flakes (about 1-1/4 cup):									
368	Kellogg's®	1 oz	28	3	110	2	Tr	Tr	Tr	Tr
369	Toasties®	1 oz	28	3	110	2	Tr	Tr	Tr	Tr
	40% Bran Flakes:									
370	Kellogg's® (about 3/4 cup)	1 oz	28	3	90	4	1	0.1	0.1	0.3
371	Post® (about 2/3 cup)	1 oz	28	3	90	3	Tr	0.1	0.1	0.2
372	Froot Loops® (about 1 cup)	1 oz	28	3	110	2	1	0.2	0.1	0.1
373	Golden Grahams® (about 3/4 cup)	1 oz	28	2	110	2	1	0.7	0.1	0.2
374	Grape-Nuts® (about 1/4 cup)	1 oz	28	3	100	3	Tr	Tr	Tr	0.1
375	Honey Nut Cheerios® (about 3/4 cup)	1 oz	28	3	105	3	1	0.1	0.3	0.3
376	Lucky Charms® (about 1 cup)	1 oz	28	3	110	3	1	0.2	0.4	0.4
377	Nature Valley® Granola (about 1/3 cup)	1 oz	28	4	125	3	5	3.3	0.7	0.7
378	100% Natural Cereal (about 1/4 cup)	1 oz	28	2	135	3	6	4.1	1.2	0.5
379	Product 19® (about 3/4 cup)	1 oz	28	3	110	3	Tr	Tr	Tr	0.1
	Raisin Bran:									
380	Kellogg's® (about 3/4 cup)	1 oz	28	8	90	3	1	0.1	0.1	0.3
381	Post® (about 1/2 cup)	1 oz	28	9	85	3	1	0.1	0.1	0.3
382	Rice Krispies® (about 1 cup)	1 oz	28	2	110	2	Tr	Tr	Tr	0.1
383	Shredded Wheat (about 2/3 cup)	1 oz	28	5	100	3	1	0.1	0.1	0.3
384	Special K® (about 1-1/3 cup)	1 oz	28	2	110	6	Tr	Tr	Tr	Tr
385	Super Sugar Crisp® (about 7/8 cup)	1 oz	28	2	105	2	Tr	Tr	Tr	0.1
386	Sugar Frosted Flakes, Kellogg's® (about 3/4 cup)	1 oz	28	3	110	1	Tr	Tr	Tr	Tr
387	Sugar Smacks® (about 3/4 cup)	1 oz	28	3	105	2	1	0.1	0.1	0.2
388	Total® (about 1 cup)	1 oz	28	4	100	3	1	0.1	0.1	0.3
389	Trix® (about 1 cup)	1 oz	28	3	110	2	Tr	0.2	0.1	0.1
390	Wheaties® (about 1 cup)	1 oz	28	5	100	3	Tr	0.1	Tr	0.2
391	Buckwheat flour, light, sifted	1 cup	98	12	340	6	1	0.2	0.4	0.4
392	Bulgur, uncooked	1 cup	170	10	600	19	3	1.2	0.3	1.2
	Cakes prepared from cake mixes with enriched flour:[35]									
	Angelfood:									
393	Whole cake, 9-3/4-in diam. tube cake	1 cake	635	38	1,510	38	2	0.4	0.2	1.0
394	Piece, 1/12 of cake	1 piece	53	38	125	3	Tr	Tr	Tr	0.1
	Coffeecake, crumb:									
395	Whole cake, 7-3/4 by 5-5/8 by 1-1/4 in	1 cake	430	30	1,385	27	41	11.8	16.7	9.6
396	Piece, 1/6 of cake	1 piece	72	30	230	5	7	2.0	2.8	1.6
	Devil's food with chocolate frosting:									
397	Whole, 2-layer cake, 8- or 9-in diam.	1 cake	1,107	24	3,755	49	136	55.6	51.4	19.7
398	Piece, 1/16 of cake	1 piece	69	24	235	3	8	3.5	3.2	1.2
399	Cupcake, 2-1/2-in diam.	1 cupcake	35	24	120	2	4	1.8	1.6	0.6
	Gingerbread:									
400	Whole cake, 8 in square	1 cake	570	37	1,575	18	39	9.6	16.4	10.5
401	Piece, 1/9 of cake	1 piece	63	37	175	2	4	1.1	1.8	1.2

[27] Nutrient added.
[30] Value based on label declaration for added nutrients.

Cholesterol	Carbohydrate	Calcium	Phosphorus	Iron	Potassium	Sodium	Vitamin A value (IU)	Vitamin A value (RE)	Thiamin	Riboflavin	Niacin	Ascorbic acid	Item No.
Milligrams	Grams	Milligrams	Milligrams	Milligrams	Milligrams	Milligrams	International units	Retinol equivalents	Milligrams	Milligrams	Milligrams	Milligrams	
0	21	23	264	[30]4.5	350	320	[30]1,250	[30]375	[30]0.37	[30]0.43	[30]5.0	[30]15	365
0	23	5	36	[27]7.5	37	213	40	[30]4	[27]0.50	[27]0.55	[27]6.6	0	366
0	20	48	134	[30]4.5	101	307	[30]1,250	[30]375	[30]0.37	[30]0.43	[30]5.0	[30]15	367
0	24	1	18	[30]1.8	26	351	[30]1,250	[30]375	[30]0.37	[30]0.43	[30]5.0	[30]15	368
0	24	1	12	[27]0.7	33	297	[30]1,250	[30]375	[30]0.37	[30]0.43	[30]5.0	0	369
0	22	14	139	[30]8.1	180	264	[30]1,250	[30]375	[30]0.37	[30]0.43	[30]5.0	0	370
0	22	12	179	[30]4.5	151	260	[30]1,250	[30]375	[30]0.37	[30]0.43	[30]5.0	0	371
0	25	3	24	[30]4.5	26	145	[30]1,250	[30]375	[30]0.37	[30]0.43	[30]5.0	[30]15	372
Tr	24	17	41	[30]4.5	63	346	[30]1,250	[30]375	[30]0.37	[30]0.43	[30]5.0	[30]15	373
0	23	11	71	1.2	95	197	[30]1,250	[30]375	[30]0.37	[30]0.43	[30]5.0	0	374
0	23	20	105	[30]4.5	99	257	[30]1,250	[30]375	[30]0.37	[30]0.43	[30]5.0	[30]15	375
0	23	32	79	[30]4.5	59	201	[30]1,250	[30]375	[30]0.37	[30]0.43	[30]5.0	[30]15	376
0	19	18	89	0.9	98	58	20	2	0.10	0.05	0.2	0	377
Tr	18	49	104	0.8	140	12	20	2	0.09	0.15	0.6	0	378
0	24	3	40	[30]18.0	44	325	[30]5,000	[30]1,501	[30]1.50	[30]1.70	[30]20.0	[30]60	379
0	21	10	105	[30]3.5	147	207	[30]960	[30]288	[30]0.28	[30]0.34	[30]3.9	0	380
0	21	13	119	[30]4.5	175	185	[30]1,250	[30]375	[30]0.37	[30]0.43	[30]5.0	0	381
0	25	4	34	[30]1.8	29	340	[30]1,250	[30]375	[30]0.37	[30]0.43	[30]5.0	[30]15	382
0	23	11	100	1.2	102	3	0	0	0.07	0.08	1.5	0	383
Tr	21	8	55	[30]4.5	49	265	[30]1,250	[30]375	[30]0.37	[30]0.43	[30]5.0	[30]15	384
0	26	6	52	[30]1.8	105	25	[30]1,250	[30]375	[30]0.37	[30]0.43	[30]5.0	0	385
0	26	1	21	[30]1.8	18	230	[30]1,250	[30]375	[30]0.37	[30]0.43	[30]5.0	[30]15	386
0	25	3	31	[30]1.8	42	75	[30]1,250	[30]375	[30]0.37	[30]0.43	[30]5.0	[30]15	387
0	22	48	118	[30]18.0	106	352	[30]5,000	[30]1,501	[30]1.50	[30]1.70	[30]20.0	[30]60	388
0	25	6	19	[30]4.5	27	181	[30]1,250	[30]375	[30]0.37	[30]0.43	[30]5.0	[30]15	389
0	23	43	98	[30]4.5	106	354	[30]1,250	[30]375	[30]0.37	[30]0.43	[30]5.0	[30]15	390
0	78	11	86	1.0	314	2	0	0	0.08	0.04	0.4	0	391
0	129	49	575	9.5	389	7	0	0	0.48	0.24	7.7	0	392
0	342	527	1,086	2.7	845	3,226	0	0	0.32	1.27	1.6	0	393
0	29	44	91	0.2	71	269	0	0	0.03	0.11	0.1	0	394
279	225	262	748	7.3	469	1,853	690	194	0.82	0.90	7.7	1	395
47	38	44	125	1.2	78	310	120	32	0.14	0.15	1.3	Tr	396
598	645	653	1,162	22.1	1,439	2,900	1,660	498	1.11	1.66	10.0	1	397
37	40	41	72	1.4	90	181	100	31	0.07	0.10	0.6	Tr	398
19	20	21	37	0.7	46	92	50	16	0.04	0.05	0.3	Tr	399
6	291	513	570	10.8	1,562	1,733	0	0	0.86	1.03	7.4	1	400
1	32	57	63	1.2	173	192	0	0	0.09	0.11	0.8	Tr	401

[35] Excepting angelfood cake, cakes were made from mixes containing vegetable shortening and frostings were made with margarine.

Table 2. Nutritive Value of the Edible Part of Food (Continued)

(Tr indicates nutrient present in trace amount.)

Item No.	Foods, approximate measures, units, and weight (weight of edible portion only)			Water	Food energy	Pro-tein	Fat	Fatty acids		
								Satu-rated	Mono-unsatu-rated	Poly-unsatu-rated
	Grain Products—Con.		Grams	Per-cent	Cal-ories	Grams	Grams	Grams	Grams	Grams
	Cakes prepared from cake mixes with enriched flour: [35]									
	Yellow with chocolate frosting:									
402	Whole, 2-layer cake, 8- or 9-in diam.	1 cake	1,108	26	3,735	45	125	47.8	48.8	21.8
403	Piece, 1/16 of cake	1 piece	69	26	235	3	8	3.0	3.0	1.4
	Cakes prepared from home recipes using enriched flour:									
	Carrot, with cream cheese frosting: [36]									
404	Whole cake, 10-in diam. tube cake	1 cake	1,536	23	6,175	63	328	66.0	135.2	107.5
405	Piece, 1/16 of cake	1 piece	96	23	385	4	21	4.1	8.4	6.7
	Fruitcake, dark: [36]									
406	Whole cake, 7-1/2-in diam., 2-1/4-in high tube cake	1 cake	1,361	18	5,185	74	228	47.6	113.0	51.7
407	Piece, 1/32 of cake, 2/3-in arc	1 piece	43	18	165	2	7	1.5	3.6	1.6
	Plain sheet cake: [37]									
	Without frosting:									
408	Whole cake, 9-in square	1 cake	777	25	2,830	35	108	29.5	45.1	25.6
409	Piece, 1/9 of cake	1 piece	86	25	315	4	12	3.3	5.0	2.8
	With uncooked white frosting:									
410	Whole cake, 9-in square	1 cake	1,096	21	4,020	37	129	41.6	50.4	26.3
411	Piece, 1/9 of cake	1 piece	121	21	445	4	14	4.6	5.6	2.9
	Pound: [38]									
412	Loaf, 8-1/2 by 3-1/2 by 3-1/4 in	1 loaf	514	22	2,025	33	94	21.1	40.9	26.7
413	Slice, 1/17 of loaf	1 slice	30	22	120	2	5	1.2	2.4	1.6
	Cakes, commercial, made with enriched flour:									
	Pound:									
414	Loaf, 8-1/2 by 3-1/2 by 3 in	1 loaf	500	24	1,935	26	94	52.0	30.0	4.0
415	Slice, 1/17 of loaf	1 slice	29	24	110	2	5	3.0	1.7	0.2
	Snack cakes:									
416	Devil's food with creme filling (2 small cakes per pkg)	1 small cake	28	20	105	1	4	1.7	1.5	0.6
417	Sponge with creme filling (2 small cakes per pkg)	1 small cake	42	19	155	1	5	2.3	2.1	0.5
	White with white frosting:									
418	Whole, 2-layer cake, 8- or 9-in diam.	1 cake	1,140	24	4,170	43	148	33.1	61.6	42.2
419	Piece, 1/16 of cake	1 piece	71	24	260	3	9	2.1	3.8	2.6
	Yellow with chocolate frosting:									
420	Whole, 2-layer cake, 8- or 9-in diam.	1 cake	1,108	23	3,895	40	175	92.0	58.7	10.0
421	Piece, 1/16 of cake	1 piece	69	23	245	2	11	5.7	3.7	0.6
	Cheesecake:									
422	Whole cake, 9-in diam.	1 cake	1,110	46	3,350	60	213	119.9	65.5	14.4
423	Piece, 1/12 of cake	1 piece	92	46	280	5	18	9.9	5.4	1.2
	Cookies made with enriched flour:									
	Brownies with nuts:									
424	Commercial, with frosting, 1-1/2 by 1-3/4 by 7/8 in	1 brownie	25	13	100	1	4	1.6	2.0	0.6
425	From home recipe, 1-3/4 by 1-3/4 by 7/8 in [36]	1 brownie	20	10	95	1	6	1.4	2.8	1.2
	Chocolate chip:									
426	Commercial, 2-1/4-in diam., 3/8 in thick	4 cookies	42	4	180	2	9	2.9	3.1	2.6

[35] Excepting angelfood cake, cakes were made from mixes containing vegetable shortening and frostings were made with margarine.
[36] Made with vegetable oil.

| | | | | | | | | Nutrients in Indicated Quantity | | | | | | |

Cho-les-terol	Carbo-hydrate	Calcium	Phos-phorus	Iron	Potas-sium	Sodium	Vitamin A value		Thiamin	Ribo-flavin	Niacin	Ascorbic acid	Item No.
							(IU)	(RE)					
Milli-grams	Grams	Milli-grams	Milli-grams	Milli-grams	Milli-grams	Milli-grams	Inter-national units	Retinol equiva-lents	Milli-grams	Milli-grams	Milli-grams	Milli-grams	
576	638	1,008	2,017	15.5	1,208	2,515	1,550	465	1.22	1.66	11.1	1	402
36	40	63	126	1.0	75	157	100	29	0.08	0.10	0.7	Tr	403
1183	775	707	998	21.0	1,720	4,470	2,240	246	1.83	1.97	14.7	23	404
74	48	44	62	1.3	108	279	140	15	0.11	0.12	0.9	1	405
640	783	1,293	1,592	37.6	6,138	2,123	1,720	422	2.41	2.55	17.0	504	406
20	25	41	50	1.2	194	67	50	13	0.08	0.08	0.5	16	407
552	434	497	793	11.7	614	2,331	1,320	373	1.24	1.40	10.1	2	408
61	48	55	88	1.3	68	258	150	41	0.14	0.15	1.1	Tr	409
636	694	548	822	11.0	669	2,488	2,190	647	1.21	1.42	9.9	2	410
70	77	61	91	1.2	74	275	240	71	0.13	0.16	1.1	Tr	411
555	265	339	473	9.3	483	1,645	3,470	1,033	0.93	1.08	7.8	1	412
32	15	20	28	0.5	28	96	200	60	0.05	0.06	0.5	Tr	413
1100	257	146	517	8.0	443	1,857	2,820	715	0.96	1.12	8.1	0	414
64	15	8	30	0.5	26	108	160	41	0.06	0.06	0.5	0	415
15	17	21	26	1.0	34	105	20	4	0.06	0.09	0.7	0	416
7	27	14	44	0.6	37	155	30	9	0.07	0.06	0.6	0	417
46	670	536	1,585	15.5	832	2,827	640	194	3.19	2.05	27.6	0	418
3	42	33	99	1.0	52	176	40	12	0.20	0.13	1.7	0	419
609	620	366	1,884	19.9	1,972	3,080	1,850	488	0.78	2.22	10.0	0	420
38	39	23	117	1.2	123	192	120	30	0.05	0.14	0.6	0	421
2053	317	622	977	5.3	1,088	2,464	2,820	833	0.33	1.44	5.1	56	422
170	26	52	81	0.4	90	204	230	69	0.03	0.12	0.4	5	423
14	16	13	26	0.6	50	59	70	18	0.08	0.07	0.3	Tr	424
18	11	9	26	0.4	35	51	20	6	0.05	0.05	0.3	Tr	425
5	28	13	41	0.8	68	140	50	15	0.10	0.23	1.0	Tr	426

[37]Cake made with vegetable shortening; frosting with margarine.
[38]Made with margarine.

Item No.	Foods, approximate measures, units, and weight (weight of edible portion only)		Water	Food energy	Pro-tein	Fat	Fatty acids		
							Satu-rated	Mono-unsatu-rated	Poly-unsatu-rated
		Grams	Per-cent	Cal-ories	Grams	Grams	Grams	Grams	Grams

Grain Products—Con.

	Cookies made with enriched flour:								
	Chocolate chip:								
427	From home recipe, 2-1/3-in diam.[25]	4 cookies	40	3	185	2	11	3.9	4.3	2.0
428	From refrigerated dough, 2-1/4-in diam., 3/8 in thick	4 cookies	48	5	225	2	11	4.0	4.4	2.0
429	Fig bars, square, 1-5/8 by 1-5/8 by 3/8 in or rectangular, 1-1/2 by 1-3/4 by 1/2 in	4 cookies	56	12	210	2	4	1.0	1.5	1.0
430	Oatmeal with raisins, 2-5/8-in diam., 1/4 in thick	4 cookies	52	4	245	3	10	2.5	4.5	2.8
431	Peanut butter cookie, from home recipe, 2-5/8-in diam.[25]	4 cookies	48	3	245	4	14	4.0	5.8	2.8
432	Sandwich type (chocolate or vanilla), 1-3/4-in diam., 3/8 in thick	4 cookies	40	2	195	2	8	2.0	3.6	2.2
	Shortbread:								
433	Commercial	4 small cookies	32	6	155	2	8	2.9	3.0	1.1
434	From home recipe[38]	2 large cookies	28	3	145	2	8	1.3	2.7	3.4
435	Sugar cookie, from refrigerated dough, 2-1/2-in diam., 1/4 in thick	4 cookies	48	4	235	2	12	2.3	5.0	3.6
436	Vanilla wafers, 1-3/4-in diam., 1/4 in thick	10 cookies	40	4	185	2	7	1.8	3.0	1.8
437	Corn chips	1-oz package	28	1	155	2	9	1.4	2.4	3.7
	Cornmeal:								
438	Whole-ground, unbolted, dry form	1 cup	122	12	435	11	5	0.5	1.1	2.5
439	Bolted (nearly whole-grain), dry form	1 cup	122	12	440	11	4	0.5	0.9	2.2
	Degermed, enriched:								
440	Dry form	1 cup	138	12	500	11	2	0.2	0.4	0.9
441	Cooked	1 cup	240	88	120	3	Tr	Tr	0.1	0.2
	Crackers:[39]								
	Cheese:								
442	Plain, 1 in square	10 crackers	10	4	50	1	3	0.9	1.2	0.3
443	Sandwich type (peanut butter)	1 sandwich	8	3	40	1	2	0.4	0.8	0.3
444	Graham, plain, 2-1/2 in square	2 crackers	14	5	60	1	1	0.4	0.6	0.4
445	Melba toast, plain	1 piece	5	4	20	1	Tr	0.1	0.1	0.1
446	Rye wafers, whole-grain, 1-7/8 by 3-1/2 in	2 wafers	14	5	55	1	1	0.3	0.4	0.3
447	Saltines[40]	4 crackers	12	4	50	1	1	0.5	0.4	0.2
448	Snack-type, standard	1 round cracker	3	3	15	Tr	1	0.2	0.4	0.1
449	Wheat, thin	4 crackers	8	3	35	1	1	0.5	0.5	0.4
450	Whole-wheat wafers	2 crackers	8	4	35	1	2	0.5	0.6	0.4
451	Croissants, made with enriched flour, 4-1/2 by 4 by 1-3/4 in	1 croissant	57	22	235	5	12	3.5	6.7	1.4
	Danish pastry, made with enriched flour:								
	Plain without fruit or nuts:								
452	Packaged ring, 12 oz	1 ring	340	27	1,305	21	71	21.8	28.6	15.6
453	Round piece, about 4-1/4-in diam., 1 in high	1 pastry	57	27	220	4	12	3.6	4.8	2.6
454	Ounce	1 oz	28	27	110	2	6	1.8	2.4	1.3
455	Fruit, round piece	1 pastry	65	30	235	4	13	3.9	5.2	2.9
	Doughnuts, made with enriched flour:								
456	Cake type, plain, 3-1/4-in diam., 1 in high	1 doughnut	50	21	210	3	12	2.8	5.0	3.0
457	Yeast-leavened, glazed, 3-3/4-in diam., 1-1/4 in high	1 doughnut	60	27	235	4	13	5.2	5.5	0.9
458	English muffins, plain, enriched	1 muffin	57	42	140	5	1	0.3	0.2	0.3
459	Toasted	1 muffin	50	29	140	5	1	0.3	0.2	0.3

[25]Made with vegetable shortening.
[38]Made with margarine.

							Nutrients in Indicated Quantity						
Cho-les-terol	Carbo-hydrate	Calcium	Phos-phorus	Iron	Potas-sium	Sodium	Vitamin A value		Thiamin	Ribo-flavin	Niacin	Ascorbic acid	Item No.
							(IU)	(RE)					
Milli-grams	Grams	Milli-grams	Milli-grams	Milli-grams	Milli-grams	Milli-grams	Inter-national units	Retinol equiva-lents	Milli-grams	Milli-grams	Milli-grams	Milli-grams	
18	26	13	34	1.0	82	82	20	5	0.06	0.06	0.6	0	427
22	32	13	34	1.0	62	173	30	8	0.06	0.10	0.9	0	428
27	42	40	34	1.4	162	180	60	6	0.08	0.07	0.7	Tr	429
2	36	18	58	1.1	90	148	40	12	0.09	0.08	1.0	0	430
22	28	21	60	1.1	110	142	20	5	0.07	0.07	1.9	0	431
0	29	12	40	1.4	66	189	0	0	0.09	0.07	0.8	0	432
27	20	13	39	0.8	38	123	30	8	0.10	0.09	0.9	0	433
0	17	6	31	0.6	18	125	300	89	0.08	0.06	0.7	Tr	434
29	31	50	91	0.9	33	261	40	11	0.09	0.06	1.1	0	435
25	29	16	36	0.8	50	150	50	14	0.07	0.10	1.0	0	436
0	16	35	52	0.5	52	233	110	11	0.04	0.05	0.4	1	437
0	90	24	312	2.2	346	1	620	62	0.46	0.13	2.4	0	438
0	91	21	272	2.2	303	1	590	59	0.37	0.10	2.3	0	439
0	108	8	137	5.9	166	1	610	61	0.61	0.36	4.8	0	440
0	26	2	34	1.4	38	0	140	14	0.14	0.10	1.2	0	441
6	6	11	17	0.3	17	112	20	5	0.05	0.04	0.4	0	442
1	5	7	25	0.3	17	90	Tr	Tr	0.04	0.03	0.6	0	443
0	11	6	20	0.4	36	86	0	0	0.02	0.03	0.6	0	444
0	4	6	10	0.1	11	44	0	0	0.01	0.01	0.1	0	445
0	10	7	44	0.5	65	115	0	0	0.06	0.03	0.5	0	446
4	9	3	12	0.5	17	165	0	0	0.06	0.05	0.6	0	447
0	2	3	6	0.1	4	30	Tr	Tr	0.01	0.01	0.1	0	448
0	5	3	15	0.3	17	69	Tr	Tr	0.04	0.03	0.4	0	449
0	5	3	22	0.2	31	59	0	0	0.02	0.03	0.4	0	450
13	27	20	64	2.1	68	452	50	13	0.17	0.13	1.3	0	451
292	152	360	347	6.5	316	1,302	360	99	0.95	1.02	8.5	Tr	452
49	26	60	58	1.1	53	218	60	17	0.16	0.17	1.4	Tr	453
24	13	30	29	0.5	26	109	30	8	0.08	0.09	0.7	Tr	454
56	28	17	80	1.3	57	233	40	11	0.16	0.14	1.4	Tr	455
20	24	22	111	1.0	58	192	20	5	0.12	0.12	1.1	Tr	456
21	26	17	55	1.4	64	222	Tr	Tr	0.28	0.12	1.8	0	457
0	27	96	67	1.7	331	378	0	0	0.26	0.19	2.2	0	458
0	27	96	67	1.7	331	378	0	0	0.23	0.19	2.2	0	459

[39] Crackers made with enriched flour except for rye wafers and whole-wheat wafers.
[40] Made with lard.

Item No.	Foods, approximate measures, units, and weight (weight of edible portion only)			Water	Food energy	Pro-tein	Fat	Fatty acids		
								Satu-rated	Mono-unsatu-rated	Poly-unsatu-rated
	Grain Products—Con.		Grams	Per-cent	Cal-ories	Grams	Grams	Grams	Grams	Grams
460	French toast, from home recipe---	1 slice--------	65	53	155	6	7	1.6	2.0	1.6
	Macaroni, enriched, cooked (cut lengths, elbows, shells):									
461	Firm stage (hot)---------------	1 cup-----------	130	64	190	7	1	0.1	0.1	0.3
	Tender stage:									
462	Cold-----------------------	1 cup-----------	105	72	115	4	Tr	0.1	0.1	0.2
463	Hot-------------------------	1 cup-----------	140	72	155	5	1	0.1	0.1	0.2
	Muffins made with enriched flour, 2-1/2-in diam., 1-1/2 in high:									
	From home recipe:									
464	Blueberry [25]-----------------	1 muffin--------	45	37	135	3	5	1.5	2.1	1.2
465	Bran [36]-----------------------	1 muffin--------	45	35	125	3	6	1.4	1.6	2.3
466	Corn (enriched, degermed cornmeal and flour) [25]------	1 muffin--------	45	33	145	3	5	1.5	2.2	1.4
	From commercial mix (egg and water added):									
467	Blueberry-------------------	1 muffin--------	45	33	140	3	5	1.4	2.0	1.2
468	Bran-----------------------	1 muffin--------	45	28	140	3	4	1.3	1.6	1.0
469	Corn-----------------------	1 muffin--------	45	30	145	3	6	1.7	2.3	1.4
470	Noodles (egg noodles), enriched, cooked-----------------------	1 cup-----------	160	70	200	7	2	0.5	0.6	0.6
471	Noodles, chow mein, canned------	1 cup-----------	45	11	220	6	11	2.1	7.3	0.4
	Pancakes, 4-in diam.:									
472	Buckwheat, from mix (with buck-wheat and enriched flours), egg and milk added-----------	1 pancake-------	27	58	55	2	2	0.9	0.9	0.5
	Plain:									
473	From home recipe using enriched flour-------------	1 pancake-------	27	50	60	2	2	0.5	0.8	0.5
474	From mix (with enriched flour), egg, milk, and oil added--------------------	1 pancake-------	27	54	60	2	2	0.5	0.9	0.5
	Piecrust, made with enriched flour and vegetable shorten-ing, baked:									
475	From home recipe, 9-in diam.----	1 pie shell-----	180	15	900	11	60	14.8	25.9	15.7
476	From mix, 9-in diam.-----------	Piecrust for 2-crust pie-----	320	19	1,485	20	93	22.7	41.0	25.0
	Pies, piecrust made with enriched flour, vegetable shortening, 9-in diam.:									
	Apple:									
477	Whole-----------------------	1 pie-----------	945	48	2,420	21	105	27.4	44.4	26.5
478	Piece, 1/6 of pie------------	1 piece---------	158	48	405	3	18	4.6	7.4	4.4
	Blueberry:									
479	Whole-----------------------	1 pie-----------	945	51	2,285	23	102	25.5	44.4	27.4
480	Piece, 1/6 of pie------------	1 piece---------	158	51	380	4	17	4.3	7.4	4.6
	Cherry:									
481	Whole-----------------------	1 pie-----------	945	47	2,465	25	107	28.4	46.3	27.4
482	Piece, 1/6 of pie------------	1 piece---------	158	47	410	4	18	4.7	7.7	4.6
	Creme:									
483	Whole-----------------------	1 pie-----------	910	43	2,710	20	139	90.1	23.7	6.4
484	Piece, 1/6 of pie------------	1 piece---------	152	43	455	3	23	15.0	4.0	1.1
	Custard:									
485	Whole-----------------------	1 pie-----------	910	58	1,985	56	101	33.7	40.0	19.1
486	Piece, 1/6 of pie------------	1 piece---------	152	58	330	9	17	5.6	6.7	3.2
	Lemon meringue:									
487	Whole-----------------------	1 pie-----------	840	47	2,140	31	86	26.0	34.4	17.6
488	Piece, 1/6 of pie------------	1 piece---------	140	47	355	5	14	4.3	5.7	2.9
	Peach:									
489	Whole-----------------------	1 pie-----------	945	48	2,410	24	101	24.6	43.5	26.5
490	Piece, 1/6 of pie------------	1 piece---------	158	48	405	4	17	4.1	7.3	4.4

[25] Made with vegetable shortening.

							Nutrients in Indicated Quantity						

Cho-les-terol	Carbo-hydrate	Calcium	Phos-phorus	Iron	Potas-sium	Sodium	Vitamin A value (IU)	(RE)	Thiamin	Ribo-flavin	Niacin	Ascorbic acid	Item No.
Milli-grams	Grams	Milli-grams	Milli-grams	Milli-grams	Milli-grams	Milli-grams	Inter-national units	Retinol equiva-lents	Milli-grams	Milli-grams	Milli-grams	Milli-grams	
112	17	72	85	1.3	86	257	110	32	0.12	0.16	1.0	Tr	460
0	39	14	85	2.1	103	1	0	0	0.23	0.13	1.8	0	461
0	24	8	53	1.3	64	1	0	0	0.15	0.08	1.2	0	462
0	32	11	70	1.7	85	1	0	0	0.20	0.11	1.5	0	463
19	20	54	46	0.9	47	198	40	9	0.10	0.11	0.9	1	464
24	19	60	125	1.4	99	189	230	30	0.11	0.13	1.3	3	465
23	21	66	59	0.9	57	169	80	15	0.11	0.11	0.9	Tr	466
45	22	15	90	0.9	54	225	50	11	0.10	0.17	1.1	Tr	467
28	24	27	182	1.7	50	385	100	14	0.08	0.12	1.9	0	468
42	22	30	128	1.3	31	291	90	16	0.09	0.09	0.8	Tr	469
50	37	16	94	2.6	70	3	110	34	0.22	0.13	1.9	0	470
5	26	14	41	0.4	33	450	0	0	0.05	0.03	0.6	0	471
20	6	59	91	0.4	66	125	60	17	0.04	0.05	0.2	Tr	472
16	9	27	38	0.5	33	115	30	10	0.06	0.07	0.5	Tr	473
16	8	36	71	0.7	43	160	30	7	0.09	0.12	0.8	Tr	474
0	79	25	90	4.5	90	1,100	0	0	0.54	0.40	5.0	0	475
0	141	131	272	9.3	179	2,602	0	0	1.06	0.80	9.9	0	476
0	360	76	208	9.5	756	2,844	280	28	1.04	0.76	9.5	9	477
0	60	13	35	1.6	126	476	50	5	0.17	0.13	1.6	2	478
0	330	104	217	12.3	945	2,533	850	85	1.04	0.85	10.4	38	479
0	55	17	36	2.1	158	423	140	14	0.17	0.14	1.7	6	480
0	363	132	236	9.5	992	2,873	4,160	416	1.13	0.85	9.5	0	481
0	61	22	40	1.6	166	480	700	70	0.19	0.14	1.6	0	482
46	351	273	919	6.8	796	2,207	1,250	391	0.36	0.89	6.4	0	483
8	59	46	154	1.1	133	369	210	65	0.06	0.15	1.1	0	484
1010	213	874	1,028	9.1	1,247	2,612	2,090	573	0.82	1.91	5.5	0	485
169	36	146	172	1.5	208	436	350	96	0.14	0.32	0.9	0	486
857	317	118	412	8.4	420	2,369	1,430	395	0.59	0.84	5.0	25	487
143	53	20	69	1.4	70	395	240	66	0.10	0.14	0.8	4	488
0	361	95	274	11.3	1,408	2,533	6,900	690	1.04	0.95	14.2	28	489
0	60	16	46	1.9	235	423	1,150	115	0.17	0.16	2.4	5	490

[36] Made with vegetable oil.

Item No.	Foods, approximate measures, units, and weight (weight of edible portion only)			Water	Food energy	Pro-tein	Fat	Fatty acids		
								Satu-rated	Mono-unsatu-rated	Poly-unsatu-rated
	Grain Products—Con.		Grams	Per-cent	Cal-ories	Grams	Grams	Grams	Grams	Grams
	Pies, piecrust made with enriched flour, vegetable shortening, 9-inch diam.:									
	Pecan:									
491	Whole	1 pie	825	20	3,450	42	189	28.1	101.5	47.0
492	Piece, 1/6 of pie	1 piece	138	20	575	7	32	4.7	17.0	7.9
	Pumpkin:									
493	Whole	1 pie	910	59	1,920	36	102	38.2	40.0	18.2
494	Piece, 1/6 of pie	1 piece	152	59	320	6	17	6.4	6.7	3.0
	Pies, fried:									
495	Apple	1 pie	85	43	255	2	14	5.8	6.6	0.6
496	Cherry	1 pie	85	42	250	2	14	5.8	6.7	0.6
	Popcorn, popped:									
497	Air-popped, unsalted	1 cup	8	4	30	1	Tr	Tr	0.1	0.2
498	Popped in vegetable oil, salted	1 cup	11	3	55	1	3	0.5	1.4	1.2
499	Sugar syrup coated	1 cup	35	4	135	2	1	0.1	0.3	0.6
	Pretzels, made with enriched flour:									
500	Stick, 2-1/4 in long	10 pretzels	3	3	10	Tr	Tr	Tr	Tr	Tr
501	Twisted, dutch, 2-3/4 by 2-5/8 in	1 pretzel	16	3	65	2	1	0.1	0.2	0.2
502	Twisted, thin, 3-1/4 by 2-1/4 by 1/4 in	10 pretzels	60	3	240	6	2	0.4	0.8	0.6
	Rice:									
503	Brown, cooked, served hot	1 cup	195	70	230	5	1	0.3	0.3	0.4
	White, enriched:									
	Commercial varieties, all types:									
504	Raw	1 cup	185	12	670	12	1	0.2	0.2	0.3
505	Cooked, served hot	1 cup	205	73	225	4	Tr	0.1	0.1	0.1
506	Instant, ready-to-serve, hot	1 cup	165	73	180	4	0	0.1	0.1	0.1
	Parboiled:									
507	Raw	1 cup	185	10	685	14	1	0.1	0.1	0.2
508	Cooked, served hot	1 cup	175	73	185	4	Tr	Tr	Tr	0.1
	Rolls, enriched:									
	Commercial:									
509	Dinner, 2-1/2-in diam., 2 in high	1 roll	28	32	85	2	2	0.5	0.8	0.6
510	Frankfurter and hamburger (8 per 11-1/2-oz pkg.)	1 roll	40	34	115	3	2	0.5	0.8	0.6
511	Hard, 3-3/4-in diam., 2 in high	1 roll	50	25	155	5	2	0.4	0.5	0.6
512	Hoagie or submarine, 11-1/2 by 3 by 2-1/2 in	1 roll	135	31	400	11	8	1.8	3.0	2.2
	From home recipe:									
513	Dinner, 2-1/2-in diam., 2 in high	1 roll	35	26	120	3	3	0.8	1.2	0.9
	Spaghetti, enriched, cooked:									
514	Firm stage, "al dente," served hot	1 cup	130	64	190	7	1	0.1	0.1	0.3
515	Tender stage, served hot	1 cup	140	73	155	5	1	0.1	0.1	0.2
516	Toaster pastries	1 pastry	54	13	210	2	6	1.7	3.6	0.4
517	Tortillas, corn	1 tortilla	30	45	65	2	1	0.1	0.3	0.6
	Waffles, made with enriched flour, 7-in diam.:									
518	From home recipe	1 waffle	75	37	245	7	13	4.0	4.9	2.6
519	From mix, egg and milk added	1 waffle	75	42	205	7	8	2.7	2.9	1.5
	Wheat flours:									
	All-purpose or family flour, enriched:									
520	Sifted, spooned	1 cup	115	12	420	12	1	0.2	0.1	0.5
521	Unsifted, spooned	1 cup	125	12	455	13	1	0.2	0.1	0.5
522	Cake or pastry flour, enriched, sifted, spooned	1 cup	96	12	350	7	1	0.1	0.1	0.3
523	Self-rising, enriched, unsifted, spooned	1 cup	125	12	440	12	1	0.2	0.1	0.5
524	Whole-wheat, from hard wheats, stirred	1 cup	120	12	400	16	2	0.3	0.3	1.1

Nutrients in Indicated Quantity

Cholesterol	Carbohydrate	Calcium	Phosphorus	Iron	Potassium	Sodium	Vitamin A value (IU)	Vitamin A value (RE)	Thiamin	Riboflavin	Niacin	Ascorbic acid	Item No.
Milligrams	Grams	Milligrams	Milligrams	Milligrams	Milligrams	Milligrams	International units	Retinol equivalents	Milligrams	Milligrams	Milligrams	Milligrams	
569	423	388	850	27.2	1,015	1,823	1,320	322	1.82	0.99	6.6	0	491
95	71	65	142	4.6	170	305	220	54	0.30	0.17	1.1	0	492
655	223	464	628	8.2	1,456	1,947	22,480	2,493	0.82	1.27	7.3	0	493
109	37	78	105	1.4	243	325	3,750	416	0.14	0.21	1.2	0	494
14	31	12	34	0.9	42	326	30	3	0.09	0.06	1.0	1	495
13	32	11	41	0.7	61	371	190	19	0.06	0.06	0.6	1	496
0	6	1	22	0.2	20	Tr	10	1	0.03	0.01	0.2	0	497
0	6	3	31	0.3	19	86	20	2	0.01	0.02	0.1	0	498
0	30	2	47	0.5	90	Tr	30	3	0.13	0.02	0.4	0	499
0	2	1	3	0.1	3	48	0	0	0.01	0.01	0.1	0	500
0	13	4	15	0.3	16	258	0	0	0.05	0.04	0.7	0	501
0	48	16	55	1.2	61	966	0	0	0.19	0.15	2.6	0	502
0	50	23	142	1.0	137	0	0	0	0.18	0.04	2.7	0	503
0	149	44	174	5.4	170	9	0	0	0.81	0.06	6.5	0	504
0	50	21	57	1.8	57	0	0	0	0.23	0.02	2.1	0	505
0	40	5	31	1.3	0	0	0	0	0.21	0.02	1.7	0	506
0	150	111	370	5.4	278	17	0	0	0.81	0.07	6.5	0	507
0	41	33	100	1.4	75	0	0	0	0.19	0.02	2.1	0	508
Tr	14	33	44	0.8	36	155	Tr	Tr	0.14	0.09	1.1	Tr	509
Tr	20	54	44	1.2	56	241	Tr	Tr	0.20	0.13	1.6	Tr	510
Tr	30	24	46	1.4	49	313	0	0	0.20	0.12	1.7	0	511
Tr	72	100	115	3.8	128	683	0	0	0.54	0.33	4.5	0	512
12	20	16	36	1.1	41	98	30	8	0.12	0.12	1.2	0	513
0	39	14	85	2.0	103	1	0	0	0.23	0.13	1.8	0	514
0	32	11	70	1.7	85	1	0	0	0.20	0.11	1.5	0	515
0	38	104	104	2.2	91	248	520	52	0.17	0.18	2.3	4	516
0	13	42	55	0.6	43	1	80	8	0.05	0.03	0.4	0	517
102	26	154	135	1.5	129	445	140	39	0.18	0.24	1.5	Tr	518
59	27	179	257	1.2	146	515	170	49	0.14	0.23	0.9	Tr	519
0	88	18	100	5.1	109	2	0	0	0.73	0.46	6.1	0	520
0	95	20	109	5.5	119	3	0	0	0.80	0.50	6.6	0	521
0	76	16	70	4.2	91	2	0	0	0.58	0.38	5.1	0	522
0	93	331	583	5.5	113	1,349	0	0	0.80	0.50	6.6	0	523
0	85	49	446	5.2	444	4	0	0	0.66	0.14	5.2	0	524

Item No.	Foods, approximate measures, units, and weight (weight of edible portion only)		Water	Food energy	Pro-tein	Fat	Fatty acids		
							Satu-rated	Mono-unsatu-rated	Poly-unsatu-rated
		Grams	Per-cent	Cal-ories	Grams	Grams	Grams	Grams	Grams
	Legumes, Nuts, and Seeds								
	Almonds, shelled:								
525	Slivered, packed--------------- 1 cup-----------	135	4	795	27	70	6.7	45.8	14.8
526	Whole------------------------- 1 oz-----------	28	4	165	6	15	1.4	9.6	3.1
	Beans, dry:								
	Cooked, drained:								
527	Black---------------------- 1 cup-----------	171	66	225	15	1	0.1	0.1	0.5
528	Great Northern------------- 1 cup-----------	180	69	210	14	1	0.1	0.1	0.6
529	Lima----------------------- 1 cup-----------	190	64	260	16	1	0.2	0.1	0.5
530	Pea (navy)----------------- 1 cup-----------	190	69	225	15	1	0.1	0.1	0.7
531	Pinto---------------------- 1 cup-----------	180	65	265	15	1	0.1	0.1	0.5
	Canned, solids and liquid:								
	White with:								
532	Frankfurters (sliced)------ 1 cup-----------	255	71	365	19	18	7.4	8.8	0.7
533	Pork and tomato sauce------ 1 cup-----------	255	71	310	16	7	2.4	2.7	0.7
534	Pork and sweet sauce------- 1 cup-----------	255	66	385	16	12	4.3	4.9	1.2
535	Red kidney----------------- 1 cup-----------	255	76	230	15	1	0.1	0.1	0.6
536	Black-eyed peas, dry, cooked (with residual cooking liquid) 1 cup-----------	250	80	190	13	1	0.2	Tr	0.3
537	Brazil nuts, shelled------------- 1 oz-----------	28	3	185	4	19	4.6	6.5	6.8
538	Carob flour--------------------- 1 cup-----------	140	3	255	6	Tr	Tr	0.1	0.1
	Cashew nuts, salted:								
539	Dry roasted------------------- 1 cup-----------	137	2	785	21	63	12.5	37.4	10.7
540	1 oz-----------	28	2	165	4	13	2.6	7.7	2.2
541	Roasted in oil---------------- 1 cup-----------	130	4	750	21	63	12.4	36.9	10.6
542	1 oz-----------	28	4	165	5	14	2.7	8.1	2.3
543	Chestnuts, European (Italian), roasted, shelled------------- 1 cup-----------	143	40	350	5	3	0.6	1.1	1.2
544	Chickpeas, cooked, drained------- 1 cup-----------	163	60	270	15	4	0.4	0.9	1.9
	Coconut:								
	Raw:								
545	Piece, about 2 by 2 by 1/2 in 1 piece---------	45	47	160	1	15	13.4	0.6	0.2
546	Shredded or grated---------- 1 cup-----------	80	47	285	3	27	23.8	1.1	0.3
547	Dried, sweetened, shredded----- 1 cup-----------	93	13	470	3	33	29.3	1.4	0.4
548	Filberts (hazelnuts), chopped---- 1 cup-----------	115	5	725	15	72	5.3	56.5	6.9
549	1 oz-----------	28	5	180	4	18	1.3	13.9	1.7
550	Lentils, dry, cooked------------- 1 cup-----------	200	72	215	16	1	0.1	0.2	0.5
551	Macadamia nuts, roasted in oil, salted----------------------- 1 cup-----------	134	2	960	10	103	15.4	80.9	1.8
552	1 oz-----------	28	2	205	2	22	3.2	17.1	0.4
	Mixed nuts, with peanuts, salted:								
553	Dry roasted------------------ 1 oz-----------	28	2	170	5	15	2.0	8.9	3.1
554	Roasted in oil--------------- 1 oz-----------	28	2	175	5	16	2.5	9.0	3.8
555	Peanuts, roasted in oil, salted-- 1 cup-----------	145	2	840	39	71	9.9	35.5	22.6
556	1 oz-----------	28	2	165	8	14	1.9	6.9	4.4
557	Peanut butter-------------------- 1 tbsp---------	16	1	95	5	8	1.4	4.0	2.5
558	Peas, split, dry, cooked--------- 1 cup-----------	200	70	230	16	1	0.1	0.1	0.3
559	Pecans, halves------------------- 1 cup-----------	108	5	720	8	73	5.9	45.5	18.1
560	1 oz-----------	28	5	190	2	19	1.5	12.0	4.7
561	Pine nuts (pinyons), shelled----- 1 oz-----------	28	6	160	3	17	2.7	6.5	7.3
562	Pistachio nuts, dried, shelled--- 1 oz-----------	28	4	165	6	14	1.7	9.3	2.1
563	Pumpkin and squash kernels, dry, hulled----------------------- 1 oz-----------	28	7	155	7	13	2.5	4.0	5.9
564	Refried beans, canned----------- 1 cup-----------	290	72	295	18	3	0.4	0.6	1.4
565	Sesame seeds, dry, hulled-------- 1 tbsp---------	8	5	45	2	4	0.6	1.7	1.9
566	Soybeans, dry, cooked, drained--- 1 cup-----------	180	71	235	20	10	1.3	1.9	5.3
	Soy products:								
567	Miso----------------------------- 1 cup-----------	276	53	470	29	13	1.8	2.6	7.3
568	Tofu, piece 2-1/2 by 2-3/4 by 1 in----------------------- 1 piece---------	120	85	85	9	5	0.7	1.0	2.9
569	Sunflower seeds, dry, hulled----- 1 oz-----------	28	5	160	6	14	1.5	2.7	9.3
570	Tahini--------------------------- 1 tbsp---------	15	3	90	3	8	1.1	3.0	3.5

[41] Cashews without salt contain 21 mg sodium per cup or 4 mg per oz.
[42] Cashews without salt contain 22 mg sodium per cup or 5 mg per oz.
[43] Macadamia nuts without salt contain 9 mg sodium per cup or 2 mg per oz.

Cholesterol	Carbohydrate	Calcium	Phosphorus	Iron	Potassium	Sodium	Vitamin A value (IU)	Vitamin A value (RE)	Thiamin	Riboflavin	Niacin	Ascorbic acid	Item No.
Milligrams	Grams	Milligrams	Milligrams	Milligrams	Milligrams	Milligrams	International units	Retinol equivalents	Milligrams	Milligrams	Milligrams	Milligrams	
0	28	359	702	4.9	988	15	0	0	0.28	1.05	4.5	1	525
0	6	75	147	1.0	208	3	0	0	0.06	0.22	1.0	Tr	526
0	41	47	239	2.9	608	1	Tr	Tr	0.43	0.05	0.9	0	527
0	38	90	266	4.9	749	13	0	0	0.25	0.13	1.3	0	528
0	49	55	293	5.9	1,163	4	0	0	0.25	0.11	1.3	0	529
0	40	95	281	5.1	790	13	0	0	0.27	0.13	1.3	0	530
0	49	86	296	5.4	882	3	Tr	Tr	0.33	0.16	0.7	0	531
30	32	94	303	4.8	668	1,374	330	33	0.18	0.15	3.3	Tr	532
10	48	138	235	4.6	536	1,181	330	33	0.20	0.08	1.5	5	533
10	54	161	291	5.9	536	969	330	33	0.15	0.10	1.3	5	534
0	42	74	278	4.6	673	968	10	1	0.13	0.10	1.5	0	535
0	35	43	238	3.3	573	20	30	3	0.40	0.10	1.0	0	536
0	4	50	170	1.0	170	1	Tr	Tr	0.28	0.03	0.5	Tr	537
0	126	390	102	5.7	1,275	24	Tr	Tr	0.07	0.07	2.2	Tr	538
0	45	62	671	8.2	774	[41]877	0	0	0.27	0.27	1.9	0	539
0	9	13	139	1.7	160	[41]181	0	0	0.06	0.06	0.4	0	540
0	37	53	554	5.3	689	[42]814	0	0	0.55	0.23	2.3	0	541
0	8	12	121	1.2	150	[42]177	0	0	0.12	0.05	0.5	0	542
0	76	41	153	1.3	847	3	30	3	0.35	0.25	1.9	37	543
0	45	80	273	4.9	475	11	Tr	Tr	0.18	0.09	0.9	0	544
0	7	6	51	1.1	160	9	0	0	0.03	0.01	0.2	1	545
0	12	11	90	1.9	285	16	0	0	0.05	0.02	0.4	3	546
0	44	14	99	1.8	313	244	0	0	0.03	0.02	0.4	1	547
0	18	216	359	3.8	512	3	80	8	0.58	0.13	1.3	1	548
0	4	53	88	0.9	126	1	20	2	0.14	0.03	0.3	Tr	549
0	38	50	238	4.2	498	26	40	4	0.14	0.12	1.2	0	550
0	17	60	268	2.4	441	[43]348	10	1	0.29	0.15	2.7	0	551
0	4	13	57	0.5	93	[43]74	Tr	Tr	0.06	0.03	0.6	0	552
0	7	20	123	1.0	169	[44]190	Tr	Tr	0.06	0.06	1.3	0	553
0	6	31	131	0.9	165	[44]185	10	1	0.14	0.06	1.4	Tr	554
0	27	125	734	2.8	1,019	[45]626	0	0	0.42	0.15	21.5	0	555
0	5	24	143	0.5	199	[45]122	0	0	0.08	0.03	4.2	0	556
0	3	5	60	0.3	110	75	0	0	0.02	0.02	2.2	0	557
0	42	22	178	3.4	592	26	80	8	0.30	0.18	1.8	0	558
0	20	39	314	2.3	423	1	140	14	0.92	0.14	1.0	2	559
0	5	10	83	0.6	111	Tr	40	4	0.24	0.04	0.3	1	560
0	5	2	10	0.9	178	20	10	1	0.35	0.06	1.2	1	561
0	7	38	143	1.9	310	2	70	7	0.23	0.05	0.3	Tr	562
0	5	12	333	4.2	229	5	110	11	0.06	0.09	0.5	Tr	563
0	51	141	245	5.1	1,141	1,228	0	0	0.14	0.16	1.4	17	564
0	1	11	62	0.6	33	3	10	1	0.06	0.01	0.4	0	565
0	19	131	322	4.9	972	4	50	5	0.38	0.16	1.1	0	566
0	65	188	853	4.7	922	8,142	110	11	0.17	0.28	0.8	0	567
0	3	108	151	2.3	50	8	0	0	0.07	0.04	0.1	0	568
0	5	33	200	1.9	195	1	10	1	0.65	0.07	1.3	Tr	569
0	3	21	119	0.7	69	5	10	1	0.24	0.02	0.8	1	570

[44]Mixed nuts without salt contain 3 mg sodium per oz.
[45]Peanuts without salt contain 22 mg sodium per cup or 4 mg per oz.

Item No.	Foods, approximate measures, units, and weight (weight of edible portion only)		Grams	Water Per-cent	Food energy Cal-ories	Pro-tein Grams	Fat Grams	Fatty acids		
								Satu-rated Grams	Mono-unsatu-rated Grams	Poly-unsatu-rated Grams
	Legumes, Nuts, and Seeds—Con.									
	Walnuts:									
571	Black, chopped-----------------	1 cup----------	125	4	760	30	71	4.5	15.9	46.9
572		1 oz-----------	28	4	170	7	16	1.0	3.6	10.6
573	English or Persian, pieces or chips-----------------------	1 cup----------	120	4	770	17	74	6.7	17.0	47.0
574		1 oz-----------	28	4	180	4	18	1.6	4.0	11.1
	Meat and Meat Products									
	Beef, cooked:[46]									
	Cuts braised, simmered, or pot roasted:									
	Relatively fat such as chuck blade:									
575	Lean and fat, piece, 2-1/2 by 2-1/2 by 3/4 in-------	3 oz-----------	85	43	325	22	26	10.8	11.7	0.9
576	Lean only from item 575----	2.2 oz---------	62	53	170	19	9	3.9	4.2	0.3
	Relatively lean, such as bottom round:									
577	Lean and fat, piece, 4-1/8 by 2-1/4 by 1/2 in--------	3 oz-----------	85	54	220	25	13	4.8	5.7	0.5
578	Lean only from item 577----	2.8 oz---------	78	57	175	25	8	2.7	3.4	0.3
	Ground beef, broiled, patty, 3 by 5/8 in:									
579	Lean-----------------------	3 oz-----------	85	56	230	21	16	6.2	6.9	0.6
580	Regular---------------------	3 oz-----------	85	54	245	20	18	6.9	7.7	0.7
581	Heart, lean, braised----------	3 oz-----------	85	65	150	24	5	1.2	0.8	1.6
582	Liver, fried, slice, 6-1/2 by 2-3/8 by 3/8 in[47]-----------	3 oz-----------	85	56	185	23	7	2.5	3.6	1.3
	Roast, oven cooked, no liquid added:									
	Relatively fat, such as rib:									
583	Lean and fat, 2 pieces, 4-1/8 by 2-1/4 by 1/4 in	3 oz-----------	85	46	315	19	26	10.8	11.4	0.9
584	Lean only from item 583----	2.2 oz---------	61	57	150	17	9	3.6	3.7	0.3
	Relatively lean, such as eye of round:									
585	Lean and fat, 2 pieces, 2-1/2 by 2-1/2 by 3/8 in	3 oz-----------	85	57	205	23	12	4.9	5.4	0.5
586	Lean only from item 585----	2.6 oz---------	75	63	135	22	5	1.9	2.1	0.2
	Steak:									
	Sirloin, broiled:									
587	Lean and fat, piece, 2-1/2 by 2-1/2 by 3/4 in-------	3 oz-----------	85	53	240	23	15	6.4	6.9	0.6
588	Lean only from item 587----	2.5 oz---------	72	59	150	22	6	2.6	2.8	0.3
589	Beef, canned, corned-----------	3 oz-----------	85	59	185	22	10	4.2	4.9	0.4
590	Beef, dried, chipped-----------	2.5 oz---------	72	48	145	24	4	1.8	2.0	0.2
	Lamb, cooked:									
	Chops, (3 per lb with bone):									
	Arm, braised:									
591	Lean and fat--------------	2.2 oz---------	63	44	220	20	15	6.9	6.0	0.9
592	Lean only from item 591----	1.7 oz---------	48	49	135	17	7	2.9	2.6	0.4
	Loin, broiled:									
593	Lean and fat--------------	2.8 oz---------	80	54	235	22	16	7.3	6.4	1.0
594	Lean only from item 593----	2.3 oz---------	64	61	140	19	6	2.6	2.4	0.4
	Leg, roasted:									
595	Lean and fat, 2 pieces, 4-1/8 by 2-1/4 by 1/4 in--------	3 oz-----------	85	59	205	22	13	5.6	4.9	0.8
596	Lean only from item 595------	2.6 oz---------	73	64	140	20	6	2.4	2.2	0.4
	Rib, roasted:									
597	Lean and fat, 3 pieces, 2-1/2 by 2-1/2 by 1/4 in--------	3 oz-----------	85	47	315	18	26	12.1	10.6	1.5
598	Lean only from item 597------	2 oz-----------	57	60	130	15	7	3.2	3.0	0.5

[46] Outer layer of fat was removed to within approximately 1/2 inch of the lean. Deposits of fat within the cut were not removed.
[47] Fried in vegetable shortening.

Cho-les-terol	Carbo-hydrate	Calcium	Phos-phorus	Iron	Potas-sium	Sodium	Vitamin A value		Thiamin	Ribo-flavin	Niacin	Ascorbic acid	Item No.
							(IU)	(RE)					
Milli-grams	Grams	Milli-grams	Milli-grams	Milli-grams	Milli-grams	Milli-grams	Inter-national units	Retinol equiva-lents	Milli-grams	Milli-grams	Milli-grams	Milli-grams	
0	15	73	580	3.8	655	1	370	37	0.27	0.14	0.9	Tr	571
0	3	16	132	0.9	149	Tr	80	8	0.06	0.03	0.2	Tr	572
0	22	113	380	2.9	602	12	150	15	0.46	0.18	1.3	4	573
0	5	27	90	0.7	142	3	40	4	0.11	0.04	0.3	1	574
87	0	11	163	2.5	163	53	Tr	Tr	0.06	0.19	2.0	0	575
66	0	8	146	2.3	163	44	Tr	Tr	0.05	0.17	1.7	0	576
81	0	5	217	2.8	248	43	Tr	Tr	0.06	0.21	3.3	0	577
75	0	4	212	2.7	240	40	Tr	Tr	0.06	0.20	3.0	0	578
74	0	9	134	1.8	256	65	Tr	Tr	0.04	0.18	4.4	0	579
76	0	9	144	2.1	248	70	Tr	Tr	0.03	0.16	4.9	0	580
164	0	5	213	6.4	198	54	Tr	Tr	0.12	1.31	3.4	5	581
410	7	9	392	5.3	309	90	[48]30,690	[48]9,120	0.18	3.52	12.3	23	582
72	0	8	145	2.0	246	54	Tr	Tr	0.06	0.16	3.1	0	583
49	0	5	127	1.7	218	45	Tr	Tr	0.05	0.13	2.7	0	584
62	0	5	177	1.6	308	50	Tr	Tr	0.07	0.14	3.0	0	585
52	0	3	170	1.5	297	46	Tr	Tr	0.07	0.13	2.8	0	586
77	0	9	186	2.6	306	53	Tr	Tr	0.10	0.23	3.3	0	587
64	0	8	176	2.4	290	48	Tr	Tr	0.09	0.22	3.1	0	588
80	0	17	90	3.7	51	802	Tr	Tr	0.02	0.20	2.9	0	589
46	0	14	287	2.3	142	3,053	Tr	Tr	0.05	0.23	2.7	0	590
77	0	16	132	1.5	195	46	Tr	Tr	0.04	0.16	4.4	0	591
59	0	12	111	1.3	162	36	Tr	Tr	0.03	0.13	3.0	0	592
78	0	16	162	1.4	272	62	Tr	Tr	0.09	0.21	5.5	0	593
60	0	12	145	1.3	241	54	Tr	Tr	0.08	0.18	4.4	0	594
78	0	8	162	1.7	273	57	Tr	Tr	0.09	0.24	5.5	0	595
65	0	6	150	1.5	247	50	Tr	Tr	0.08	0.20	4.6	0	596
77	0	19	139	1.4	224	60	Tr	Tr	0.08	0.18	5.5	0	597
50	0	12	111	1.0	179	46	Tr	Tr	0.05	0.13	3.5	0	598

[48] Value varies widely.

Item No.	Foods, approximate measures, units, and weight (weight of edible portion only)		Water	Food energy	Pro-tein	Fat	Fatty acids		
							Satu-rated	Mono-unsatu-rated	Poly-unsatu-rated
		Grams	Per-cent	Cal-ories	Grams	Grams	Grams	Grams	Grams
	Meat and Meat Products—Con.								
	Pork, cured, cooked:								
	Bacon:								
599	Regular----------------------	3 medium slices	19	13	110	6	9	3.3	4.5	1.1
600	Canadian-style---------------	2 slices--------	46	62	85	11	4	1.3	1.9	0.4
601	Ham, light cure, roasted:								
	Lean and fat, 2 pieces, 4-1/8 by 2-1/4 by 1/4 in--------	3 oz------------	85	58	205	18	14	5.1	6.7	1.5
602	Lean only from item 601------	2.4 oz----------	68	66	105	17	4	1.3	1.7	0.4
603	Ham, canned, roasted, 2 pieces, 4-1/8 by 2-1/4 by 1/4 in-----	3 oz------------	85	67	140	18	7	2.4	3.5	0.8
	Luncheon meat:								
604	Canned, spiced or unspiced, slice, 3 by 2 by 1/2 in----	2 slices--------	42	52	140	5	13	4.5	6.0	1.5
605	Chopped ham (8 slices per 6 oz pkg)---------------------	2 slices--------	42	64	95	7	7	2.4	3.4	0.9
	Cooked ham (8 slices per 8-oz pkg):								
606	Regular-------------------	2 slices--------	57	65	105	10	6	1.9	2.8	0.7
607	Extra lean---------------	2 slices--------	57	71	75	11	3	0.9	1.3	0.3
	Pork, fresh, cooked:								
	Chop, loin (cut 3 per lb with bone):								
	Broiled:								
608	Lean and fat---------------	3.1 oz----------	87	50	275	24	19	7.0	8.8	2.2
609	Lean only from item 608----	2.5 oz----------	72	57	165	23	8	2.6	3.4	0.9
	Pan fried:								
610	Lean and fat---------------	3.1 oz----------	89	45	335	21	27	9.8	12.5	3.1
611	Lean only from item 610----	2.4 oz----------	67	54	180	19	11	3.7	4.8	1.3
	Ham (leg), roasted:								
612	Lean and fat, piece, 2-1/2 by 2-1/2 by 3/4 in------------	3 oz------------	85	53	250	21	18	6.4	8.1	2.0
613	Lean only from item 612------	2.5 oz----------	72	60	160	20	8	2.7	3.6	1.0
	Rib, roasted:								
614	Lean and fat, piece, 2-1/2 by 3/4 in--------------------	3 oz------------	85	51	270	21	20	7.2	9.2	2.3
615	Lean only from item 614------	2.5 oz----------	71	57	175	20	10	3.4	4.4	1.2
	Shoulder cut, braised:								
616	Lean and fat, 3 pieces, 2-1/2 by 2-1/2 by 1/4 in---------	3 oz------------	85	47	295	23	22	7.9	10.0	2.4
617	Lean only from item 616------	2.4 oz----------	67	54	165	22	8	2.8	3.7	1.0
	Sausages (See also Luncheon meats, items 604-607):								
618	Bologna, slice (8 per 8-oz pkg)	2 slices--------	57	54	180	7	16	6.1	7.6	1.4
619	Braunschweiger, slice (6 per 6-oz pkg)--------------------	2 slices--------	57	48	205	8	18	6.2	8.5	2.1
620	Brown and serve (10-11 per 8-oz pkg), browned-----------	1 link----------	13	45	50	2	5	1.7	2.2	0.5
621	Frankfurter (10 per 1-lb pkg), cooked (reheated)------------	1 frankfurter---	45	54	145	5	13	4.8	6.2	1.2
622	Pork link (16 per 1-lb pkg), cooked[50]--------------------	1 link----------	13	45	50	3	4	1.4	1.8	0.5
	Salami:								
623	Cooked type, slice (8 per 8-oz pkg)------------------	2 slices--------	57	60	145	8	11	4.6	5.2	1.2
624	Dry type, slice (12 per 4-oz pkg)--------------------	2 slices--------	20	35	85	5	7	2.4	3.4	0.6
625	Sandwich spread (pork, beef)---	1 tbsp----------	15	60	35	1	3	0.9	1.1	0.4
626	Vienna sausage (7 per 4-oz can)	1 sausage-------	16	60	45	2	4	1.5	2.0	0.3
	Veal, medium fat, cooked, bone removed:								
627	Cutlet, 4-1/8 by 2-1/4 by 1/2 in, braised or broiled-------	3 oz------------	85	60	185	23	9	4.1	4.1	0.6
628	Rib, 2 pieces, 4-1/8 by 2-1/4 by 1/4 in, roasted----------	3 oz------------	85	55	230	23	14	6.0	6.0	1.0

[49] Contains added sodium ascorbate. If sodium ascorbate is not added, ascorbic acid content is negligible.

Nutrients in Indicated Quantity

Cho-les-terol	Carbo-hydrate	Calcium	Phos-phorus	Iron	Potas-sium	Sodium	Vitamin A value (IU)	Vitamin A value (RE)	Thiamin	Ribo-flavin	Niacin	Ascorbic acid	Item No.
Milli-grams	Grams	Milli-grams	Milli-grams	Milli-grams	Milli-grams	Milli-grams	Inter-national units	Retinol equiva-lents	Milli-grams	Milli-grams	Milli-grams	Milli-grams	
16	Tr	2	64	0.3	92	303	0	0	0.13	0.05	1.4	6	599
27	1	5	136	0.4	179	711	0	0	0.38	0.09	3.2	10	600
53	0	6	182	0.7	243	1,009	0	0	0.51	0.19	3.8	0	601
37	0	5	154	0.6	215	902	0	0	0.46	0.17	3.4	0	602
35	Tr	6	188	0.9	298	908	0	0	0.82	0.21	4.3	[49]19	603
26	1	3	34	0.3	90	541	0	0	0.15	0.08	1.3	Tr	604
21	0.	3	65	0.3	134	576	0	0	0.27	0.09	1.6	[49]8	605
32	2	4	141	0.6	189	751	0	0	0.49	0.14	3.0	[49]16	606
27	1	4	124	0.4	200	815	0	0	0.53	0.13	2.8	[49]15	607
84	0	3	184	0.7	312	61	10	3	0.87	0.24	4.3	Tr	608
71	0	4	176	0.7	302	56	10	1	0.83	0.22	4.0	Tr	609
92	0	4	190	0.7	323	64	10	3	0.91	0.24	4.6	Tr	610
72	0	3	178	0.7	305	57	10	1	0.84	0.22	4.0	Tr	611
79	0	5	210	0.9	280	50	10	2	0.54	0.27	3.9	Tr	612
68	0	5	202	0.8	269	46	10	1	0.50	0.25	3.6	Tr	613
69	0	9	190	0.8	313	37	10	3	0.50	0.24	4.2	Tr	614
56	0	8	182	0.7	300	33	10	2	0.45	0.22	3.8	Tr	615
93	0	6	162	1.4	286	75	10	3	0.46	0.26	4.4	Tr	616
76	0	5	151	1.3	271	68	10	1	0.40	0.24	4.0	Tr	617
31	2	7	52	0.9	103	581	0	0	0.10	0.08	1.5	[49]12	618
89	2	5	96	5.3	113	652	8,010	2,405	0.14	0.87	4.8	[49]6	619
9	Tr	1	14	0.1	25	105	0	0	0.05	0.02	0.4	0	620
23	1	5	39	0.5	75	504	0	0	0.09	0.05	1.2	[49]12	621
11	Tr	4	24	0.2	47	168	0	0	0.10	0.03	0.6	Tr	622
37	1	7	66	1.5	113	607	0	0	0.14	0.21	2.0	[49]7	623
16	1	2	28	0.3	76	372	0	0	0.12	0.06	1.0	[49]5	624
6	2	2	9	0.1	17	152	10	1	0.03	0.02	0.3	0	625
8	Tr	2	8	0.1	16	152	0	0	0.01	0.02	0.3	0	626
109	0	9	196	0.8	258	56	Tr	Tr	0.06	0.21	4.6	0	627
109	0	10	211	0.7	259	57	Tr	Tr	0.11	0.26	6.6	0	628

[50] One patty (8 per pound) of bulk sausage is equivalent to 2 links.

Item No.	Foods, approximate measures, units, and weight (weight of edible portion only)		Water	Food energy	Pro-tein	Fat	Fatty acids		
							Satu-rated	Mono-unsatu-rated	Poly-unsatu-rated
	Mixed Dishes and Fast Foods	Grams	Per-cent	Cal-ories	Grams	Grams	Grams	Grams	Grams
	Mixed dishes:								
629	Beef and vegetable stew, from home recipe-----------------	1 cup-----------	245	82	220	16	11	4.4	4.5	0.5
630	Beef potpie, from home recipe, baked, piece, 1/3 of 9-in diam. pie[51] -------------	1 piece---------	210	55	515	21	30	7.9	12.9	7.4
631	Chicken a la king, cooked, from home recipe-------------	1 cup-----------	245	68	470	27	34	12.9	13.4	6.2
632	Chicken and noodles, cooked, from home recipe------------	1 cup-----------	240	71	365	22	18	5.1	7.1	3.9
	Chicken chow mein:								
633	Canned-----------------------	1 cup-----------	250	89	95	7	Tr	0.1	0.1	0.8
634	From home recipe------------	1 cup-----------	250	78	255	31	10	4.1	4.9	3.5
635	Chicken potpie, from home recipe, baked, piece, 1/3 of 9-in diam. pie[51] -------------	1 piece---------	232	57	545	23	31	10.3	15.5	6.6
636	Chili con carne with beans, canned----------------------	1 cup-----------	255	72	340	19	16	5.8	7.2	1.0
637	Chop suey with beef and pork, from home recipe------------	1 cup-----------	250	75	300	26	17	4.3	7.4	4.2
	Macaroni (enriched) and cheese:								
638	Canned[52] ---------------------	1 cup-----------	240	80	230	9	10	4.7	2.9	1.3
639	From home recipe[38] -----------	1 cup-----------	200	58	430	17	22	9.8	7.4	3.6
640	Quiche Lorraine, 1/8 of 8-in diam. quiche[51] -------------	1 slice---------	176	47	600	13	48	23.2	17.8	4.1
	Spaghetti (enriched) in tomato sauce with cheese:								
641	Canned----------------------	1 cup-----------	250	80	190	6	2	0.4	0.4	0.5
642	From home recipe------------	1 cup-----------	250	77	260	9	9	3.0	3.6	1.2
	Spaghetti (enriched) with meat-balls and tomato sauce:								
643	Canned----------------------	1 cup-----------	250	78	260	12	10	2.4	3.9	3.1
644	From home recipe------------	1 cup-----------	248	70	330	19	12	3.9	4.4	2.2
	Fast food entrees:								
	Cheeseburger:								
645	Regular----------------------	1 sandwich------	112	46	300	15	15	7.3	5.6	1.0
646	4 oz patty------------------	1 sandwich------	194	46	525	30	31	15.1	12.2	1.4
	Chicken, fried. See Poultry and Poultry Products (items 656-659).								
647	Enchilada---------------------	1 enchilada-----	230	72	235	20	16	7.7	6.7	0.6
648	English muffin, egg, cheese, and bacon-------------------	1 sandwich------	138	49	360	18	18	8.0	8.0	0.7
	Fish sandwich:								
649	Regular, with cheese---------	1 sandwich------	140	43	420	16	23	6.3	6.9	7.7
650	Large, without cheese--------	1 sandwich------	170	48	470	18	27	6.3	8.7	9.5
	Hamburger:								
651	Regular----------------------	1 sandwich------	98	46	245	12	11	4.4	5.3	0.5
652	4 oz patty------------------	1 sandwich------	174	50	445	25	21	7.1	11.7	0.6
653	Pizza, cheese, 1/8 of 15-in diam. pizza[51] ----------------	1 slice---------	120	46	290	15	9	4.1	2.6	1.3
654	Roast beef sandwich------------	1 sandwich------	150	52	345	22	13	3.5	6.9	1.8
655	Taco-------------------------	1 taco---------	81	55	195	9	11	4.1	5.5	0.8

[38] Made with margarine.
[51] Crust made with vegetable shortening and enriched flour.

Cho-les-terol	Carbo-hydrate	Calcium	Phos-phorus	Iron	Potas-sium	Sodium	Vitamin A value (IU)	(RE)	Thiamin	Ribo-flavin	Niacin	Ascorbic acid	Item No.
Milli-grams	Grams	Milli-grams	Milli-grams	Milli-grams	Milli-grams	Milli-grams	Inter-national units	Retinol equiva-lents	Milli-grams	Milli-grams	Milli-grams	Milli-grams	
71	15	29	184	2.9	613	292	5,690	568	0.15	0.17	4.7	17	629
42	39	29	149	3.8	334	596	4,220	517	0.29	0.29	4.8	6	630
221	12	127	358	2.5	404	760	1,130	272	0.10	0.42	5.4	12	631
103	26	26	247	2.2	149	600	430	130	0.05	0.17	4.3	Tr	632
8	18	45	85	1.3	418	725	150	28	0.05	0.10	1.0	13	633
75	10	58	293	2.5	473	718	280	50	0.08	0.23	4.3	10	634
56	42	70	232	3.0	343	594	7,220	735	0.32	0.32	4.9	5	635
28	31	82	321	4.3	594	1,354	150	15	0.08	0.18	3.3	8	636
68	13	60	248	4.8	425	1,053	600	60	0.28	0.38	5.0	33	637
24	26	199	182	1.0	139	730	260	72	0.12	0.24	1.0	Tr	638
44	40	362	322	1.8	240	1,086	860	232	0.20	0.40	1.8	1	639
285	29	211	276	1.0	283	653	1,640	454	0.11	0.32	Tr	Tr	640
3	39	40	88	2.8	303	955	930	120	0.35	0.28	4.5	10	641
8	37	80	135	2.3	408	955	1,080	140	0.25	0.18	2.3	13	642
23	29	53	113	3.3	245	1,220	1,000	100	0.15	0.18	2.3	5	643
89	39	124	236	3.7	665	1,009	1,590	159	0.25	0.30	4.0	22	644
44	28	135	174	2.3	219	672	340	65	0.26	0.24	3.7	1	645
104	40	236	320	4.5	407	1,224	670	128	0.33	0.48	7.4	3	646
19	24	97	198	3.3	653	1,332	2,720	352	0.18	0.26	Tr	Tr	647
213	31	197	290	3.1	201	832	650	160	0.46	0.50	3.7	1	648
56	39	132	223	1.8	274	667	160	25	0.32	0.26	3.3	2	649
91	41	61	246	2.2	375	621	110	15	0.35	0.23	3.5	1	650
32	28	56	107	2.2	202	463	80	14	0.23	0.24	3.8	1	651
71	38	75	225	4.8	404	763	160	28	0.38	0.38	7.8	1	652
56	39	220	216	1.6	230	699	750	106	0.34	0.29	4.2	2	653
55	34	60	222	4.0	338	757	240	32	0.40	0.33	6.0	2	654
21	15	109	134	1.2	263	456	420	57	0.09	0.07	1.4	1	655

[52]Made with corn oil.

Item No.	Foods, approximate measures, units, and weight (weight of edible portion only)		Grams	Water Percent	Food energy Calories	Protein Grams	Fat Grams	Fatty acids Saturated Grams	Monounsaturated Grams	Polyunsaturated Grams
	Poultry and Poultry Products									
	Chicken:									
	Fried, flesh, with skin:[53]									
	Batter dipped:									
656	Breast, 1/2 breast (5.6 oz with bones)	4.9 oz	140	52	365	35	18	4.9	7.6	4.3
657	Drumstick (3.4 oz with bones)	2.5 oz	72	53	195	16	11	3.0	4.6	2.7
	Flour coated:									
658	Breast, 1/2 breast (4.2 oz with bones)	3.5 oz	98	57	220	31	9	2.4	3.4	1.9
659	Drumstick (2.6 oz with bones)	1.7 oz	49	57	120	13	7	1.8	2.7	1.6
	Roasted, flesh only:									
660	Breast, 1/2 breast (4.2 oz with bones and skin)	3.0 oz	86	65	140	27	3	0.9	1.1	0.7
661	Drumstick, (2.9 oz with bones and skin)	1.6 oz	44	67	75	12	2	0.7	0.8	0.6
662	Stewed, flesh only, light and dark meat, chopped or diced	1 cup	140	67	250	38	9	2.6	3.3	2.2
663	Chicken liver, cooked	1 liver	20	68	30	5	1	0.4	0.3	0.2
664	Duck, roasted, flesh only	1/2 duck	221	64	445	52	25	9.2	8.2	3.2
	Turkey, roasted, flesh only:									
665	Dark meat, piece, 2-1/2 by 1-5/8 by 1/4 in	4 pieces	85	63	160	24	6	2.1	1.4	1.8
666	Light meat, piece, 4 by 2 by 1/4 in	2 pieces	85	66	135	25	3	0.9	0.5	0.7
	Light and dark meat:									
667	Chopped or diced	1 cup	140	65	240	41	7	2.3	1.4	2.0
668	Pieces (1 slice white meat, 4 by 2 by 1/4 in and 2 slices dark meat, 2-1/2 by 1-5/8 by 1/4 in)	3 pieces	85	65	145	25	4	1.4	0.9	1.2
	Poultry food products:									
	Chicken:									
669	Canned, boneless	5 oz	142	69	235	31	11	3.1	4.5	2.5
670	Frankfurter (10 per 1-lb pkg)	1 frankfurter	45	58	115	6	9	2.5	3.8	1.8
671	Roll, light (6 slices per 6 oz pkg)	2 slices	57	69	90	11	4	1.1	1.7	0.9
	Turkey:									
672	Gravy and turkey, frozen	5-oz package	142	85	95	8	4	1.2	1.4	0.7
673	Ham, cured turkey thigh meat (8 slices per 8-oz pkg)	2 slices	57	71	75	11	3	1.0	0.7	0.9
674	Loaf, breast meat (8 slices per 6-oz pkg)	2 slices	42	72	45	10	1	0.2	0.2	0.1
675	Patties, breaded, battered, fried (2.25 oz)	1 patty	64	50	180	9	12	3.0	4.8	3.0
676	Roast, boneless, frozen, seasoned, light and dark meat, cooked	3 oz	85	68	130	18	5	1.6	1.0	1.4
	Soups, Sauces, and Gravies									
	Soups:									
	Canned, condensed:									
	Prepared with equal volume of milk:									
677	Clam chowder, New England	1 cup	248	85	165	9	7	3.0	2.3	1.1
678	Cream of chicken	1 cup	248	85	190	7	11	4.6	4.5	1.6
679	Cream of mushroom	1 cup	248	85	205	6	14	5.1	3.0	4.6
680	Tomato	1 cup	248	85	160	6	6	2.9	1.6	1.1

[53] Fried in vegetable shortening.

Cholesterol	Carbohydrate	Calcium	Phosphorus	Iron	Potassium	Sodium	Vitamin A value (IU)	Vitamin A value (RE)	Thiamin	Riboflavin	Niacin	Ascorbic acid	Item No.
Milligrams	Grams	Milligrams	Milligrams	Milligrams	Milligrams	Milligrams	International units	Retinol equivalents	Milligrams	Milligrams	Milligrams	Milligrams	
119	13	28	259	1.8	281	385	90	28	0.16	0.20	14.7	0	656
62	6	12	106	1.0	134	194	60	19	0.08	0.15	3.7	0	657
87	2	16	228	1.2	254	74	50	15	0.08	0.13	13.5	0	658
44	1	6	86	0.7	112	44	40	12	0.04	0.11	3.0	0	659
73	0	13	196	0.9	220	64	20	5	0.06	0.10	11.8	0	660
41	0	5	81	0.6	108	42	30	8	0.03	0.10	2.7	0	661
116	0	20	210	1.6	252	98	70	21	0.07	0.23	8.6	0	662
126	Tr	3	62	1.7	28	10	3,270	983	0.03	0.35	0.9	3	663
197	0	27	449	6.0	557	144	170	51	0.57	1.04	11.3	0	664
72	0	27	173	2.0	246	67	0	0	0.05	0.21	3.1	0	665
59	0	16	186	1.1	259	54	0	0	0.05	0.11	5.8	0	666
106	0	35	298	2.5	417	98	0	0	0.09	0.25	7.6	0	667
65	0	21	181	1.5	253	60	0	0	0.05	0.15	4.6	0	668
88	0	20	158	2.2	196	714	170	48	0.02	0.18	9.0	3	669
45	3	43	48	0.9	38	616	60	17	0.03	0.05	1.4	0	670
28	1	24	89	0.6	129	331	50	14	0.04	0.07	3.0	0	671
26	7	20	115	1.3	87	787	60	18	0.03	0.18	2.6	0	672
32	Tr	6	108	1.6	184	565	0	0	0.03	0.14	2.0	0	673
17	0	3	97	0.2	118	608	0	0	0.02	0.05	3.5	[54]0	674
40	10	9	173	1.4	176	512	20	7	0.06	0.12	1.5	0	675
45	3	4	207	1.4	253	578	0	0	0.04	0.14	5.3	0	676
22	17	186	156	1.5	300	992	160	40	0.07	0.24	1.0	3	677
27	15	181	151	0.7	273	1,047	710	94	0.07	0.26	0.9	1	678
20	15	179	156	0.6	270	1,076	150	37	0.08	0.28	0.9	2	679
17	22	159	149	1.8	449	932	850	109	0.13	0.25	1.5	68	680

[54] If sodium ascorbate is added, product contains 11 mg ascorbic acid.

Item No.	Foods, approximate measures, units, and weight (weight of edible portion only)		Water	Food energy	Pro-tein	Fat	Fatty acids		
							Satu-rated	Mono-unsatu-rated	Poly-unsatu-rated
	Soups, Sauces, and Gravies—Con.	Grams	Per-cent	Cal-ories	Grams	Grams	Grams	Grams	Grams
	Soups:								
	Canned, condensed:								
	Prepared with equal volume of water:								
681	Bean with bacon------------	1 cup-----------	253	84	170	8	6	1.5	2.2	1.8
682	Beef broth, bouillon, consomme-----------------	1 cup-----------	240	98	15	3	1	0.3	0.2	Tr
683	Beef noodle----------------	1 cup-----------	244	92	85	5	3	1.1	1.2	0.5
684	Chicken noodle-------------	1 cup-----------	241	92	75	4	2	0.7	1.1	0.6
685	Chicken rice---------------	1 cup-----------	241	94	60	4	2	0.5	0.9	0.4
686	Clam chowder, Manhattan----	1 cup-----------	244	90	80	4	2	0.4	0.4	1.3
687	Cream of chicken-----------	1 cup-----------	244	91	115	3	7	2.1	3.3	1.5
688	Cream of mushroom----------	1 cup-----------	244	90	130	2	9	2.4	1.7	4.2
689	Minestrone-----------------	1 cup-----------	241	91	80	4	3	0.6	0.7	1.1
690	Pea, green-----------------	1 cup-----------	250	83	165	9	3	1.4	1.0	0.4
691	Tomato---------------------	1 cup-----------	244	90	85	2	2	0.4	0.4	1.0
692	Vegetable beef-------------	1 cup-----------	244	92	80	6	2	0.9	0.8	0.1
693	Vegetarian-----------------	1 cup-----------	241	92	70	2	2	0.3	0.8	0.7
	Dehydrated:								
	Unprepared:								
694	Bouillon-------------------	1 pkt-----------	6	3	15	1	1	0.3	0.2	Tr
695	Onion----------------------	1 pkt-----------	7	4	20	1	Tr	0.1	0.2	Tr
	Prepared with water:								
696	Chicken noodle-------------	1 pkt (6-fl-oz)	188	94	40	2	1	0.2	0.4	0.3
697	Onion----------------------	1 pkt (6-fl-oz)	184	96	20	1	Tr	0.1	0.2	0.1
698	Tomato vegetable-----------	1 pkt (6-fl-oz)	189	94	40	1	1	0.3	0.2	0.1
	Sauces:								
	From dry mix:								
699	Cheese, prepared with milk---	1 cup-----------	279	77	305	16	17	9.3	5.3	1.6
700	Hollandaise, prepared with water-----------------	1 cup-----------	259	84	240	5	20	11.6	5.9	0.9
701	White sauce, prepared with milk-----------------	1 cup-----------	264	81	240	10	13	6.4	4.7	1.7
	From home recipe:								
702	White sauce, medium[55]--------	1 cup-----------	250	73	395	10	30	9.1	11.9	7.2
	Ready to serve:								
703	Barbecue-------------------	1 tbsp----------	16	81	10	Tr	Tr	Tr	0.1	0.1
704	Soy------------------------	1 tbsp----------	18	68	10	2	0	0.0	0.0	0.0
	Gravies:								
	Canned:								
705	Beef-----------------------	1 cup-----------	233	87	125	9	5	2.7	2.3	0.2
706	Chicken--------------------	1 cup-----------	238	85	190	5	14	3.4	6.1	3.6
707	Mushroom-------------------	1 cup-----------	238	89	120	3	6	1.0	2.8	2.4
	From dry mix:								
708	Brown----------------------	1 cup-----------	261	91	80	3	2	0.9	0.8	0.1
709	Chicken--------------------	1 cup-----------	260	91	85	3	2	0.5	0.9	0.4
	Sugars and Sweets								
	Candy:								
710	Caramels, plain or chocolate---	1 oz-----------	28	8	115	1	3	2.2	0.3	0.1
	Chocolate:								
711	Milk, plain----------------	1 oz-----------	28	1	145	2	9	5.4	3.0	0.3
712	Milk, with almonds---------	1 oz-----------	28	2	150	3	10	4.8	4.1	0.7
713	Milk, with peanuts---------	1 oz-----------	28	1	155	4	11	4.2	3.5	1.5
714	Milk, with rice cereal-------	1 oz-----------	28	2	140	2	7	4.4	2.5	0.2
715	Semisweet, small pieces (60 per oz)-----------------	1 cup or 6 oz---	170	1	860	7	61	36.2	19.9	1.9
716	Sweet (dark)---------------	1 oz-----------	28	1	150	1	10	5.9	3.3	0.3
717	Fondant, uncoated (mints, candy corn, other)-----------------	1 oz-----------	28	3	105	Tr	0	0.0	0.0	0.0
718	Fudge, chocolate, plain--------	1 oz-----------	28	8	115	1	3	2.1	1.0	0.1
719	Gum drops------------------	1 oz-----------	28	12	100	Tr	Tr	Tr	Tr	0.1

[55] Made with enriched flour, margarine, and whole milk.

Nutrients in Indicated Quantity

Cholesterol	Carbohydrate	Calcium	Phosphorus	Iron	Potassium	Sodium	Vitamin A value (IU)	Vitamin A value (RE)	Thiamin	Riboflavin	Niacin	Ascorbic acid	Item No.
Milligrams	Grams	Milligrams	Milligrams	Milligrams	Milligrams	Milligrams	International units	Retinol equivalents	Milligrams	Milligrams	Milligrams	Milligrams	
3	23	81	132	2.0	402	951	890	89	0.09	0.03	0.6	2	681
Tr	Tr	14	31	0.4	130	782	0	0	Tr	0.05	1.9	0	682
5	9	15	46	1.1	100	952	630	63	0.07	0.06	1.1	Tr	683
7	9	17	36	0.8	55	1,106	710	71	0.05	0.06	1.4	Tr	684
7	7	17	22	0.7	101	815	660	66	0.02	0.02	1.1	Tr	685
2	12	34	59	1.9	261	1,808	920	92	0.06	0.05	1.3	3	686
10	9	34	37	0.6	88	986	560	56	0.03	0.06	0.8	Tr	687
2	9	46	49	0.5	100	1,032	0	0	0.05	0.09	0.7	1	688
2	11	34	55	0.9	313	911	2,340	234	0.05	0.04	0.9	1	689
0	27	28	125	2.0	190	988	200	20	0.11	0.07	1.2	2	690
0	17	12	34	1.8	264	871	690	69	0.09	0.05	1.4	66	691
5	10	17	41	1.1	173	956	1,890	189	0.04	0.05	1.0	2	692
0	12	22	34	1.1	210	822	3,010	301	0.05	0.05	0.9	1	693
1	1	4	19	0.1	27	1,019	Tr	Tr	Tr	0.01	0.3	0	694
Tr	4	10	23	0.1	47	627	Tr	Tr	0.02	0.04	0.4	Tr	695
2	6	24	24	0.4	23	957	50	5	0.05	0.04	0.7	Tr	696
0	4	9	22	0.1	48	635	Tr	Tr	0.02	0.04	0.4	Tr	697
0	8	6	23	0.5	78	856	140	14	0.04	0.03	0.6	5	698
53	23	569	438	0.3	552	1,565	390	117	0.15	0.56	0.3	2	699
52	14	124	127	0.9	124	1,564	730	220	0.05	0.18	0.1	Tr	700
34	21	425	256	0.3	444	797	310	92	0.08	0.45	0.5	3	701
32	24	292	238	0.9	381	888	1,190	340	0.15	0.43	0.8	2	702
0	2	3	3	0.1	28	130	140	14	Tr	Tr	0.1	1	703
0	2	3	38	0.5	64	1,029	0	0	0.01	0.02	0.6	0	704
7	11	14	70	1.6	189	117	0	0	0.07	0.08	1.5	0	705
5	13	48	69	1.1	259	1,373	880	264	0.04	0.10	1.1	0	706
0	13	17	36	1.6	252	1,357	0	0	0.08	0.15	1.6	0	707
2	14	66	47	0.2	61	1,147	0	0	0.04	0.09	0.9	0	708
3	14	39	47	0.3	62	1,134	0	0	0.05	0.15	0.8	3	709
1	22	42	35	0.4	54	64	Tr	Tr	0.01	0.05	0.1	Tr	710
6	16	50	61	0.4	96	23	30	10	0.02	0.10	0.1	Tr	711
5	15	65	77	0.5	125	23	30	8	0.02	0.12	0.2	Tr	712
5	13	49	83	0.4	138	19	30	8	0.07	0.07	1.4	Tr	713
6	18	48	57	0.2	100	46	30	8	0.01	0.08	0.1	Tr	714
0	97	51	178	5.8	593	24	30	3	0.10	0.14	0.9	Tr	715
0	16	7	41	0.6	86	5	10	1	0.01	0.04	0.1	Tr	716
0	27	2	Tr	0.1	1	57	0	0	Tr	Tr	Tr	0	717
1	21	22	24	0.3	42	54	Tr	Tr	0.01	0.03	0.1	Tr	718
0	25	2	Tr	0.1	1	10	0	0	0.00	Tr	Tr	0	719

Item No.	Foods, approximate measures, units, and weight (weight of edible portion only)		Water	Food energy	Pro-tein	Fat	Fatty acids Satu-rated	Mono-unsatu-rated	Poly-unsatu-rated
		Grams	Per-cent	Cal-ories	Grams	Grams	Grams	Grams	Grams
	Sugars and Sweets—Con.								
	Candy:								
720	Hard--------------------	1 oz------------	28	1	110	0	0	0.0	0.0	0.0
721	Jelly beans-------------	1 oz------------	28	6	105	Tr	Tr	Tr	Tr	0.1
722	Marshmallows------------	1 oz------------	28	17	90	1	0	0.0	0.0	0.0
723	Custard, baked----------	1 cup----------	265	77	305	14	15	6.8	5.4	0.7
724	Gelatin dessert prepared with gelatin dessert powder and water-------	1/2 cup--------	120	84	70	2	0	0.0	0.0	0.0
725	Honey, strained or extracted-----	1 cup----------	339	17	1,030	1	0	0.0	0.0	0.0
726		1 tbsp---------	21	17	65	Tr	0	0.0	0.0	0.0
727	Jams and preserves------	1 tbsp---------	20	29	55	Tr	Tr	0.0	Tr	Tr
728		1 packet-------	14	29	40	Tr	Tr	0.0	Tr	Tr
729	Jellies-----------------	1 tbsp---------	18	28	50	Tr	Tr	Tr	Tr	Tr
730		1 packet-------	14	28	40	Tr	Tr	Tr	Tr	Tr
731	Popsicle, 3-fl-oz size-----------	1 popsicle-----	95	80	70	0	0	0.0	0.0	0.0
	Puddings:								
	Canned:								
732	Chocolate--------------------	5-oz can--------	142	68	205	3	11	9.5	0.5	0.1
733	Tapioca---------------------	5-oz can--------	142	74	160	3	5	4.8	Tr	Tr
734	Vanilla---------------------	5-oz can--------	142	69	220	2	10	9.5	0.2	0.1
	Dry mix, prepared with whole milk:								
	Chocolate:								
735	Instant----------------	1/2 cup--------	130	71	155	4	4	2.3	1.1	0.2
736	Regular (cooked)-----------	1/2 cup--------	130	73	150	4	4	2.4	1.1	0.1
737	Rice--------------------	1/2 cup--------	132	73	155	4	4	2.3	1.1	0.1
738	Tapioca-----------------	1/2 cup--------	130	75	145	4	4	2.3	1.1	0.1
	Vanilla:								
739	Instant-----------------	1/2 cup--------	130	73	150	4	4	2.2	1.1	0.2
740	Regular (cooked)-----------	1/2 cup--------	130	74	145	4	4	2.3	1.0	0.1
	Sugars:								
741	Brown, pressed down-----------	1 cup----------	220	2	820	0	0	0.0	0.0	0.0
	White:								
742	Granulated-------------------	1 cup----------	200	1	770	0	0	0.0	0.0	0.0
743		1 tbsp----------	12	1	45	0	0	0.0	0.0	0.0
744		1 packet-------	6	1	25	0	0	0.0	0.0	0.0
745	Powdered, sifted, spooned into cup-------------	1 cup----------	100	1	385	0	0	0.0	0.0	0.0
	Syrups:								
	Chocolate-flavored syrup or topping:								
746	Thin type-------------------	2 tbsp---------	38	37	85	1	Tr	0.2	0.1	0.1
747	Fudge type------------------	2 tbsp---------	38	25	125	2	5	3.1	1.7	0.2
748	Molasses, cane, blackstrap-----	2 tbsp---------	40	24	85	0	0	0.0	0.0	0.0
749	Table syrup (corn and maple)---	2 tbsp---------	42	25	122	0	0	0.0	0.0	0.0
	Vegetables and Vegetable Products								
750	Alfalfa seeds, sprouted, raw-----	1 cup----------	33	91	10	1	Tr	Tr	Tr	0.1
751	Artichokes, globe or French, cooked, drained-------------	1 artichoke-----	120	87	55	3	Tr	Tr	Tr	0.1
	Asparagus, green:								
	Cooked, drained:								
	From raw:								
752	Cuts and tips-------------	1 cup----------	180	92	45	5	1	0.1	Tr	0.2
753	Spears, 1/2-in diam. at base-------------------	4 spears--------	60	92	15	2	Tr	Tr	Tr	0.1
	From frozen:								
754	Cuts and tips-----------	1 cup----------	180	91	50	5	1	0.2	Tr	0.3
755	Spears, 1/2-in diam. at base-------------------	4 spears--------	60	91	15	2	Tr	0.1	Tr	0.1
756	Canned, spears, 1/2-in diam. at base-------------------	4 spears--------	80	95	10	1	Tr	Tr	Tr	0.1
757	Bamboo shoots, canned, drained---	1 cup----------	131	94	25	2	1	0.1	Tr	0.2

[56] For regular pack; special dietary pack contains 3 mg sodium.

Cho-les-terol	Carbo-hydrate	Calcium	Phos-phorus	Iron	Potas-sium	Sodium	Vitamin A value (IU)	Vitamin A value (RE)	Thiamin	Ribo-flavin	Niacin	Ascorbic acid	Item No.
Milli-grams	Grams	Milli-grams	Milli-grams	Milli-grams	Milli-grams	Milli-grams	Inter-national units	Retinol equiva-lents	Milli-grams	Milli-grams	Milli-grams	Milli-grams	
0	28	Tr	2	0.1	1	7	0	0	0.10	0.00	0.0	0	720
0	26	1	1	0.3	11	7	0	0	0.00	Tr	Tr	0	721
0	23	1	2	0.5	2	25	0	0	0.00	Tr	Tr	0	722
278	29	297	310	1.1	387	209	530	146	0.11	0.50	0.3	1	723
0	17	2	23	Tr	Tr	55	0	0	0.00	0.00	0.0	0	724
0	279	17	20	1.7	173	17	0	0	0.02	0.14	1.0	3	725
0	17	1	1	0.1	11	1	0	0	Tr	0.01	0.1	Tr	726
0	14	4	2	0.2	18	2	Tr	Tr	Tr	0.01	Tr	Tr	727
0	10	3	1	0.1	12	2	Tr	Tr	Tr	Tr	Tr	Tr	728
0	13	2	Tr	0.1	16	5	Tr	Tr	Tr	0.01	Tr	1	729
0	10	1	Tr	Tr	13	4	Tr	Tr	Tr	Tr	Tr	1	730
0	18	0	0	Tr	4	11	0	0	0.00	0.00	0.0	0	731
1	30	74	117	1.2	254	285	100	31	0.04	0.17	0.6	Tr	732
Tr	28	119	113	0.3	212	252	Tr	Tr	0.03	0.14	0.4	Tr	733
1	33	79	94	0.2	155	305	Tr	Tr	0.03	0.12	0.6	Tr	734
14	27	130	329	0.3	176	440	130	33	0.04	0.18	0.1	1	735
15	25	146	120	0.2	190	167	140	34	0.05	0.20	0.1	1	736
15	27	133	110	0.5	165	140	140	33	0.10	0.18	0.6	1	737
15	25	131	103	0.1	167	152	140	34	0.04	0.18	0.1	1	738
15	27	129	273	0.1	164	375	140	33	0.04	0.17	0.1	1	739
15	25	132	102	0.1	166	178	140	34	0.04	0.18	0.1	1	740
0	212	187	56	4.8	757	97	0	0	0.02	0.07	0.2	0	741
0	199	3	Tr	0.1	7	5	0	0	0.00	0.00	0.0	0	742
0	12	Tr	Tr	Tr	Tr	Tr	0	0	0.00	0.00	0.0	0	743
0	6	Tr	Tr	Tr	Tr	Tr	0	0	0.00	0.00	0.0	0	744
0	100	1	Tr	Tr	4	2	0	0	0.00	0.00	0.0	0	745
0	22	6	49	0.8	85	36	Tr	Tr	Tr	0.02	0.1	0	746
0	21	38	60	0.5	82	42	40	13	0.02	0.08	0.1	0	747
0	22	274	34	10.1	1,171	38	0	0	0.04	0.08	0.8	0	748
0	32	1	4	Tr	7	19	0	0	0.00	0.00	0.0	0	749
0	1	11	23	0.3	26	2	50	5	0.03	0.04	0.2	3	750
0	12	47	72	1.6	316	79	170	17	0.07	0.06	0.7	9	751
0	8	43	110	1.2	558	7	1,490	149	0.18	0.22	1.9	49	752
0	3	14	37	0.4	186	2	500	50	0.06	0.07	0.6	16	753
0	9	41	99	1.2	392	7	1,470	147	0.12	0.19	1.9	44	754
0	3	14	33	0.4	131	2	490	49	0.04	0.06	0.6	15	755
0	2	11	30	0.5	122	[56]278	380	38	0.04	0.07	0.7	13	756
0	4	10	33	0.4	105	9	10	1	0.03	0.03	0.2	1	757

Item No.	Foods, approximate measures, units, and weight (weight of edible portion only)			Water	Food energy	Protein	Fat	Fatty acids		
								Saturated	Mono-unsaturated	Poly-unsaturated
	Vegetables and Vegetable Products—Con.		Grams	Percent	Calories	Grams	Grams	Grams	Grams	Grams
	Beans:									
	Lima, immature seeds, frozen, cooked, drained:									
758	Thick-seeded types (Fordhooks)	1 cup	170	74	170	10	1	0.1	Tr	0.3
759	Thin-seeded types (baby limas)	1 cup	180	72	190	12	1	0.1	Tr	0.3
	Snap:									
	Cooked, drained:									
760	From raw (cut and French style)	1 cup	125	89	45	2	Tr	0.1	Tr	0.2
761	From frozen (cut)	1 cup	135	92	35	2	Tr	Tr	Tr	0.1
762	Canned, drained solids (cut)	1 cup	135	93	25	2	Tr	Tr	Tr	0.1
	Beans, mature. See Beans, dry (items 527-535) and Black-eyed peas, dry (item 536).									
	Bean sprouts (mung):									
763	Raw	1 cup	104	90	30	3	Tr	Tr	Tr	0.1
764	Cooked, drained	1 cup	124	93	25	3	Tr	Tr	Tr	Tr
	Beets:									
	Cooked, drained:									
765	Diced or sliced	1 cup	170	91	55	2	Tr	Tr	Tr	Tr
766	Whole beets, 2-in diam.	2 beets	100	91	30	1	Tr	Tr	Tr	Tr
767	Canned, drained solids, diced or sliced	1 cup	170	91	55	2	Tr	Tr	Tr	0.1
768	Beet greens, leaves and stems, cooked, drained	1 cup	144	89	40	4	Tr	Tr	0.1	0.1
	Black-eyed peas, immature seeds, cooked and drained:									
769	From raw	1 cup	165	72	180	13	1	0.3	0.1	0.6
770	From frozen	1 cup	170	66	225	14	1	0.3	0.1	0.5
	Broccoli:									
771	Raw	1 spear	151	91	40	4	1	0.1	Tr	0.3
	Cooked, drained:									
	From raw:									
772	Spear, medium	1 spear	180	90	50	5	1	0.1	Tr	0.2
773	Spears, cut into 1/2-in pieces	1 cup	155	90	45	5	Tr	0.1	Tr	0.2
	From frozen:									
774	Piece, 4-1/2 to 5 in long	1 piece	30	91	10	1	Tr	Tr	Tr	Tr
775	Chopped	1 cup	185	91	50	6	Tr	Tr	Tr	0.1
	Brussels sprouts, cooked, drained:									
776	From raw, 7-8 sprouts, 1-1/4 to 1-1/2-in diam.	1 cup	155	87	60	4	1	0.2	0.1	0.4
777	From frozen	1 cup	155	87	65	6	1	0.1	Tr	0.3
	Cabbage, common varieties:									
778	Raw, coarsely shredded or sliced	1 cup	70	93	15	1	Tr	Tr	Tr	0.1
779	Cooked, drained	1 cup	150	94	30	1	Tr	Tr	Tr	0.2
	Cabbage, Chinese:									
780	Pak-choi, cooked, drained	1 cup	170	96	20	3	Tr	Tr	Tr	0.1
781	Pe-tsai, raw, 1-in pieces	1 cup	76	94	10	1	Tr	Tr	Tr	0.1
782	Cabbage, red, raw, coarsely shredded or sliced	1 cup	70	92	20	1	Tr	Tr	Tr	0.1
783	Cabbage, savoy, raw, coarsely shredded or sliced	1 cup	70	91	20	1	Tr	Tr	Tr	Tr

[57] For green varieties; yellow varieties contain 101 IU or 10 RE.
[58] For green varieties; yellow varieties contain 151 IU or 15 RE.
[59] For regular pack; special dietary pack contains 3 mg sodium.

Cho-les-terol	Carbo-hydrate	Calcium	Phos-phorus	Iron	Potas-sium	Sodium	Vitamin A value		Thiamin	Ribo-flavin	Niacin	Ascorbic acid	Item No.
							(IU)	(RE)					
Milli-grams	Grams	Milli-grams	Milli-grams	Milli-grams	Milli-grams	Milli-grams	Inter-national units	Retinol equiva-lents	Milli-grams	Milli-grams	Milli-grams	Milli-grams	
0	32	37	107	2.3	694	90	320	32	0.13	0.10	1.8	22	758
0	35	50	202	3.5	740	52	300	30	0.13	0.10	1.4	10	759
0	10	58	49	1.6	374	4	[57]830	[57]83	0.09	0.12	0.8	12	760
0	8	61	32	1.1	151	18	[58]710	[58]71	0.06	0.10	0.6	11	761
0	6	35	26	1.2	147	[59]339	[60]470	[60]47	0.02	0.08	0.3	6	762
0	6	14	56	0.9	155	6	20	2	0.09	0.13	0.8	14	763
0	5	15	35	0.8	125	12	20	2	0.06	0.13	1.0	14	764
0	11	19	53	1.1	530	83	20	2	0.05	0.02	0.5	9	765
0	7	11	31	0.6	312	49	10	1	0.03	0.01	0.3	6	766
0	12	26	29	3.1	252	[61]466	20	2	0.02	0.07	0.3	7	767
0	8	164	59	2.7	1,309	347	7,340	734	0.17	0.42	0.7	36	768
0	30	46	196	2.4	693	7	1,050	105	0.11	0.18	1.8	3	769
0	40	39	207	3.6	638	9	130	13	0.44	0.11	1.2	4	770
0	8	72	100	1.3	491	41	2,330	233	0.10	0.18	1.0	141	771
0	10	205	86	2.1	293	20	2,540	254	0.15	0.37	1.4	113	772
0	9	177	74	1.8	253	17	2,180	218	0.13	0.32	1.2	97	773
0	2	15	17	0.2	54	7	570	57	0.02	0.02	0.1	12	774
0	10	94	102	1.1	333	44	3,500	350	0.10	0.15	0.8	74	775
0	13	56	87	1.9	491	33	1,110	111	0.17	0.12	0.9	96	776
0	13	37	84	1.1	504	36	910	91	0.16	0.18	0.8	71	777
0	4	33	16	0.4	172	13	90	9	0.04	0.02	0.2	33	778
0	7	50	38	0.6	308	29	130	13	0.09	0.08	0.3	36	779
0	3	158	49	1.8	631	58	4,370	437	0.05	0.11	0.7	44	780
0	2	59	22	0.2	181	7	910	91	0.03	0.04	0.3	21	781
0	4	36	29	0.3	144	8	30	3	0.04	0.02	0.2	40	782
0	4	25	29	0.3	161	20	700	70	0.05	0.02	0.2	22	783

[60] For green varieties; yellow varieties contain 142 IU or 14 RE.
[61] For regular pack; special dietary pack contains 78 mg sodium.

Item No.	Foods, approximate measures, units, and weight (weight of edible portion only)		Water	Food energy	Pro-tein	Fat	Fatty acids		
							Satu-rated	Mono-unsatu-rated	Poly-unsatu-rated
	Vegetables and Vegetable Products—Con.	Grams	Per-cent	Cal-ories	Grams	Grams	Grams	Grams	Grams
	Carrots:								
	Raw, without crowns and tips, scraped:								
784	Whole, 7-1/2 by 1-1/8 in, or strips, 2-1/2 to 3 in long	1 carrot or 18 strips--------	72	88	30	1	Tr	Tr	Tr	0.1
785	Grated----------------------	1 cup-----------	110	88	45	1	Tr	Tr	Tr	0.1
	Cooked, sliced, drained:								
786	From raw-------------------	1 cup-----------	156	87	70	2	Tr	0.1	Tr	0.1
787	From frozen----------------	1 cup-----------	146	90	55	2	Tr	Tr	Tr	0.1
788	Canned, sliced, drained solids	1 cup-----------	146	93	35	1	Tr	0.1	Tr	0.1
	Cauliflower:								
789	Raw, (flowerets)---------------	1 cup-----------	100	92	25	2	Tr	Tr	Tr	0.1
	Cooked, drained:								
790	From raw (flowerets)---------	1 cup-----------	125	93	30	2	Tr	Tr	Tr	0.1
791	From frozen (flowerets)------	1 cup-----------	180	94	35	3	Tr	0.1	Tr	0.2
	Celery, pascal type, raw:								
792	Stalk, large outer, 8 by 1-1/2 in (at root end)-------------	1 stalk---------	40	95	5	Tr	Tr	Tr	Tr	Tr
793	Pieces, diced------------------	1 cup-----------	120	95	20	1	Tr	Tr	Tr	0.1
	Collards, cooked, drained:								
794	From raw (leaves without stems)	1 cup-----------	190	96	25	2	Tr	0.1	Tr	0.2
795	From frozen (chopped)----------	1 cup-----------	170	88	60	5	1	0.1	0.1	0.4
	Corn, sweet:								
	Cooked, drained:								
796	From raw, ear 5 by 1-3/4 in--	1 ear-----------	77	70	85	3	1	0.2	0.3	0.5
	From frozen:								
797	Ear, trimmed to about 3-1/2 in long------------------	1 ear-----------	63	73	60	2	Tr	0.1	0.1	0.2
798	Kernels--------------------	1 cup-----------	165	76	135	5	Tr	Tr	Tr	0.1
	Canned:								
799	Cream style------------------	1 cup-----------	256	79	185	4	1	0.2	0.3	0.5
800	Whole kernel, vacuum pack----	1 cup-----------	210	77	165	5	1	0.2	0.3	0.5
	Cowpeas. See Black-eyed peas, immature (items 769,770), mature (item 536).								
801	Cucumber, with peel, slices, 1/8 in thick (large, 2-1/8-in diam.; small, 1-3/4-in diam.)--	6 large or 8 small slices	28	96	5	Tr	Tr	Tr	Tr	Tr
802	Dandelion greens, cooked, drained	1 cup-----------	105	90	35	2	1	0.1	Tr	0.3
803	Eggplant, cooked, steamed-------	1 cup-----------	96	92	25	1	Tr	Tr	Tr	0.1
804	Endive, curly (including esca-role), raw, small pieces-------	1 cup-----------	50	94	10	1	Tr	Tr	Tr	Tr
805	Jerusalem-artichoke, raw, sliced	1 cup-----------	150	78	115	3	Tr	0.0	Tr	Tr
	Kale, cooked, drained:								
806	From raw, chopped--------------	1 cup-----------	130	91	40	2	1	0.1	Tr	0.3
807	From frozen, chopped-----------	1 cup-----------	130	91	40	4	1	0.1	Tr	0.3
808	Kohlrabi, thickened bulb-like stems, cooked, drained, diced--	1 cup-----------	165	90	50	3	Tr	Tr	Tr	0.1
	Lettuce, raw:								
	Butterhead, as Boston types:								
809	Head, 5-in diam--------------	1 head----------	163	96	20	2	Tr	Tr	Tr	0.2
810	Leaves-----------------------	1 outer or 2 inner leaves--	15	96	Tr	Tr	Tr	Tr	Tr	Tr
	Crisphead, as iceberg:								
811	Head, 6-in diam-------------	1 head----------	539	96	70	5	1	0.1	Tr	0.5
812	Wedge, 1/4 of head----------	1 wedge---------	135	96	20	1	Tr	Tr	Tr	0.1
813	Pieces, chopped or shredded--	1 cup-----------	55	96	5	1	Tr	Tr	Tr	0.1
814	Looseleaf (bunching varieties including romaine or cos), chopped or shredded pieces---	1 cup-----------	56	94	10	1	Tr	Tr	Tr	0.1

[62] For regular pack; special dietary pack contains 61 mg sodium.
[63] For yellow varieties; white varieties contain only a trace of vitamin A.

							Nutrients in Indicated Quantity						
Cho-les-terol	Carbo-hydrate	Calcium	Phos-phorus	Iron	Potas-sium	Sodium	Vitamin A value		Thiamin	Ribo-flavin	Niacin	Ascorbic acid	Item No.
							(IU)	(RE)					
Milli-grams	Grams	Milli-grams	Milli-grams	Milli-grams	Milli-grams	Milli-grams	Inter-national units	Retinol equiva-lents	Milli-grams	Milli-grams	Milli-grams	Milli-grams	
0	7	19	32	0.4	233	25	20,250	2,025	0.07	0.04	0.7	7	784
0	11	30	48	0.6	355	39	30,940	3,094	0.11	0.06	1.0	10	785
0	16	48	47	1.0	354	103	38,300	3,830	0.05	0.09	0.8	4	786
0	12	41	38	0.7	231	86	25,850	2,585	0.04	0.05	0.6	4	787
0	8	37	35	0.9	261	[62]352	20,110	2,011	0.03	0.04	0.8	4	788
0	5	29	46	0.6	355	15	20	2	0.08	0.06	0.6	72	789
0	6	34	44	0.5	404	8	20	2	0.08	0.07	0.7	69	790
0	7	31	43	0.7	250	32	40	4	0.07	0.10	0.6	56	791
0	1	14	10	0.2	114	35	50	5	0.01	0.01	0.1	3	792
0	4	43	31	0.6	341	106	150	15	0.04	0.04	0.4	8	793
0	5	148	19	0.8	177	36	4,220	422	0.03	0.08	0.4	19	794
0	12	357	46	1.9	427	85	10,170	1,017	0.08	0.20	1.1	45	795
0	19	2	79	0.5	192	13	[63]170	[63]17	0.17	0.06	1.2	5	796
0	14	2	47	0.4	158	3	[63]130	[63]13	0.11	0.04	1.0	3	797
0	34	3	78	0.5	229	8	[63]410	[63]41	0.11	0.12	2.1	4	798
0	46	8	131	1.0	343	[64]730	[63]250	[63]25	0.06	0.14	2.5	12	799
0	41	11	134	0.9	391	[65]571	[63]510	[63]51	0.09	0.15	2.5	17	800
0	1	4	5	0.1	42	1	10	1	0.01	0.01	0.1	1	801
0	7	147	44	1.9	244	46	12,290	1,229	0.14	0.18	0.5	19	802
0	6	6	21	0.3	238	3	60	6	0.07	0.02	0.6	1	803
0	2	26	14	0.4	157	11	1,030	103	0.04	0.04	0.2	3	804
0	26	21	117	5.1	644	6	30	3	0.30	0.09	2.0	6	805
0	7	94	36	1.2	296	30	9,620	962	0.07	0.09	0.7	53	806
0	7	179	36	1.2	417	20	8,260	826	0.06	0.15	0.9	33	807
0	11	41	74	0.7	561	35	60	6	0.07	0.03	0.6	89	808
0	4	52	38	0.5	419	8	1,580	158	0.10	0.10	0.5	13	809
0	Tr	5	3	Tr	39	1	150	15	0.01	0.01	Tr	1	810
0	11	102	108	2.7	852	49	1,780	178	0.25	0.16	1.0	21	811
0	3	26	27	0.7	213	12	450	45	0.06	0.04	0.3	5	812
0	1	10	11	0.3	87	5	180	18	0.03	0.02	0.1	2	813
0	2	38	14	0.8	148	5	1,060	106	0.03	0.04	0.2	10	814

[64] For regular pack; special dietary pack contains 8 mg sodium.
[65] For regular pack; special dietary pack contains 6 mg sodium.

Item No.	Foods, approximate measures, units, and weight (weight of edible portion only)			Water	Food energy	Pro-tein	Fat	Fatty acids		
								Satu-rated	Mono-unsatu-rated	Poly-unsatu-rated
	Vegetables and Vegetable Products—Con.		Grams	Per-cent	Cal-ories	Grams	Grams	Grams	Grams	Grams
	Mushrooms:									
815	Raw, sliced or chopped	1 cup	70	92	20	1	Tr	Tr	Tr	0.1
816	Cooked, drained	1 cup	156	91	40	3	1	0.1	Tr	0.3
817	Canned, drained solids	1 cup	156	91	35	3	Tr	0.1	Tr	0.2
818	Mustard greens, without stems and midribs, cooked, drained	1 cup	140	94	20	3	Tr	Tr	0.2	0.1
819	Okra pods, 3 by 5/8 in, cooked	8 pods	85	90	25	2	Tr	Tr	Tr	Tr
	Onions:									
	Raw:									
820	Chopped	1 cup	160	91	55	2	Tr	0.1	0.1	0.2
821	Sliced	1 cup	115	91	40	1	Tr	0.1	Tr	0.1
822	Cooked (whole or sliced), drained	1 cup	210	92	60	2	Tr	0.1	Tr	0.1
823	Onions, spring, raw, bulb (3/8-in diam.) and white portion of top	6 onions	30	92	10	1	Tr	Tr	Tr	Tr
824	Onion rings, breaded, par-fried, frozen, prepared	2 rings	20	29	80	1	5	1.7	2.2	1.0
	Parsley:									
825	Raw	10 sprigs	10	88	5	Tr	Tr	Tr	Tr	Tr
826	Freeze-dried	1 tbsp	0.4	2	Tr	Tr	Tr	Tr	Tr	Tr
827	Parsnips, cooked (diced or 2 in lengths), drained	1 cup	156	78	125	2	Tr	0.1	0.2	0.1
828	Peas, edible pod, cooked, drained	1 cup	160	89	65	5	Tr	0.1	Tr	0.2
	Peas, green:									
829	Canned, drained solids	1 cup	170	82	115	8	1	0.1	0.1	0.3
830	Frozen, cooked, drained	1 cup	160	80	125	8	Tr	0.1	Tr	0.2
	Peppers:									
831	Hot chili, raw	1 pepper	45	88	20	1	Tr	Tr	Tr	Tr
	Sweet (about 5 per lb, whole), stem and seeds removed:									
832	Raw	1 pepper	74	93	20	1	Tr	Tr	Tr	0.2
833	Cooked, drained	1 pepper	73	95	15	Tr	Tr	Tr	Tr	0.1
	Potatoes, cooked:									
	Baked (about 2 per lb, raw):									
834	With skin	1 potato	202	71	220	5	Tr	0.1	Tr	0.1
835	Flesh only	1 potato	156	75	145	3	Tr	Tr	Tr	0.1
	Boiled (about 3 per lb, raw):									
836	Peeled after boiling	1 potato	136	77	120	3	Tr	Tr	Tr	0.1
837	Peeled before boiling	1 potato	135	77	115	2	Tr	Tr	Tr	0.1
	French fried, strip, 2 to 3-1/2 in long, frozen:									
838	Oven heated	10 strips	50	53	110	2	4	2.1	1.8	0.3
839	Fried in vegetable oil	10 strips	50	38	160	2	8	2.5	1.6	3.8
	Potato products, prepared:									
	Au gratin:									
840	From dry mix	1 cup	245	79	230	6	10	6.3	2.9	0.3
841	From home recipe	1 cup	245	74	325	12	19	11.6	5.3	0.7
842	Hashed brown, from frozen	1 cup	156	56	340	5	18	7.0	8.0	2.1
	Mashed:									
	From home recipe:									
843	Milk added	1 cup	210	78	160	4	1	0.7	0.3	0.1
844	Milk and margarine added	1 cup	210	76	225	4	9	2.2	3.7	2.5
845	From dehydrated flakes (without milk), water, milk, butter, and salt added	1 cup	210	76	235	4	12	7.2	3.3	0.5
846	Potato salad, made with mayonnaise	1 cup	250	76	360	7	21	3.6	6.2	9.3
	Scalloped:									
847	From dry mix	1 cup	245	79	230	5	11	6.5	3.0	0.5
848	From home recipe	1 cup	245	81	210	7	9	5.5	2.5	0.4

[66] For regular pack; special dietary pack contains 3 mg sodium.
[67] For red peppers; green peppers contain 350 IU or 35 RE.
[68] For green peppers; red peppers contain 4,220 IU or 422 RE.

Cholesterol	Carbohydrate	Calcium	Phosphorus	Iron	Potassium	Sodium	Vitamin A value (IU)	Vitamin A value (RE)	Thiamin	Riboflavin	Niacin	Ascorbic acid	Item No.
Milligrams	Grams	Milligrams	Milligrams	Milligrams	Milligrams	Milligrams	International units	Retinol equivalents	Milligrams	Milligrams	Milligrams	Milligrams	
0	3	4	73	0.9	259	3	0	0	0.07	0.31	2.9	2	815
0	8	9	136	2.7	555	3	0	0	0.11	0.47	7.0	6	816
0	8	17	103	1.2	201	663	0	0	0.13	0.03	2.5	0	817
0	3	104	57	1.0	283	22	4,240	424	0.06	0.09	0.6	35	818
0	6	54	48	0.4	274	4	490	49	0.11	0.05	0.7	14	819
0	12	40	46	0.6	248	3	0	0	0.10	0.02	0.2	13	820
0	8	29	33	0.4	178	2	0	0	0.07	0.01	0.1	10	821
0	13	57	48	0.4	319	17	0	0	0.09	0.02	0.2	12	822
0	2	18	10	0.6	77	1	1,500	150	0.02	0.04	0.1	14	823
0	8	6	16	0.3	26	75	50	5	0.06	0.03	0.7	Tr	824
0	1	13	4	0.6	54	4	520	52	0.01	0.01	0.1	9	825
0	Tr	1	2	0.2	25	2	250	25	Tr	0.01	Tr	1	826
0	30	58	108	0.9	573	16	0	0	0.13	0.08	1.1	20	827
0	11	67	88	3.2	384	6	210	21	0.20	0.12	0.9	77	828
0	21	34	114	1.6	294	[66]372	1,310	131	0.21	0.13	1.2	16	829
0	23	38	144	2.5	269	139	1,070	107	0.45	0.16	2.4	16	830
0	4	8	21	0.5	153	3	[67]4,840	[67]484	0.04	0.04	0.4	109	831
0	4	4	16	0.9	144	2	[68]390	[68]39	0.06	0.04	0.4	[69]95	832
0	3	3	11	0.6	94	1	[70]280	[70]28	0.04	0.03	0.3	[71]81	833
0	51	20	115	2.7	844	16	0	0	0.22	0.07	3.3	26	834
0	34	8	78	0.5	610	8	0	0	0.16	0.03	2.2	20	835
0	27	7	60	0.4	515	5	0	0	0.14	0.03	2.0	18	836
0	27	11	54	0.4	443	7	0	0	0.13	0.03	1.8	10	837
0	17	5	43	0.7	229	16	0	0	0.06	0.02	1.2	5	838
0	20	10	47	0.4	366	108	0	0	0.09	0.01	1.6	5	839
12	31	203	233	0.8	537	1,076	520	76	0.05	0.20	2.3	8	840
56	28	292	277	1.6	970	1,061	650	93	0.16	0.28	2.4	24	841
0	44	23	112	2.4	680	53	0	0	0.17	0.03	3.8	10	842
4	37	55	101	0.6	628	636	40	12	0.18	0.08	2.3	14	843
4	35	55	97	0.5	607	620	360	42	0.18	0.08	2.3	13	844
29	32	103	118	0.5	489	697	380	44	0.23	0.11	1.4	20	845
170	28	48	130	1.6	635	1,323	520	83	0.19	0.15	2.2	25	846
27	31	88	137	0.9	497	835	360	51	0.05	0.14	2.5	8	847
29	26	140	154	1.4	926	821	330	47	0.17	0.23	2.6	26	848

[69]For green peppers; red peppers contain 141 mg ascorbic acid.
[70]For green peppers; red peppers contain 2,740 IU or 274 RE.
[71]For green peppers; red peppers contain 121 mg ascorbic acid.

Item No.	Foods, approximate measures, units, and weight (weight of edible portion only)		Grams	Water Per-cent	Food energy Cal-ories	Pro-tein Grams	Fat Grams	Fatty acids Satu-rated Grams	Mono-unsatu-rated Grams	Poly-unsatu-rated Grams
	Vegetables and Vegetable Products—Con.									
849	Potato chips	10 chips	20	3	105	1	7	1.8	1.2	3.6
	Pumpkin:									
850	Cooked from raw, mashed	1 cup	245	94	50	2	Tr	0.1	Tr	Tr
851	Canned	1 cup	245	90	85	3	1	0.4	0.1	Tr
852	Radishes, raw, stem ends, rootlets cut off	4 radishes	18	95	5	Tr	Tr	Tr	Tr	Tr
853	Sauerkraut, canned, solids and liquid	1 cup	236	93	45	2	Tr	0.1	Tr	0.1
	Seaweed:									
854	Kelp, raw	1 oz	28	82	10	Tr	Tr	0.1	Tr	Tr
855	Spirulina, dried	1 oz	28	5	80	16	2	0.8	0.2	0.6
	Southern peas. See Black-eyed peas, immature (items 769,770), mature (item 536).									
	Spinach:									
856	Raw, chopped	1 cup	55	92	10	2	Tr	Tr	Tr	0.1
	Cooked, drained:									
857	From raw	1 cup	180	91	40	5	Tr	0.1	Tr	0.2
858	From frozen (leaf)	1 cup	190	90	55	6	Tr	0.1	Tr	0.2
859	Canned, drained solids	1 cup	214	92	50	6	1	0.2	Tr	0.4
860	Spinach souffle	1 cup	136	74	220	11	18	7.1	6.8	3.1
	Squash, cooked:									
861	Summer (all varieties), sliced, drained	1 cup	180	94	35	2	1	0.1	Tr	0.2
862	Winter (all varieties), baked, cubes	1 cup	205	89	80	2	1	0.3	0.1	0.5
	Sunchoke. See Jerusalem-arti-choke (item 805).									
	Sweetpotatoes:									
	Cooked (raw, 5 by 2 in; about 2-1/2 per lb):									
863	Baked in skin, peeled	1 potato	114	73	115	2	Tr	Tr	Tr	0.1
864	Boiled, without skin	1 potato	151	73	160	2	Tr	0.1	Tr	0.2
865	Candied, 2-1/2 by 2-in piece	1 piece	105	67	145	1	3	1.4	0.7	0.2
	Canned:									
866	Solid pack (mashed)	1 cup	255	74	260	5	1	0.1	Tr	0.2
867	Vacuum pack, piece 2-3/4 by 1 in	1 piece	40	76	35	1	Tr	Tr	Tr	Tr
	Tomatoes:									
868	Raw, 2-3/5-in diam. (3 per 12 oz pkg.)	1 tomato	123	94	25	1	Tr	Tr	Tr	0.1
869	Canned, solids and liquid	1 cup	240	94	50	2	1	0.1	0.1	0.2
870	Tomato juice, canned	1 cup	244	94	40	2	Tr	Tr	Tr	0.1
	Tomato products, canned:									
871	Paste	1 cup	262	74	220	10	2	0.3	0.4	0.9
872	Puree	1 cup	250	87	105	4	Tr	Tr	Tr	0.1
873	Sauce	1 cup	245	89	75	3	Tr	0.1	0.1	0.2
874	Turnips, cooked, diced	1 cup	156	94	30	1	Tr	Tr	Tr	0.1
	Turnip greens, cooked, drained:									
875	From raw (leaves and stems)	1 cup	144	93	30	2	Tr	0.1	Tr	0.1
876	From frozen (chopped)	1 cup	164	90	50	5	1	0.2	Tr	0.3
877	Vegetable juice cocktail, canned	1 cup	242	94	45	2	Tr	Tr	Tr	0.1
	Vegetables, mixed:									
878	Canned, drained solids	1 cup	163	87	75	4	Tr	0.1	Tr	0.2
879	Frozen, cooked, drained	1 cup	182	83	105	5	Tr	0.1	Tr	0.1
880	Waterchestnuts, canned	1 cup	140	86	70	1	Tr	Tr	Tr	Tr

[1] Value not determined.
[72] With added salt; if none is added, sodium content is 58 mg.
[73] For regular pack; special dietary pack contains 31 mg sodium.
[74] With added salt; if none is added, sodium content is 24 mg.

Cho-les-terol	Carbo-hydrate	Calcium	Phos-phorus	Iron	Potas-sium	Sodium	Vitamin A value (IU)	Vitamin A value (RE)	Thiamin	Ribo-flavin	Niacin	Ascorbic acid	Item No.
Milli-grams	Grams	Milli-grams	Milli-grams	Milli-grams	Milli-grams	Milli-grams	Inter-national units	Retinol equiva-lents	Milli-grams	Milli-grams	Milli-grams	Milli-grams	
0	10	5	31	0.2	260	94	0	0	0.03	Tr	0.8	8	849
0	12	37	74	1.4	564	2	2,650	265	0.08	0.19	1.0	12	850
0	20	64	86	3.4	505	12	54,040	5,404	0.06	0.13	0.9	10	851
0	1	4	3	0.1	42	4	Tr	Tr	Tr	0.01	0.1	4	852
0	10	71	47	3.5	401	1,560	40	4	0.05	0.05	0.3	35	853
0	3	48	12	0.8	25	66	30	3	0.01	0.04	0.1	(1)	854
0	7	34	33	8.1	386	297	160	16	0.67	1.04	3.6	3	855
0	2	54	27	1.5	307	43	3,690	369	0.04	0.10	0.4	15	856
0	7	245	101	6.4	839	126	14,740	1,474	0.17	0.42	0.9	18	857
0	10	277	91	2.9	566	163	14,790	1,479	0.11	0.32	0.8	23	858
0	7	272	94	4.9	740	72 683	18,780	1,878	0.03	0.30	0.8	31	859
184	3	230	231	1.3	201	763	3,460	675	0.09	0.30	0.5	3	860
0	8	49	70	0.6	346	2	520	52	0.08	0.07	0.9	10	861
0	18	29	41	0.7	896	2	7,290	729	0.17	0.05	1.4	20	862
0	28	32	63	0.5	397	11	24,880	2,488	0.08	0.14	0.7	28	863
0	37	32	41	0.8	278	20	25,750	2,575	0.08	0.21	1.0	26	864
8	29	27	27	1.2	198	74	4,400	440	0.02	0.04	0.4	7	865
0	59	77	133	3.4	536	191	38,570	3,857	0.07	0.23	2.4	13	866
0	8	9	20	0.4	125	21	3,190	319	0.01	0.02	0.3	11	867
0	5	9	28	0.6	255	10	1,390	139	0.07	0.06	0.7	22	868
0	10	62	46	1.5	530	73 391	1,450	145	0.11	0.07	1.8	36	869
0	10	22	46	1.4	537	74 881	1,360	136	0.11	0.08	1.6	45	870
0	49	92	207	7.8	2,442	75 170	6,470	647	0.41	0.50	8.4	111	871
0	25	38	100	2.3	1,050	76 50	3,400	340	0.18	0.14	4.3	88	872
0	18	34	78	1.9	909	77 1,482	2,400	240	0.16	0.14	2.8	32	873
0	8	34	30	0.3	211	78	0	0	0.04	0.04	0.5	18	874
0	6	197	42	1.2	292	42	7,920	792	0.06	0.10	0.6	39	875
0	8	249	56	3.2	367	25	13,080	1,308	0.09	0.12	0.8	36	876
0	11	27	41	1.0	467	883	2,830	283	0.10	0.07	1.8	67	877
0	15	44	68	1.7	474	243	18,990	1,899	0.08	0.08	0.9	8	878
0	24	46	93	1.5	308	64	7,780	778	0.13	0.22	1.5	6	879
0	17	6	27	1.2	165	11	10	1	0.02	0.03	0.5	2	880

[75] With no added salt; if salt is added, sodium content is 2,070 mg.
[76] With no added salt; if salt is added, sodium content is 998 mg.
[77] With salt added.

Item No.	Foods, approximate measures, units, and weight (weight of edible portion only)		Water	Food energy	Pro-tein	Fat	Fatty acids		
							Satu-rated	Mono-unsatu-rated	Poly-unsatu-rated
	Miscellaneous Items	Grams	Per-cent	Cal-ories	Grams	Grams	Grams	Grams	Grams
	Baking powders for home use:								
	Sodium aluminum sulfate:								
881	With monocalcium phosphate monohydrate	1 tsp	3	2	5	Tr	0	0.0	0.0	0.0
882	With monocalcium phosphate monohydrate, calcium sulfate	1 tsp	2.9	1	5	Tr	0	0.0	0.0	0.0
883	Straight phosphate	1 tsp	3.8	2	5	Tr	0	0.0	0.0	0.0
884	Low sodium	1 tsp	4.3	1	5	Tr	0	0.0	0.0	0.0
885	Catsup	1 cup	273	69	290	5	1	0.2	0.2	0.4
886		1 tbsp	15	69	15	Tr	Tr	Tr	Tr	Tr
887	Celery seed	1 tsp	2	6	10	Tr	1	Tr	0.3	0.1
888	Chili powder	1 tsp	2.6	8	10	Tr	Tr	0.1	0.1	0.2
	Chocolate:								
889	Bitter or baking	1 oz	28	2	145	3	15	9.0	4.9	0.5
	Semisweet, see Candy, (item 715).								
890	Cinnamon	1 tsp	2.3	10	5	Tr	Tr	Tr	Tr	Tr
891	Curry powder	1 tsp	2	10	5	Tr	Tr	(1)	(1)	(1)
892	Garlic powder	1 tsp	2.8	6	10	Tr	Tr	Tr	Tr	Tr
893	Gelatin, dry	1 envelope	7	13	25	6	Tr	Tr	Tr	Tr
894	Mustard, prepared, yellow	1 tsp or individual packet	5	80	5	Tr	Tr	Tr	0.2	Tr
	Olives, canned:								
895	Green	4 medium or 3 extra large	13	78	15	Tr	2	0.2	1.2	0.1
896	Ripe, Mission, pitted	3 small or 2 large	9	73	15	Tr	2	0.3	1.3	0.2
897	Onion powder	1 tsp	2.1	5	5	Tr	Tr	Tr	Tr	Tr
898	Oregano	1 tsp	1.5	7	5	Tr	Tr	Tr	Tr	0.1
899	Paprika	1 tsp	2.1	10	5	Tr	Tr	Tr	Tr	0.2
900	Pepper, black	1 tsp	2.1	11	5	Tr	Tr	Tr	Tr	Tr
	Pickles, cucumber:								
901	Dill, medium, whole, 3-3/4 in long, 1-1/4-in diam.	1 pickle	65	93	5	Tr	Tr	Tr	Tr	0.1
902	Fresh-pack, slices 1-1/2-in diam., 1/4 in thick	2 slices	15	79	10	Tr	Tr	Tr	Tr	Tr
903	Sweet, gherkin, small, whole, about 2-1/2 in long, 3/4-in diam.	1 pickle	15	61	20	Tr	Tr	Tr	Tr	Tr
	Popcorn. See Grain Products, (items 497-499).								
904	Relish, finely chopped, sweet	1 tbsp	15	63	20	Tr	Tr	Tr	Tr	Tr
905	Salt	1 tsp	5.5	0	0	0	0	0.0	0.0	0.0
906	Vinegar, cider	1 tbsp	15	94	Tr	Tr	0	0.0	0.0	0.0
	Yeast:								
907	Baker's, dry, active	1 pkg	7	5	20	3	Tr	Tr	0.1	Tr
908	Brewer's, dry	1 tbsp	8	5	25	3	Tr	Tr	Tr	0.0

[1]Value not determined.

Nutrients in Indicated Quantity

Cholesterol	Carbohydrate	Calcium	Phosphorus	Iron	Potassium	Sodium	Vitamin A value (IU)	Vitamin A value (RE)	Thiamin	Riboflavin	Niacin	Ascorbic acid	Item No.
Milligrams	Grams	Milligrams	Milligrams	Milligrams	Milligrams	Milligrams	International units	Retinol equivalents	Milligrams	Milligrams	Milligrams	Milligrams	
0	1	58	87	0.0	5	329	0	0	0.00	0.00	0.0	0	881
0	1	183	45	0.0	4	290	0	0	0.00	0.00	0.0	0	882
0	1	239	359	0.0	6	312	0	0	0.00	0.00	0.0	0	883
0	1	207	314	0.0	891	Tr	0	0	0.00	0.00	0.0	0	884
0	69	60	137	2.2	991	2,845	3,820	382	0.25	0.19	4.4	41	885
0	4	3	8	0.1	54	156	210	21	0.01	0.01	0.2	2	886
0	1	35	11	0.9	28	3	Tr	Tr	0.01	0.01	0.1	Tr	887
0	1	7	8	0.4	50	26	910	91	0.01	0.02	0.2	2	888
0	8	22	109	1.9	235	1	10	1	0.01	0.07	0.4	0	889
0	2	28	1	0.9	12	1	10	1	Tr	Tr	Tr	1	890
0	1	10	7	0.6	31	1	20	2	0.01	0.01	0.1	Tr	891
0	2	2	12	0.1	31	1	0	0	0.01	Tr	Tr	Tr	892
0	0	1	0	0.0	2	6	0	0	0.00	0.00	0.0	0	893
0	Tr	4	4	0.1	7	63	0	0	Tr	0.01	Tr	Tr	894
0	Tr	8	2	0.2	7	312	40	4	Tr	Tr	Tr	0	895
0	Tr	10	2	0.2	2	68	10	1	Tr	Tr	Tr	0	896
0	2	8	7	0.1	20	1	Tr	Tr	0.01	Tr	Tr	Tr	897
0	1	24	3	0.7	25	Tr	100	10	0.01	Tr	0.1	1	898
0	1	4	7	0.5	49	1	1,270	127	0.01	0.04	0.3	1	899
0	1	9	4	0.6	26	1	Tr	Tr	Tr	0.01	Tr	0	900
0	1	17	14	0.7	130	928	70	7	Tr	0.01	Tr	4	901
0	3	5	4	0.3	30	101	20	2	Tr	Tr	Tr	1	902
0	5	2	2	0.2	30	107	10	1	Tr	Tr	Tr	1	903
0	5	3	2	0.1	30	107	20	2	Tr	Tr	0.0	1	904
0	0	14	3	Tr	Tr	2,132	0	0	0.00	0.00	0.0	0	905
0	1	1	1	0.1	15	Tr	0	0	0.00	0.00	0.0	0	906
0	3	3	90	1.1	140	4	Tr	Tr	0.16	0.38	2.6	Tr	907
0	3	[78]17	140	1.4	152	10	Tr	Tr	1.25	0.34	3.0	Tr	908

[78]Value may vary from 6 to 60 mg.

Table 3.—Yield of Cooked Meat per Pound of Raw Meat as Purchased

Retail cut and method of cooking	Yield after cooking (less drippings)	
	Parts weighed	Weight
Chops or steaks for broiling or frying:		*Ounces*
With bone and relatively large amount of fat, such as pork or lamb chops; beef rib, sirloin, or porterhouse steaks.	Lean, bone, and fat	10-12
	Lean and fat	7-10
	Lean only	5-7
Without bone and with very little fat, such as round of beef, veal steaks.	Lean and fat	12-13
	Lean only	9-12
Ground meat for broiling or frying, such as beef, lamb, or pork patties.	Patties	9-13
Roast for oven cooking (no liquid added):		
With bone and relatively large amount of fat, such as beef rib, loin, chuck; lamb shoulder, leg; pork, fresh or cured.	Lean, bone, and fat	10-12
	Lean and fat	8-10
	Lean only	6-9
Without bone.	Lean and fat	10-12
	Lean only	7-10
Cuts for pot roasting, simmering, braising, stewing:		
With bone and relatively large amount of fat, such as beef chuck, pork shoulder.	Lean, bone, and fat	10-11
	Lean and fat	8-9
	Lean only	6-8
Without bone and with relatively small amount of fat, such as trimmed beef, veal.	Lean with adhering fat	9-11

The Psychology of Stress & Nutrition

Table 4.—Recommended Daily Dietary Allowances (RDA)[1]

(Designed for the maintenance of good nutrition of practically all healthy persons in the United States.)

Sex-age category	Persons Age (Years From)	To	Weight Kilograms	Pounds	Height Centimeters	Inches	Food energy Calories	Protein Grams	Minerals Calcium Milligrams	Phosphorus Milligrams	Iron Milligrams	Vitamin A Retinol equivalents[2]	International units[3]	Thiamin Milligrams	Riboflavin Milligrams	Niacin Milligrams	Ascorbic acid Milligrams
Infants	0	0.5	6	13	60	24	kg × 115 lb × 52.3	kg × 2.2 lb × 1.0	360	240	10	420	1,400	0.3	0.4	6	35
	0.5	1	9	20	71	28	kg × 105 lb × 47.7	kg × 2.0 lb × 0.9	540	360	15	400	2,000	.5	.6	8	35
Children	1	3	13	29	90	35	1,300	23	800	800	15	400	2,000	.7	.8	9	45
	4	6	20	44	112	44	1,700	30	800	800	10	500	2,500	.9	1.0	11	45
	7	10	28	62	132	52	2,400	34	800	800	10	700	3,300	1.2	1.4	16	45
Males	11	14	45	99	157	62	2,700	45	1,200	1,200	18	1,000	5,000	1.4	1.6	18	50
	15	18	66	145	176	69	2,800	56	1,200	1,200	18	1,000	5,000	1.4	1.7	18	60
	19	22	70	154	177	70	2,900	56	800	800	10	1,000	5,000	1.5	1.7	19	60
	23	50	70	154	178	70	2,700	56	800	800	10	1,000	5,000	1.4	1.6	18	60
	51 +		70	154	178	70	[4]2,400	56	800	800	10	1,000	5,000	1.2	1.4	16	60
Females	11	14	46	101	157	62	2,200	46	1,200	1,200	18	800	4,000	1.1	1.3	15	50
	15	18	55	120	163	64	2,100	46	1,200	1,200	18	800	4,000	1.1	1.3	14	60
	19	22	55	120	163	64	2,100	44	800	800	18	800	4,000	1.1	1.3	14	60
	23	50	55	120	163	64	2,000	44	800	800	18	800	4,000	1.0	1.2	13	60
	51 +		55	120	163	64	[4]1,800	44	800	800	10	800	4,000	1.0	1.2	13	60
Pregnant							+ 300	+ 30	+ 400	+ 400	[5]18+	+ 200	+ 1,000	+ .4	+ .3	+ 2	+ 20
Lactating							+ 500	+ 20	+ 400	+ 400	18	+ 400	+ 2,000	+ .5	+ .5	+ 5	+ 40

1. Source: Adapted from Recommended Dietary Allowances, 9th ed., 1980, 185 pp. Washington DC: National Academy of Sciences, National Research Council. Also available in libraries. This publication tabulates the RDA for selected nutrients, discusses the basis for all RDA, and reviews current knowledge of the dietary needs for other nutrients.

2. 1 retinol equivalent = 1 μg retinol or 6 μg beta-carotene.

3. 1 international unit = 0.3 μg retinol or 0.6 μg beta-carotene.

4. After age 75 years, energy requirement is 2,050 calories for males and 1,600 calories for females.

5. The increased requirement cannot be met by ordinary diets; therefore the use of supplemental iron is recommended.

NOTE—The Recommended Daily Dietary Allowances (RDA) should not be confused with the U.S. Recommended Daily Allowances (U.S. RDA). The RDA are amounts of nutrients recommended by the Food and Nutrition Board of the National Research Council and are considered adequate for maintenance of good nutrition in healthy persons in the United States. The allowances are revised from time to time in accordance with newer knowledge of nutritional needs.

The U.S. RDA are the amounts of protein, vitamins, and minerals established by the Food and Drug Administration as standards for nutrition labeling. These allowances were derived from the RDA set by the Food and Nutrition Board. The U.S. RDA for most nutrients approximates the highest RDA of the sex-age categories in this table, excluding the allowances for pregnant and lactating females. Therefore, a diet that furnishes the U.S. RDA for a nutrient will furnish the RDA for most people and more than the RDA for many. U.S. RDA are protein, 45 grams (eggs, fish, meat, milk, poultry), 65 grams (other foods); vitamin A, 5,000 International Units; thiamin, 1.5 milligrams; riboflavin, 1.7 milligrams; niacin, 20 milligrams; ascorbic acid, 60 milligrams; calcium, 1 gram; phosphorus, 1 gram; iron, 18 milligrams. For additional information on U.S. RDA, see the "Federal Register," vol. 38, no. 49 (March 14, 1973), pp. 6959-6960, and Agriculture Information Bulletin 382, "Nutrition Labeling—Tools for Its Use."

Table 5—Food Sources of Additional Nutrients

Vitamins

Vitamin B$_6$	Vitamin B$_{12}$	Vitamin D
	(present in foods of animal origin only)	
Bananas		Egg yolk
Fish (most)		Liver
Liver and kidney	Cheese	Saltwater fish
Meat	Fish	Vitamin D milk
Poultry	Liver and kidney	
Potatoes and sweetpotatoes	Meat	
	Milk	
Whole-grain cereals	Shellfish	
Yeast	Whole egg and egg yolk	

Vitamin E	Folacin
Margarine	Dark-green vegetables
Nuts	Dry beans and peas
Peanuts and peanut butter	Liver
Vegetable oils	Wheat germ
Whole-grain cereals	Yeast

Minerals

Iodine	Magnesium	Zinc
Iodized salt	Bananas	Cocoa
Seafood	Cocoa	Dry beans and peas
	Dark-green vegetables (most)	Meat
	Dry beans and peas	Poultry
	Milk	Shellfish
	Nuts	Whole-grain cereals
	Whole-grain cereals	

Table 6—Amount of Fat That Provides 30 and 35 Percent of Calories at Specified Calorie Levels

Calories per day in diet	Amount of fat that provides—	
	30% of calories	35% of calories
	Grams	Grams
1,500	50	58
2,000	67	78
2,500	83	97
3,000	100	117

The Psychology of Stress & Nutrition

This page intentionally left blank.

Emotions and Stress

Figure   A

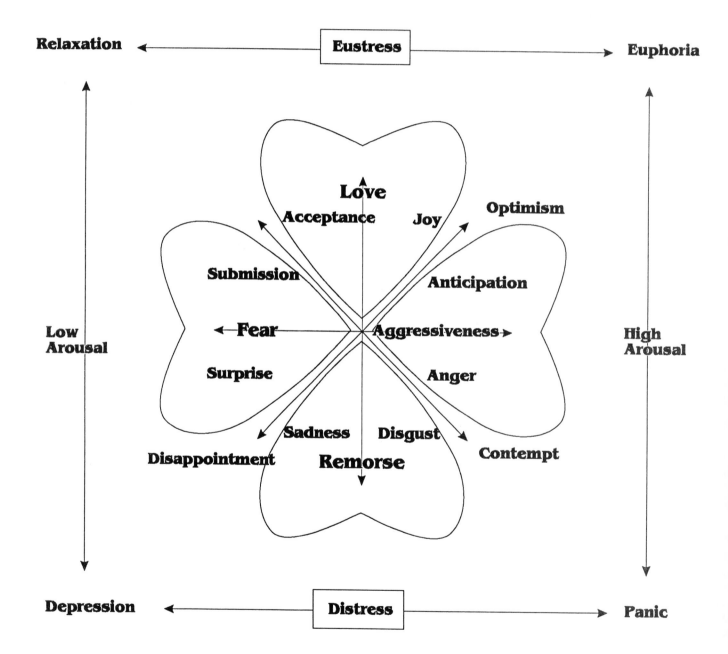

Relaxation ← Eustress → Euphoria

Low Arousal ↕ High Arousal

Love
Acceptance   Joy   Optimism
Submission   Anticipation
Fear ← → Aggressiveness
Surprise   Anger
Sadness   Disgust
Disappointment   Remorse   Contempt

Depression ← Distress → Panic

Acupress for Eustress

Figure B

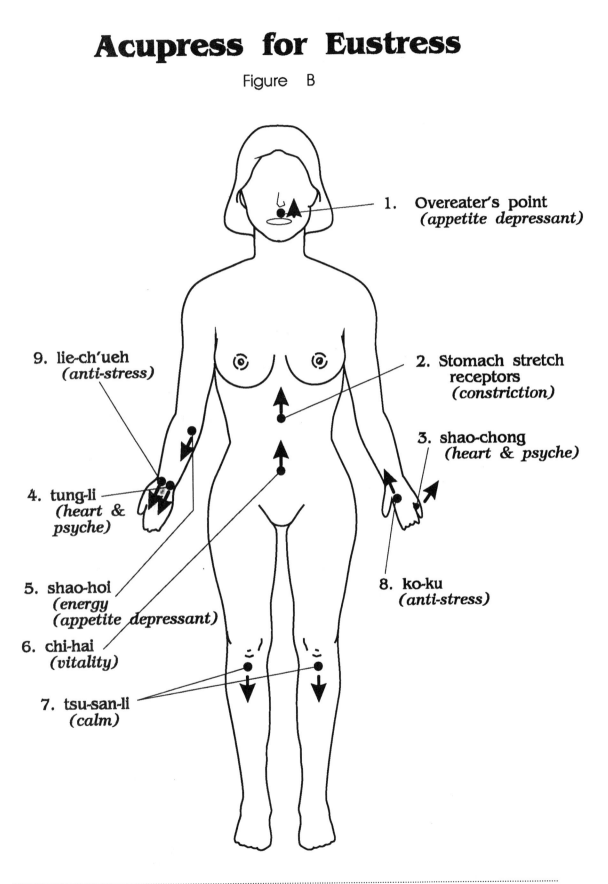

1. **Overeater's point**
   (appetite depressant)

9. **lie-ch'ueh**
   (anti-stress)

2. **Stomach stretch receptors**
   (constriction)

3. **shao-chong**
   (heart & psyche)

4. **tung-li**
   (heart & psyche)

5. **shao-hoi**
   (energy (appetite depressant)

6. **chi-hai**
   (vitality)

8. **ko-ku**
   (anti-stress)

7. **tsu-san-li**
   (calm)

NOTES

Chapter 1: Introduction

1. Don Diespecker, *The Psychology of Health* (Wallongong: Unpublished Manuscript, 1986), p. 17.

2. *Ibid.*, p. 33-34

3. Hans Selye, *Stress Without Distress* (Bergenfield: New American Library, 1974), p. 14.

4. Bill Stokes, "It's a Wonderful Life — With Prevention," *Spokesman-Review* (Spokane: Cowles, December 2, 1986), p. F1.

5. *Ibid.*

6. *Ibid.*

7. U.S. Department of Health and Human Services, "Heart Disease, No. 1 Killer," *Spokesman-Review* (Spokane: Cowles, January 6, 1986), p. A8.

8. Department of Agriculture, "Is the U.S. Eating Better?" *Spokesman-Review* (Spokane: Cowles, December 2, 1986), p. F1.

9. Covert Bailey, *Fit or Fat?* (Boston: Houghton Mifflin Co., 1978), p. 83.

10. Marion Burros, "Despite Concerns About Fat, Eating Habits Haven't Changes," *Spokesman-Review* (Spokane: Cowles, October 29, 1985), p. 4F.

11. Kenneth R. Pelletier, *Mind as Healer, Mind as Slayer* (New York: Del, 1977), p. 40.

12. Department of Agriculture, "Is the U.S. Eating Better?" *Spokesman-Review* (Spokane: Cowles, December 2, 1986), p. F1

13. *Ibid.*

14. Peggy Mann, The Dismal Truth About Teen-Age Health, *Reader's Digest* (Pleasantville: The Reader's Digest Association, March 1986), pp. 103-107.

15. *Ibid.*, p. 104.

16. *Ibid.*, p. 105*f*.

17. *Ibid.*, p. 106.

18. *Ibid.*, p. 104

19. *Ibid.*, p. 106.

20. *Ibid.*, p. 106*f*.

21. *Ibid.*, p. 106.

22. *Ibid.*, pp. 106-107.

23. *Ibid.*, p. 107.

Chapter 2: Ubiquitous Stress

1. Roy L. Walford, *Maximum Life Span* (New York: Avon Books, 1983), p. 177.

2. *Ibid.*

3. David Monagan, "Fatal Emotions," *Reader's Digest* (Pleasantville: The Reader's Digest Association, August 13, 1986), p. 125.

4. Judy J. Wurtman, *The Carbohydrate Craver's Diet* (Boston: Houghton Mifflin Co., 1983), p. 4.

5. Kenneth R. Pelletier, *Mind as Healer, Mind as Slayer* (New York: Dell, 1977), p. 40.

6. D. C. Jarvis, *Arthritis and Folk Medicine* (Greenwich: Fawcett, 1960), p. 75.

7. Barbara Brown, *Between Health and Illness* (Boston: Houghton Mifflin, 1985), pp. 144-155.

8. Susan Zarrow, "The Achiever's Guide to a Tranquil Mind," (*Prevention* (Emmaus: Rodale, March 1986), pp. 72-77.

9. Daniel Goleman, "Research Affirms Power of Positive Thinking," *The New York Times*, (New York: New York Times, February 3, 1987), pp. C5.

10. Lawrance Galton, *1001 Health Tips* (New York: Simon and Schuster, 1984), p. 212.

11. Charles T. McGee, *How to Survive Modern Technology* (New Canaan: Keats, 1979), p. 94.

12. John A. McDougal and Mary A. McDougal, *The McDougal Plan* (Piscataway: New Century, 1983), p. 179.

13. Carl J. Reich (personal correspondence) (Calgary: February 1984).

14. Robert Stephan, (personal interview) (Spokane: Spring 1988).

15. *Ibid.*

16. Covert Bailey, *Fit or Fat?* (Boston: Houghton Mifflin, 1978), p. 79.

17. Walt Murra, "Upstream Research Uncovers Some Social Health Secrets," *Spokane Health Today* (Spokane: Spokane Health Today, April 1986), p. 10.

18. *Ibid.*

Chapter 3: The Physiology of Stress

1. C. Van Toller, *Introduction to the Autonomic Nervous System and Behaviour* (New York: John Wiley and Sons, 1979), p. 98.

2. Charles Kilo, *Educating the Diabetic Patient* (New York: Science Medicine, 1982), p. 13.

3. *Ibid.*, p. 9.

4. Scott Prichard, "What's the Scoop on Sugar?" *Spokesman-Review* (Spokane: Cowles, January 20, 1987), p. F1.

5. William Kronholm, "White Man's Diet Harmful to Indians," *Associated Press* (Santa Barbara: News Press, April 21, 1985).

6. Charles Kilo, *Education the Diabetic Patient* (New York: Science and Medicine, 1982), p. 10.

7. Associated Press, "Diet Allows Some Sugar for Diabetics," *Spokesman-Review* (Spokane: Cowles, December 11, 1986), p. F1.

8. Covert Bailey, *Fit or Fat* (Boston: Houghton Mifflin, 1978), p. 83.

9. Scott Prichard, "The American Passion for Protein: Exploding the Myth," *Spokesman-Review* (Spokane: Cowles, March 17, 1987), p. F1.

10. James V. McConnel, *Understanding Human Behavior* (New York: Holt, Rinehart and Winston, 1986), p. 274.

11. Robert Hass, *Eat to Win* (New York: New American Library, 1983), p. 209.

12. Nicholas R. Hall and Allen L. Goldstein, "Thinking Well, The Chemical Links Between Emotion and Health," *The Sciences* (New York: New York Academy of Science, March/April 1986), p. 38.

13. Hans Selye, *Stress Without Distress* (Bergenfield: New American Library, 1974), pp. 11-51.

14. Herman Aihara, *Acid and Alkaline* (Denver: The Nutri-Books, 1986), p. 12.

15. *Ibid.*, p. 88.

16. Hans Selye, *Stress Without Distress* (Bergenfield: New American Library, 1974), p. 27.

17. Carlton Fredericks and Herman Goodman, *Low Blood Sugar and You* (New York: Grosset and Dunlap, 1979), p. 218.

Chapter 4: From Bad Stress to Good Stress

1. Hans Selye, *Stress Without Distress* (Bergenfield: New American Library, 1974), pp. 11-51.

2. *Ibid.*

3. Sigmund Stephen Miller with Julian Asher Miller and Don Ethan Miller, *Life Span Plus* (New York: Macmillan, 1986), p. 122.

4. Hans Selye, *The Stress of My Life* (New York: Van Nostrand and Rineholt, 1979).

5. *Ibid.*

6. Charles Rodale, "Good Stress: Why You Need it to Stay Strong," *Prevention* (Emmaus: The Rodale Press), p. 28.

7. *Ibid.*, pp. 28-29.

8. *Ibid.*, p. 29.

9. *Ibid.*, p. 32.

10. Jane B. Burka and Lenora M. Yuen, "A Procrastinator's Guide to Telling Time, *Working Woman*, (September 1984), p. 78.

11. Robert G. Allen, "You Can Rise to the Challenge," Parade Magazine (Spokane: Cowles, April 20, 1987), p. 20.

12. *Ibid.*

13. *Ibid.*

14. *Ibid.*, p. 211

15. *Ibid.*

16. *Ibid.*

17. Norman Cousins, "Healing and Believing," *The Saturday Evening Post* (Indianapolis: The Saturday Review, April 1982), p. 31.

18. *Ibid.*, p. 32.

19. *Ibid.*, p. 48.

1. Robert Ornstein, *Psychology: The Study of Human Experience* (New York: Harcourt Brace Jovanovich, 1985), pp. 534-535.

2. Michael Colgan (column) by Carlton Fredericks, "Supplementing Endorsed at a VERY Orthodox University," *Prevention* (Emmaus: Rodale, January 1983), p. 31.

3. Judith J. Wurtman, *The Carbohydrate Craver's Diet* (Boston: Houghton Mifflin, 1983), p. 4.

4. *Ibid.*

5. *Ibid.*, p. 29.

6. *Ibid.*, p. 31.

7. *Ibid.*, p. 176.

8. *Ibid.*, p. 177.

9. Judy J. Wurtman, *Managing Your Mind and Mood Through Food* (New York: Rawson, 1986), p. 24.

10. Frank Bahr, *Dr. Bahr's Acu-Diet* (New York: William Morrow, 1978).

11. *Ibid.*, p. 154.

12. *Ibid.*

13. *Ibid.*, pp. 11-13.

14. *Ibid.*

15. Judith J. Wurtman, *The Carbohydrate Craver's Diet* (Boston: Houghton Mifflin, 1983).

16. Frank R. Bahr, *Dr. Bahr's Acu-Diet* (New York: William Morrow, 1978).

17. *Ibid.*

Chapter 6: Biokinesiology

1. John F. Thie, *Touch for Health* (Marina del Rey: DeVorss, 1979), p. 6.

2. *Ibid.*, p. 7.

3. Wayne W. Topping, *Stress Release* (Bellingham: Topping International Institute, 1985).

4. *Ibid.*, p. 16.

5. *Ibid.*, p. 19.

6. *Ibid.*, p. 22.

7. *Ibid.*, pp. 27-28.

8. John F. Thie, *Touch for Health* (Marina del Rey: Devorss, 1979), p. 36.

9. Hubert Swartout, *Guide to Health* (Mountain View: Pacific Press, 1938), p. 34.

10. John F. Thie, *Touch for Health* (Marina del Rey: Devorss, 1979), p. 10.

11. *Ibid.*

12. Wayne W. Topping, *Stress Release* (Bellingham: Topping International Institute, 1985), p. 42.

13. *Ibid.*, pp. 45-46.

14. *Ibid.*

15. *Ibid.*

Chapter 7: The Immune System

1. Peter Jaret, "Our Immune System: the Wars Within," *National Geographic* (Washington, DC: National Geographic Society, June 1986), pp. 732-734.

2. Stuart Berger, *Dr. Berger's Immune System Diet* (New York: New American Library, 1986).

3. Karl Goodskin, "Study Profiles Women Prone to Cervical Cancer," *Journal of Psychosomatic Research* (Stanford: Association for Psychosomatic Research, 1987), pp. 67-76.

4. Henry Dreyer, "Do You Have a Type C (Cancer Prone) Personality?" *Redbook* (Mary 1988), p. 108(4)

5. *Ibid.*

6. *Ibid.*

7. *Ibid.*

8. Earl Ubell, "When Your Immune System Fails," *Parade Magazine* (Spokane: Cowles, January 18, 1987), pp. 16-18.

9. Department of Health and Welfare, *Self-Care Manual for Arthritic Patients* (Salt Lake City: Intermountain Regional Medical Program, 1975).

10. Nicholas Hall and Allen Goldstein, "Thinking Well, The Chemical Links Between Emotion and Health," *The Sciences* (New York: New York Academy of Sciences, March/April 1986), p. 40.

11. *Ibid.*, p. 34.

Chapter 8: Allergies—Aliens Against Self

1. Kurt W. Donsbach, *Allergies* (Huntington Beach: The International Health Sciences, Inc., 1980), p. 9.

2. C. E. Bates, *Depression: The Crucial Role of Nutrition* (Vancouver, BC: Kask Graphics, Ltd., 1986), p. 45.

3. C. E. Bates, *Radically Determined Abnormal Fatty Acid and Prostaglandin Metabolism and Food Allergies Linked to Autoimmune Inflammatory, and Psychiatric Disorders Among British Columbia Indians*, (Campbell River, BC: unpublished report, 1987), p. 1.

4. *Ibid.*, p. 4.

5. *Ibid.*, p. 6.

6. *Ibid.*

7. *Ibid.*

8. *Ibid.*

9. Jeannie Barone, "Nutrition News — Less Fat, Less Illness," *American Health* (New York: R.D. Publication, April 1990) p. 112.

Chapter 9: Unsaturated Fat—A Wolf in Sheep's Clothing

1. Denham Harman, Shelton Hedricks, Dennis E. Eddy, and Jon Seibald, "Free Radical Theory On Central Nervous System Functioning," *Journal of the American Geriatric Society* (New York: New York Academy of Sciences, 1976).

2. Durk Pearson and Sandy Shaw, *The Life Extension Companion* (New York: Laboratory for the Advancement of Biomedical Research, 1984).

3. Robert Hass, *Eat to Win* (New York: New American Library, 1983), p. 130.

4. *Ibid.*, p. 131.

5. Denham Harman, Shelton Hedricks, Dennis E. Eddy, and John Seibald, "Free Radical Theory On Central Nervous System Functioning," *Journal of the American Geriatric Society* (New York: New York Academy of Sciences, 1976).

6. *Ibid.*

7. Covert Bailey, *Fit or Fat* (Boston: Houghton Mifflin, 1978), p. 83.

8. Nathan Pritikin with Patrick M. McGrady, Jr. *The Pritikin Program for Diet and Exercise* (New York: Bantam Books, 1979), p. 9.

9. Myron Brenton and the Editors of Prevention Magazine, *Aging Slowing* (Emmaus: Rodale Press, 1983), p. 42.

10. Pearson and Shaw, *The Life Extension Companion* (New York: Laboratory for the Advancement of Biomedical Research, 1984).

11. Denham Harmon, Shelton Hedricks, Dennis E. Eddy, and John Seibald, "Free Radical Theory On Central Nervous System Functioning," *Journal of the American Geriatric Society* (New York: New York Academy of Sciences, 1976).

12. Hans Selye, *The Stress of my Life* (New York: Van Nostrand and Rineholt, 1979).

13. Ray L. Walford, *Maximum Life Span* (New York: Avon Books, 1983), p. 140.

14. *Ibid.*, pp. 86-87.

15. *Ibid.*, pp. 140-141.

16. *Ibid.*, pp. 110-111.

17. *Ibid.*, pp. 154-155.

18. *Ibid.*

19. Dan Adair, "Spring Health Care," *Spokesman-Review* (Spokane: Cowles, March 11, 1990), pp. S1-10.

20. Robert Stack, *Controlling Fat for Life* (Arizona Bariatric Physicians, 1987).

21. Susan E. Gebhart and Ruth E. Matthews, *Nutritive Value of Foods* (Pullman: Washington State College of Agriculture Cooperative Extension, April 1989). (Material is available as USDA G0072, Washington State University Cooperative Extension EB1518, PNW357 from Washington State University, Oregon State University, and the University of Idaho.)

Chapter 10: The Balanced Diet—Stress Control

1. Dan Adair, "Spring Health Care," *Spokesman-Review* (Spokane: Cowles, March 11, 1990), p. S4.

2. Garry Gordon, *Nutritional Evaluation by Computer Analysis for Sarah A. Culton* (Hayward: MineraLab, Inc., February 2, 1984).

Chapter 11: Conclusions and Implications

1. Marilyn vos Savant, "Ask Marilyn," *Parade Magazine* (Spokane: Cowles, March 18, 1990), p. 18.

2. Sharon Timmons, "What this Class Has Meant To Me," (Spokane: Unpublished, December 9, 1987.

BIBLIOGRAPHY

John Adair, "Spring Health Care '90," *Spokesman-Review*, (Spokane: Cowles March 11, 1990), pp. S1-10)

Herman Aihara, *Acid and Alkaline* (Denver: The Nutri-Books, 1980.)

Robert G. Allen, "You Can Rise To The Challenge," *Parade Magazine Spokesman-Review* (Spokane: Cowles, April 20, 1987), pp. 20-22.

American Heart Association and National Academy of Science, "Daily Nutrition Countdown," *Family Circle* (New York: New York Times, April 15, 1986.)

Associated Press, "Diet Allows Some Sugar for Diabetics," *Spokesman-Review* (Spokane, Cowles, December 11, 1986) p. F1.

Associated Press, "Study Connects Hostile Teens to High Cholesterol in Adults," *Spokesman-Review* (Spokane: Cowles, November 15, 1990), p. F1.

Frank R. Bahr, *Dr. Bahr's Acu-Diet* (New York: William Morrow and Co., 1978.)

Covert Bailey, *Fit or Fat?* (Boston: Houghton Mifflin Co., 1978.)

Covert Bailey, *The Fit-or-Fat Diet* (Boston: Houghton Mifflin Co., 1984).

Covert Bailey, *Target Recipes* (Boston: Houghton Mifflin Co., 1985.)

Jeanine Barone, "Nutrition News: Less Fat, Less Illness" *American Health* (New York: RD Publications, April 1990), p. 112.

C.E. (Chuck) Bates, *Depression: The Crucial Role of Nutrition* (Vancouver, BC: Kask Graphics Ltd., 1986).

C.E. Bates, *Radically Determined Abnormal Fatty Acid and Prostaglandin Metabolism and Food Allergies Linked to Autoimmune Inflammatory, and Psychiatric Disorders Among British Columbia Indians* (Campbell River, BC: unpublished report, 1987).

Stuart Berger, *Dr. Berger's Immune Power Diet* (New York: New American Library, 1986).

Myron Brenton and the Editors of Prevention Magazine, *Aging Slowing* (Emmaus: Rodale Press, 1983).

Barbara Brown, *Between Health and Illness* (Boston: Houghton Mifflin Co., 1985).

Jane B. Burka and Lenora M. Yuen, "A Procrastinator's Guide to Telling Time," *Working Woman* (September 1984), p. 78.

Marion Burros, "Despite concerns About Fat, Eating Habits Haven't Changed," *Spokesman-Review* (Spokane: Cowles Publishing Co., October 29, 1985), p. 4F.

E. Cheraskin, W. M. Ringsdorf, with Arlene Brecher, *Psycho-dietetics* (New York: Bantam Books, 1974).

Michael Colgan (column) by Carlton Fredericks, "Supplementing Endorsed at a VERY Orthodox University," *Prevention* (Emmaus: Rodale, January 1983), p. 31

Dennis Coon, *Introduction to Psychology* (San Francisco: West Publishing Co., 1986).

Eleanor Cousins, "The Irrepressible Spoof Strikes Again," *The Saturday Evening Post* (April, 1982), pp. 26-29, 105.

Norman Cousins, "Healing and Believing" *The Saturday Evening Post* (Indianapolis: The Saturday Review, April 1982), pp. 31-32, 48, 111.

Norman Cousins, *Human Options: An Autobiographical Notebook* (New York: W. W. Norton and Co., 1986).

Norman Cousins, *Human Options* (New York: Berkeley Books, 1986).

Norman Cousins, "My Incredible Self-Cure, *Family Circle* (New York: New York Times, June 3, 1980) pp. 8, 122-125.

Helena Curtis, *Invitation to Biology* (New York: Worth Publishers, 1977).

Martha Davis, Elizabeth R. Eshelmna, and Matthew McKay, *The Relaxation and Stress Reduction Workbook* (Oakland: New Harbinger Publishers, 1982).

Arthur S. DeMoss Foundation *Power for Living* (Atlanta: American Vision, 1983).

Department of Agriculture, "Is the U.S. Eating Better?" *Spokesman-Review* (Spokane: Cowles Publishing, December 2, 1986), p. B1.

Don Diespecker, *The Psychology of Health* (Wollongong, Australia: Unpublished manuscript, 1986).

Kurt W. Donsbach, *Allergies* (Huntington Beach: The International Institute of Natural Health Sciences, 1980).

Henry Dreher, "Do You Have a Type C (Cancer Prone) Personality?" *Redbook* May 1988), p. 108 (4).

Henry Dreher, *The Complete Guide to Cancer Prevention* (New York: Harper and Row, 1988).

Carlton Fredericks and Herman Goodman, *Low Blood Sugar and You* (New York: Grosset and Dunlap, 1969).

Carlton Fredericks, *New and Complete Nutrition Handbook* (Conago Park: Major Books, 1976).

Carlton Fredericks, *New Low Blood Sugar and You* (New York: Putman Publishing Group, 1985).

Lawrence Galton, *1001 Health Tips* (New York: Simon and Schuster, 1984).

Susan E. Gebhart and Ruth E. Matthews, *Nutritive Value of Foods* (Pullman: Washington State College of Agriculture Cooperative Extension, April 1989). (This material is available as USDA G0072; Washington State University Cooperative Extension EB1518; and as PNW357 from Washington State University, Oregon State University, and the University of Idaho.)

Ann Gilroy, *Adelle Davis' Let's Stay Healthy* (New York: Harcourt Brace Jovanovich, Inc., 1981).

Daniel Goleman, "Research Affirms Power of Positive Thinking," *The New York Times* (New York: New York Times, February 3, 1987), pp. C1, C5.

Karl Goodskin, "Study Profiles of Women Prone to Cervical Cancer," *Journal of Psychosomatic Research* (Stanford: Association for Psychosomatic Research, 1987), pp. 67-76.

Gary F. Gordon, *Nutritional Evaluation by Computer Analysis for Sarah A. Culton* (Hayward: MineraLab, Inc., February 2, 1984).

Nicholas R. Hall and Allen L. Goldstein, "Thinking Well, The Chemical Links Between Emotion and Health," *The Sciences* (New York: New York Academy of Sciences, March/April 1986), pp. 34-40.

Harold W. Harper and Michael Culbert, *How You Can Beat the Killer Diseases* (New Rochelle: Arlington House Publishers, 1977).

Robert Hass, *Eat to Win* (New York: New American Library, 1983).

Heart Institute Specialists, *The Heart Institute Diet* (Seattle: Providence Medical Center, 1991).

Holy Bible, Commonly known as the authorized (King James) version (Nashville: The Gideons International, 1984).

Peter Jaret, "Our Immune System: the Wars Within," *National Geographic* (Washington, DC: National Geographic Society, June, 1986), pp. 705-734.

D. C. Jarvis, *Arthritis and Folk Medicine* (Greenwich: Fawcett Publications, Inc., 1960).

D. C. Jarvis, *Folk Medicine* (New York: Fawcett Columbine, 1958).

Charles Kilo, *Education the Diabetic Patient* (New York: Science and Medicine, 1982).

John D. Kirshmann, *Nutrition Almanac* (New York: McGraw-Hill Book Co., 1975).

John D. Kirschmann with Lavon J. Dunne, *Nutrition Almanac, Second Edition* (New York: McGraw-Hill Book Co., 1984).

Knight-Ridder, "Huge Weight-loss Industry Criticized by Health Experts," *Spokesman-Review* (Spokane: Cowles Publishing Co., March 27, 1990), p. A12.

Suzanne Kobosa and Salvatore Maddi, *The Hardy Executive: Health Under Stress* (Chicago: Dow Jones-Irwin, 1984).

William Kronholm, "White Man's Diet Harmful to Indians," *Associated Press* Santa Barbara: New Press, April 21, 1985).

Charles T. Kuntzleman, "Guide to Family Fitness," *Reader's Digest* (Pleasantville: The Reader's Digest Association, Inc., January 1986).

Frances Moore Lappe, *Diet for a Small Planet* (New York: Ballantine Books, Inc., 1971).

Michael Lesser, *Nutrition and Vitamin Therapy* (New York: Bantam Books, 1980).

Robert B. Malmo, "Obituary: Hans Hugo Selye (1907-1982), *American Psychologist* (Arlington: American Psychological Association, Inc., Volume 41, January 1986), pp. 92-93.

Marshall Mandell and Lynne Waller Scanlon, *Dr. Mandell's 5-Day Allergy Relief System* (New York: Simon and Schuster, 1979).

Peggy Mann, "The Dismal Truth About Teen-Age Health," *Reader's Digest* (Pleasantville: The Reader's Digest Association, March 1986), pp. 103-107.

James V. McConnell, *Understanding Human Behavior* (New York: Holt, Rhinehart, and Winston, 1986).

John A. McDougal and Mary A. McDougal, *The McGougal Plan* (Piscataway: New Century Publishers, Inc., 1983)

Charles T. McGee, *How to Survive Modern Technology* (New Canaan: Keats Publishing, Inc., 1979).

Sir Peter Medawar, "When We Are Old," *Atlantic,* March 1984, pp. 16-20.

Sigmund Stephen Miller with Julian Asher Miller and Don Ethan Miller, *Life Span Plus* (New York: MacMillan Publishing Co., 1986).

David Monagan, "Fatal Emotions," *Reader's Digest* (Pleasantville: The Reader's Digest Association, 1986), pp. 123-126.

Walt Murra, "Upstream Research Uncovers Some Social Health Secrets," *Spokane Health Today* (Spokane: Spokane Health Today Publishers, April 1986), pp.10-11.

Robert Ornstein, *Psychology: The Study of Human Experience* (New York: Harcourt Brace Javanovich, 1985).

Durk Pearson and Sandy Shaw, *The Life Extension Companion* (New York: Laboratory for the Advancement of Biomedical Research, 1984).

Kenneth R. Pelletier, *Mind as Healer, Mind as Slayer* (New York: Dell Publishing Co., 1977).

Scott Prichard, "Even in Moderation Alcohol Affects Functions," *Spokesman Review* (Spokane: Cowles Publishing Co., January 20, 1987), p. B1.

Scott Prichard, "The American Passion for Protein, Exploding the Myth," *Spokesman Review* (Spokane: Cowles Publishing Co., March 17, 1987), p. F1.

Scott Pritchard, "What's the Scoop on Sugar?" *Spokesman-Review* (Spokane: Cowles Publishing Co., January 20, 1987), p. B1.

Nathan Pritikin with Patrick M. McGrady, Jr., *The Pritikin Program for Diet and Exercise* (New York: Bantam Books, Inc., 1979).

Carl J. Reich (Personal correspondence) (Calgary Alberta: Medical Center, February 7, 1984).

Paul Raeburn, "Kicking Coffee Can Lower Blood Pressure," *Spokesman-Review* (Spokane: Cowles Publishing Co., November 18, 1986), p. B1.

Michael Regan, "Can We Live Longer?" *Parade Magazine* (Spokane: Cowles Publishing Co., June 12, 1988), p. 20.

Charles Rodale, "Your Inner Source to Fight Disease, "*Prevention Magazine* (Emmaus: The Rodale Press, Inc., February 1986).

Robert Rose, "The Experts Give Their Best Educational Advice — Moderation." *Spokesman-Review* (Spokane: Cowles Publishing Co., November 18, 1986), p. B1.

Marilyn vos Savant, "Ask Marilyn, " *Parade Magazine* (Spokane: Cowles Publishing Co., March 18, 1990), p. 18.

Alexander Schaus, *Diet, Crime, and Delinquency* (Berkeley: Parker House, 1980).

Hans Seyle, *The Stress of My Life* (New York: Van Nostrand and Rinehart, 1979).

Hans Seyle, *Stress Without Distress* (Bergenfield: New American Library, 1974).

Don Smith, "Stroke Prevention: the Importance of Risk Factors," *Stroke Clinical Updates* (Englewood: National Stroke Association, January 1991), pp. 17-20.

Ronald E. Smith, Erwin G. Sarason, and Barbara Sarason, *The Frontiers of Behavior* (New York: Harper and Row, 1986).

Robert Stark, *Controlling Fat for Life* (Arizona Bariatric Physicians, 1987).

Barbara Sternberg, "Five Diet Demons and How to Lick Them," *Family Circle* (New York: New York Times, January 20, 1986).

Bill Stokes, "It's a Wonderful Life — With Prevention," *Spokesman-Review* (Spokane: Cowles Publishing Co., December 2, 1986), p. F1.

Hubert Swartout, *Guide to Health* (Mountain View: Pacific Press Publishing, 1938)

John F. Thie, *Touch for Health* (Marina Del Rey: DeVorss and Co., 1979).

Sharon Timmons, "What this Class has Meant to Me," (Spokane: Unpublished, December 9, 1987).

C. Van Toller, *The Nervous Body, An Introduction to the Autonomic Nervous System and Behaviour* (New York: John Wiley and Sons, 1979).

Wayne Topping, *Biokinesiology Workbook* (Bellingham: Topping International Institute, 1985).

Gerard J. Torters and Micholas P. Anagnostakos, *Principles of Anatomy and Physiology* (New York: Harper and Row, 1984), pp. 23-26, 368.

Earl Ubell, "The Immune System," *Parade Magazine* (Spokane: Cowles Publishing Co., April 21, 1985) pp. 16-18.

Earl Ubell, "When Your Immune System Fails," *Parade Magazine* (Spokane: Cowles Publishing Co., January 6, 1986), p. A8.

Roy L. Walford, *Maximum Life Span* (New York: Avon Books, 1983).

Judy Wurtman, *The Carbohydrate Craver's Diet* (Boston: Houghton Mifflin Co., 1983).

Susan Zarrow, "The Achiever's Guide to a Tranquil Mind," *Prevention* (Emmaus: Rodale Press, Inc., March 1986), pp. 72-77.

Sam Ziff and Michael F. Ziff, *The Hazards of Silver/Amalgam Fillings: Restorative Dentistry Without Silver Amalgam Fillings* (Orlando: Bio-Probe, Inc., 1986. References and/or Notes

Index

C

The Psychology of Stress & Nutrition

ABOUT THE AUTHOR

Sarah A. Culton holds a Doctorate in Education degree, with a major in psychology (guidance and counseling), from the University of Idaho. She also has undergraduate minors in English and Home Economics — a compatible combination for the writing of this book. Since the age of 18, she has been teaching and counseling young people of all ages. After a "bout" with rheumatoid arthritis, she retired after 21 years as a psychology professor at Spokane Falls Community College, in Spokane, Washington. Since then, she has been researching and writing this book. Now that her arthritis is in remission, she is continuing with her writing, as well as doing volunteer counseling and psychological work in schools near her home — she is a certified school psychologist in the State of Washington. She and her husband of over 40 years live in a lovely turn-of-the-century home, located on 40 acres at the foot of Dominion Mountain, near Colville, Washington, in Stevens County. They raised a son and a daughter, with whom they spend a great deal of time; and also enjoy traveling in their motor home. Dr. Culton's utmost concern for the welfare of others is her major motivating force. In her book, she documents from research how to achieve better health through stress control — exercise, relaxation, and above all, good nutrition.

Memberships

American Association for Counseling and Development
American Association for World Health
American Psychologic Association
American Public Health Association
Christian Association for Psychological Studies
Foundation for Chiropractic Education and Research
International Academy of Nutrition and Preventive Medicine
International Council of Psychologists
International Stress Management Association
National Stroke Association
Nutrition for Optimal Health Association
Society for Nutrition Education
Society for Psycho-physiological Research
Washington Education/National Education Association

Presentations

Stress and Psychosomatic Health Issues, Annual Convention, San Francisco, CA, August 13, 1991.

Stroke Prevention through Education, 3rd Annual Stroke Rehabilitation Conference, The Medical Center of Central Massachusetts, Framington, MA, October 17-18, 1991.

The Psychology of Stress and Nutrition, International Stress Management Association Conference, Paris, France, September 1-3, 1992. (tentative)